Abbott's Gambit
The 2013 Australian Federal Election

Abbott's Gambit

The 2013 Australian Federal Election

Edited by Carol Johnson and John Wanna (with Hsu-Ann Lee)

Published by ANU Press
The Australian National University
Canberra ACT 0200, Australia
Email: anupress@anu.edu.au
This title is also available online at http://press.anu.edu.au

---

National Library of Australia Cataloguing-in-Publication entry

Title: Abbott's gambit : the 2013 Australian federal election / Editors, Carol Johnson and John Wanna (with Hsu-Ann Lee).

ISBN: 9781925022100 (paperback) 9781925022094 (ebook)

Subjects: Australia--Parliament--Elections--2013.
Elections--Australia--2013.
Political campaigns--Australia--21st century.
Australia--Politics and government--21st century.

Other Creators/Contributors:
Johnson, Carol, 1955- editor.
Wanna, John, editor.
Lee, Hsu-Ann, editor.

Dewey Number: 324.994

All rights reserved. No part of this publication may be reproduced, stored in a retrieval system or transmitted in any form or by any means, electronic, mechanical, photocopying or otherwise, without the prior permission of the publisher.

Cover design and layout by ANU Press

This edition © 2015 ANU Press

Contents

Preface and Acknowledgements ix
Contributors xiii
Introduction: Analysing the 2013 Australian Federal Election 1
    Carol Johnson, John Wanna and Hsu-Ann Lee

Part 1. Campaign Themes and Context

1. An Overview of the 2013 Federal Election Campaign: Ruinous politics, cynical adversarialism and contending agendas 17
    Jennifer Rayner and John Wanna

2. The Battle for Hearts and Minds 35
    Carol Johnson

3. The Leadership Contest: An end to the 'messiah complex'? . . 49
    Paul Strangio and James Walter

Part 2. Vital Images of the Campaign—The Media, Campaign Advertising, Polls, Predictions and the Cartoons

4. The Empire Strikes Back: Mainstream media still matters 67
    Wayne Errington

5. New Media in the Electoral Context: The new normal 81
    Peter John Chen

6. Campaign Advertising and Communication Strategies in the Election of 2013 95
    Sally Young

7. Making Policy and Winning Votes: Election promises and political strategies in the 2013 campaign 109
    Nicholas Reece

8. How the Pollsters Called the Horse Race: Changing polling technologies, cost pressures, and the concentration on the two-party-preferred 123
    Murray Goot

9. All That Glitters: Betting markets and the 2013
   Australian federal election 143
   Simon Jackman

10. Nearly All About Kevin:
    The election as drawn by Australian cartoonists 161
    Haydon Manning and Robert Phiddian

Part 3. Party Perspectives

11. The Liberal Campaign in the 2013 Federal Election 191
    Brian Loughnane

12. The Labor Party Campaign and Aftermath. 203
    George Wright

13. The 2013 Federal Election: The Greens campaign 211
    Andrew Bartlett

Part 4. Regional Variations in Voting Trends

14. The Electoral Geography of the 2013 Election:
    Voting patterns in the states and regions for
    the Lower House. 225
    Dean Jaensch with Narelle Miragliotta and Rae Wear

15. Regional Place-Based Identities and Party Strategies
    at the 2013 Federal Election. 249
    Geoff Robinson

16. The Contest for Rural Representation: The celebrated
    contest over Indi and the fate of the independents 275
    Jennifer Curtin and Brian Costar

17. The Advent of Two New Micro Parties:
    The Palmer United Party and Katter's Australia Party 293
    Tom King

Part 5. Salient Issues

18. An Impecunious Election: The significance of fiscal and
    economic issues 311
    John Wanna

19. Ethnic Voting and Asylum Issues. 323
    James Jupp

20. The Environment in the 2013 Election: Controversies
    over climate change, the carbon tax and conservation. . . . 341
    Nick Economou

21. Unstable Bipartisanship or Off the Agenda?
    Social issues during the 2013 election campaign. 359
    Rob Manwaring, Gwen Gray and Lionel Orchard

22. Gender and the 2013 Election: The Abbott 'mandate' 375
    Kirsty McLaren and Marian Sawer

Part 6. The Results

23. Explaining the Results 393
    Antony Green

24. Documenting the Inevitable: Voting behaviour at the
    2013 Australian election 411
    Clive Bean and Ian McAllister

Conclusion: Reflections on Abbott's Gambit—Mantras,
    manipulation and mandates 425
    Carol Johnson and John Wanna

Preface and Acknowledgements

This volume is the latest in a published series of Australian election studies which have contemporaneously analysed Australian federal elections across almost seven decades. This volume represents the 15th edited collection of essays analysing 16 Australian national elections dating back to 1958 (with the series beginning effectively from the pivotal election of 1972 and since then missing only two elections, 1974 and 1984, to the present day—a complete list of previous titles is appended below). The series involves Australia's leading political science academics, as well as contributions from senior political journalists and expert practitioners including serving and former politicians and their political staffers. The series has always blended analysis from political players and key insiders who often participated in campaigns themselves as decision-makers and combatants, along with academics able to stand back and reflect on the political contest, tracing longer-term trends, themes and resonances. The objective of each study was to explain the dynamics of a particular electoral contest (and its subsequent outcome) by discussing a range of background factors and contributory influences as well as exploring the significance of the proximate factors that helped shape the eventual result of the campaign.

The previous post-election volume, *Julia 2010: The caretaker election* (edited by Marian Simms and John Wanna), also published by ANU Press, highlighted the electoral backlash that eventually resulted in a hung parliament and a minority Labor Government lasting from September 2010 to September 2013. Julia Gillard, after seizing the prime ministership from Kevin Rudd at the end of his first term in office, went directly into the 2010 campaign without a clear narrative, while also facing accusations she was duplicitous and doubts over the legitimacy and effectiveness of her leadership. Her conservative opponent, Tony Abbott, had not shone in the popularity stakes but had united a previously fractious opposition and made it electorally competitive. The resulting hung parliament, with the Coalition holding 73 seats, Labor on 72 and five largely conservative crossbenchers, fashioned together a minority Labor Government which was without an electoral mandate and quickly lost electoral support. Three years later, the 2013 federal election reflected the electoral culmination of Tony Abbott's successful oppositional campaign against an increasingly dysfunctional Labor minority Government. With Labor's caucus desperately ditching Gillard and returning Rudd to the prime ministership on the eve of the election, Abbott was able to profit from Labor's disarray. For the conservatives, the 2013 election completed a strategy of ousting Labor from office that had begun in 2010, and allowed a regenerated Coalition to be installed as the alternative government. However, the result also indicated a widespread disaffection across the electorate with the political leaders of the day and with the major political parties including the Greens. There was both a mood of resignation and an element of political retribution at play in the 2013 federal election; it produced an electoral volatility that seemed all but unremarkable to many Australians but totally perplexed many overseas observers of Australian politics.

The explanations behind the outcome of the 2013 election are manifold and contextual. Simple explanations are notoriously misleading—such as Labor lost the election purely because of its internal disunity, or that the conservatives won by their relentless negativity. In fact, in some parts of Australia there was no change or hardly any in party representation whereas others had massive swings and not necessarily where they were expected. Paradoxically, Labor actually won increased support in a few constituencies, whereas the Coalition gained only a relatively small swing towards it even though it could comfortably form government. Accordingly, the expert contributors to this volume together offer a comprehensive assessment of the 2013 election with a richness of perspectives and analytical approaches only such a collection of intentionally diverse contributors can provide. They explore the key themes of the electoral contest, the battle over ideas and values, the campaign strategies of the political parties, the policy and platform differences, the clash between the two leaders, the media coverage and advertising strategies, societal and demographic factors, changing voting patterns and regional variations, and the salience of issues and interests.

Previous volumes analysing Australian federal elections have long been characterised by a commendable breadth in both the approaches and methodologies adopted and the large range of factors analysed by the contributors. While the studies identify key themes that were present in specific elections, the current editors, like their predecessors, remain convinced that election outcomes are determined by multiple factors and a complex web of influences (some even contradictory or countervailing). Consequently, useful insights into the nature and outcome of election campaigns can best be gained by a using a wide lens of perspectives and a range of quantitative and qualitative approaches. That is why this book has an unusually large number of contributors compared with many election studies overseas (see e.g. Nelson 2013; Allen and Barrie 2010). It is also the reason why the editors have made a deliberate effort to include many newer voices to accompany the more established members of the political science profession who have specialised in political and electoral research. Hence, the present volume focuses on key themes and topics which other electoral studies overseas have also identified as increasingly important, such as new modes of political communication (see e.g. Wring, Mortimore and Atkinson 2011; Levine and Roberts 2012), as well as detailed voting studies and analysis of issues ranging from political economy to ethnicity and gender. Encouraging a range of studies and approaches has also resulted in this collection meeting the needs of a diverse readership. In general, the chapters are designed to be read by an informed public, journalists, political advisors and politicians as well as by the book's primary audience of academics and undergraduate students. In short, the editors and authors have endeavoured to ensure that the chapters are both academically rigorous and that they engage a broader audience interested in the key processes of Australian democracy. Nonetheless, given the diversity of approaches taken, some chapters will, by their very nature, have a more technical nature than others. The latter chapters include those by Murray Goot and Simon Jackman on the accuracy of the opinion polls and the predictive capacities of the betting markets. Even here, however, informed readers will be able to follow the general argument while some of the more technical content will be of interest both to professional pollsters and to academic specialists (indeed, Jackman's article engages with major overseas literature on the accuracy of betting markets compared with the polls).

In planning the content of the volume we surveyed the contents of each earlier electoral study back to 1972 to examine their range and breadth of coverage (and mix of authors), plus an extensive sample of similar electoral studies compiled in overseas jurisdictions. The topics canvassed usually include polling, voters, parties, debates, campaigning, media and final results. We tried to ensure that the range of topics covered in comparative studies was in some way replicated in this volume, to provide greater systematisation and for the purposes of comparative analysis. Draft chapters were extensively workshopped by the collective contributors and some invited commentators at a two-day seminar in early November 2013, funded by the Academy of Social Sciences in Australia, with support also from the Australia and New Zealand School of Government (ANZSOG) at The Australian National University. ANZSOG also provided the facilities at ANU and editorial assistance. The editors wish to thank Hsu-Ann Lee for exceptional editorial assistance, Claire Dixon for logistical support, John Beaton and Margaret Blood from the Academy, Justin Pritchard for earlier research assistance, and also various other people who helped with specific tasks, including Skye Laris, Bernie Shaw, Stuart Smith, Erin Farley, Adam Masters and Alison Plumb. We also wish to thank those discussants and attendees who contributed to the earlier workshop, including Robin Archer from the London School of Economics (LSE). Murray Goot, John Warhurst and Marian Simms were helpful in planning and preparation of this volume, and we wish to thank the expert referees, the Social Sciences Editorial Board and the staff of ANU Press for their invaluable assistance in bringing this manuscript to publication.

Carol Johnson and John Wanna

April 2014

***

Previous Australian electoral studies in this series include:

Australia Votes: The 1958 Federal Election, edited by D Rawson, 1961 (the first book-length study of a federal election but not part of any series).

Labor to Power: Australia's 1972 Election, edited by H Mayer, 1973 (the second book-length study but again not part of an ongoing series, and also published in *Politics,* Vol 8 (1), 1973).

Australia at the Polls: The National Elections of 1975, edited by HR Penniman, 1977.

The Australian National Elections of 1977, edited by HR Penniman, 1979.

Australia at the Polls: The National Elections of 1980 and 1983, edited by HR Penniman, 1983.

Australia Votes: The 1987 Federal Election, edited by I McAllister and J Warhurst, 1988.

The Greening of Australian Politics: The 1990 Federal Election, edited by C Bean, I McAllister and J Warhurst, 1990.

The 1993 Federal Election, Special Edition of the *Australian Journal of Political Science*, Vol 29, 1994, guest editor C Bean.

The Politics of Retribution: The 1996 Australian Federal Election, edited by C Bean, M Simms, S Bennett and J Warhurst, 1997.

Howard's Agenda: The 1998 Australian Election, edited by M Simms and J Warhurst, 2000.

2001: The Centenary Election, edited by J Warhurst and M Simms, 2002.

Mortgage Nation: The 2004 Australian Election, edited by M Simms and J Warhurst, 2005.

Kevin 07: The 2007 Australian Election, in the *Australian Journal of Cultural History*, Part 1 Vol 27 (3) 2009, and Part 2 Vol 28 (1) 2010, guest editor M Simms.

Julia 2010: The caretaker election, edited by M Simms and J Wanna, 2012.

NB: An earlier list of this series and some details about the electoral studies is included in Murray Goot's entry 'Election Studies', in Brian Galligan and Winsome Roberts (eds), 2007, *The Oxford Companion to Australian Politics*, Melbourne: Oxford University Press.

Contributors

Andrew Bartlett was a Queenland Senator with the Australian Democrats for over 10 years, being Parliamentary Leader from 2002–04, as well as holding many other positions within the party. On the Democrats' demise, he joined the Greens, standing as a candidate twice. He is currently the Convenor of the Queensland Greens.

Clive Bean is a professor of Political Science and Director of Undergraduate Studies at the Queensland University of Technology. He is a director of the Australian Election Study, which has surveyed the Australian electorate each election year since 1987.

Peter John Chen is a senior lecturer in Government and International Relations at the University of Sydney. He is the author of *Australian Politics in a Digital Age* (2013) and *Electronic Engagement: A Guide for Public Managers* (2007).

Brian Costar is a professor at Swinburne University's Institute for Social Research and specialises in Australian politics and elections and parliamentary studies. He has co-authored a number of publications on the rise of independents including *Rebels with a Cause: Independents in Australian Politics* (2004).

Jennifer Curtin is an associate professor in Comparative Politics and Public Policy at the University of Auckland. Previously, she taught Politics and Policy at Monash University and the University of Canberra and held a postdoctoral position at The Australian National University. Her research has focused on the representation of women in formal political institutions and policy making environments, and rural and regional representation, and the rise of independents, in Australian and New Zealand politics.

Nick Economou is a senior lecturer in the School of Political and Social Inquiry, Monash University. He has published books and journal articles on national and state government in Australia and is a media commentator on Australian national and state politics, contributing regularly to the ABC, 3AW, the BBC, *The Conversation*, and various newspapers.

Wayne Errington is a senior lecturer in Politics and Public Policy at the University of Adelaide. He is the author of numerous articles on political communication, political parties and leadership, and co-author of *John Winston Howard: The Definitive Biography*.

Murray Goot is Distinguished Professor and Australian Research Council Australian Professorial Fellow at the Department of Modern History, Politics and International Relations, Macquarie University. He is widely recognised as one of Australia's leading academic analysts of public opinion and has written widely in this area.

Gwendolyn Gray AO is an adjunct fellow in the School of Politics and International Relations at The Australian National University, where she previously taught and wrote on Australian and international health and welfare policies, particularly on the way policies affect women. She has been a member of the Australian women's health movement for over 20 years, serving on the executives of Sexual Health and Family Planning ACT, Sexual Health and Family Planning Australia and the Australian Women's Health Network.

Antony Green is an election analyst with the Australian Broadcasting Corporation. He is a leading psephologist and has analysed elections for the ABC since 1989. He has contributed election analysis to publications such as the *Sydney Morning Herald* and *Crikey*, and his blog can be found at: blogs.abc.net.au/antonygreen/.

Simon Jackman is a professor of Political Science and (by courtesy) of Statistics at Stanford University. Jackman's teaching and research centres on the application of statistical methods in the social sciences, with a particular focus on issues in democratic politics (public opinion, election campaigns, political participation, and electoral systems). Jackman worked as a polling analyst for *Huffington Post* ahead of the US 2012 presidential election and for *Guardian Australia* during the 2013 Australian federal election. He can be contacted by email: jackman@stanford.edu.

Dean Jaensch AO is Professor (Academic Status) of Politics at Flinders University. He is the author and co-author of 20 books, and of numerous chapters and articles, mainly on themes of Australian politics. He has edited four books and a professional journal. For over 40 years he has had a wide involvement with public political education, and with political and electoral analysis and commentary. He has a constant relationship with the media, commenting on political matters.

Carol Johnson is a professor of Politics at the University of Adelaide. She is a former president of the Australian Political Studies Association, the peak body of Australian political scientists; a Fellow of the Academy of Social Sciences in Australia and currently serves on the Academy's Executive Committee. Her key research interests lie in the areas of Australian politics, ideology and discourse, gender and sexuality, and the politics of emotion. Her key books include *Governing Change: From Keating to Howard* (2000) and *The Labor Legacy: Curtin, Chifley, Whitlam, Hawke* (1989).

James Jupp AM, FASSA is a regular contributor to Australian election studies and specialises in the politics of 'ethnic' areas and issues. He is an adjunct associate professor in the Australian Demographic and Social Research Institute at ANU and formerly taught political science at universities in Melbourne, York (UK) and Waterloo (Canada). His many publications include *The Australian People* (1988 and 2001), *From White Australia to Woomera* (2002 and 2007) and *The Encyclopedia of Religion in Australia* (2009).

Tom King is a PhD student in the School of Politics and International Relations at The Australian National University. He was previously a public servant for 30 years, working in the Australian Taxation Office and the Department of Social Security.

Hsu-Ann Lee holds a Bachelor of Laws/Bachelor of Arts (Spanish Honours) from The Australian National University and is currently a research assistant for the Australia and New Zealand School of Government (ANZSOG) at ANU.

Brian Loughnane is the Federal Director of the Liberal Party of Australia and was the Coalition's National Campaign Director for the 2004, 2007, 2010 and 2013 federal elections. He has been a party member for over 30 years, serving in various roles at both state and federal level.

Haydon Manning, of the Department of Politics and Public Policy at Flinders University, is a frequent commentator on South Australian and national politics whose main research interests focus on political attitudes, voting behaviour, South Australian and federal elections, political parties, environmental politics, and political cartoons.

Rob Manwaring teaches politics and public policy at Flinders University, South Australia. His forthcoming book on British and Australian Labour and democratic renewal will be published in 2014.

Ian McAllister is Distinguished Professor of Political Science at The Australian National University, and from 1997 until 2004 was Director of the Research School of Social Sciences at ANU. He is a director of the Australian Election Study, which has surveyed the Australian electorate each election year since 1987.

Kirsty McLaren is undertaking a PhD on social movements in sub-Saharan Africa, in the School of Politics and International Relations at The Australian National University. As a research associate with the Mapping the Australian Women's Movement project, she contributed to *The Women's Movement in Protest, Institutions and the Internet*.

Narelle Miragliotta is a lecturer in Australian Politics at Monash University. Her research interests are in the area of political institutions, with a focus on political parties, parliament, and elections and electoral systems, particularly in Australia.

Lionel Orchard teaches Public Policy at Flinders University, South Australia. Lionel has published widely, particularly in the area of housing policy in Australia. His most recent book *Australian Public Policy: Progressive Ideas in the Neoliberal Ascendency* is an edited collection with Chris Miller on Australian public policy.

Robert Phiddian, Deputy Dean of the School of Humanities at Flinders University, researches political satire particularly in the contexts of 18th century British literature and contemporary Australian political cartoons.

Jennifer Rayner is a doctoral candidate with the Centre for the Study of Australian Politics at The Australian National University, where she researches election campaign strategy in Australian state and federal politics.

Nicholas Reece is a Public Policy fellow at the University of Melbourne. He has significant experience in election campaigns with previous roles including Director of Strategy for Prime Minister Julia Gillard and Party Secretary and Campaign Director for the Australian Labor Party in Victoria.

Geoff Robinson is a senior lecturer in Politics and Australian Studies at Deakin University, Waurn Ponds campus. He is a regular media commentator on Australian politics and author of *When the Labor Party Dreams: Class, Politics and Policy in New South Wales 1930–1932* (2008). He can be followed on Twitter: @geoffpolhist.

Marian Sawer AO is Emeritus Professor in the School of Politics and International Relations at The Australian National University. Her most recent book (co-edited with Sarah Maddison) is *The Women's Movement in Protest, Institutions and the Internet: Australia in Transnational Perspective* (2013).

Paul Strangio is an associate professor of Politics in the School of Social Sciences at Monash University. A specialist in Australian political history he has written widely on political leadership and political parties. His most recent book, *Neither Power Nor Glory: 100 Years of Political Labor in Victoria, 1856–1956* (Melbourne University Press, 2012) won the 2013 Henry Mayer Book Prize for Australian Politics.

James Walter is a professor of Politics in the School of Social Sciences at Monash University. He has written widely on leadership, biography, and political ideas. His most recent book, *What were they thinking? The politics of ideas in Australia* (2010) won the 2011 Henry Mayer Book Prize for Australian Politics.

John Wanna holds the Sir John Bunting Chair of Public Administration at The Australian National University, and is the National Research Director for the Australia and New Zealand School of Government (ANZSOG). He has published widely on Australian politics and public policy.

Rae Wear teaches and researches Queensland and Australian politics in the School of Political Science and International Studies at the University of Queensland. She has written books, chapters and articles on Queensland's premiers, state and federal politics, Australian political parties and populism.

George Wright is the General Secretary of the Australian Labor Party. He was previously Director of Policy and Communications at the Australian Council of Trade Unions and Press Secretary to the Prime Minister in the Rudd Labor Government.

Sally Young is a reader in Political Science in the School of Social and Political Sciences at the University of Melbourne. She was the Research Director for the University's 2013 Election Watch project. Funding for the project, and for subsequent research (including this chapter), was provided by the Melbourne School of Government.

Introduction: Analysing the 2013 Australian federal election

Carol Johnson, John Wanna and Hsu-Ann Lee

Australians historically do not change governments lightly. Yet the 2013 federal election heralded a change of government—only the seventh time Australians have voted to change their national government since the Second World War. Tony Abbott, who had been Opposition Leader since 1 December 2009, became Australia's 28th Prime Minister on 18 September 2013 leading a Liberal–National Coalition with a comfortable majority in the lower house of parliament but well short of a majority in the upper house. The election result occurred after a surreal seven-and-a-half months of campaigning (actually 227 days) in which the Coalition largely held its collective nerve, while the Labor Government continued to implode through internal divisions and acrimony. To all intents and purposes the campaign was not fought principally on policy issues, but on personalities and the tarnished record of the Rudd–Gillard governments.

The result was largely a foregone conclusion (although events or major blunders could have thrown it off course). For months opinion polls indicated a comfortable Coalition victory. And three months out from polling day, betting markets predicted a Coalition win giving it the short odds of $1.25 compared to the longer odds for Labor of $3.75. Pollsters and pundits were convinced the Coalition would form the next government, as were many voters who responded to survey questions about who they expected to win the forthcoming election.

But the tectonic shift in the bigger picture of Australian voting intentions was not the only story of the 2013 election. Underneath this seismic movement were many other different stories and contradictory occurrences. Australia produced no uniform swing across the nation; regions voted differently and with various degrees of disaffection. Some sitting members unexpectedly hung on to their seats while others who were expected to hold theirs easily lost to local challengers. Labor expected to lose many of its frontbench performers in a rout, but apart from a couple of outer ministers largely kept its frontbench intact after the poll. Once again, as we discuss in subsequent chapters, voters continued to turn away from the major party blocs, preferring instead to vote for minor parties, micro parties and independents. In the Senate vote, brand new parties formed on the cusp of the election garnered support and almost unknown candidates fronting micro parties won seats in parliament due to some tactical gaming ploys. So, for an election that many predicted was a *fait accompli* for the conservatives, there were many complicating dimensions and facets that capture our interest and are worth exploring to explain the eventual outcome. This is the project of this book as it traverses the various aspects of the 2013 federal election.

Ideally, to fully appreciate the analysis of a specific study of a national election, readers should have some understanding of the main contours and institutional rules of the electoral system in question, and consequently the ways the system works to produce actual outcomes. Each and every electoral system has its own peculiarities and codified specifics, which can remain opaque to the specialist and lay reader alike. Many contextual conditions and formal requirements, as well as the composite electoral procedures that impose detailed rules and disciplines on participants, can be hugely influential in the intended outcomes. Systems produce effects, some intended, some unintended; whether it nurtures or circumscribes the number of political parties, or makes it harder or easier for minor parties and independents to gain representation, or allows parties to fill inopportune vacancies expediently without going back to the voters, these are all systemic institutional factors that affect outcomes; they profoundly structure the behaviour of the proximate players in the electoral process and shape our analysis as observers.

Hence, we would like to point out that while the analyses in the chapters that follow draw significantly on the relevant international literatures, there are many specific features of the Australian political system worth explaining for the benefit of those—including overseas readers—who may be less familiar with the Australian electoral system and its legislative context. It is important to recognise that the Australian political system contains a number of unique characteristics which significantly affect the outcome of elections—the 2013 federal election is no exception. We canvass these specific features initially in this introduction.

Understanding the importance of Australia's electoral system to its electoral outcomes

Australia has a long history of electoral innovation (Kelly 2012; Sawer 2001), including in regard to unusual voting systems and a reliance on independent electoral administration. Voting in the House of Representatives (the lower house in the bicameral system) uses a system of preferential voting in individual constituencies, rather than simple majority or first-past-the-post voting (plurality voting systems) or proportional representational voting. Australian voters are required to rank candidates for a particular seat by giving numbered preferences—such as numbering their ballot sequentially: 1, 2, 3, 4, 5, etc.— according to their individual preferences. In 2013 an average of eight candidates contested each lower house seat, a new record number of candidates standing for election. Voters who do not correctly register a full set of preferences are often deemed to have made an informal vote. If a candidate receives over 50 per cent of first preference votes (a clear majority of preference 1 votes on the first count of ballot papers) they are duly elected. If no one is elected outright on the first count (i.e. no one gains 50 per cent +1), then the votes of losing candidates are re-allocated, beginning with the second preferences of the lowest scoring candidate whose preferences are transferred at full value, with this elimination process continuing until a candidate manages to exceed 50 per cent (with, of course, the least popular candidates progressively being excluded).

Hence in the Australian electoral system it is uncommon but not unknown for a candidate who comes second or third in the initial ballot to win a seat 'on preferences'—for example, see Chapter 16, where an independent candidate defeated a sitting Liberal MP in the Victorian seat of Indi. This particular aspect of Australia's preferential voting system encourages *negative voting* (against those voters most dislike) and operates to ensure that the 'least un-preferred' candidate is elected to a seat in parliament (i.e. winning candidates receive less of a positive endorsement as a prospective member than the judgment that they are the 'least worst' candidate standing for the election). It is a perverse system in the minds of many overseas observers more used to positive forms of voting expression. It is neither proportional nor straight-forwardly majoritarian, but endorses the 'least worst' candidate in the eyes of the electorate—where every subsequent preference (second, third, fourth, etc.) counts for the same value as the first preference cast if the intended candidate is eliminated.

Australian governments since the 1940s have been formed by two major party blocs, either a conservative grouping led by the Liberal Party of Australia (in 'permanent' coalition with the Nationals, a rural-based party formerly known as the Country Party, and a sprinkling of other country liberals), or somewhat less commonly by the Australian Labor Party, an amalgam of separate state divisions, rival union factions and constituency branches. Due to the preferential voting system, the voting result that is crucial for determining election outcomes is *not* the primary vote (the percentage of first preference votes a party receives)—although a low primary vote can be the first sign a party is unelectable—but rather the two-party-preferred vote (the percentage of the votes that eventually goes to Labor or the Coalition after the full distribution of preferences). Accordingly, almost exclusively the media and polling organisations focus on the latter figure and not the former, as Goot discusses in Chapter 8.

In addition, it is important for general readers to remember that voting in Australia is compulsory, in terms of both registration or enrolment and actual voting (see further Hill 2010)—at least insofar as voters have to attend a polling booth and have their name ticked off, although some may not hand in a valid ballot paper.

The voting system for the Senate (an entirely elected upper house) is even more complicated. Because the Senate consists of 12 Senators from each of the six original states and two Senators from each of the two territories (a total of 76 Senators), a simple preferential system would not work. Crucially, unlike in the House of Representatives, more than one person needs to be elected from each geographical area. Consequently, a system of quasi-proportional representation is used, in which the voter places sequentially numbered preferences against all candidates' names (or votes for a party bloc of names—see below). Successful candidates have to gain a certain proportion of the actual votes cast (the 'quota'). The Senate quota is worked out on the basis of candidates winning a certain proportion of the overall formal vote for that jurisdiction, given the number of candidates that have to be elected (note that only half of the state-based Senators face voters in a normal half-Senate election).[1] If the required number of candidates do not attain full quotas outright, votes above the quota and votes of the least popular candidates are re-allocated according to the flow of preferences marked by the voter or party of choice. Hence, the Senate vote is partially proportional (but not exclusively because states have different proportionalities) *and* partially preferential (in that once the candidates with outright quotas are elected, the remainder of seats are allocated by preferential redistribution).

The complicated Senate voting system is very beneficial for minor parties in that they can get their candidates elected with a much smaller proportion of the state-wide vote than if they were standing for the House of Representatives, where one has to win more than 50 per cent of the formal vote after preferences are distributed. Thus, Andrew Bartlett in Chapter 13 celebrates the fact that the Greens in 2013 made history in holding as many as *10* seats (of 76) in the Senate, and in becoming the first minor party to retain their lower house seat (*one* of a total of 150 seats). On the other hand, both the Palmer United Party and Katter's Australia Party polled better in the House of Representatives than in the Senate—a 'surprising' outcome, but one which secured them just one seat each in the lower house (see Chapter 17 by Tom King).

However, the system is even more complicated because the large number of candidates standing for Senate positions resulted in, from 1984 onwards, the

---

[1] The basic formula for determining a quota for election to the Senate is as follows:
Total number of formal votes cast
Divided by the number of candidates +1, then add one vote to qualify as a complete quota.
So, if 100,000 valid votes are cast and six senators are to be elected, then 100,000 is divided by 7, +1 vote; or an actual quota of 14,286 votes.

introduction of a system where voters could simply allocate preferences to party blocs, called 'above the line voting', rather than having to allocate preferences to each candidate 'below the line'.[2] Parties then allocate how their preferences should be distributed to other candidates—a system which has been criticised for lacking transparency and which, in the 2013 election, also led to accusations of rorting as a number of minor parties inflated their results by exchanging preferences with each other (see Antony Green's chapter for more information).

The proliferation of minor parties has been further encouraged by the relatively 'light touch' nature of Australian party regulation and electoral spending. This is particularly the case in regard to campaign funding from private sources where, as Gauja (2010: 191) points out, Australia has a relatively *laissez-faire* approach, more similar to that in the UK than Canada or New Zealand, or even the US.[3] As Gauja (2010: 166) notes:

> Unlike the regulatory regimes of comparable common law nations, there is no legislative restriction placed on the amounts that may be donated to Australian political parties or their expenditure during election campaigns.

Instead, Australian campaign regulation relies heavily on election campaign disclosure laws, which some argue have been undermined by a provision allowing anonymous donations of up to $12,400 (Gauja 2010: 166–9). Importantly, in terms of the newly formed Palmer United Party (see King's chapter), established by claimed billionaire Clive Palmer, there is also no cap on how much candidates can contribute to their (or their party's) campaigns, unlike in Canada (Parliamentary Information and Research Service 2006).

There are also relatively few barriers to registered electors standing as candidates or creating new parties, with implications for the number of micro parties and genuine independents standing (see the chapters by Jennifer Curtin and Brian Costar, as well as Tom King and Antony Green on the proliferation of micro parties). The *Electoral and Referendum Amendment (Improving Electoral Procedure) Act 2013* merely amended the *Commonwealth Electoral Act 1918* (the *Electoral Act*) and the *Referendum (Machinery Provisions) Act 1984* (the *Referendum Act*) to increase the dollar amount a person nominating as a Senator had to deposit from $1,000 to $2,000, and for House of Representatives nominees from $500 to $1,000 (AEC 2013a). A political party can be registered with the

---

2 The 'below the line' system often leads to votes being ruled invalid ('informal') if correct sequential numbers are not allocated to all candidates properly—for example, if there is an inadvertent doubling up or omission of some numbers.
3 For a detailed analysis of Australian electoral and financial regulations see Parliamentary Library, Parliament of Australia (2012); Orr (2010) and Tham, Costar and Orr (2011). For a detailed analysis of the comparative regulations covering public funding, as opposed to private funding of parties in Australia, Canada, New Zealand, the UK and US, see Gauja (2010: 144–57).

Australian Electoral Commission to participate in federal elections merely on the basis that it has a written constitution setting out the aims of the party and either at least one member who has been elected to federal parliament, or at least 500 members who are not listed in another party's application for registration (AEC 2013b).

Finally, the Australian Electoral Commission, which conducts and scrutinises Australian elections, once traditionally enjoyed a high level of trust amongst the Australian public as well as the various professionals who study election processes and outcomes. This trust was badly damaged during the 2013 election process by a series of mishaps and instances of incompetence. Some candidates publicly complained about the procedures of the AEC. Then, the AEC 'lost' some 1,370 Senate votes critical to the preference count in Western Australia when it found that they had gone missing between the original count and a recount, although poor material management systems, rather than fraud, was found to be the reason (AEC 2013c and 2013d). Despite the fact that the missing ballot papers constituted only around 0.01 per cent of total votes cast in the state, the loss of these ballots in Western Australia was unusually significant because the result was crucial to the balance of power in the Senate—specifically whether Labor could retain their second seat. Indeed, the publication date of this volume was pushed back so that the outcome could be taken into account.

As Antony Green explains in Chapter 23, the contest for the final two Western Australian Senate places was extremely close, at one point a matter of a single vote potentially determining the distribution of preferences and thus the end result. Labor and the Greens (sitting Senators Louise Pratt and Scott Ludlam, respectively), Palmer United (Zhenya Wang) and the Australian Sports Party (Wayne Dropulich) were all in the running. The initial count gave these two seats to Palmer United and the Australian Sports Party; the recount saw the Greens beat PUP to hold on to their Senate place. A new West Australian half-Senate election awarded by the High Court produced another permutation—Labor again failed to keep their second seat, the Liberals retained their three positions and both the Greens and PUP were successful, providing an interesting crossbench for the new Coalition Government to deal with.

The scandal of the 'lost votes' cost both the Federal Electoral Commissioner and the Western Australian State Manager their jobs and the AEC became the subject of an investigatory joint house parliamentary committee inquiry. The re-election in Western Australia was held in April 2014 at an additional cost of $23 million. At this re-election, the AEC once again proved lax in its administration of cast ballots, and around 75 voters had to vote for a third time.

Having set out the broad background to Australian federal elections, it is now necessary to proceed to analyse key features of the 2013 election in particular.

Main themes explored in chapters

The overall aims of this book are to analyse the 2013 federal election and provide explanations as to why a change of government took place. We chose the title *Abbott's Gambit* because it conveys succinctly the defining strategy of the eventual winner. It evokes the atmosphere of the hung parliament of 2010–13, where the conservative opposition successfully drew its adversarial battlelines in the years leading up to the ballot. It also recognises that it was not the out-going government, but rather Abbott as the challenger who set the tone of the election and determined the agendas—no mean feat for an opposition leader. His polarising, take-no-prisoners, approach to politics was a high-stakes gamble that ultimately paid off for the Opposition Leader at his second tilt at high office. In taking this gambit Abbott faced the risk that his strategy might implode or self-destruct (*à la* Latham in 2004) or alienate constituents. The gambit not only shaped the context in which he was to fight the 2013 election, but also had significant implications beyond the election day itself in sullying the environment in which he was to commence government. His cynical gambit was certainly a cunning ploy from opposition, but paradoxically may have served to poison the well as he commences his term in government.

This book identifies the following key issues and trends that were of particular importance in this election, and that constitute key themes that will be explored in subsequent chapters:

- The effect of the Labor–Green–independent minority government and voter perceptions of dysfunctionality, serial scandals and duplicity;
- The personalisation of politics, and its relationship to leadership issues—with popularity, 'likeability', trust, image, identity and performance becoming major determinative factors for the public's voting intentions;
- The historically low opinion of politics in the electorate and declining trust in government;
- The importance of hyper-adversarialism in party politics, and concocted 'fear' or 'scare' campaigns to pander basely to a disaffected electorate;
- The decline in party identification, voter loyalties and 'habit voting', leading to greater electoral volatility among sections of the electorate and a preparedness to cast 'protest' votes for minor party candidates or independents;
- The mediatisation of politics (and trivialisation of politics) in which both traditional and new social media had influential but different roles to play;
- The superficial marketisation of politics, in which fabricated policies are developed and communicated based on forms of pre-tested market research

(and, despite the preponderance of the techniques of marketisation and 'spin', the Labor Government's inability to communicate its achievements);
- The incessant professionalisation of politics, including the growing disparity between our career political representatives and the electorate and the importing of campaigning and communication techniques from overseas;
- The crucial importance of competitive parties defining (or conjuring) areas of key policy difference, while neutralising others through apparent bipartisan support;
- The importance of the campaign tactics and detailed campaign preparations of the major parties, including candidate selection and targeted 'sandbagging' of vulnerable seats;
- The role of party discipline as a stultifying influence on politics and political debate, but also the rise of egotistical identities encouraging intra-party rivalries and disunity;
- The importance of political geography and changing constituency demographics, including the clashes of values and preferences (e.g. over the environment or social policies), but also the influences of gender, ethnicity, education and social class;
- The importance of 'hip-pocket' or economic motivations for voting;
- The roles and agendas of minor parties, independents/crossbenchers who have recently enjoyed much political influence; and,
- Overall, the increasing disintegration or fragmentation of the rigid two-party system and the historical left-right voting divide in Australian politics.

Several chapters emphasise the paralysing effect of minority government and voter perceptions of dysfunction and scandal. Jennifer Rayner and John Wanna point out the crucial role played by issues of agenda-setting and framing in shaping voter perceptions. Carol Johnson points out that an essential feature of the way in which Abbott mobilised emotion was firstly to evoke voters' anxiety (by depicting the previous Labor governments as characterised by uncertainty, dysfunction and chaos) and then secondly to evoke the politics of reassurance (by promising voters that a Coalition Government would be safe and dependable).

Paul Strangio and James Walter emphasise how important voters' perceptions of dysfunction were in shaping leadership issues during the initial periods of the campaign. Such leadership issues reflect a general trend towards the personalisation of politics. Claims about the relative popularity and celebrity status of Kevin Rudd compared with Julia Gillard played a major role in Labor's decision to change leaders shortly before the election. However, as Walter and Strangio point out, the combination of Rudd's poor campaigning and Abbott's low popularity led to commentators reassessing the importance of leadership effects in the course of the 2013 campaign. Leadership issues also intersected with issues of party discipline. Labor's internal disunity and leadership tensions undermined its campaign while Abbott's strong self-discipline and the control of tensions within the Liberal Party and Coalition contributed in no small part to the Coalition's victory. As Haydon Manning and Robert Phiddian emphasise, these issues about leadership, disunity and discipline were also reflected in the cartoonists' graphic history of the campaign, in addition to the normal hyperbole and pantomime.

Opinion poll ratings were also crucial in Labor's decision to replace Gillard as leader with the recycled Rudd. Despite the prominence given to polling in media analyses of the lead-up to the election, Murray Goot notes in his chapter that there were problems with the polls' accuracy. On the one hand, the focus on two-party-preferred results attempted to minimise the risk of predicting outcomes, particularly in a situation where Labor's primary vote was so low. The polls were less successful in accurately predicting the outcomes in marginal seats, partly because of some voter reversion and Labor's success in 'sandbagging' particular seats via successful local campaigns, as discussed in George Wright's chapter, and partly because of complex regional and demographic factors discussed in the chapters by Dean Jaensch *et al*. and by James Jupp. Many of the polls had also been conducted before a late surge in minor party support that partly reflected a disillusion with the major parties that is discussed in the chapters by Tom King and by Jennifer Curtin and Brian Costar. Simon Jackman points out in his chapter that summarising diverse opinion poll results also played a major role in influencing betting markets, which some have argued are more reliable than the polls themselves at predicting election outcomes. However, in the 2013 election these betting markets often posted misleading odds in specific seats.

Carol Johnson's chapter focuses on the importance of 'fear' and 'scare' campaigns in engaging a disaffected electorate. Drawing on international literature on the importance of the politics of emotion in election campaigning, Johnson suggests that the eliciting of emotion was not only an important strategy for engaging the electorate but also an important means by which ideological differences between the parties were evoked. For example, the Coalition could raise neo-liberal themes via fear campaigns on issues such as a claimed excessive government debt or taxes, without necessarily explicitly spelling out the ideological differences between the parties that underpinned them. Johnson argues that this partly helps to explain the lack of explicit ideological differentiation between the major parties on some issues that has been noted by other commentators in the book (see chapters by Jennifer Rayner and John Wanna and by Gwen Gray, Rob Manwaring and Lionel Orchard). In particular, as Gray, Manwaring and Orchard point out, the Coalition pursued a small target strategy on many social issues, including previously controversial ones such as health or education, in an attempt to neutralise points of policy difference. More explicitly ideological statements by key Liberal politicians tended to be made before (Hockey 2012) or after the election (Abbott 2014) rather than during it.

Media also played a crucial role in engaging the electorate, reflecting an increasing mediatisation of politics. Wayne Errington points out that the traditional media did still play an important role in the campaign as, indeed, frequent accusations of media bias against the Murdoch press revealed. However, Peter John Chen argues that social media was not only important as a key site of election commentary, but that it also became an essential technique of campaigning and a key site of electoral practices, with parties often drawing on the experience of equivalent parties overseas.

Party election strategies are also being driven by another aspect of communication, characterised by the marketisation of politics, in which policies are developed and communicated based on forms of market research. Sally Young analyses how parties are still using traditional television advertising as well as new forms of information technology. Above all, campaign advertising and communication strategies are now focusing on using market research and targeting particular sets of voters. Nicholas Reece continues this theme, pointing out the role that market research is increasingly playing in *shaping*, not just selling, policy. Such communication and marketing strategies, and their influence on election policy, reflect an increasing professionalisation of politics, which includes the buying-in of overseas expertise (as Young's, Chen's and Reece's chapters all emphasise). Yet this professionalisation has also contributed to a growing disparity between our political representatives and the electorate, which can fuel the electorate's disaffection, noted throughout this volume.

The analysis of how policy was sold also illustrates the crucial importance of the winning parties defining areas of policy difference, while neutralising others. This is a point emphasised in Gwen Gray's, Rob Manwaring's and Lionel Orchard's analysis of social policy in the 2013 election, where some issues such as health and education were effectively neutralised by either downplaying their importance or declaring bipartisan support. Gender was another social issue that the parties handled carefully during the campaign. Kirsty McLaren and Marian Sawer argue that, in the aftermath of Gillard's misogyny speech, both Abbott and Rudd attempted to minimise gender as an issue during the 2013 election. Nonetheless, gender remained a significant factor in terms of the campaign's masculine undertones. Furthermore, women's continuing under-representation (including the presence of only one woman in Abbott's original cabinet) and the marginalising of women's policy compared with previous years indicate that Australian politics is still male dominated—perhaps reflecting the nature of Australian society. Meanwhile, James Jupp's chapter notes the (largely unsuccessful) attempts by the Liberal Party to win over ethnic voters via the selection of candidates from appropriate ethnic backgrounds. He also notes the major parties attempts to out-do each other in terms of introducing tough asylum seeker policies.

Labor's relatively late leadership change meant that Rudd had difficulty capitalising on social policy initiatives that were associated with the Gillard Government. Labor struggled to counter the Liberals' handling of economic policy issues, in which the Coalition became the owners of stable and sound economic management, while Labor was stuck with the image of being the fiscally irresponsible party that had persistently presided over rising debt levels while continuing to announce unfunded future liabilities (and these issues of budgetary management also had major implications for the fear campaigns analysed by Johnson). Given the crucial importance of economic and fiscal debates in the 2013 election, it was considered necessary to provide a detailed analysis of economic issues in a separate chapter (see the chapter by John Wanna). Moreover, Nick Economou argues that the politics of climate change also continued to be a major economic issue in terms of the carbon tax, even after Gillard was removed from office. Indeed, other environmental issues tended to be downplayed compared with climate change and the imposition of the associated carbon tax—a policy shift by Labor that was often painted as an expedient act of duplicity. Given that it 'universalised' the cost of a key environmental policy, the carbon tax may even have played a major role in Labor's defeat. It also allowed Abbott to maintain that his government would honour its commitments—an undertaking that has since proved difficult for the conservatives to uphold.

Previous volumes in the election series have analysed regional voting trends primarily on a state-by-state basis. However, increasingly demographic and regional divides cross state and territory boundaries, and cannot be easily confined to these jurisdictional entities. Indeed, Geoff Robinson's chapter delivers a particularly interesting account of the changing role of regional factors in Australian political history and the implications for today. Consequently, rather than devoting separate chapters to analysing the results and electoral effects in each state and territory, the current volume aims to analyse voting trends by way of categories such as swing states and non-swing states (to assist in determining where was the outcome decided); mortgage-belt voting; rural-urban voting; voting according to demographics of age, gender, ethnicity, education and socio-economic status. A number of contributors to this volume have engaged in the analysis of regional factors, under the oversight of Dean Jaensch, with Narelle Miragliotta and Rae Wear also contributing essential insights. The study concludes that there were relatively similar patterns of party support in rural clusters, provincial city clusters and metropolitan clusters. The existence of such clusters emphasises the importance of facts that are not confined to—and indeed often cross—state boundaries. While results in New South Wales played a key role in determining the election outcome, Labor did not suffer the massive losses expected by some in western Sydney. Those findings are confirmed by other chapters. For example, James Jupp has undertaken a detailed study of voting across 'ethnic' electorates, pointing out that Labor largely retained the 'ethnic' vote, and this helps to explain the western Sydney result. Similarly, Curtin and Costar's chapter emphasises the degree to which rural constituencies can feel alienated by major party campaigns, and can view viable independents as an alternative, as the result in the electorate of Indi demonstrated in the 2013 election.

Antony Green's chapter provides a detailed analysis of the voting outcome. Green notes that, while Labor did not do as poorly as predicted by some commentators and polls, particularly those which came out prior to the change back to Rudd, it did obtain an exceptionally low first preference vote. Meanwhile support for independents and minor parties reached record highs (the latter assisted by weaknesses in Australia's electoral system). Clive Bean and Ian McAllister's chapter throws further light on the election outcome by providing a detailed analysis of the findings of the Australian Electoral Survey (AES), including comparisons with key findings in previous elections. The AES explores the political attitudes of those with a certain interest in Australian politics and provides survey data on the range of information sources on which these people base their opinions and voting intentions.

The 2013 volume includes not only the academic assessments outlined above but also the insider analyses offered by key party players themselves, namely chapters by Brian Loughnane, Federal Director of the Liberal Party; George Wright, National Secretary of the Australian Labor Party and Andrew Bartlett, Convenor of the Queensland Greens and an experienced political campaigner who was previously a Queensland Senator for the Australian Democrats. The contributions from Loughnane, Wright and Bartlett provide expert practitioner insights into the parties' own thinking and campaign strategies and will be further discussed in the final chapter.

Conclusion

As this brief overview of the campaign suggests, the 2013 election outcome was influenced by a wide range of factors—many contextual and deep-seated in nature, but some more proximate and transitory in their immediate impacts. It was fairly clear months before the election was called that Labor would lose the election and Abbott would win; but the change of leadership from Gillard to Rudd, the campaign dynamics and differential regional volatility, as well as the continued rise of minor and micro parties, all contributed to the final result. Abbott's strategy of running a tightly controlled campaign in which Labor was constructed as an internecine and dysfunctional rabble and the Coalition as the only united team on the political stage able to form a mature adult government, clearly played a major role in bringing about a change of government. It was a message that helped to regenerate an opposition into an alternative government and one that certainly appealed to sections of a disaffected electorate. Nevertheless a sizeable proportion of the electorate (over one-fifth in the House vote and almost one-third in the Senate) voted for parties or candidates other than the two major political party blocs, or voted informally. This reflects a degree of disillusionment with the established parties and contributed towards the lower primary vote swing gained by the Liberal–Nationals (around +1.5 per cent, and only 3.61 per cent in two-party-preferred terms). These are issues that will be returned to in the final chapter of this volume.

References

Abbott, Tony. 2014. 'Address to the World Economic Forum'. Davos, Switzerland, 23 January 2014, viewed 27 March 2014: <www.pm.gov.au/media/2014-01-23/address-world-economic-forum-davos-switzerland-0>.

Allen, Nicholas and Bartle, John. 2011. *Britain at the Polls 2010*. London: Sage.

Australian Electoral Commission. 2013a. 'Commonwealth electoral legislation— changes since the 2010 federal election'. Updated 24 July, viewed 15 December 2013: <www.aec.gov.au/elections/australian_electoral_system/legislation-changes.htm>.

Australian Electoral Commission. 2013b. 'Party registration overview'. Updated 22 April, viewed 15 December 2013: <www.aec.gov.au/Parties_and_Representatives/party_registration/overview.htm>.

Australian Electoral Commission. 2013c. 'AEC releases voting preference information recorded for WA missing votes'. Media release, 8 November, viewed 26 March 2014: <www.aec.gov.au/media/media-releases/2013/files/e11-08.pdf>.

Australian Electoral Commission. 2013d. *Inquiry into the 2013 WA Senate Election December 2013*. Report commissioned by the Australian Electoral Commission and produced by MJ Keelty AO. Viewed 26 March 2014: <www.aec.gov.au/about_aec/Publications/Reports_On_Federal_Electoral_Events/2013/files/inquiry-into-the-2013-wa-senate-election.pdf>.

Gauja, Anika. 2010. *Political Parties and Elections: Legislating for Representative Democracy*. Farnham: Ashgate.

Hill, Lisa. 2010. 'Public Acceptance of Compulsory Voting: Explaining the Australian Case'. *Representation* 46(4): 425–38.

Kelly, Norm. 2012. *Directions in Australian Electoral Reform*. Canberra: ANU E-Press.

Levine, Steven and Roberts, Nigel S. 2012. *Key to Victory: The New Zealand General Election of 2008*. Wellington: Victoria University Press.

Nelson, Michael. 2013. *The Elections of 2012*. Los Angeles: CQ Press.

Orr, Graeme. 2010. *The Law of Politics: Elections, Parties and Money in Australia*. Sydney: Federation Press.

Parliamentary Information and Research Service, Parliament of Canada. 2006. 'Political financing and campaign regulation'. Prepared by Sebastian Spano, Law and Government Division, 23 February, viewed 27 March 2014: <www.parl.gc.ca/Content/LOP/researchpublications/prb0579-e.htm#limits1>.

Parliamentary Library, Parliament of Australia. 2012. 'Electoral and political financing: the Commonwealth regime and its reforms'. Background Note, prepared by Brenton Holmes, Politics and Public Administration Section, 30 March, viewed 15 December 2013: <www.aph.gov.au/About_Parliament/Parliamentary_Departments/Parliamentary_Library/pubs/BN/2011-2012/ElectoralFinancing#_Toc320870078>.

Sawer, Marian (ed.). 2001. *Elections Full, Free and Fair*. Sydney: Federation Press.

Tham, Joo-Cheong, Costar, Brian and Orr, Graeme (eds). 2011. *Electoral Democracy: Australian Prospects*. Melbourne: Melbourne University Press.

Wring, Dominic, Mortimore, Roger and Atkinson, Simon (eds). 2011. *Political Communication in Britain: The Leader's Debates, the Campaign and the Media in the 2010 General Election*. Basingstoke: Palgrave Macmillan.

Part 1. Campaign Themes and Context

1. An Overview of the 2013 Federal Election Campaign: Ruinous politics, cynical adversarialism and contending agendas

Jennifer Rayner and John Wanna

It was often suggested in the Australian media that the 2013 federal election campaign began effectively on 30 January 2013, when the then-Prime Minister Julia Gillard took the unprecedented step of announcing the election date in a speech to the National Press Club eight months out from polling day. Others may suggest that the campaign truly began when Kevin Rudd returned to the prime ministership on 26 June after a bitter war of attrition within his party. But looking back on how the election unfolded, it seems clear that the campaign began in earnest three years earlier on 7 September 2010, when the Greens and three key independent MPs sided with Labor to deliver Australia its first hung parliament since 1943. That was the day that Tony Abbott's Coalition, with one more seat than Labor in the House, began its tireless crusade to bring down the Gillard, and for the following three years it rarely wavered in this aim.

Viewed in this light, the events of an intensively clamorous election year begin to make sense. The ALP spent much of 2013 looking for a tipping point that would reverse Tony Abbott's steady and inexorable march towards The Lodge, and allow it to break free from a constrictive political agenda set by the Coalition. This search led to a confused and nerve-racking year of activity for Labor which culminated in the displacement of Julia Gillard and the reinstalling of Kevin Rudd to the leadership, followed by a chaotic campaign which seemed to veer from one eccentric policy announcement to the next without any coherent or unifying theme.

By contrast, the Coalition sought to minimise the chances of a turning point occurring by sticking with its tried-and-tested techniques of the past few years: simple slogans backed by scant policy, ruthless discipline to maintain party unity, a highly adversarial focus on three wedge issues and an unrelenting emphasis on the Government's failings. Having framed the election as a referendum on Labor's past six years in office and having set the criteria against which its performance would be (unfavourably) judged, the Coalition arguably needed to do little else but stay the course for victory, while guarding against any hint of overconfidence.

We explore how this dynamic evolved throughout the years and months leading up to election day 7 September 2013, and what the Coalition's victory demonstrates about the enduring importance of agenda-setting, framing and issue ownership in political campaigning. These analytical frames help to indicate how political leaders and parties come to define or 'own' issues in ways which enhance their strategic advantage relative to their competitors and shape popular understandings (Dery 2000; Harris, Fury and Lock 2006). Agenda-setting explores how political actors shape the public discourse and issue agenda; framing and issue ownership involve the selective emphasis of information 'to promote a particular problem definition, causal interpretation, moral evaluation and/or treatment recommendation' (Entman 1993: 52). The key point is that the way leaders talk about issues inherently shapes how they are understood by the public and the range of actions considered feasible in response, and this provides parties with an important strategic tool during election campaigns.

Legacies of the Labor government 2007–13

The roots of the Coalition's successful agenda-setting and framing efforts were planted in the rather fertile political soil provided by the Labor Government's six years in office, and so it is necessary to look back to the period leading up to the 2010 election to identify their first green shoots.

After barnstorming to power in 2007 with an ambitious agenda for change and political renewal, the Rudd Government quickly found itself mired in the global financial crisis and struggling to deliver promised reform on a wide range of policy fronts. To avoid a recession, the Government worked fast in producing five major stimulus packages between October 2008 and February 2009, which included the distribution of $900 cheques to low-paid Australian taxpayers and massive new spending on school and housing infrastructure. While the nation avoided recession as a result of these stimulus measures, the speed with which they were implemented led to instances of amateurishness, poor administration, swindling and even deaths—four young men died in separate incidents while installing roof insulation under a stimulus scheme to improve home energy efficiency. The Coalition began to attack the Government's supposed profligacy and irresponsibility in implementing the stimulus programs. Senior Coalition figures such as Christopher Pyne, Joe Hockey and Julie Bishop used Question Time and the media to continually bait the Rudd ministry about its 'pink batts fiasco' and 'school hall rip-offs', and framed the stimulus spending as the latest example of a panicky Labor Government squandering the surplus built up by its more prudent Liberal predecessors (see Bishop 2008; Hockey 2009; Pyne

2009). As a consequence, the Government received little credit for the enormous achievement of avoiding recession, while also acquiring the beginnings of a reputation for chaotic policy delivery and poor economic management.

Labor's first term affected the Government in other damaging ways. To expedite decision-making during the financial crisis, Rudd centralised decision-making around a kitchen cabinet of four senior ministers: himself, his deputy Julia Gillard, Treasurer Wayne Swan and Finance Minister Lindsay Tanner. However, these arrangements did not end once the threat of economic doom receded, and the rest of cabinet was increasingly excluded from important policy decisions (Tingle 2010; Tanner 2012). At the same time, Rudd began to irritate his back bench caucus members over the lack of consultation and his chaotic governing style (McKew 2013).

By 2009—still only its second year in office—the Government appeared to be losing its way, making erratic decisions and failing to address important issues of policy implementation. Rudd stumbled dramatically over policies to mitigate climate change, failing twice to introduce a carbon emissions trading scheme and then shelving further plans to address this critical policy issue in the face of public discontent over projected cost of living increases. One of the Coalition's cut-through campaign messages of 2013 which tagged Kevin Rudd as 'Captain Chaos' had its genesis in this earlier period, when it seemed as though the energy and enthusiasm of 2007 had acquired a more manic edge.

Events came to a head when Rudd was dramatically ousted as leader in June 2010 by Julia Gillard at the behest of Labor's powerful factions. Becoming Prime Minister after the sudden 'coup', Gillard struggled to make an impression from the outset and at the August 2010 election Labor was reduced to minority government status.[1] Gillard managed to patch together a loose 'coalition' of sorts, denying the Liberals a victory after 17 drawn-out days of negotiation. Almost from the moment that the minority Government was formed, Abbott began describing it as a 'bad government' mired in 'chaos', headed by a woman offering nothing but 'broken promises' who was 'beholden to the Greens'. This depiction of Gillard's Government as weak, unstable and chaotic became a familiar Coalition trope throughout the following three years—Hansard alone records more than 400 instances of Liberal and National MPs using the four phrases highlighted above between 7 September 2010 and the last sitting of parliament in 2013 (Hansard, 43rd Parliament of Australia).

In addition to casting a negative frame around the concept of minority government, the Coalition also chiselled away at Labor's policy credibility by ensuring that three issues stayed at the top of the political agenda: the

---

[1] The ALP narrowly won the two-party-preferred vote at 50.12 to 49.88 per cent, but actually won one fewer seat than the Coalition with 72 to 73 seats respectively.

economy, asylum seekers and the carbon tax. These issues had been emphasised prominently in the Coalition's 2010 election campaign, and Abbott refused to relinquish them once back in opposition, cementing his 'ownership' of them politically (Newspoll 2013a). During the three years of the Gillard Government, 64 per cent of all opposition questions asked during Question Time were about these same three issues, while Abbott and his shadow ministers also issued hundreds of media releases, briefings, advertisements and even billboards drawing attention to them. The Coalition's framing of these issues was unambiguously negative: a rise in the number of asylum seekers arriving by boat was presented as a 'border security disaster', the fiscal situation and escalating public debt attained the status of a 'budget emergency', and the carbon tax which Abbott promised to 'axe' was blamed for 'driving up the price of electricity bills by $300 a year' and 'ripping the heart and soul out of small business' (see Hockey 2013; Abbott and Hockey 2011; Morrison 2011).[2] The thrashing of these core issues advantaged the Coalition while it highlighted the stark tension between the party's traditional, materialist support base and its more recent, post-materialist one (Charnock and Ellis 2004). It also provided the opportunity for the Opposition to hammer Labor for placing environmental issues ahead of the cost of living concerns of ordinary voters.

The Gillard Government worked conscientiously to pursue its own distinct policy agenda, committing to a major overhaul of education funding, developing the National Disability Insurance Scheme and accelerating the roll-out of the National Broadband Network, amongst other achievements. But in the face of the Coalition's relentless aggression, Labor seemed unable to gain traction with its alternative agendas.[3] Gillard spent a significant proportion of her term talking about Coalition-owned issues and her opponent's agendas. This suggests the Government was continually reinforcing both the salience of these issues as benchmarks of governing competence, and the Coalition's ownership of them in the eyes of voters (Walgrave, Lefevere and Nuytemans 2009).

Labor seemed unable to move the public conversation past the Coalition's favoured issues, and struggled to neutralise Abbott's negative framing of them. On occasions the Government appeared to play right into his hands. For instance, Treasurer Wayne Swan spent over two years steadfastly promising to deliver a budget surplus by mid-2013 before unceremoniously ditching this commitment in December 2012—a backflip which only served to reinforce the Coalition's

---

[2] It also allowed the Coalition to mount an effective personal attack on Gillard as a 'liar', 'hypocrite' and 'untrustworthy' head of government.

[3] To give an illustration of this, between August 2010 and June 2013 we identified 5,332 articles in Australia's capital city newspapers which featured Gillard discussing asylum seeker issues, 4,713 discussing her Government's management of the economy, and 4,567 focusing on the carbon tax. By contrast, the same papers published 3,853 articles which featured Gillard discussing her party's education agenda, 1,314 on the National Broadband Network, and just 904 on the National Disability Insurance Scheme. Search conducted via Ebsco Host Australia New Zealand Reference Centre, hosted by the National Library of Australia.

claim Labor could not manage the country's finances effectively. Similarly, the Government pursued a range of measures to manage asylum seekers which foundered in the implementation and did not stop arrivals, and so lent weight to Abbott's rhetoric about the Government failing to 'stop the boats'. On the carbon tax, the Government attempted to neutralise the Coalition's negative frame and provide a more positive one by positioning the tax as a necessary response to global warming and a sign of Australia's good global citizenship. However, the Government's frame was relatively academic and thematic in that it relied upon theoretical claims about environmental benefits and comparing the Australian scheme against international benchmarks (Gillard 2011; Combet 2011). By contrast, the Coalition's frame was almost entirely episodic, as it appeared to have an endless supply of anxious pensioners and frustrated small business owners to trot out as evidence of the tax's negative effects (see Abbott 2012; Abbott 2011; Hunt 2013). The personal content of episodic frames gives them far greater emotional resonance and endurance than thematic ones (Aarøe 2011), which perhaps helps to explain why the Gillard Government was not successful in re-framing this damaging political issue.

During the period of minority government, Labor was also wrestling with the internal consequences of sacking Kevin Rudd and exiling him to the back bench. On this issue the Coalition needed to do little except stand back and allow voters an unimpeded view of Labor's cannibalisation. Deeply resentful at being ousted from office and determined to regain the nation's top job at any cost, Rudd first challenged Gillard in late February 2012. Resoundingly losing that ballot, Rudd continued to agitate against Gillard behind the scenes, prompting a bungled 'non-coup' in March 2013 when his backers pushed him to challenge again but he ultimately chose not to stand (Wanna 2013: 620–1). Recognising that unity and stability would be an asset when contrasted with Labor's internal toxicity, the Coalition took pains to emphasise the party's 'strong and united leadership team' during this period. Abbott kept reminding voters that his shadow front bench had remained unchanged since he assumed the leadership in 2009 (with potential aspirants such as Malcolm Turnbull remaining firmly 'within the tent'), in sharp contrast with the five ministerial re-shuffles necessitated by Labor's in-fighting.

As a result of these tumultuous contextual events, the Labor Government entered the election year with its public standing at record lows, a reputation for chaos, division and inconsistency, and a policy agenda littered with unresolved issues which favoured its opponents. By contrast, the Coalition commenced the year with a strong and unified team, a simple and consistent set of messages that it had repeated *ad nauseum* for the previous three years, and a rhetorical set of solutions to the policy issues it worked so diligently to keep on the political agenda. With the momentum clearly running its way, the Coalition simply needed to ensure that nothing would alter the electoral playing field. The Government, on the other hand, urgently needed to find some way to level it in order to be competitive.

The longest campaign before Labor's caucus finally capitulates to Rudd

In desperation, Labor attempted the first of its 'game-changing' moves on 30 January, when Prime Minister Gillard took the unprecedented step of announcing the election date for 14 September—then some eight months away. Traditionally in Australian politics, governments guard the election date closely and attempt to spring it on their opponents at a strategically advantageous moment. But by giving away that small advantage, Gillard apparently hoped to demonstrate that she was in control of the political agenda and pressure the Coalition into revealing the details of the policies it had been touting for the previous three years (Rayner 2013). There was much speculation that her announcement was aimed at discouraging the Rudd forces from mounting any further challenges and forcing the party to lock in behind her for the campaign (Grattan 2013; Wanna 2013).

Gillard's gamble in foreshadowing the election date so early did not succeed on any of these counts. Remembering Paul Keating's demolition of John Hewson's detailed *Fightback!* package in 1993,[4] the Coalition refused to rise to the bait and release its costings or detailed plans, denying ammunition to the Government with which it might attack the Opposition's credibility. Despite the Government not being in formal caretaker mode, Gillard also found it increasingly difficult to progress her own political agenda on issues such as the Gonski schools funding package, disability care and media reform because many of the key stakeholders decided to 'dig in' and wait for the expected change of government rather than engage in constructive negotiations with Labor (Coorey *et al.* 2013; Hywood 2013; Shanahan 2013; Williams 2013).

Furthermore, in the last days of the last parliamentary sitting week, the querulous Rudd forces rallied again for a final tilt and convinced a narrow majority of the nervous caucus to support his leadership bid. This was a last-ditch effort to minimise Labor seat losses after independent polling showed the Government could lose up to 24 marginal seats—one-third of its representation in the lower house of parliament. The party appeared to believe that returning

---

4   Tony Abbott was Hewson's press secretary at the time and so had a vivid, first-hand experience of the sport that governments can make with opposition policy.

to Rudd would put it back in the game electorally by drawing a line under the negativity of the minority government and neutralising the personal animosity towards Gillard (the so-called 'save the furniture' strategy).

In the caucus ballot Rudd received 57 votes but Gillard still managed 45 votes from her ardent loyalists and, significantly, carried most of her ministers with her. Reactions to Labor's revolving leadership circus went from relief from Labor pragmatists who felt the change gave them better campaign prospects (Hawker 2013), to some belated praise for Gillard as Australia's first female prime minister and condemnation for those who had sought to bring her down. To the electorate, the reinstallation of Rudd reinforced the impression that Labor was inherently unstable and 'unworthy' to govern, and so the leadership switch did not appear to alter the electoral dynamic substantively (Newspoll 2013b). Labor's persistent disunity and dysfunctionality would remain a powerful factor in the election campaign (Wright 2013).

While the Government was wrestling to deliver its policy agenda and manage Labor's internal ructions, the Coalition simply stepped up the pace of its long-running campaign while maintaining consistency in its form and content. Abbott began the year by releasing the party's election policy summary on Australia Day, and then embarked on a 'mini-campaign' in the key eastern states to promote this plan. The policy summary entitled *Our Plan: Real solutions for all Australians* contained all of the party's signature policies which had been announced since 2010, including a generous paid parental scheme, abolishing the carbon tax and replacing it with a Direct Action Plan to cut carbon emissions, stopping the asylum seeker boats and restoring the budget to surplus (Liberal Party of Australia 2013). But despite these policies having been developed years in advance, the Coalition did not include any substantive detail on their implementation in the campaign document. Abbott also resisted pressure to release the party's costings until the second last day of the formal campaign. The Coalition seemed to understand that the detail of its policies was not as important as the symbolism of having a plan, in sharp contrast with Labor's apparent lack of direction. Importantly too, the Coalition's continued focus on an already-announced agenda lent weight to Abbott's promise to lead a stable, 'no surprises' government (Abbott 2013a).

One lingering negative for the Coalition was Tony Abbott's personal standing with the electorate, as public polling showed that some segments of the community remained deeply distrustful of him both because of his conservative social and religious views, and his reputation as a political brawler. As Kirsty McLaren and Marian Sawer note in Chapter 22, from the time of the campaign mini-launch in January the party worked to counter this by presenting Abbott as calm, reasonable and moderate in his views; showing him to be 'a daggy dad' rather than a 'dangerous ideologue'. Abbott's wife, daughters, lesbian sister and feminist chief of staff were all called into service to demonstrate his good relationships with women and evolving view of issues such as marriage equality and abortion (*Australian Women's Weekly* 2013; Hayes 2013; Maiden 2013). This came across as a concocted attempt to wear down public resistance to Abbott and remove any final barriers to voting Liberal for soft and swinging voters; some critics claimed that Abbott would not be able to sustain the façade throughout the campaign (Howitt 2013; Smith 2013). While he remained quite unpopular by historical standards, the Liberal Party's charm offensive appeared to be relatively successful in rehabilitating Abbott's image as his approval ratings increased from 29 per cent in January 2013 to 44 per cent by the final week of the campaign (Newspoll 2013c).

Throughout 2013 the public opinion polls such as Newspoll, Nielsen, Morgan and Galaxy were a constant source of good cheer for the Coalition, as they regularly showed the margin between it and the Government fluctuating between 55–45 and 60–40 per cent. On occasion, Labor's primary vote was down to 29–31 per cent compared to the Coalition's primary support of 45 per cent, with the two-party-preferred vote holding at 43 per cent to Labor against 57 per cent for the Coalition. Only once during the year—immediately after Rudd's return—did Newspoll show the Government drawing level with the Coalition, and only one of the published polls showed Labor leading at any point during the year (Morgan on 1 July 2013, with Labor at 51.5 to 48.5).

Despite an initial honeymoon, Rudd failed to restore Labor's electoral prospects to the heights the Government may have hoped for. But his return created a brief period of potential advantage which he sought to press by calling the election for 7 September 2013, a week earlier than Gillard had nominated. In the final section, we briefly canvass the key events of the formal campaign and demonstrate how these barely shifted the by then established dynamic between the Government and its opponents.

Fear, loathing and empty slogans on the campaign trail

Rudd's return hobbled Labor's campaign effort in two significant ways. At a practical level, 110 of the party's 150 campaign staff reportedly quit upon learning of Gillard's ousting by Rudd, leaving Labor scrambling to fill key roles just weeks out from the formal campaign (Wright 2013). Demonstrating his old controlling instincts, Rudd brought in his own team of advisors—including long-time confidant Bruce Hawker—who reportedly operated as a parallel and competing campaign unit to that within the ALP's headquarters (Hawker 2013; Snow 2013).

More significantly, Rudd's return meant that the ALP could no longer campaign on its signature achievements of the past term: introducing the National Disability Insurance Scheme and progress made on the implementation of the Gonski education funding plan. These major national initiatives were intimately linked with Julia Gillard's prime ministership, and so building the campaign around these would have only served to highlight Labor's rotating leadership. Instead, the party opened its campaign by focusing on national leadership, with Rudd promising 'a better way, a smarter way, a new way to secure Australia's future' (Australian Labor Party 2013). As Sally Young and Nicholas Reece detail in Chapters 6 and 7, the 'New Way' pitch was an obvious throwback to Labor's successful 'New Leadership' campaign of 2007 and an attempt to replace the toxic odour of the minority government with the heady optimism of 'Kevin07'. However, many campaign-watchers commented on the effrontery of Rudd's claim given his central role in the ugliness of the past few years, and so the 'New Way' emphasis on change was quickly dropped (Hartcher 2013).

In its place, Labor opted for a deeply negative attack on the Coalition, accusing it of having a secret 'slash and burn' agenda which would decimate government services, raise the goods and services tax (GST) to 12 per cent, and rip away supports for families such as the School Kids Bonus. Labor's TV advertisements identified Abbott as a cruel fiend who would lead an onslaught against Australian living standards—with the most emphasised slogan being 'If Abbott wins, you lose'. To support this attack, Rudd held a joint press conference with Treasurer Chris Bowen and Finance Minister Penny Wong to announce that they had identified a $10 billion 'black hole' in the Coalition's costings which could only be addressed by 'cuts, cuts and more cuts' (Rudd 2013a). The announcement was apparently intended to puncture the Coalition's financial credibility and undermine its claim to offer stable, responsible government. But it backfired spectacularly when the heads of the Treasury and Finance departments publicly declared that their agencies had not been involved in costing the policies and that Labor's figures could not be relied upon (Department of the Treasury 2013). The party was left looking incompetent and more than a little desperate, particularly as Rudd continued to quote the $10 billion figure in interviews and campaign speeches. Indeed, cynicism all round about claims and counter-claims made by politicians saw the establishment of a raft of 'fact checker' web sites that variously investigated campaign statements for their accuracy (see *Canberra Times* 4 September 2013: 24–5).

Aside from its attacks on the Coalition, the Labor campaign lacked a consistent, unifying theme as Rudd's daily announcements ranged over health, jobs, education, infrastructure and much else besides without settling long on any of these issues. In stark contrast with 2007 when every Labor policy was carefully detailed and costed, Rudd made three major announcements which appeared to have been thought up on the spot: promising to introduce marriage equality legislation within the first 100 days of a new parliament; proposing to establish a Special Economic Zone in the Northern Territory; and suggesting that Sydney's Garden Island naval base could be relocated to Queensland (Rudd 2013b, 2013c and 2013d). Each of these policies were apparently intended to appeal to specific segments of the community who, together, would build a coalition of support for Labor, while also allowing it to seize the political agenda back from the Coalition. But these policies did not knit into a cohesive plan for a third term of government, or engage with the everyday concerns of soft and swinging voters. Furthermore, the lack of detail and major cost implications firmly reinforced the Coalition's framing of Labor as being immature and reckless at the helm of government.

For the Coalition's part, it simply continued with the course it had planned several years before: highlighting Labor's supposed failings on the economy, its duplicity over the carbon tax, and inability to stem the flow of asylum seekers, while spruiking both the unity and experience of its own team, and the benefits of key commitments such as its generous paid parental leave scheme. Labor's only real response to these issues was to re-intensify its attacks against Abbott, as it had failed to either neutralise these issues or develop effective policy solutions to them over the preceding months. Interestingly, the Coalition did not seek to directly capitalise on Labor's leadership instability or run a character assassination on Rudd—despite having a wealth of archive material available featuring members of Rudd's own party giving their frank assessments of his character. Instead, from the time of Rudd's return to the prime ministership Abbott adopted a weary and slightly incredulous tone when dealing with the issue, and simply called on voters to 'end the soap opera' by voting for 'strong, stable and competent government' (Aston 2013). It was also clear from the body language and verbal jousts at the three public debates that both leaders loathed each other and found it hard to take their opponent seriously.

As has now become customary, both major parties launched their campaigns well inside the formal campaign period and both opted to do so in the battleground state of Queensland—the Coalition two weeks out from polling day on Sunday 25 August, and Labor on 1 September. The launches offered little that was new either in policy or messaging, which was probably just as well because record high early voting meant that many Australians had already cast their ballots by the time these launches were held. According to the Australian Electoral Commission, more than 275,000 people had lodged an early vote by 25 August, and over one million people had done so by 1 September (Australian Electoral Commission 2013a and 2013b). In total, more than 3.2 million Australians voted before polling day in 2013, a significant increase on the 2.5 million who did so in 2010 (Australian Electoral Commission 2013c). As discussed by other contributors in more detail in section four, this sharp rise in early voting appears to indicate that voters had made up their minds well in advance and simply wished to get the election over with—something which is supported by the relative consistency of the opinion poll results for both major parties over the preceding year.

As the campaign neared its end, the apparent inevitability of a Coalition victory caused a shift in focus to some of the other players on the electoral field. Perhaps in response to voter dissatisfaction with all participants in the hung parliament, there was an increased prominence afforded to minor and micro parties in the election, although the majority of these parties were single issue groups which only managed to stand candidates for the Senate. They did not receive much attention from the media or major parties until it emerged that Glen Druery, a New South Wales consultant, was engineering a preference-swapping alliance between them to channel support away from the larger parties (Norrington and Lewis 2013). The alliance was ultimately successful in securing the election of micro party senators in every state—an outcome which subsequently led to calls for reform of Australia's compulsory preferential and ticket voting systems. Contesting their first federal elections, Katter's Australia Party and the Palmer United Party also attracted attention for their larger-than-life leaders and unorthodox campaign techniques, but relatively few seasoned observers took either party seriously as a major electoral prospect.

The Australian Greens found themselves hemmed in from all sides in the 2013 campaign, as the Coalition's negative framing of the Gillard minority Government also damaged its minor party supporting partner, while the proliferation of new and special interest parties diminished the Greens' appeal as the party with which to park a protest vote. Furthermore, having gained its first lower house MP in 2010, the party was determined to retain the seat of Melbourne but needed to do so on primary votes as both major parties decided to preference all other candidates before the Greens, including their main antagonists. In an apparent effort to break the association with Labor, the Greens had formally withdrawn from their parliamentary agreement in February 2013 and committed the party to pursuing a different path from either of the major parties (Milne 2013). This was most notably seen in the debate about asylum seekers throughout the year, when the Greens advocated a humanitarian policy which was far more compassionate than those proposed by both the Coalition and the ALP. This arguably assisted Adam Bandt in retaining Melbourne, but appears to have hurt the party elsewhere as its national vote on election day fell back more than three per cent from the 2010 result (Miragliotta 2013). The 'battle for Melbourne' was closely watched in the final weeks of the campaign as it was seen as one of the few opportunities for a Labor gain, but by pouring a reported $1 million into the seat, the Greens were able to retain the seat.

A change of government was obvious within hours of the polls closing on election night, and by 10 pm Kevin Rudd had conceded defeat. The atmosphere at his concession speech was somewhat more triumphal than mournful however, as Labor had avoided a feared electoral wipe-out on the scale seen in the previous Queensland and New South Wales state elections. Although Labor had recorded its lowest vote in 100 years, the party ultimately won 55 seats to the Coalition's 90 with all former cabinet members retaining their seats, giving it the resources to be a 'viable fighting force for the future' (Rudd 2013e). Prime Minister-elect Tony Abbott used his acceptance speech to declare that Australia was 'under new management and ... once more open for business' and reiterate his intention to lead a government 'of no surprises and no excuses' (Abbott 2013b). While there would be a few shocks for the Coalition in the final wash-up of counting—frontbencher Sophie Mirabella suffered a nine per cent swing to be defeated by independent Cathy McGowan and Queensland MP Ted O'Brien narrowly lost Fairfax to Clive Palmer—there could be no denying the scale and decisiveness of Abbott's win. It was a calculated gambit largely orchestrated over two consecutive stages—firstly, the 2010 election to even the contest, then the 2013 election to cement the victory. Abbott's triumph was largely one of attrition.

Conclusion

In looking back at the 2013 federal election it would be easy to explain Labor's 'thumping defeat' as a product of its leadership instability, and the continual changes in policy and focus which flowed from this (Shanahan 2014). Immediately after the election, several Labor figures were quick to suggest this narrative of events, with the outgoing Minister for Health Tanya Plibersek claiming the party deserved '9 out of 10 for governing the country [but] 0 out of 10 for governing ourselves' (ABC TV 2013b). There can be no denying that the Labor Government comprehensively allowed its chances of re-election for a third term to evaporate by appearing to spend more time fighting than governing, and certainly this widespread perception explains much about the final result. However, this 'governments lose office' narrative does not give sufficient credit to the Coalition for applying the pressure which so often caused the Government to crack, or for its discipline and strategic nous in leveraging the Government's internal travails to its own advantage.

As we have suggested, the Coalition was largely responsible for focusing attention on three iconic issues and keeping them at the forefront of the political agenda—the economy, asylum seekers and the carbon tax. Each of these issues was damaging to Labor and they were promoted as litmus tests of the Government's incompetence in dealing with policy problems. What's more, Abbott's opposition successfully framed these issues in such a way as to inflict maximum political pressure on the Government, often forcing it to adopt policy positions which were unsustainable, unworkable or downright ill-considered. The Coalition under Abbott had the discipline to unite behind a clear and consistent set of themes which connected both to its values and the aspirations of many Australians, and it had the sense to know when to step back and simply allow voters full view of Labor's internal grief. In doing so, the Coalition not only demonstrated the enduring importance of agenda-setting, issue ownership and framing in elections, it also convinced sufficient voters that it *did* have what it takes to deliver 'grown-up government'. Given the stark contrast this created with Labor, it is hardly surprising that so many Australians opted for change.

References

60 Minutes. 2013. 'The contender'. Television broadcast, Nine Network, 5 March. Presented by Liz Hayes.

Aarøe, Lene. 2011. 'Investigating frame strength: the case of episodic and thematic frames'. *Political Communication* 28(2): 207–26.

Abbott, Tony. 2011. 'Questions without notice—carbon pricing'. Hansard, 43rd Parliament of Australia. 28 February.

Abbott, Tony. 2012. 'Questions without notice—carbon pricing'. Hansard, 43rd Parliament of Australia. 10 October.

Abbott, Tony. 2013a. 'Address to the federal campaign rally, Lidcombe'. 27 January.

Abbott, Tony. 2013b. 'Federal Election 2013—victory speech'. 7 September.

Abbott, Tony and Hockey, Joe. 2011. 'Julia Gillard's carbon tax'. Transcript of joint doorstop interview, 1 March.

Abbott, Tony and Rudd, Kevin. 2013. 'Leaders Debate'. National Press Club, 11 August, viewed 14 October 2013: <www.kevinrudd.org.au/latest3_110813>.

ABC TV. 2013. *Australia Votes 2013*. Television broadcast, 7 September. Interview with Health Minister Tanya Plibersek.

Aston, Heath. 2013. 'Libs rally to end "soap opera"'. *Sydney Morning Herald*, 29 June.

Australian Electoral Commission (AEC). 2013a. 'Early voting numbers increase as remote and overseas polling starts'. Media release, 27 August, viewed 2 April 2014: <www.aec.gov.au/media/media-releases/2013/e08-27.htm>.

AEC. 2013b. 'Early voting tracking to record levels as polling day preparations ramp up'. Media release, 5 September, viewed 2 April: <www.aec.gov.au/media/media-releases/2013/e09-05a.htm>.

AEC. 2013c. 'Key facts and figures—2013 federal election'. Viewed 20 November: <www.aec.gov.au/Elections/Federal_Elections/2013/files/e2013-key-facts.pdf>.

Australian Labor Party. 2013. *A New Way*. Campaign advertisement, viewed 18 November: <www.youtube.com/watch?v=WMGCByEkWKA>.

Australian Women's Weekly. 2013. 'Is Tony Abbott a changed man?', 11 March.

Bishop, Julie. 2008. 'Mid-year economic and fiscal outlook'. Transcript of doorstop interview, 5 November.

Budge, Ian and Farlie, Dennis J. 1983. *Explaining and predicting elections*. London: Allen & Unwin.

Charnock, David and Ellis, Peter. 2004. 'Postmaterialism and postmodernisation in Australian electoral politics'. *Electoral Studies* 23(1): 45–72.

Combet, Greg. 2011. 'Questions without notice—carbon pricing'. Hansard, 43rd Parliament of Australia, 12 September.

Coorey, Phil, Whitbourn, Michaela and Mather, Joanna. 2013. 'Labor states join Gonski backlash'. *Australian Financial Review,* 19 April.

Department of the Treasury. 2013. 'Statement on costings by the Department of the Treasury and the Department of Finance and Deregulation'. Media release, 29 August, viewed 2 April 2014: <www.treasury.gov.au/PublicationsAndMedia/MediaReleases/2013/Costings-Statement>.

Dery, David. 2000. 'Agenda setting and problem definition'. *Policy Studies* 21(1): 37–47.

Entman, Robert M. 1993. 'Framing: towards clarification of a fractured paradigm'. *Journal of Communication* 43(4): 51–8.

Gillard, Julia. 2011. 'Questions without notice—carbon pricing'. Hansard, 43rd Parliament of Australia, 1 March.

Grattan, Michelle. 2013. 'Well executed? Or executed well?' *The Age*, 31 January.

Hansard. 2010–13. *Parliamentary Debates of the 43rd Australian Parliament 2010–2013*. Canberra: Parliament of Australia.

Harris, Phil, Fury, Donna and Lock, Andrew. 2006. 'Do political parties and the press influence the public agenda?' *Journal of Political Marketing* 5(3): 1–28.

Hawker, Bruce. 2013. *The Rudd Rebellion: the campaign to save Labor*. Melbourne: Melbourne University Press.

Hayes, Danny. 2008. 'Party reputations, journalistic expectations: how issue ownership influences election news'. *Political Communication* 25(4): 377–400.

Hockey, Joe. 2009. 'Cloud of debt hangs heavy'. *The Sun Herald*, 6 September.

Hockey, Joe. 2013. 'Address to the Australian Mines and Metals Association National Conference'. Melbourne, 17 May. Transcript available online, viewed 1 April 2014: <www.joehockey.com/media/speeches/details.aspx?s=116>.

Howitt, Clint. 2013. 'The polishing of Tony Abbott'. *Independent Australia*, 25 May, viewed 17 November 2013: <www.independentaustralia.net/2013/politics/tony-abbott-as-prime-minister/>.

Hunt, Greg. 2012. 'NSW power bills skyrocket due to carbon tax'. Media release, 13 June, viewed 2 April: <www.liberal.org.au/latest-news/2012/06/13/nsw-power-bills-skyrocket-due-carbon-tax-0>.

Hunt, Greg. 2013. 'Questions without notice—carbon pricing'. Hansard, 43rd Parliament of Australia, 20 March.

Hywood, Greg. 2013. *Evidence before the Environment and Communications Legislation Committee inquiry into the Public Interest Media Advocate Bill 2013*, 18 March. Canberra: Parliament of Australia.

Lateline. 2013. 'Opposition leader's image'. Television program transcript, ABC, 30 April, viewed 1 April 2014: <www.abc.net.au/lateline/content/2013/s3748802.htm>. Reporter Suzanne Smith.

Liberal Party of Australia. 2013. *Our Plan: Real solutions for all Australians*. Canberra: Liberal Party of Australia.

Maiden, Samantha. 2013. 'With Tony Abbott on my side'. *The Sunday Telegraph*, 6 January.

McKew, Maxine. 2013. *Tales from the political trenches*. Melbourne: Melbourne University Press.

Milne, Christine. 2013. 'Address to the National Press Club'. Canberra, 19 February.

Miragliotta, Narelle. 2013. 'Election 2013 brings a mixed result for the Greens'. *The Conversation,* 9 September, viewed 19 November 2013: <theconversation.com/election-2013-brings-a-mixed-result-for-the-greens-17524>.

Morrison, Scott. 2010. 'Business as usual for people smugglers under Gillard'. Media release, 5 October, viewed 2 April 2014: <www.liberal.org.au/latest-news/2010/10/05/business-usual-people-smugglers-under-gillard-0>.

Newspoll. 2013a. *Political and issues trends. Best party to handle federal issues.* Summary 9–11 August 2013, viewed 19 November 2013: <polling.newspoll.com.au/image_uploads/130803%20Issues.pdf>.

Newspoll. 2013b. *Political and issues trends. Federal voting intention.* 11 to 13 January–9 to 11 August, viewed 19 November 2013: <www.newspoll.com.au/opinion-polls-2/opinion-polls-2/>.

Newspoll. 2013c. *Political and issues trends. Satisfaction with leader of the opposition.* 11 to 13 January–9 to 11 August, viewed 19 November 2013: <www.newspoll.com.au/opinion-polls-2/opinion-polls-2/>.

Norrington, Brad and Lewis, Rosie. 2013. 'Minor parties pay consultant to engineer preference swap deals'. *The Australian,* 4 September.

Petrocik, John R, Benoit, William L and Hansen, Glenn J. 2003. 'Issue ownership and Presidential campaigning, 1952–2000'. *Political Science Quarterly* 118(4): 599–626.

Pyne, Christopher. 2009. 'School hall building program falling down'. Media release, 14 June, viewed 2 April 2014: <www.pyneonline.com.au/media/media-releases/releases>.

Rayner, Jennifer. 2013. 'In an escalating political arms race, Gillard blinks first'. *The Drum*, 30 January 2013, viewed 15 November 2013: <www.abc.net.au/unleashed/4491676.html>.

Riker, William H. 1986. *The art of political manipulation.* New Haven: Yale University Press.

Roy Morgan Research. 2013a. 'Morgan Poll: Rudd pushes ALP ahead of L-NP'. *The Monthly*, 1 July, viewed 9 October 2013: <www.themonthly.com.au/blog/roy-morgan-research/2013/07/01/1372660748/morgan-poll-rudd-pushes-alp-ahead-l-np>.

Roy Morgan Research. 2013b. 'Morgan Poll—Parties locked at 50/50 after week one'. *The Monthly*, 12 August, viewed 9 October 2013: <www.themonthly.com.au/blog/roy-morgan-research/2013/08/12/1376262827/morgan-poll-parties-locked-5050-after-week-one>.

Rudd, Kevin. 2013a. '$10 billion error in the Opposition's savings'. Transcript of joint press conference, 29 August.

Rudd, Kevin. 2013b. 'Growing the North: a plan for Northern Australia'. Media release, 15 August, viewed 2 April 2014: <d3n8a8pro7vhmx.cloudfront.net/ australianlaborparty/pages/995/attachments/original/1376694666/MR_-_ Growing_the_North.pdf>.

Rudd, Kevin. 2013c. 'Deploying Australia's Navy to secure our nation'. Media release, 27 August.

Rudd, Kevin. 2013d. 'Kevin Rudd's concession speech'. *Australian Labor Party,* 7 September, viewed 1 April 2014: <www.alp.org.au/kevin_rudd_s_ concession_speech>.

Rudd, Kevin. 2013e. 'Address to Caucus' , Canberra, 13 September, viewed 23 December 2014: <australianpolitics.com/downloads/alp/13-09-13_address-to-caucus_kevin-rudd2.pdf>.

Shanahan, Dennis. 2013. 'Campbell Newman joins Gonski revolt as Queensland threatens June deadline'. *The Australian*, 3 June.

Snow, Deborah. 2013. 'How Kevin Rudd's 2013 election campaign imploded'. *The Sydney Morning Herald,* 9 September.

Tanner, Lindsay. 2012. *Politics with purpose: occasional observations on private and public life.* Melbourne: Scribe Publications.

Walgrave, Stefaan, Lefevere, Jonas and Nuytemans, Michiel. 2009. 'Issue ownership stability and change: how political parties claim and maintain issues through media appearances'. *Political Communication* 26(2): 153–72.

Wanna, John. 2013. 'Utter despondency over Labor's leadership woes'. *Australian Journal of Politics and History* 59(4): 618–25.

Williams, Kim. 2013. *Evidence before the Environment and Communications Legislation Committee inquiry into the Public Interest Media Advocate Bill 2013.* 18 March. Canberra: Parliament of Australia.

Wright, George. 2013. 'Address to the National Press Club'. Canberra, 29 October, viewed December 2013: <d3n8a8pro7vhmx.cloudfront.net/ australianlaborparty/pages/1890/attachments/original/1383017072/George_ Wright__Address_to_NPC_Transcript.pdf>.

2. The Battle for Hearts and Minds

Carol Johnson

Winning hearts

It is increasingly recognised that emotion plays a very important role in politics and at election time in particular. Emotion (for example, in terms of feeling fear, anxiety, hope, empathy, pride) is central to election policy debates. Politicians evoke emotions such as fear and anxiety to encourage opposition to government debt or to garner support for tougher border security measures. They evoke feelings of hope to foster support for the vision of the future enshrined in party policies. They encourage feelings of pride to support arguments based on national identity. They encourage feelings of empathy for some groups that are seen as legitimate and deny empathy to those who aren't, with implications ranging from policies on asylum seekers and welfare recipients to policies supporting 'mainstream' voters (see further Johnson 2005 and 2010).

International research has emphasised the important role played by emotion in political advertising (Brader 2006) and election campaigning more broadly (Westen 2007). Further research demonstrates that emotion plays a key role in encouraging the electorate to engage with political issues and in influencing electors' decisions to change political views and allegiances (Marcus *et al.* 2000; Marcus 2002; Neuman *et al.* 2007; Brader 2006). Westen (2007: 125) goes so far as to claim that 'the data … are crystal clear: people vote for the candidate who elicits the right feelings, not the candidate who presents the best arguments'. Redlawsk (2006: 10) draws on recent neurophysiological research to come to a slightly more balanced approach—albeit one that still emphasises the importance of emotion—arguing that politics is 'about feeling every bit as much as it is about thinking.' Consequently, *feeling* is the key aspect of emotion on which this chapter will focus.

It should therefore not surprise us that appeals to emotion were regularly used by politicians from both major parties during the 2013 Australian election campaign, although obviously this is only one of many aspects of campaign strategy that will be discussed. Nonetheless, it will be argued here that the use of emotion was highly significant because it was so closely tied to the battle for minds. In particular, the battle of ideas and its underlying ideological components tended not to be fully articulated in the 2013 election campaign (see the following chapter by Strangio and Walter). However, an analysis of election policy discourse reveals that ideology was still playing a significant, if somewhat subterranean, role. It was simply that, rather than explicitly spelling out opposing views in depth, politicians often attempted to evoke differing ideological positions by mobilising differing fear campaigns and differing forms of the politics of reassurance.[1] In short, party-specific political positions were evoked via party-specific forms of emotional frameworks that closely intersected with forms of ideology (see Johnson 2010).

Tony Abbott had identified what were to be key features of the emotional framework underlying his 2013 campaign in a policy speech he gave a year earlier:

> John Howard was onto something when he said that he wanted Australians to feel more 'relaxed and comfortable' about our country. People naturally seek the reassurance that their job is safe, their doctor is available, their children go to a good school, their neighbourhood is friendly, and their country is secure … These days, there's an even deeper sense of public unease about where we're headed, only the uncertainty is more economic than cultural (Abbott 2012).

Abbott's campaign to win hearts by using emotion therefore centred around two main strategies. The first was to encourage voters to feel afraid and anxious by emphasising the Coalition's argument that Labor posed a threat to the economy (e.g. via government debt) and to border security (failing to 'stop the boats'). The second strategy was to neutralise Labor fear campaigns against the Coalition, based on arguments that the Coalition would make substantial budget cuts, by encouraging voters to feel reassured that a Coalition Government would continue to provide jobs, good education and health services.

There was far less focus than during previous Howard campaigns on evoking cultural insecurities and anxieties, for example, in terms of 'culture war' arguments about national identity or arguing that politically correct special interests were stealing government resources from mainstream Australians (see further Johnson 2007: 39–73). Nevertheless there were residual hints of such culture war arguments, such as comments Christopher Pyne (cited in Owen 2013) made about alleged biases in the national school curriculum. Abbott (2013b) also accused Labor of encouraging division on the basis of factors such as gender and class, thereby downplaying forms of social inequality while also trying to counter Labor critiques of Abbott's conservative position on gender issues. However, the Abbott campaign mainly focused on reworking two other

---

[1] Fear campaigns are being dealt with as a political campaigning strategy in this chapter and are analysed accordingly. An assessment of the legitimacy or otherwise of the fears and anxieties being evoked by politicians is beyond its scope. This chapter also focuses on analysing political discourse but it should be noted that the politics of emotion is also evoked via images and other forms of non-verbal communication.

old Howard election strategies: attempting to motivate a fear of Labor economic incompetence and government debt, and a fear of asylum seekers. The ongoing impact of the global financial crisis (GFC), including the after-effects of Rudd stimulus package expenditure combined with drastically falling government revenues, provided particularly fertile ground for the Liberals to highlight issues of government debt.

In addition, Abbott had spent much of his period as Opposition Leader encouraging feelings of insecurity by suggesting that the minority Labor Government was both dysfunctional and likely to fall at any time—although it actually served a full term and passed over 500 pieces of legislation. Nonetheless, Labor's leadership instability, publicly expressed disunity and differences of opinion, combined with scandals over Peter Slipper and Craig Thomson, were fertile ground for the Opposition Leader to exploit. During the campaign itself, Abbott (2013b) built on his previous arguments, suggesting that the deposing of Julia Gillard and the reinstalling of Kevin Rudd were further evidence that it was 'faceless men' rather than the people who were running the country, and stated that a third of cabinet ministers had resigned. He claimed that there was a 'rent in our polity' and 'a political crisis' (Abbott 2013b). The consequence was that 'an exasperated people are looking for stability and certainty and the only place they will find that stability and that certainty is with the Liberal National Coalition' (Abbott 2013b). Or, as he spelled out in more detail elsewhere:

> There is only one way that Australians can be sure to leave the chaos, the division, the failures, the bloodletting and the politics behind, for good, and that is to change the government. Only the coalition can be trusted when we say: there will be no deals with the Greens, no deals with flaky independents, no deals whatsoever … Above all we will return stable, certain, competent government so all Australians can again plan their futures with confidence (Abbott 2013d).

Such statements provide classic examples of Abbott's key strategy of first encouraging feelings of anxiety then providing and encouraging feelings of reassurance. The Liberals particularly emphasised the importance of feelings of economic reassurance and security. Abbott (2013b) stated that voters should ask themselves 'Who can make your future more secure? Who can make your life better? Who can ease your cost-of-living pressures and who can make your job more safe?' The answer was the Coalition, since only a new government could 'restore the hope, reward and opportunity that should be your birthright' (Abbott 2013a). As was the case previously with Howard, the Liberals were encouraging a feeling of nostalgia for a past golden age (see further Johnson 2007: 40–50). In Howard's (2006) case, the nostalgia was for the values of 'old Australia'. However, in 2013, the Liberals were not only evoking the certainties of the distant past—they were also claiming that Australia could return to (what they depicted as) the more recent certainties of the Howard period, by leaving behind the Rudd period in which Australia was governed by 'captain chaos' (Liberal Party of Australia 2013). Mobilising nostalgia fitted particularly well with the politics of reassurance. The implication was that Labor had robbed Australians of feelings of security, certainty and pride in their national identity, while the Liberals were depicted as the source of feelings of hope.

At the same time Abbott set out to reassure those who might have been impacted by Labor scare campaigns by suggesting that a Coalition Government would benefit all Australians. There was no re-stating of earlier comments by Joe Hockey (2012) that suggested there would need to be massive cuts to welfare and entitlements as Australia competed with Asian neighbours who spent a far smaller proportion of GDP on welfare and other benefits. Rather, Abbott (2013a) claimed: 'We must be a country that rewards people for having a go—but we must never leave anyone behind'. He reassured workers that 'your pay and conditions will be safe under a Coalition Government and that as far as is humanly possible we want your jobs to be secure' (Abbott 2013c). He affirmed that Australia was 'an immigrant nation' and that the opportunities Australia offered to newcomers were what made Australia 'a beacon of hope and optimism right around the world' (Abbott 2013b).

In evoking feelings of protection, Abbott drew on a particular form of fatherly protective masculinity (see further Johnson 2013), in which male heads of household look after their families. As Tony Abbott's daughter Frances stated at the Liberal Party campaign launch, after listing the support Abbott had given his daughters: 'My Dad looks out for everyone and I know he will look out for you' (cited in Nine MSN 2013). Abbott's version of protective masculinity was further strengthened by his hyper-masculine image of surf lifesaver and volunteer firefighter. As Sawer and McLaren's chapter points out, Abbott also made considerable efforts to try to reassure female voters that he wasn't too threatening or aggressively masculine, in the aftermath of Gillard's accusations that he was sexist and a misogynist. Meanwhile, his loving support for his lesbian sister, Christine, was used as evidence that he wasn't intolerant of gays and lesbians (*60 Minutes* 2013), while still using his opposition to same-sex marriage to reassure social conservatives who were anxious about the pace of social change.

In short, Abbott's overall strategy was to first evoke fear and anxiety and then to be the person who offered reassurance, attempting to neutralise Labor's scare campaign in the process. In Abbott's (2013a) words:

> I will spend the next two weeks reassuring people that there is a better way while Mr Rudd will spend the next two weeks trying to scare you about what might happen if he doesn't keep his job.

Abbott claimed during one of the leadership debates that as a result Rudd had no vision for Australia: 'If all you've got is a scare, you've got no vision for the future' (Abbott and Rudd 2013b). By contrast, the Liberal campaign focused on suggesting that they had a positive vision of, and plan for, the direction Australia should take (Loughnane 2013).

Both Gillard and Rudd faced dilemmas in attempting to counter Abbott's politics of emotion. Gillard was well aware of the ways in which Abbott was attempting to mobilise fear and anxiety. She understood that 'Australians have been screamed at now by the Opposition for more than a year. They've been told that they need to be very afraid … we all know a good fear campaign when we see one' (Gillard 2012). Such strategies were even more effective, in her view, because 'Australians … are still feeling anxious from the days of the Global Financial Crisis' (Gillard 2012). She appeared to have hoped that time, and Labor's compensation packages, would prove Abbott's scare campaign on the carbon price/tax to be unfounded (Shanahan 2011). However, Abbott (2011) had retaliated by suggesting—as part of the politics of reassurance—that the carbon tax was an issue of 'trust', and only the Liberals could be trusted to keep their promises. Gillard hoped to succeed in making voters anxious about Abbott by arguing that he was negative, aggressive and dangerously sexist. However, as we have seen, Abbott (2013b) responded by conveying a family-friendly image and arguing that Labor was encouraging division on the basis of gender. Gillard attempted her own politics of reassurance by stressing that Labor governments had a long history of introducing measures that addressed peoples' fears of facing hard times, via measures such as aged pensions, Medicare and now the disability insurance scheme (Gillard cited in O'Reilly 2012). However, Abbott partly undermined this strategy by embracing the disability insurance scheme as a bipartisan policy (see further the contribution by Gray, Manwaring and Orchard in Chapter 21).

Labor was also somewhat hamstrung in attempting to counter Abbott in that Rudd initially seemed to avoid running on Labor's policy record during the Gillard years. However, Labor began to emphasise that record again towards the end of the campaign. Despite his own promise to run a positive agenda, Rudd spent a great deal of the lead-up to the campaign trying to neutralise what he argued were Abbott's scare campaigns:

> Mr Abbott is a formidable politician—he is the nation's most formidable exponent of negative politics, and negative politics above all designed to induce feelings of worry, anxiety and fear in the community. He and the Liberal Party have concluded that fear is a far better political bet than engaging on a debate on the facts (Rudd 2013a).

For example, Rudd argued that there was not a 'budget emergency' over debt as Tony Abbott had claimed in his 2013 Budget Reply Speech (Parliament of Australia 2013). Rudd (2013a) provided figures to demonstrate that Australia's economic performance actually compared very favourably with that of other western economies and that Australia's level of government debt was also low by comparison. Rudd (2013a) argued that Abbott's strategy was to 'Run away from the facts. But keep pumping out the fear'.

Nonetheless, Rudd had his own version of a fear campaign, in this case regarding the cuts which Labor argued that an Abbott Government would introduce. He argued that Abbott was doing everything he could to avoid proper financial scrutiny because if 'you the Australian people knew the dimensions of what he and his government are planning by way of cuts … you would not vote for him' (Rudd 2013c). Rudd's (2013c) message to the Australian people was therefore a simple one:

> if you are in doubt after all this evasion on how Mr Abbott's massive cuts would hurt your jobs, your schools and your hospitals and the economy in this most fragile of global economic times, don't vote for him.

By contrast, Rudd (2013c) argued that his own key mission was to ensure that voters' jobs were secure. With that in mind, Rudd (2013a) argued that Labor had steered Australia through the GFC and only Labor could be trusted to steer Australia through the end of the China-led resources boom and to build a diverse, 21st century economy that was not overly dependent on mining and had good infrastructure, including high speed internet. It would be an Australia where there was a 'fair go for all', where people could access good health care and a good education regardless of income, and there would be no discrimination on the basis of gender, race or sexuality (Rudd 2013b). It was an argument, however, that Rudd did not win.

Winning minds

As other chapters will make clear, election policies and campaigns are influenced by a range of factors, including purely pragmatic—not to say opportunistic—ones that can also be shaped by a range of methods designed to ascertain public opinion (see e.g. Chapter 1 by Rayner and Wanna and Chapter 7 by Reece). The Coalition also made strategic decisions in an attempt to neutralise some key policy differences in areas such as education and health (see Chapter 21 by Gray, Manwaring and Orchard). However, it would be unfortunate to lose sight of the fact that there were also underlying ideological differences between the Liberal and Labor parties. This chapter therefore takes issue with those who argue that there has been a fundamental convergence between Labor and the Liberals that has dissolved any meaningful ideological differences between the major parties.[2] Rather, as suggested previously, this chapter will argue that ideological differences frequently underlay the different emotional frameworks that were being evoked. In particular, ideological differences influenced what voters were encouraged to feel fear and anxiety about, as well as the forms of the politics of reassurance that were offered.

Ideology is often implicated in the politics of emotion (see Johnson 2010). So, for example, neo-liberal political ideology is often associated with encouraging fear of debt and big, intrusive government, while feelings of hope are seen to lie in encouraging individual initiative and self-reliance in a market context. By contrast, social democratic ideology is often associated with encouraging feelings of security via assurances that government will promise a safety net in times of market failure (Johnson 2012). Similarly conservative social and political values can be articulated through fear of the 'other', for example, asylum seekers—a fear which Labor chose to combat in the 2013 election via the harsh measures of the 'PNG solution' (see Chapter 19 by Jupp), rather than by attempting to diffuse it and encourage empathy for those fleeing persecution. There were therefore strong ideological underpinnings to the forms of the politics of emotion that have been discussed previously, that are intertwined with both the politics of fear and the politics of reassurance.

Kevin Rudd alluded to such ideological differences between Labor and the Liberals during one of the leaders' debates. He characterised the difference as being between a nation-building agenda and one focused on budget cuts and claimed that:

> This debate is one which has a long resonance ... in the competing traditions of Australian political history. We're not simply looking at an isolated series of events today. They are part and parcel of two competing political ideas on the role of government in both the economy and society ... (Rudd 2013c).

He also argued that making savage cuts was consistent with previous Coalition Government actions, according to the 'consistent Conservative script', given the commission of audit and subsequent major budget cuts established by the Howard Government (Rudd 2013c). Rudd (Abbott and Rudd 2013c) explicitly identified Abbott's position as 'ideological', arguing that massive cuts could

---

2 For an excellent account, and independent analysis, of views on the ideological convergence of major parties see Goot (2004). For an analysis of the ongoing influence of ideology in Australian politics see Edwards (2013).

drive the Australian economy into recession and that 'I understand the *ideology*, I understand the policy but it is the wrong policy and it's doubly wrong at this time' [emphasis added].

The ideological differences that underlay Rudd and Abbott's positions at the 2013 election had emerged much more explicitly, in 2009, in a debate over the best way to respond to the GFC. As is well known, Kevin Rudd (and Wayne Swan) had both argued for a Keynesian-influenced response to the GFC, using a substantial government stimulus package (Rudd 2009; Taylor and Uren 2010). Furthermore, Rudd (2009) argued that the GFC had largely been caused by neo-liberal deregulation and made a Keynesian case for the need for ongoing government regulation and intervention in order to smooth out the cyclical downturns of capitalism. Rudd's arguments were quite consistent with previous critiques he had made of neo-liberal ideology (Rudd 2006a, 2006b and 2006c) although he had downplayed explicit statements of such positions during the 2007 election campaign.

Significantly, before he became Opposition Leader, Abbott (2009) had penned a stinging critique of Rudd's arguments regarding the nature of, and policy prescriptions for, the GFC, depicting Rudd as a 'misguided, would-be Messiah' who had 'confused a cyclical (if severe) downturn with a fundamental crisis of capitalism'. Abbott (2009) had been particularly critical of Rudd's arguments in support of social democratic government interventions in the economy, arguing that Rudd was putting forward 'socialist' arguments. Abbott (2009) went on to deny that neo-liberal ideology had shaped government policy in Australia, while suggesting that individuals and businesses generally made better decisions regarding their best interests than government could; that debt-fuelled spending would exacerbate problems and that 'a permanent tax cut is more likely to encourage the initiative culture that will soonest restore strong economic growth', along with measures such as lower interest rates and cutting government regulation. In short, although he would deny the tag, Abbott was putting forward arguments that are commonly associated with neo-liberalism (see Harvey 2005; Crouch 2011).

By the 2013 campaign launch, Abbott's (2013a) ideological position was articulated less explicitly, but he did claim that under a Coalition Government 'each year, government will be a smaller percentage of our economy'. He also pledged to cut the carbon and mining taxes, as well as to cut red tape because:

> We understand, deep in our DNA, that you can't have a strong society and strong communities without strong economies to sustain them and you can't have a strong economy without profitable private businesses. We know that a stronger economy is not about picking winners but about helping everyone to get ahead (Abbott 2013a).

Parties these days rarely use the term 'ideology' about their own position, preferring to retain a negative, pejorative use of the term that can be used against their opponents, while their own position is depicted as being both pragmatic and the truth. However, terms such as 'DNA' (Abbott 2013a) or 'values' (see Rudd 2013b) are often used to refer to underlying ideological differences about, for example, the respective roles of government and the market, as the following passage from Abbott also makes clear:

> This … is the clearest choice in a generation and it is not just between two different teams and two different policies. It is not just between unity and stability on one side and division and dysfunction on the other. It is a choice about fundamental values. It is a choice about what we believe in as a people and as a nation. And I say to the Australian people the Labor Party right now is addicted to big government. They just can't help themselves. Here in the Coalition we believe in strong citizens, Labor is only interested in wealth redistribution. But we the people understand that you have got to create the wealth before you can distribute it. Labor obsesses about the state but we the people understand that it is in community that Australian people will be strong, and strong communities and strong individuals are what we need if the social fabric of this great nation is to improve in the months and years ahead (Abbott 2013b).

Abbott's position was consistent with many arguments that would have been put forward by the Howard Government (see Johnson 2007).

However, Rudd faced problems in articulating his position because of a widely acknowledged ideological crisis of social democracy at an international level (Lavelle 2008: 1; Nahles and Cruddas 2012: viii), which has also been noted in the Australian context by commentators as diverse as journalist and labour historian Troy Bramston (2011) and Liberal Party Federal Director Brian Loughnane (2013: 4, 14). The crisis partly revolves around social democratic parties' attempts to address the relationship between government and market, following the partial embrace of a watered down form of neo-liberalism (in which the Australian and New Zealand labour parties were pioneers). That partial embrace of neo-liberalism by Labor, especially from the Hawke and Keating period onwards (Lavelle 2005), made it harder for Swan and Rudd to argue for the re-embracing of some Keynesian strategies, particularly in regard to justifying running deficits and major government funding for nation-building projects. It also arguably made it harder to justify the mining tax (even if this was partly designed to redistribute mining profits to other sectors of the economy) and a carbon price (even if the longer-term pricing mechanism was to be a market-based emissions trading scheme).

That partial embrace of neo-liberal ideology by previous Labor governments also had implications for the politics of emotion because it helped to reinforce a fear of government debt along with a fear of, and resentment towards, high taxing governments. The election outcome suggests that part of Rudd's problem in arguing his case was that Abbott's evoking of the fear of government debt and taxes appears to have been far more successful than Rudd's older social democratic strategy of attempting to make people feel secure and reassured by promising government intervention and benefits to ameliorate the impacts of dysfunctional markets. Abbott (admittedly greatly assisted by Labor's own major problems in regard to program delivery and catastrophic levels of internal disunity) seems to have succeeded in arguing that it was government rather than the market that was dysfunctional. The roles of ideology and emotion were therefore closely intertwined. In the process, Abbott won both the battle for hearts and the battle for minds.

References

60 Minutes. 2013. 'Tony Abbott'. Television broadcast, Nine Network, Sydney, 9 March. Presented by Liz Hayes. Viewed 15 December 2013: <sixtyminutes.ninemsn.com.au/article/8623144/tony-abbott>.

Abbott, Tony. 2009. 'Misguided, would-be messiah'. *The Australian*, 7 February, viewed 21 October 2013: <www.theaustralian.com.au/archive/business/misguided-would-be-messiah/story-e6frgagx-1111118780014>.

Abbott, Tony. 2011. 'Tony Abbott's carbon tax address'. Transcript, *SBS news online*, 11 July, viewed 15 December 2013: <www.sbs.com.au/news/article/2011/07/11/transcript-tony-abbotts-carbon-tax-address>.

Abbott, Tony. 2012. 'The Coalition's plans for stronger communities'. *Tony Abbott, Federal Member for Warringah and Leader of the Opposition—News*, 6 June, viewed 28 July 2012: <www.tonyabbott.com.au/LatestNews/Speeches/tabid/88/articleType/ArticleView/articleId/8746/Landmark-Speech--Address-to-the-Pratt-Foundation-Melbourne.aspx>.

Abbott, Tony. 2013a. 'Address to the Federal Coalition Campaign Launch'. 25 August, viewed 14 October 2013: <www.liberal.org.au/latest-news/2013/08/25/tony-abbott-address-2013-federal-coalition-campaign-launch>.

Abbott, Tony 2013b. 'Address to Victorian Federal campaign rally'. 2 July, viewed 14 October 2013: <www.liberal.org.au/latest-news/2013/07/02/tony-abbott-transcript-address-victorian-federal-campaign-rally-melbourne>.

Abbott, Tony. 2013c. 'Address to workers, Narangba, Queensland'. 5 September, viewed 6 September 2013: <www.tonyabbott.com.au/LatestNews/Speeches/tabid/88/articleType/ArticleView/articleId/9494/Address-to-workers-Narangba-Queensland.aspx>.

Abbott, Tony, 2013d. 'At your service and offering a better way. A Statement by Tony Abbott'. *The Australian*, 5 August: 6.

Abbott, Tony and Rudd, Kevin. 2013a. 'Leaders' Debate'. National Press Club, 11 August, viewed 14 October 2013: <www.kevinrudd.org.au/latest3_110813>.

Abbott, Tony and Rudd, Kevin. 2013b. 'Peoples' Forum'. Brisbane Broncos Leagues Club, 21 August, viewed 14 October 2013: <www.kevinrudd.org.au/latest1_220813>.

Abbott, Tony and Rudd, Kevin. 2013c. 'People's Forum'. Rooty Hill RSL Club, 28 August, viewed 14 October 2013: <www.kevinrudd.org.au/latest3_280813>.

Bowen, Chris. 2013. 'Press Conference'. Canberra, 2 August, viewed 14 October 2013: <ministers.treasury.gov.au/DisplayDocs.aspx?doc=transcripts/2013/022.htm&pageID=004&min=cebb&Year=&DocType=>.

Brader, Ted. 2006. *Campaigning for Hearts and Minds: How Emotional Appeals in Political Ads Work*. Chicago: University of Chicago Press.

Bramston, Troy. 2011. *Looking for the Light on the Hill: Modern Labor's Challenges*. Melbourne: Scribe.

Clarke, Simon *et al*. 2006. 'Moving Forward in the Study of Emotion'. In Simon Clarke *et al*. (eds), *Emotion, Politics and Society*, Basingstoke: Palgrave Macmillan.

Crouch, Colin. 2011. *The Strange Non-Death of Neo-Liberalism*. Cambridge: Polity Press.

Edwards, Lindy. 2013. *The Passion of Politics: the Role of Ideology and Political Theory in Australia*. Sydney: Allen & Unwin.

Gillard, Julia. 2012. 'Address to Australian Council of Trade Unions Congress'. Sydney, 15 May, viewed 24 July 2012: <www.pm.gov.au/press-office/address-australian-council-trade-unions-congress-sydney>.

Goot, Murray. 2004. 'Party convergence reconsidered'. *Australian Journal of Political Science* 39(1): 49–73.

Harvey, David. 2005. *A Brief History of Neoliberalism*. Oxford: Oxford University Press.

Hoggett, Paul. 2009. *Politics, Identity, and Emotion*. Boulder: Paradigm.

Howard, John. 2006. 'A sense of balance: The Australian Achievement in 2006'. Address to the National Press Club, 25 January, viewed 18 December 2013: <pandora.nla.gov.au/pan/10052/20060321-0000/www.pm.gov.au/news/speeches/speech1754.html>.

Johnson, Carol. 2005. 'Narratives of identity: Denying empathy in conservative discourses on race, class and sexuality'. *Theory and Society* 34(1): 37–61.

Johnson, Carol. 2007. *Governing Change: From Keating to Howard*. Revised edn. Perth: Network Books.

Johnson, Carol. 2010. 'The politics of affective citizenship: From Blair to Obama'. *Citizenship Studies* 14(5): 495–509.

Johnson, Carol. 2012. 'Social Democracy in Uncertain Global Times: Governing the Politics and Economics of Emotion'. Paper presented to the IPSA 22nd World Congress of Political Science, Madrid, July. Viewed 17 December 2013: <paperroom.ipsa.org/papers/paper_13011.pdf>.

Johnson, Carol. 2013. 'From Obama to Abbott: Gender Identity and the Politics of Emotion'. *Australian Feminist Studies* 28(75): 14–29.

Hockey, Joe. 2012. *Lateline*, Australian Broadcasting Corporation (ABC), Sydney, 18 April, viewed 27 October 2013: <www.abc.net.au/lateline/content/2012/s3480665.htm>.

Lavelle, Ashley. 2005. 'Social Democrats and Neo-Liberalism: A Case Study of the Australian Labor Party'. *Political Studies* 53(4): 753–71.

Lavelle, Ashley. 2008. *The Death of Social Democracy: Political Consequences in the 21st Century*. Abingdon Oxon: Ashgate.

Liberal Party of Australia. 2013. *Captain Chaos*. Television advertisement, viewed 18 December 2013: <www.youtube.com/watch?v=I_W-Wf4hDOs>.

Loughnane, Brian. 2013. 'Address to the National Press Club'. Canberra, 23 October, viewed 26 October 2013: <lpaweb-static.s3.amazonaws.com/Brian%20Loughnane%20-%20National%20Press%20Club%20Address%20-%2023%20October%202013.pdf>.

Marcus, George. 2002. *The Sentimental Citizen: Emotion in Democratic Politics*. Philadelphia: Pennsylvania University Press.

Marcus, George *et al*. 2000. *Affective Intelligence and Political Judgment*. Chicago: University of Chicago Press.

Nahles, Andrea and Cruddas, Jon. 2012. 'Preface: Social Democracy in our Times'. In Henning Meyer and Jonathan Rutherford (eds), *The Future of European Social Democracy: Building the Good Society*, Basingstoke: Palgrave Macmillan.

Neuman, W Russell *et al*. 2007. *The Affect Effect: Dynamics of Emotion in Political Thinking and Behavior*. Chicago: University of Chicago Press.

Nine MSN. 2013. 'Softer Side of Abbott on Show'. *Nine MSN News Online*, viewed 25 August 2013: <news.ninemsn.com.au/national/2013/08/25/08/18/abbott-to-float-tradie-loans-scheme>.

O'Reilly, Sue. 2012. 'Gillard's driving ambition to take the fear out of disability'. *The Australian*, 19–20 May, Inquirer: 12.

Owen, Michael. 2013. 'Christopher Pyne warns teachers against impeding reform'. *The Australian*, 4 September, viewed 25 October 2013: <www.theaustralian.com.au/national-affairs/election-2013/christopher-pyne-warns-teachers-against-impeding-reform/story-fn9qr68y-1226710077163#mm-premium>.

Parliament of Australia. 2013. *House of Representatives Hansard*. 16 May: 3571.

Redlawsk, David P (ed.). 2006. *Feeling Politics: Emotion in Political Information Processing*. New York: Palgrave Macmillan.

Rudd, Kevin. 2006a. 'Address to the Centre for Independent Studies'. 16 November, viewed 5 July 2007: <www.cis.org.au/events/policymakers/krudd_lecture.pdf>.

Rudd, Kevin. 2006b. 'Child of Hayek'. *The Australian*, 20 December: 12.

Rudd, Kevin. 2006c. 'Howard's Brutopia: The Battle of Ideas in Australian Politics'. *The Monthly*, November: 46–50.

Rudd, Kevin. 2009. 'The Global Financial Crisis'. *The Monthly*, February: 20–8.

Rudd, Kevin. 2013a. 'The Australian Economy in Transition: Building a new National Competitiveness Agenda'. Canberra, 11 July, viewed 13 July 2013: <www.pm.gov.au/press-office/address-national-press-club>.

Rudd, Kevin. 2013b. 'Building for Australia's future'. ALP campaign launch, Brisbane, 1 September, viewed 4 September 2013: <www.kevinrudd.org.au/building_australia_s_future>.

Rudd, Kevin. 2013c. 'National Press Club Address'. Canberra, 5 September, viewed 9 September 2013: <www.kevinrudd.org.au/latest4_05091>.

Shanahan, Dennis. 2011. 'Gillard's long game is a big gamble'. *The Australian*, 21 May, viewed 15 December 2013: <www.theaustralian.com.au/national-affairs/opinion/gillards-long-game-is-a-big-gamble/story-e6frgd0x-1226059944024>.

Sunrise. 2013. Television program, Channel 7, Sydney, 6 September. Interview with Kevin Rudd. Viewed 9 September 2013: <www.kevinrudd.org.au/latest3_060913>.

Taylor, Lenore and Uren, David. 2010. *Shitstorm: Inside Labor's Darkest Days*. Melbourne: MUP.

Westen, Drew. 2007. *The Political Brain: The Role of Emotion in Deciding the Fate of the Nation*. New York: Public Affairs.

Young. Sally. 2004. *The Persuaders: Inside the Hidden Machine of Political Advertising*. Melbourne: Pluto Press.

3. The Leadership Contest: An end to the 'messiah complex'?

Paul Strangio and James Walter

Prime Minister Kevin Rudd had only just fired the starting gun on the 2013 election campaign, but commentators were already in no doubt about the nature of the campaign that would unfold during the ensuing five weeks: 'This federal election will be the most presidential in style, communications and frenzy in our history' (Dusevic 2013). In Australia we have grown accustomed over recent decades to media representations of each national election as a new high water mark in 'presidential' campaigning. The 2013 campaign was certainly no exception; the term 'presidential' was a ubiquitous reference point for journalists, especially in their descriptions of the Labor Party's pitch for re-election (see the controversy between Kefford and Dowding in the *Australian Journal of Political Science* 2013).

Given the tumultuous backstory to the election this was hardly surprising. While the roles of the executed and the executioner had been reversed in a reprisal of the dynamics of the 2010 federal poll, the 2013 election was announced within a handful of weeks of a party room coup to depose another Labor prime minister. On this occasion, caucus had voted to overthrow Julia Gillard and reinstate Kevin Rudd after a lengthy campaign of internal destabilisation by the Rudd-aligned forces (see Walsh 2013) against Gillard and escalating panic at published and internal opinion polling suggesting that the ALP faced electoral annihilation if it persisted with her leadership. If Gillard's (2013) subsequent assessment of the rationale for her removal glossed over her missteps in office, she nonetheless was correct in her assertion that the party room had capitulated to Rudd's apparent popularity: 'it was not done because caucus now believed Kevin Rudd had the greater talent for governing ... It was done—indeed expressly done—on the basis that Labor might do better at the election'. That his colleagues had thrice previously rejected him in favour of Gillard (counting the 'no-show challenge' of March 2013) underscored that the fundamental calculation for resurrecting Rudd as leader was that his personal appeal could retrieve Labor's dire electoral circumstances. The expectations of what improvement he might deliver ranged from the optimistic (that the ALP might now have a shot at winning the election with Rudd) to the modest (that the losses would be minimised or, to employ another phrase that became ubiquitous during the campaign, that he would 'save the furniture'). Whatever the scale of expectation, the positioning of Rudd as the government's saviour provided the narrative frame for the leadership contest in the 2013 election and, as we will see, also influenced the conduct of the campaign.

Rudd's highly personalised campaign

At least initially the 'saviour narrative' and reality appeared to coalesce. Rudd's reclaiming of the prime ministership catalysed a dramatic shift in the published opinion polls. By mid-July, only a fortnight after the change in Labor leadership, Newspoll recorded a nine per cent surge in the ALP's primary vote, which translated into the government level-pegging with the Coalition in two-party-preferred terms (Shanahan 2013a). Rudd had opened up a 22-point lead over Tony Abbott as preferred prime minister, contrasting with the 45 to 33 per cent lead Abbott enjoyed over Gillard in the final Newspoll before her fall. The perception that Rudd's renaissance had been a so-called 'game-changer' was reinforced by reports that the ALP was recalibrating its resource allocation, with the focus shifting from 'sandbagging' vulnerable seats to targeting 'winnable' seats, particularly in the Prime Minister's home state of Queensland. Columnists interpreted the turnaround as evidence of the ascendancy of a personality-driven, leader-centred politics:

> Am I the only person to be amazed by the way—if the polls are to be believed—the swapping of a leader has transformed the Labor government's electoral prospects from dead in the water to level-pegging? Is that all it takes? Can the mere replacement of an unpopular woman with a popular man make a world of difference? … It's possible Rudd's improvement in the polls won't last but, regardless, we're witnessing a fascinating case study in the power of personality and perception versus reality … Talk about the triumph of presidential politics (Gittins 2013).

Rudd's predominance (and the distancing from his predecessor) was reinforced in July as the Prime Minister acted decisively and rapidly to cauterise lingering political and policy problems that had plagued Gillard's incumbency. He dealt with the 'boat people' via the PNG 'solution' and 'killed off' the carbon tax by advancing the date for a transition to an emissions trading scheme. That the Labor Party had 'surrendered itself to Kevin Rudd' (Kelly 2013a) was perhaps most emphatically illustrated by caucus endorsing his audacious scheme for reform to the party rules governing the election of leaders that promised to stem the chronic instabilities of recent years but also afforded him 'untouchable power if he wins the election' (Kelly 2013a). As Rudd commanded the political landscape with his rush of announcements and with the polls swinging towards the government, some commentary suggested the Coalition had been caught flat-footed by the leadership change and renewed questions were asked about the electability of the relatively unpopular Abbott (Kenny 2013a; Tingle 2013). However, later accounts would suggest that Liberal Party strategists had not only factored in Rudd's return, but had also calculated that the frenetic activity of the Prime Minister would pique pre-existing doubts about his leadership style dating back to his first period as Prime Minister: 'the more Rudd ran around fixing and announcing and creating mob scenes, the more he fitted into a "chaos" story' (Williams 2013).

Following on from the Labor caucus's capitulation to Rudd and his dominant performance throughout July, by the time the campaign proper got under way on 5 August it had become axiomatic in media analysis that the government's fortunes were tied to a 'presidential' campaign. For example, one of the doyens of political commentary, columnist Paul Kelly (2013b), marked the announcement of the election by writing:

> Rudd's core calculation is highly personalised. Rudd believes he can best Abbott. Convinced the more the public sees Rudd–Abbott debate the more it will move to Labor, Rudd wants a presidential campaign.

What took longer to emerge was that not only would the ALP's campaign be individual-dominated in its public presentation, but also in the direction of its strategy and conduct. The relatively late leadership change had dislocated the ALP organisation's election planning. Only weeks before Gillard's downfall, Labor's party headquarters in Melbourne had staged a full campaign dress rehearsal complete with 150 staff. In another telling indicator of how personal leadership allegiance had come to trump party loyalty during the Rudd–Gillard civil war, however, some two-thirds of those staff departed when Gillard was deposed (Kenny 2013b). In addition to requiring a replenishment of personnel, Rudd's resurrection changed the whole tenor of the ALP's campaign. Plans for an electorate-based emphasis and a championing of the reform achievements of the (Gillard) Labor government were now to be overshadowed by a focus on Rudd (see Norrington 2013). In his post-election address to the National Press Club, the ALP's National Secretary and director of the 2013 campaign, George Wright, explained:

> It had to emphasise Kevin Rudd and his strengths and work the party's strategy into making the most of these, not the other way around. To do anything else would have been implausible. For the party to install a new leader in such drawn-out and dramatic circumstances—well, our leader was always going to be in the spotlight (G Wright 2013).

What was more, Labor headquarters accepted that 'Prime Minister Kevin Rudd had earned the right—you could say he had accepted a duty—to campaign on his strategy' (G Wright 2013).

Consistent with his leadership history, the Prime Minister had no compunction in exercising that 'right'. Along with his chief lieutenant, Bruce Hawker, the consultant who had helped Rudd's toppling of Gillard, the Prime Minister appropriated tasks that normally would have been the preserve of Labor's campaign headquarters: altering travel schedules, handpicking candidates (such as the former Queensland ALP premier Peter Beattie), recasting strategies and messages, 'freewheeling' on policy and rewriting advertisements (Bramston 2013; Snow 2013; Williams 2013). According to one account, 'Rudd's own hand remained firmly on the tiller at all times, micro-managing both the smallest and biggest issues, conveying little trust outside his own inner sanctum' (Williams 2013). A senior Labor figure later complained: 'Look if Rudd knew how to fly the campaign plane and Hawker knew how to navigate, they would have thrown out the pilot, and the two of them would have flown the plane themselves' (Bramston 2013).

The Rudd campaign rapidly began to crumble under the weight of expectations and succumb to internal contradictions. Even before the writs were issued, opinion polls indicated that the initial surge of support triggered by his return to office was ebbing away. There were reports too about concerns within Labor circles that the Prime Minister had erred tactically by delaying the calling of the election and that his frantic round of activity during July had depleted his resources (Shanahan 2013b; 2013c). Worse was to come, as Rudd's reputation as a formidable campaigner, based on his 2007 election triumph, unravelled during August. He performed scratchily in the first leaders' debate. Hawker (2013) later revealed that during preparation for the event Rudd was distracted by his embroilment in candidate pre-selection issues. His announcement of a series of grandiose but apparently unplanned and unrelated ideas (a differential tax rate for the Northern Territory; moving the navy base on Garden Island in Sydney to Brisbane; a high-speed rail network down the east coast of Australia) were criticised as policy 'thought bubbles' and seemed redolent of the chaos and incoherence of his mode of governance. By the second week of the campaign, reports surfaced of a breakdown in communications between the Prime Minister's travelling party and Labor's headquarters with 'insiders' quoted as being concerned by 'snap decisions being taken by a small team of [Rudd's] confidantes (sic)' (Massola and Heath 2013).

Yet another problematic aspect of Rudd's highly personalised campaign performance was his default to meet-and-greet occasions where he was typically mobbed by members of the public (often panting youngsters) whose intent seemed to have less to do with politics than a desire to be photographed with a 'famous' person. These repetitive appearances militated against prime ministerial gravitas; it was as if Rudd in his keenness to exploit his supposed popularity had lost perspective on the line between celebrity and national leadership. Gillard (2013) pointedly warned her party subsequently against seduction by 'the fripperies of selfies and content-less social media'. In a related if novel twist, Rudd's media vanity fuelled a small cottage industry of speculative pseudo-psychoanalysis of the Prime Minister. The most extreme (Albrechtsen 2013) suggested he had the traits of a 'psychopath'. It also later emerged that the Liberal Party had solicited a report from a 'friendly psychiatrist' who diagnosed from afar that the Labor leader was 'suffering a personality disorder known as "grandiose narcissism"' and 'proposed tactics to leverage Rudd's personality' (Williams 2013).

By the second half of the campaign the Prime Minister's self-belief must have been under siege as Labor's support sank in the polls and his own popularity rating descended to record lows. Expressing the revised consensus of media commentators, *The Age*'s Michael Gordon (2013) attributed the collapse in the government's position to 'the folly of Labor's initial campaign strategy of focusing entirely on the Rudd persona ... almost independent of the Labor Party'. In the final fortnight of the campaign there seemed to be tacit admission of this miscalculation as the ALP campaign was reorientated towards a concentration on the themes of job protection and the risks of spending cuts under a Coalition government. A week out from polling day Rudd delivered perhaps his most disciplined performance of the campaign at Labor's official launch, the shift in emphasis from personal to party highlighted by the Prime Minister identifying his cause with a catalogue of totemic Labor reforms: the aged pension;[1] the Snowy Mountains hydro electrical scheme; Medicare; national superannuation; and DisabilityCare. The verdict from the pundits, however, was that the change had come too late (Kelly 2013c).

Abbott's disciplined campaign as leader

How did Tony Abbott's campaign compare? In the wake of Rudd's return to the prime ministership and the initial bounce in the opinions polls for the government, the media stylised the election as a contest between a celebrity PM and an unpopular but ruthlessly effective opposition leader. As one headline proclaimed, 'It's the pop star v the pragmatist' (Dusevic 2013). Based on data from the Australian Election Study (AES) surveys, at the 2010 election Abbott had been the least popular opposition leader since Andrew Peacock

---

1 A common Labor misappropriation: the aged pension was legislated for by Alfred Deakin's second Liberal-Protectionist ministry in June 1908.

two decades earlier (McAllister 2011: 249). Despite the Coalition establishing a clear and consistent advantage over the Gillard government in the opinion polls thereafter, Abbott's poor personal ratings remained a talking point and there was sporadic speculation that his leadership might become vulnerable in the event of the ALP reinstating Rudd. When that change materialised in June 2013, it was not long before some commentators suggested that the Liberal Party ought to dispense with Abbott and replace him with the more electorally appealing shadow communications spokesperson and former leader, Malcolm Turnbull (Short 2013).

Consistent with this framing, when the election was called it was widely noted that Abbott's opening statement was much less leader-centric than that of his rival: 'Abbott knows he is unpopular with most voters, so, unlike Rudd, he emphasises his "team", which he referred to six times, and the Coalition, which rated another half-dozen mentions' (Hartcher 2013a). While Abbott's references to 'the team' persisted over the following month and his colleagues such as Julie Bishop and Joe Hockey (though not Nationals leader, Warren Truss) featured more prominently than their Labor counterparts, the Coalition's was nevertheless a leader-oriented campaign. Abbott's media coverage, announcements and staged appearances dominated. In striking contrast with the erratic performance of the Prime Minister, however, Abbott stayed resolutely on message and resisted Rudd's efforts to force the campaign onto the ground he preferred. ALP National Secretary George Wright (2013) would later concede that the Coalition's was a 'brilliantly disciplined' campaign. Whereas Rudd's extemporising on the ground created confusion in Labor's organisation, Abbott marched closely in step with a well-oiled and highly experienced Liberal Party campaign team headquartered in Melbourne (Baker 2013).

Arguably, Abbott's relentless harping on key issues—boat arrivals, the carbon tax and alleged economic mismanagement—had been road-tested in 2010 and had already dictated the terms of debate before the campaign even started. Abbott and his Coalition colleagues simply refused to shift ground when challenged on subsidiary issues such as climate change, the National Broadband Network (NBN), education or health. Abbott's was a simple message largely devoid of policy detail (and evasive about costings), but it was coherent and consistent. With the one exception of the expensive paid parental leave (PPL) scheme, which provoked internal division and some negative reaction, there was no policy drift. With his events scripted meticulously and choreographed by the Liberals' campaign operatives, nor were there any substantial gaffes by Abbott. He did come under fire for what appeared to be thoughtlessly sexist remarks, yet these seemed less the result of bungling than designed to provoke predictable reactions from the 'politically correct' who could then be made to appear ridiculous. Perhaps Abbott's most premeditated 'off-the-cuff' line of the campaign was delivered during the second leaders' debate when he interrupted a prolix Rudd by interjecting 'Does this guy ever shut up?' While Labor seized on the 'outburst' as a lapse of control by Abbott, the likelihood is that it had been calculated to exploit preconceptions that the Prime Minister was 'all talk and no action' (Packham and Walker 2013).

In addition, there was always the gift of Labor's record of internal disunity on which Abbott could capitalise. It was said that the Coalition campaign had prepared advertisements drawing on the rich body of analyses of Rudd's character failings from his own Labor colleagues, but opted instead to allow Rudd free rein to demonstrate just these traits in the campaign. Whether true or not, Abbott needed only occasionally to refer to Labor's successive depositions of leaders or to repeat his line, 'Do you want another three years like the last six?', to call the whole sorry saga to mind. At the Liberal Party's official launch, according to Paul Kelly (2013d), Abbott 'turned Labor's campaign themes against itself' by demanding 'If the people who've worked with Mr Rudd didn't trust him, why should you?'

As the Coalition's victory became seemingly inevitable (and in the immediate aftermath of that success) there was a rush of commentary about Abbott—some revisionist, some point-scoring—about how he had been underestimated, about how he had exploded the myth of his 'unelectability' and about how he had metamorphosed from the one-time impulsive and accident-prone 'Mad Monk' into a disciplined, even restrained, performer. To get to The Lodge, he had achieved a character transition on the scale of Bob Hawke's renunciation of booze and womanising (e.g. Kelly 2013d; Shanahan 2013d; Taylor 2013). Perhaps the most remarkable and ironic aspect of that 'transformation' given the terms on which the campaign had mostly been fought is that by its end stages the opinion polls were showing that not only had he overtaken Rudd in the preferred prime minister rating, but he was the least unpopular of two unpopular leaders.

The one-time 'ugly duckling' did indeed triumph on election day. The respective performances of both leaders when the results were clear recapitulated the atmosphere of the campaign. Rudd spoke at unseemly length, with surreal invocations of Labor tradition and his 'great party' belying the leader-centric nature of his campaigning (and the larger history of his prime ministerships), in an atmosphere verging on hysteria—almost as if, given the adulation of supporters, it had been a kind of victory ('Jeez, I thought we lost,' he remarked in response to a wild bout of cheering). It seemed a denial of reality. Still the pugilist, Abbott rejoiced in announcing that the Labor primary vote had plumbed its lowest level in a hundred years and declared that 'grown-up government' was back and that 'Australia was open for business' (Maley 2013; T Wright 2013).

The significance of the 2013 leadership contest

How might one rate 'success' in this leadership contest? In the obvious sense, given the Coalition electoral victory, Abbott 'won'—indeed, it is likely that the result was largely determined before the campaign proper began. Abbott had laid that groundwork by being one of the most effective opposition leaders of the post-war period. That he had succeeded principally through aggression and an enthusiastic resort to incivility, rather than through ideological and policy creativity, arguably disqualifies him from the ranks of the great opposition leaders who crafted a message that mobilised a constituency (like Menzies) or developed a compelling program of reform (like Whitlam). Ultimately, Labor's self-immolation ensured that Abbott was not called to account for the threadbare nature of his vision or the relative paucity of his policy portfolio. At the same time, it was widely accepted that Abbott's unremitting 'attack dog' style had been a major impediment to the electorate warming to him. The public remained cool about him right up to the election even though, as we have seen, he had eclipsed Rudd in the popularity stakes by the campaign's closing stages. A leading pollster noted he was the first federal Opposition Leader in four decades to win office with a net negative approval rating (Hartcher 2013b). Abbott's persistent unpopularity was corroborated by comparing the data on leadership ratings from the 2013 AES (Bean *et al*. 2014) with its predecessors dating back to 1987 (McAllister 2011: 246–50). They indicate that, while marginally more popular than he had been at the 2010 election, Abbott had maintained the dubious mantle as the second worst rated opposition leader over the past quarter of a century behind Peacock in 1990. Moreover, while only three opposition leaders had won office during that period—Howard in 1996, Rudd in 2007 and Abbott in 2013—Abbott was easily the least popular to achieve that feat.

As for Rudd, there was at least some consolation in that the defeat was not as crushing as had been predicted by the final polls. Inevitably, debate ensued about whether his reinstalment had been justified after all. Though inevitably speculative, George Wright (2013) told the National Press Club that the leadership change had averted 'potential losses' of the order of another 25 seats. In that sense, the 'saviour narrative' was not completely extinguished. Yet it had been reduced to a pale version of what it had been in the heady first weeks following Rudd's revival, and there was a predictable riposte from his detractors that Labor's predicament under Gillard would never have become so acute without his relentless campaign of internal subversion. Moreover, at a larger level, there was also a different conclusion to be drawn: that the campaign, and indeed the entire story of the ALP's chequered incumbency since 2007, had exposed the dangers of excessive leader orientation.

The 'personalisation' and 'mediatisation' of politics

The 2013 campaign was a striking manifestation of two closely related trends: firstly, of parties interpreting their link with the people as largely dependent on 'the leader'; and secondly, of what is often summarised as 'mediatised' politics (Mazzoleni and Schulz 1999; Helms 2012; Boumens et al. 2013). It was not only the contingency of Rudd's last-minute regaining of the prime ministership that sealed the 'presidential' character of the campaign. Over recent decades, party practices evolved as economic development eroded their characteristic class and status concerns and the party attachments these had once fostered. As Campus (2010: 224) has argued:

> Voters lost the reference points with which they used to orient themselves ... At that point, party and coalition leaders appeared as an anchor, a shortcut to making voting decisions without being obliged to fully understand ... the transformation of the party system.

The leader would set the agenda in responding to citizens' issue concerns. The media also 'played an essential role in the transition from a model of political communication based on parties to one based on leaders' (Campus 2010: 224). There was increasing evidence of a personalisation of politics (Dalton et al. 2000), which comprised a convenient marriage with mediatisation—that is, stories about personalities being more integral to the commercial media culture than analysis of policy. Communications professionals capitalising on the media, especially television, would assist the leader in building 'a virtual personal relationship with the citizenry' (Campus 2010: 227). The outcome, however, was that 'political logic' (the communication of policy objectives) would succumb to 'media logic' (the imperatives of the story) and so 'mediatisation' is 'the colonisation of politics by the mass media culture' (Campus 2010: 228).

Labor's civil war of 2010–13, depending substantially on Rudd's command of 'media logic' and then feeding into the 2013 election campaign, is essential to the 2013 narrative. Rudd, in the 2007 election campaign, proved a master of mediatised politics. That victory, built on the back of his longer-term resort to 'mediated visibility' as a television regular, was a striking instance of the increasing personalisation of politics that Dalton and colleagues (2000) have described. *Kevin07* was not only predominantly about Rudd, demonstrating conclusively that he could command public attention, but also revealed his capacities to build a 'virtual relationship' with the voters and to 'personify' the Labor brand. Its perplexing culmination was his persisting ability to win positive regard at large, from people who had never met him, while provoking the antipathy of many of those who worked closely with him.

But 'media logic' would be cruel to his government. Rudd's consuming obsession with the media cycle and concern about the way decisions would impact on popularity led to difficult decisions being squibbed. The hard work of turning promising ideas into good policy and planning their implementation was secondary. Government administration was chaotic but he would not relinquish control. Looking outwards rather than towards his colleagues, he failed to see when the tide was turning against him. Julia Gillard, seeing a 'government that had lost its way', rode a party room insurgency to replace him. Yet the leadership repertoire demanded by mediatised politics was something that she could never master. Gillard in turn failed not so much in administration and policy achievement, but in achieving a personal tie with the voters and as communicator-in-chief. Rudd worked relentlessly to destabilise Gillard, yet despite this remained successful in courting the media (with his story of a leader wronged) and in rebuilding his popularity. To that extent, his command of media logic was compelling. And so, as outlined earlier, he was returned to power to rescue the party.

The expectation was that, whatever his shortcomings in government, Rudd would again prove a formidable campaigner. The danger, always, is that such a focus on the leader deflects attention from other players, ensuring that every glitch, every misstep, is sheeted home to the leader alone. There were, as we have seen, plenty of glitches and missteps in his campaign. Furthermore, as the Liberal Party had anticipated, the longer Rudd reoccupied the limelight the more the electorate was reminded of the fragilities of his governing persona and the gloss of popularity rapidly wore off. In order to successfully be seen as the embodiment of the party, leaders have to appear 'authentic', they have to publicly 'demonstrate and persuade citizens that they really are true to themselves and act accordingly, and that their convictions and beliefs are actually reflected in the [party's] policies' (Helms 2012: 658). Was it realistic to expect that Rudd could satisfy this criterion in 2013? Given the denunciation that had been heaped upon him in the successive confrontations with Gillard, only a disciplined, unified and temperate campaign could recapture the 'authenticity' (true to himself and with convictions reflecting those of his party) needed to prevail. Instead, as observed earlier, he was erratic rather than consistent, generating splits between his inner circle and Labor's campaign HQ, issuing 'thought bubbles' that disrupted considered policy, and confusing celebrity (as he was mobbed on the 'meet-and-greet' trail) with authority at the expense of gravitas. He and his team may have tried to build the 'story' of the 'Rudd rebellion' against the perverse politics of the previous six years (see Hawker 2013), but in responding to the imperatives of this specious narrative they revealed the costs of sacrificing political logic. The boom and bust pattern of voter estimates of Rudd suggested by AES data (Bean *et al*. 2014; McAllister 2011: 249)—between 2007 and 2013 he went from the most popular leader in the quarter of a century of AES surveys to being the lowest rated prime minister at an election—gives dramatic expression to the inherent vulnerability of the personalising leader.

Abbott's story presents in many ways as a sharp contrast. Though the Liberal Party's rapid leadership transitions in opposition during 2007–09 (Brendan Nelson to Turnbull to Abbott) suggest a search for a 'leader solution', the resort to what many wrote off as the 'unelectable' Abbott appeared to defy 'media logic'. What is more, Abbott proceeded not to court popularity but instead to practise a form of intransigent opposition such as we have rarely seen. He held on to the leadership despite nagging doubts that his unpopularity was a millstone around his party's electoral aspirations.

Nevertheless, the Coalition's 2013 campaign was as heavily leader-focused as Labor's, and in that sense catered to the implicit proposition that it matters more which person gets into power than which party (see Boumans et al. 2013: 203). It featured contrived events calculated to emphasise Abbott's centrality and authority, albeit with a greater appearance of synchronisation between his beliefs and convictions and those of his party than Rudd was able to manage. Abbott also followed a staple of the mediatised mode—private lives as a resource to be exploited in constructing political identity (Campus 2010: 223)—with carefully staged revelations of his domestic life, especially his relationships with his wife and daughters, designed to humanise the 'hard' image his aggressive opposition stance had encouraged. While stressing his team, the extent to which the story was Abbott himself ensured they were rarely noticed, risking (like Rudd) the danger that failure would be seen as his alone. The professionalism of the Liberal campaign and his apparent willingness to be closely managed averted this risk, but does it remain a live possibility for Abbott now that he is in government?

It is the Labor debacle, however, that in the final analysis provides the most compelling leadership story of the 2013 election. In particular, Rudd's rollercoaster trajectory illuminates graphically the principal problem with the personalisation integral to mediatised politics: it is inherently more volatile than were the patterns of the past. Party affiliation, once closely tied to social identity, used to be relatively stable. Now that identity effects have diminished and the leader's personality figures alongside the party in determining allegiance, it should be recognised that fidelity to personality oscillates more rapidly and with greater amplitude when a leader's all too human failings become apparent (Blondel and Thiebault 2009: 58). Backlash against the leader is an ever present danger. Labor's failure to appreciate this, and its inability to contain and control its leaders' idiosyncrasies except through dramatic and catastrophic depositions, provides a cautionary tale about the reliance on 'leader effects' and the danger of capitulating to media logic. As the ALP went about finding a successor to Rudd following its election loss, Bill Shorten, the successful candidate, suggested that his party had heeded that lesson: 'If I am elected leader,' he vowed, 'you will hear less about I and more about we. The era of the messiah is over' (*The Australian* 2013). Time will tell if that is true.

References

Albrechtsen, Janet. 2013. 'Voters are waking up to the real Rudd'. *The Australian*, 21 August.

Australian Journal of Political Science. 2013. 'The Presidentialisation of Australian Politics' 48(2): 135–51. Article by Glenn Kefford, with comment by Keith Dowding and rejoinder by Kefford.

Baker, Mark. 2013. 'Mission accomplished'. *The Age*, 9 September.

Bean, Clive, McAllister, Ian, Pietsch, Juliet and Gibson, Rachel. 2014. *Australian Election Study, 2013: Codebook*. Canberra: Australian Data Archive, The Australian National University.

Blondel, Jean and Thiebault, Jean-Louis. 2009. *Political Leadership, Parties and Citizens: The Personalisation of Leadership*. Hoboken: Taylor & Francis.

Boumans, Jelle W Boomgaarden, Hajo G and Vliegenthart, Rens. 2013. 'Media Personalisation in Context: A Cross-National Comparison between the UK and the Netherlands, 1992–2007'. *Political Studies* 61(1): 198–216.

Bramston, Troy. 2013. 'Captain Chaos major pain for ground control'. *The Australian*, 9 September.

Campus, Donatella. 2010. 'Personalization of Politics in Italy and France: The Cases of Berlusconi and Sarkozy'. *International Journal of Press/Politics* 15(2): 219–35.

Dalton, Russell, McAllister, Ian and Wattenberg, Martin. 2000. 'The consequences of partisan dealignment'. In Russell Dalton and Martin Wattenberg (eds), *Parties without Partisans: Political Change in Advanced Industrial Democracies*. Oxford: Oxford University Press.

Dusevic, Tom. 2013. 'It's the pop star v the pragmatist as perception dominates political reality'. *The Australian*, 5 August.

Gillard, Julia. 2013. 'Julia Gillard writes on power, purpose and Labor's future'. *Guardian Australia*, 14 September, viewed December 2014: <www.theguardian.com/world/2013/sep/13/julia-gillard-labor-purpose-future>.

Gittins, Ross. 2013. 'Polls have changed, but Labor hasn't'. *The Age*, 22 July.

Gordon, Michael. 2013. 'The beauty contest is over, now it's a character test'. *The Age*, 24 August.

Hartcher, Peter. 2013a. 'Spot the difference between a reborn contrite Kev and Team Tony'. *The Sydney Morning Herald*, 5 August.

Hartcher, Peter. 2013b. 'Not the popular choice: emphatic win but approval rating could be a lot better'. *The Sydney Morning Herald*, 9 September.

Hawker, Bruce. 2013. *The Rudd Rebellion: The Campaign to Save Labor*. Melbourne: Melbourne University Press.

Helms, Ludger. 2012. 'Democratic Political Leadership in the New Media Age: A Farewell to Excellence?' *British Journal of Politics and International Relations* 14: 651–70.

Kelly, Paul. 2013a. 'Rudd to be most powerful PM'. *The Australian,* 10 July.

Kelly, Paul. 2013b. 'Kevin plots our greatest election heist'. *The Australian,* 5 August.

Kelly, Paul. 2013c. 'Kevin Rudd's rallying cry comes too late'. *The Australian,* 2 September.

Kelly, Paul. 2013d. 'Torching the "unelectability" myth of Tony Abbott'. *The Australian,* 26 August.

Kenny, Mark. 2013a. 'Abbott under pressure as game changes'. *The Age*, 10 July.

Kenny, Mark. 2013b. 'Chaos led to exodus of true believers'. *The Sydney Morning Herald*, 31 October.

Loughnane, Brian. 2013. 'Address to the National Press Club'. Canberra, 23 October, viewed 26 October 2013: <www.liberal.org.au/latest-news/2013/10/23/2013-federal-election-address-brian-loughnane-federal-director?utm_source=Liberal+Party+E-news&utm_campaign=8a6661f086-Post+NPC+Speech+Transcript&utm_medium=email&utm_term=0_51af948dc8-8a6661f086-57529133>.

Maley, Jacqueline. 2013. 'It's another wait for Planet Kevin'. *The Sunday Age*, 8 September.

Massola, James and Heath, Joanna. 2013. 'Rudd camp unravels in the thick of it'. *Australian Financial Review*, 16 August.

Mazzoleni, Gianpietro and Schulz, Winfried. 1999. 'Mediatization of Politics: A Challenge for Democracy?' *Political Communication* 16(3): 247–61.

McAllister, Ian. 2011. *The Australian Voter: 50 Years of Change*. Sydney: UNSW Press.

Norrington, Brad. 2013. 'Strategy to put new PM front and centre'. *The Australian*, 28 June.

Packham, Ben and Walker, Jamie. 2013. 'Labor seeks to exploit Tony Abbott's "shut up" debate outburst'. *The Australian*, 22 August.

Shanahan, Dennis. 2013a. 'Election race neck-and-neck as Rudd streaks away from Abbott'. *The Australian*, 9 July.

Shanahan, Dennis. 2013b. 'After the coup, the resurrection comes to a halt'. *The Australian*, 23 July.

Shanahan, Dennis. 2013c. 'ALP fears as campaign wobbles'. *The Australian*, 7 August.

Shanahan, Dennis. 2013d. 'Win or Lose, it's Tony's triumph'. *The Australian*, 6 September.

Short, Michael. 2013. 'Liberal Party's best bet: switch to Turnbull'. *The Age*, 16 July.

Snow, Deborah. 2013. 'How Kevin Rudd's 2013 election campaign imploded'. *The Australian*, 9 September.

Taylor, Lenore. 2013. 'Tony Abbott: the journey from rank outsider to Australia's new leader'. *Guardian Australia*, 8 September, viewed December 2013: <www.theguardian.com/world/2013/sep/08/tony-abbott-australias-new-prime-minister>.

The Australian. 2013. 'Messiah complex: Bill Shorten a PM for the powerless or just a rude, naughty boy?' 26 September.

Tingle, Laura. 2013. 'Net negatives of Abbott's electability worsen'. *Australian Financial Review*, 26 July.

Walsh, Kerry-Anne. 2013. *The Stalking of Julia Gillard: How the media and Team Rudd contrived to bring down the Prime Minister*. Sydney: Allen & Unwin.

Williams, Pamela. 2013. 'How Kevin Rudd's campaign unravelled'. *Australian Financial Review*, 9 September.

Wright, George. 2013. 'Address to the National Press Club'. Canberra, 29 October, viewed December 2013: <d3n8a8pro7vhmx.cloudfront.net/australianlaborparty/pages/1890/attachments/original/1383017072/George_Wright__Address_to_NPC_Transcript.pdf>.

Wright, Tony. 2013. 'Unrestrained celebration as Liberal hero makes his point'. *The Sunday Age*, 8 September.

Part 2. Vital Images of the Campaign—The Media, Campaign Advertising, Polls, Predictions and the Cartoons

4. The Empire Strikes Back: Mainstream media still matters

Wayne Errington

With so much attention being paid to the new forms of media transforming the public sphere, we can forget that most Australians follow election campaigns the old-fashioned way. According to the Australian Election Study (AES), those electors reporting that they follow election campaigns in the traditional media 'a good deal' are well down from the highs of the 1960s but they still dwarf those relying on the internet. In the 2013 election those who followed the election 'a good deal' on television amounted to 30 per cent, 15 per cent for radio and 17 per cent for newspapers. Close interest in all traditional media at election time has fallen consistently since 2007. While those claiming to have followed the election 'a good deal' has risen steadily, that group only reached 14 per cent in 2013 (McAllister and Cameron 2014). In an otherwise lacklustre 2013 campaign, the power and appropriate role of television, radio and newspapers became one of the major talking points. The News Corporation Australia (henceforth News Corp) press, in particular, was determined to show that old media still mattered, featuring partisan advocacy reminiscent of the 1975 post-Dismissal campaign against Labor. This chapter first reflects on the changing nature of media power, especially efforts by parties and commentators to set the campaign agenda, and then discusses the quality of the mass media coverage and the influence of the News Corp outlets in particular.

For those who love their politics, the 2013 election provided a cornucopia of media sources to take in every policy announcement, every debate or community forum, and every baby kissed. Political junkies could admire the professionalism of the likes of David Spears on *Sky News*; listen as the ABC bent over backwards to be fair to all points of view; watch (and read) Richo (Graham Richardson) indulge his dislike of Julia Gillard; or read (and watch) Andrew Bolt indulge his dislike of just about everybody. All this whilst monitoring our Twitter feeds and checking in on the many new forums for reporting and analysis online. On the 24-hour news channels, we witnessed the entirety of the press conference where journalists complained about having to quiz political leaders on policy documents they had been given only moments before. Later on the six o'clock commercial television news—watched, according to OzTams ratings, by more than ten times the audience of the 24-hour news channels—we received only a brief précis of the same policy announcement, followed by a quick analysis of the politics surrounding it, not the policy itself.

Despite the rise of the internet and social media, television remains important enough to dominate the rhythms of an election campaign. Policy announcements, photo opportunities, speeches and fundraisers are timed for the desired coverage (or lack thereof) by the nightly television news. Digital technology has made news a relatively cheap way for television networks to fill their quotas for domestically produced content. Thus, we see early morning, breakfast, late morning, afternoon and late news able to cover breaking election stories, though rarely in any depth. However, it is the three million strong audiences on free-to-air evening television that provide the greatest exposure. The dominance of television amongst an increasingly diverse media provides the campaigns with both tactical and financial challenges. The parties need to engage voters for whom social media is the primary source of information, while attracting the attention of mainstream media consumers, inevitably through expensive television advertising. One audience expects a conversation about politics; the other would prefer to eat their dinner in peace. The result of the 2010 election was a reminder that Australian elections are sometimes decided by the slimmest of margins, so every vote counts and little is left to chance even by a party that finds itself streets ahead in the published opinion polls.

The 2013 federal election was the first election campaign in which the major Australian newspapers published not only printed editions but also operated news websites behind various kinds of paywall. This development represented a further polarisation of media consumption between the political news 'haves' and 'have-nots'. If you are reading this, you probably fall into the former category. You may hear about Alan Jones's indiscretions because they are reported on *Media Watch*, not because you find his 2GB breakfast show compelling. Arguably, the transformation of the media with its more refracted technologies and outlets, with different old and new platforms and divided between the 'haves' and 'have-nots', has encouraged the parties to change the ways they campaign and the messages they disseminate. Into this space we are also witnessing the arrival of much more partisan commentators, strident in their opinions and taking every opportunity to convince undecided voters of the merits of their preferred team or candidate.

Assessing the power of the media

The nature of the media's power remains elusive in spite of thousands of studies across a range of academic disciplines.[1] Short-term media effects of most interest during an election campaign depend on the characteristics of the audience and

---

1 See Valkenberg and Peter (2013) for a recent review of media effects research, and Bennett and Iyengar (2010) for a taste of the debate.

the context of the message or image. Education, partisanship, psychology and perceptions of the source of the message all influence the way voters process information (Scheufele and Tewksbury 2007: 16). Even so, journalism is one of the few professions ranking as low in public trust as politics. Yet, just as voters can distrust politicians in general but like a particular leader, most voters rely on a trusted media source for information about politics. Much of the partisanship in election coverage, particularly in the so-called 'quality press', is directed at audiences already committed to voting a particular way. Thus, *The Australian* and the *Australian Financial Review* have a disproportionately Liberal-voting audience, while the *Sydney Morning Herald* and Melbourne's *Age* now cater more to Labor and Green voters (Young 2011: 93). More problematic for the parties, and for understanding media effects on election results, are the tastes and attitudes of apathetic or swinging voters, many of whom do not closely follow the campaign.

Agenda-setting and agenda-priming

An increasingly media-savvy public is aware of the role of the media in setting and framing the agenda. Agenda-setting, though, is a complex process. It is not the exclusive domain of the gatekeepers inside media organisations, as political leaders, interest groups, voters and other actors also attempt to influence media content. Journalists enjoy revealing the attempts of political parties at media management but often have little choice but to succumb to that management when they are continually under pressure to break stories. Election campaigns are a combination of intense micro-management and inevitable unpredictability. The 2013 campaign provided a good example of the latter when New South Wales Premier Barry O'Farrell unexpectedly confronted Kevin Rudd on the Sydney Harbour foreshore over a hastily announced policy to move military establishments from Sydney to Brisbane.

Less well known than agenda-setting is *agenda-priming*, where voter preferences may depend on which issue (or issues) saturates the media during the campaign (Iyengar and Simon 2000: 157). The 2001 Australian federal election won by John Howard provides a good illustration of agenda-priming, when immigration, border control and national security issues which favoured the Coalition played a disproportionate role in the campaign. The extent to which late-deciding voters were affected by this coverage is difficult to discern exactly (Denemark *et al*. 2007: 94–5). In 2013, only 14 per cent of voters chose asylum seekers among the three issues most important to them in an Essential poll dominated by the economy, taxation and education. We can infer much about what private party polling in marginal seats reveals about swinging voters from the way leaders have responded to the asylum seeker issues in recent elections. With agenda-priming in mind, even widely ridiculed policies such as buying up Indonesian fishing boats and comments from the candidate for Lindsay that refugees were causing traffic problems in western Sydney would have done the Coalition little harm. In 2013, the media, while usually indulging the agenda-setting tactics of the major party leaders, tended to return swiftly to some of the issues identified by voters as more important.

The out-going Labor Government responded to its precarious position in the published opinion polls by continually shifting emphasis, their supposed ill-discipline becoming a familiar campaign narrative. Rudd warned voters about the effect on the price of Vegemite that would be caused by the Coalition's failure to rule out changes to the GST. With little preparation or forethought, he launched policies promoting the development of northern Australia that senior Labor figures had ridiculed earlier in the year when the Coalition foreshadowed similar measures. There was no sustained argument from the Government about its achievements, and little sense of building on its television advertising accusing the Coalition of planning all manner of cuts to public services.

Economic management was the mainstay of the campaign (see Wanna's chapter). Journalists were determined to question the Opposition about the release of policy costings but were unable to divert the Coalition from their plans to detail their budget late in the campaign. By contrast, education and health were not covered by the mainstream media to the extent that polling indicated public interest in those issues. While bipartisanship on school education would be exposed as a mirage after the election, the parliamentary Labor Party had chosen to remove the leader who could speak with most credibility on education.

Effect of declining media resources

A further dimension of the power of the media during an election is the relative resources of the political parties, interest groups and media outlets. The financial problems of media companies have caused a decline in specialist reporters on issues such as defence, science and health, as well as the retrenchment of experienced journalists. This specialisation was historically the strength of quality newspapers. The campaign environment intensifies this problem with journalists expected to digest policy announcements at a moment's notice to file for news channels or websites. In response to declining revenue caused by online competition for both readers and advertisers, Australian newspapers have made hundreds of editorial positions redundant. While the role of News Corp during the campaign prompted discussion of that company's newspaper circulation (reaching two-thirds of the metropolitan population nationwide), the more important statistic was the 10 per cent decline in circulation across the board in the year to June 2013 (Audit Bureau of Circulation 2013). Radio and television have not been immune to these confronting forces but the unique role of newspapers in setting the agenda for electronic media gives the decline of newspapers greater political salience. It was not that long ago that scholars highlighted the great advantages that the 'PR State' (governments heavily investing in public relations, accumulating media advisors, setting up public sector media units and exploiting the use of government advertising), provides to governments compared to opposition parties and the fourth estate (see, for example, Ward 2007; Errington and van Onselen 2007). A neutral observer of the plights of the Rudd and Gillard Governments may have been unaware of this phenomenon. In both 2010 and 2013, the Labor caucus chose to give away the advantage of incumbency by electing new (and recycled) leaders.

After his resurrection in June 2013, Kevin Rudd made some rapid fire policy announcements about carbon pricing and the fringe benefits tax. Journalists were quick to point out that such announcements from a newly installed prime minister with no intention of recalling parliament prior to polling day had the authority of election promises more so than settled policy. In contrast, sending asylum seekers to Papua New Guinea could be achieved within existing legislation. One particularly cynical use of incumbency was the $30 million government advertising campaign to promote the new policy (Lewis 2013). Notionally aimed at asylum seekers with the message 'If you come here by boat without a visa YOU WON'T BE SETTLED IN AUSTRALIA' (but initially carried only in English), the placement of the advertisements in domestic newspapers was met with well-deserved ridicule. A government that seemed to have learned from the experience of the Howard Government—that spending millions on government advertising only makes voters angry—*un*learned the lesson just weeks before the 2013 election.

The televised debates in the 2013 campaign

Leader debates during the election campaign provide the two major parties with a more equal media footing than they otherwise have during the balance of the parliamentary term. The first leaders' debate in 2013 was almost universally derided for shallow, predictable questions from journalists and scripted responses from the leaders. As the headline on Sid Maher's (2013) analysis for *The Australian* put it, 'a night of waffle, scare campaigns and cost evasion'. Channel Nine's Laurie Oakes chimed in with some horse-race commentary, declaring Abbott the winner because his 'three-word slogans' amounted to 'sharper, clearer messages' even though he thought Rudd won on policy substance. The debate format chosen prevented sustained questioning of the leaders. Part of the waffle from both leaders came in their anodyne responses to a question on aged care that exposed the gap between the parties' policy ambitions and Treasury's lack of revenue. There was little follow-up on this issue in the rest of the campaign. Combined with the widespread view that a defeat for the Government seemed inevitable, the number of Australian Election Study respondents claiming to have watched a leaders' debate in 2013 was near an historic low at 32 per cent (McAllister and Cameron 2014).

Two subsequent debates—which have been rare in recent elections because incumbent prime ministers usually wish to minimise opportunities for their opponent to share a platform—were hosted by *Sky News* from RSL/Leagues mega clubs in Brisbane and Sydney. These were in format and content much livelier affairs. Questions from the general public, notionally swinging voters but inevitably featuring some partisans, were often pointed and some left the leaders floundering as they circled one another on the stage. In such a forum a leader cannot be seen to ignore a question from a voter and revert to talking points. They have to empathise with this audience in a way they need not with a panel of journalists. In one exchange, by refusing to join an audience member in condemning foreign investment in Australian farmland, Abbott looked prime ministerial compared to Rudd's populist posturing. This audience-centred format, which has been part of American presidential debates for decades, is likely to be used more often in Australian campaigns in the future. After the staid first debate, however, the main television networks had generally lost interest in what the leaders had to say—relegating the debates to their secondary digital channels, with about a quarter of the audience viewing them.

The news emerging from all the debates was predictably trivial—raising such items as whether Rudd flouted the rules by referring to speaking notes or whether Abbott was wise to tell the prime minister to shut up. In the way these things are usually appraised, Rudd's failure to deliver a 'knock-out blow' ensured that Abbott was considered the main beneficiary. Given the complete absence of wit among contemporary Australian political leaders—incapable of delivering a line like Ronald Reagan's 1984 promise not to use his opponent's youth and inexperience against him—just what a knock-out blow would look like in these debates is unclear. It was not only the debates, though, where reporting on the campaign showed a predilection towards the trivial.

The trivial pursuits of reporters

Julia Gillard hoped that nominating a September 2013 election date as early as January of that year would allow her Government to turn the nation's attention to government strengths and opposition weaknesses in policy. She was sorely disappointed, though, by her own party's capacity to make a spectacle of itself and by the press gallery's capacity to find alternatives to policy debate. There was some reflection among journalists, most notably ABC TV's Chris Uhlmann, about their own role in promoting leadership instability. Kerry-Anne Walsh (2013) indicted the entire press gallery for their role in 'stalking' Gillard. Former Minister for Finance and Deregulation Lindsay Tanner complained after the 2010 election that 'the media are retreating into an entertainment frame that has little tolerance for complex social and economic issues' (2011: 1). The trend towards trivialisation is clear enough, although the role that political leaders have played in enabling it bears some analysis.

Since those who avidly consume political media are less likely to change their vote than those who do their best to ignore coverage of politics, even much of the supposedly serious political programing can be more like entertainment than public affairs. Horse-race style coverage was common in the quality media in 2013, with every new poll making headline news. The traditional squabbling over Senate preference deals gained, in hindsight, greater than usual importance. Yet, as blogger and author Greg Jericho pointed out, for those who were interested, Election 2013 was 'policy heaven' yet 'fewer were consuming this detailed coverage' (2013). Substantial differences between the parties on broadband, taxation and parental leave were probed by journalists at press conferences with the party leaders. One effect of digital media is to create hours of extra air time that forces parties to offer up a wider range of spokespeople than during past campaigns which focused exclusively on the leaders. Journalist for *The Australian* and *Sky News* presenter, Peter van Onselen, complained via Twitter that an analysis piece of his comparing party policies received less feedback than anything he wrote about polling or party strategy during the campaign (van Onselen 2013).

Similarly, while the leaders of the two major parties dominated radio and television air time, the minor party candidates and independents also received a good deal of coverage. Some of this attention derived from the celebrity status of Clive Palmer and Julian Assange, whose profile on *60 Minutes* did not outweigh the fractiousness of his Wikileaks Party. Journalists were enticed by free travel aboard Palmer's private jet although his business dealings generally received more attention than his policy platform.

There is a middle ground between the self-styled seriousness of interview programs and broadsheet newspapers, and the frippery of FM radio. Given the wide media choices available, it is important for politicians to communicate with those voters who do not pay much attention to formal news programing. Channel Ten's *The Project* provides a unique medium, aimed at a young adult audience and including plenty of political content, if not a lot of analytical depth. Joe Hockey and Kevin Rudd were regulars during the campaign—not so Tony Abbott.

Abbott, like Rudd when he was Opposition Leader, had adopted a strategy of rarely engaging in lengthy interviews on ABC television and radio on programs such as *AM, 7.30, Lateline* and *Insiders*. This was partly a reaction to an interview with Kerry O'Brien in 2010 when Abbott questioned his own veracity. It may also suggest that Coalition strategists simply do not value these interviews as regular fare, preferring AM talkback radio to make their arguments. Nevertheless, Abbott handled such interviews perfectly well during the 2013 campaign and overall he was quizzed often enough on his policies during the campaign. The fact that he was disciplined in his responses, and didn't sway from his plan not to release policy costings until late in the campaign doesn't mean that the media didn't do its best to hold him to account. However, providing voters with a thorough understanding of what was at stake was another matter.

The costings debate raised interesting issues about the assumptions underlying budget forecasts and the fairest way to deal with the issue during an election campaign, but few outlets took the time to properly analyse the rival claims. Browbeaten by partisans into the safety of vacuous reporting of claim and counter-claim about the alleged lies of the other side, even ABC Television was of little help. For analysis they often turned to Labor and Liberal-leaning commentators who agreed the costings debate was in a terrible state. ABC Radio current affairs provided much better analysis than either the main ABC TV channel or the 24-hour news network through finance reporter Stephen Long.

Interestingly, the 2013 campaign saw the emergence of rival fact-checking organisations that were supposedly aimed at keeping the political parties and the media commentariat honest. Yet, there was not much evidence that these aspirations were achieved. Commentators barracking for one side or the other were always unlikely to be cowed by 'fact-checking'. The fact-checkers themselves tended to take an overly literal view of their brief and spend much of their time arguing over interpretations of key words. The ABC's *Fact Check* site wound up its thorough analysis of Labor's claims about the Coalition's supposed '$70 billion black hole' with this delightfully unreflective line: 'Only when the Coalition releases its spending and taxing plans in full will Labor be able to criticise its policies accurately' (ABC 2013). A greater endorsement of the Coalition's campaign strategy could not have been written. Nevertheless, this combination of media platforms signals a promising avenue for greater depth of coverage for those interested. ABC television news featured reports on *Fact Check* research. Channel Seven joined with *Politifact* for regular, if brief, reports on the major policy issues, in an effort to get beyond the claim and counter-claim that has become the staple of television news reporting.

Editorialising in newspaper reporting

Kevin Rudd's return to the prime ministership posed an interesting dilemma for News Corp. Chairman Rupert Murdoch had signalled his distaste for the Gillard Government clearly enough—through his personal Twitter feed and the uniformly negative attitude of his Australian newspapers' editorials. In June, he tweeted: 'Australian public now totally disgusted with Labor Party wrecking country with its sordid intrigues. Now for a quick election' (Murdoch 2013). Murdoch dispatched legendary editor Col Allan to Australia from New York just before the campaign began. His task was reportedly to add some spark to the tabloids, something they didn't really seem to need.

Any doubts about whether Rudd's return would lead to a softer line were dispelled by the front page of Sydney's *Daily Telegraph* the day after Rudd announced the election date. The headline read: 'Finally you have the chance to … KICK THIS MOB OUT' (5 August 2013). The lead-in to the banner in small print, implying that the paper was being guided by its readers in calling for a change of government, was a deft touch in demagoguery.

The Fairfax newspapers gave unusual prominence to criticism of their rival publisher's approach to the campaign. Their criticism was hard to justify since late in her prime ministership, *The Age* had delivered a similarly presumptuous direction to the Labor caucus to dump Gillard. As Walsh (2013) noted, Fairfax's Peter Hartcher played as important a role as any journalist in the destabilisation of Gillard. Fairfax's conservative commentator Paul Sheehan (2013) alleged that News Corp's loss of faith in Labor was motivated by the competitive challenge that the National Broadband Network (NBN) threatened to the one profitable part of News Corp Australia—Foxtel. While this seems a slim motive for such a vociferous campaign, it did go some way to explaining why News Corp appeared unconcerned about alienating the hundreds of thousands of loyal Labor voters who buy their newspapers. It would appear that many newspapers in the News Corp empire, such as *The Australian,* have been retained for influence rather than profit. That principle may now apply to the Australian tabloids as well.

Rudd took up the theme of News Corp's power on the campaign trail. Labor had long bristled at the lack of balance in News Corp's political coverage, culminating in the tabloids' response to the Government's 2013 proposals to give modest legislative force to newspaper content regulation. Comparisons of Communications Minister Stephen Conroy to various odious dictators captured the tone of News Corp's coverage of that issue. Rudd's indulgence in media criticism was emblematic of his total lack of campaign strategy. It also made him look like a whinger.

Whether the tone of News Corp's editorial position influenced or followed the views of their readership over the course of six years of Labor Government is difficult to judge. A majority of News Corp papers supported a change of government in 2007, with some shifting back to the Coalition in 2010. More importantly, in terms of longer-term media effects on politics, the tone of day-to-day reporting on issues such as the home insulation scheme, school building projects and carbon pricing became particularly hostile throughout Gillard's term as prime minister. Roy Morgan Research found that the majority of News Corp tabloid readership, with the exception of the *Hobart Mercury*, supported the Coalition parties prior to the campaign (2013). *The Australian*, with its smaller audience but important agenda-setting role, amplified every complaint from the business sector into a national crisis.

In spite of the apparently unified senior editorial view, the News Corp tabloids varied in tone from city to city: more vociferous in Sydney and Brisbane, less so in Adelaide, Perth, Hobart and, at least during the campaign, in Melbourne. State-based election results lent weight to the idea that the tabloids had a limited effect, with the swings against Labor larger in Tasmania and Victoria than in New South Wales and Queensland. Yet those results also reflected the fact that the southern states swung towards Labor in 2010, and so contained more swinging voters yet to wield their baseball bats. Still, the voters of the Brisbane seat of Forde seemed to agree with the front-page banner of the *Courier-Mail* exclaiming: 'Send in the Clown', prompted by Kevin Rudd's announcement that Peter Beattie would be the candidate for the Coalition-held seat (Wardill 2013).

Analysis in the News Corp tabloids followed the pattern set by the front page editorialising. While we learned some detail about Abbott's home life in 'Tough guy Tony Abbott's secret is out', featuring a photograph of the Opposition Leader training with an army regiment in Darwin, the *Daily Telegraph* also agonised over the question of 'Kevin Rudd: Hero or Psychopath?' With admirable objectivity, the *Telegraph* concluded that the prime minister's mental state was 'an open-ended question' (Carswell 2013). Prior to the election, the *Telegraph* featured a series entitled 'Wreck-it Rudd', playing on a recent children's movie title, reminding voters of Rudd's record on asylum seekers, home insulation and other policy areas during his first stint as prime minister, as well as his proposed changes to the fringe benefits tax. Even *The Australian* could not keep up the pretence of former Coalition staffer Chris Kenny providing objective analysis in a column entitled 'Picking the Spin'. This feature was put on the back-burner after the first week of the campaign.

Kevin Rudd was not News Corp's only target. Having the temerity to start his own party in competition with the Coalition put Clive Palmer close to the top of *The Australian*'s ever-growing list of enemies. Hedley Thomas (2013) pointed out that billionaire 'Professor' Palmer was neither a billionaire nor a professor. The change of tone in the paper's coverage of Palmer after the Queenslander quit the Liberal National Party at the end of 2011—including prominent and exhaustive coverage of the magnate's legal battles—was clear enough. When Wayne Swan attacked Palmer, along with mining magnate and Australia's richest woman Gina Reinhardt, in 2011 for supporting policies that increase inequality, *The Australian* cried class warfare.

Reflecting the diversity of their readership, the News Corp tabloids stopped some way short of blatant one-sidedness. All the News Corp Sunday tabloids carried a compassionate feature about a baby lost when a boat carrying asylum seekers was struck by a storm in Indonesian waters. Sydney's *Daily Telegraph* joined in the fun of the hunt for Jaymes Diaz, the Liberal candidate for Greenway in Sydney's west who early in the campaign gained worldwide attention for his heroic failure to nominate more than one of the six points of the Coalition's asylum seeker policy in a television interview. He was thereafter hardly spotted until polling day, encouraging a competition among media outlets to spot him campaigning—one of a number of Coalition candidates under instructions from campaign headquarters to refuse interview requests from national media outlets. Some of the best policy analysis of the campaign came from the national economics correspondent for News Corp, Jessica Irvine, who lashed both major parties for their failure to face up to the long-term constraints on fiscal policy.

Conclusion

Old media showed it still counted in its coverage of the 2013 campaign. These traditional media outlets are now successfully integrating with new media and social media to provide excellent coverage of election campaigns—both in real-time coverage of events and in policy analysis—for that minority of the electorate sufficiently interested in intensive coverage. While the power of News Corp was a point of interest in the campaign, it is their ongoing reporting over the parliamentary cycle, rather than their attention-grabbing headlines, which frames and influences the political agenda. Recent changes in media technology are further polarising the Australian electorate between those maximising these opportunities and those who are exposed only to occasional messages about politics, often from a partisan or ephemeral source. In a nation where voting is compulsory, these trends are worthy of further reflection.

References

Australian Broadcasting Corporation (ABC). 2013. 'Kevin Rudd's $70 billion black hole claim not credible'. 14 August, viewed 7 January 2014: <www.abc.net.au/news/2013-08-14/kevin-rudd-70-billion-black-hole-claim-not-credible/4871852>.

Bennett, W Lance and Iyengar, Shanto. 2010. 'The Shifting Foundations of Political Communication: Responding to a defense of the media effects paradigm'. *Journal of Communication* 60(1): 35–9.

Carswell, Andrew. 2013. 'Kevin Rudd: hero or psychopath?' *Daily Telegraph*, 10 August, viewed 7 January 2014: <www.dailytelegraph.com.au/news/nsw/kevin-rudd-hero-or-psychopath/story-fni0cx12-1226694584192>.

Denemark, David, Ward, Ian and Bean, Clive. 2007. 'Election Campaigns and Television News Coverage: The case of the 2001 Australian election'. *Australian Journal of Political Science* 42(1): 89–109.

Errington, Wayne and van Onselen, Peter. 2007. 'The Democratic State as a Campaign Tool: The permanent campaign in Australia'. *Journal of Commonwealth and Comparative Politics* 45(1): 78–91.

Iyengar, Shanto and Simon, Adam. 2000. 'New Perspectives and Evidence on Political Communication and Campaign Effects'. *Annual Review of Psychology* 51: 149–69.

Jericho, Greg. 2013. 'In (qualified) praise of the press gallery'. *The Drum*, 11 September, viewed 11 September 2013: <www.abc.net.au/news/2013-09-11/jericho-in-qualified-praise-of-the-press-gallery/4948676>.

Lewis, Steve. 2013. 'Kevin Rudd's ads promoting PNG deal to cost taxpayers $30m'. *News.com.au*, 11 August, viewed 11 August 2013: <www.news.com.au/national/kevin-rudd8217s-ads-promoting-png-deal-to-cost-taxpayers-30m/story-fnho52ip-1226695091761>.

Maher, Sid. 2013. 'A night of waffle, scare campaigns and cost evasion'. *The Australian*, 12 August, viewed 27 February 2014: <www.theaustralian.com.au/national-affairs/election-2013/a-night-of-waffle-scare-campaigns-and-cost-evasion/story-fn9qr68y-1226695199954>.

McAllister, Ian and Cameron, Sarah. 2014. *Trends in Australian Political Opinion: Results From the Australian Election Study 1987–2013*. Canberra: The Australian National University.

Murdoch, Rupert. 2013. 'Australian public now totally disgusted with Labor Party wrecking country with its sordid intrigues. Now for a quick election.' 27 June, Twitter post: @rupertmurdoch.

Roy Morgan Research. 2013. 'The Political Profiles of Newspapers'. *Roy Morgan Profiles*, 28 August.

Scheufele, Dietram and Tewksbury, David. 2007. 'Framing, Agenda-Setting, and Priming: The evolution of three media effects models'. *Journal of Political Communication* (57): 9–20.

Sheehan, Paul. 2013. 'A 21st century fox playing chicken'. *The Sydney Morning Herald*, 5 August, viewed 5 August 2013: <www.smh.com.au/comment/a-21st-century-fox-playing-chicken-20130804-2r7ir.html>.

Tanner, Lindsay. 2011. *Sideshow: Dumbing down democracy*. Melbourne: Scribe.

Thomas, Hedley. 2013. 'Why we need to worry about the real Clive Palmer'. *The Australian*, 5 September, viewed 5 September 2013: <www.theaustralian.com.au/news/investigations/why-we-need-to-worry-about-the-real-clive-palmer/story-fn6tcxar-1226710922127>.

Valkenburg, Patti and Peter, Jochen. 2013. 'Five Challenges for the Future of Media Effects Research'. *International Journal of Communication* 7: 197–215.

van Onselen, Peter. 2013. 'For all the complaining the media don't focus on policy, my feature (comparing policies) today had less feedback than any other I've done!' 2 September, Twitter post: @vanonselenp.

Walsh, Kerry-Anne. 2013. *The Stalking of Julia Gillard: How the media and Team Rudd contrived to bring down the Prime Minister*. Sydney: Allen & Unwin.

Ward, Ian. 2007. 'Mapping the Australian PR State'. In Sally Young (ed.), *Government Communication in Australia*, Melbourne: Cambridge University Press.

Wardill, Steven. 2013. 'Prime Minister Kevin Rudd begs spinner Peter Beattie to help rescue Labor'. *Courier-Mail*, 9 August, viewed 15 January: <www.couriermail.com.au/news/queensland/prime-minister-kevin-rudd-begs-spinner-peter-beattie-to-help-rescue-labor/story-fnihsrf2-1226693889409>.

Young, Sally. 2011. *How Australia Decides: Election reporting and the media*. Melbourne: Cambridge University Press.

5. New Media in the Electoral Context: The new normal

Peter John Chen

The political impact and use of new media technologies—the internet, social media and mobile communication—have been subject to specific attention in the coverage of federal elections for nearly a decade now. Over this time, the use of new media has moved from being a novelty for parties, candidates, civil society organisations and established media to becoming an important—if still secondary—aspect of political communication in the electoral process. This new significance is seen in the professionalisation of channel management by political actors, heightened risk management by political organisations, and increased use of international knowledge transfer and learning. These changes represent an example of the adaptation of wholly new communication technologies into the political environment, and the interplay between technological possibilities and the structural context (Gibson 2002; Chen 2013).

Building on this tradition, this chapter examines the role of new media in the 2013 campaign, focusing on the use of online media channels by central party campaign teams and in the news media. Following Gibson and Cantijoch's (2011) question about the role of new media in the 2010 election, I argue that new media has finally 'arrived' as an essential element of the contemporary electoral practices of Australian political parties, with visible and significant impacts on the conduct of the 2013 election and elections to come. This has significant political implications for the competitiveness and representation of electoral politics, albeit constrained by Australia's two-party system. The chapter identifies the way established parliamentary parties are able to rapidly adopt new techniques and co-opt practices from civil society groups, entrenching the political status quo in a changing media landscape. In other words, the chapter provides evidence of the 'normalisation hypothesis' of political adoption of new technology (Gibson and McAllister 2011). At the same time, interesting developments in the reporting of elections are occurring within parts of the Australian news media that may be challenging the way parties are able to act as 'primary definers' of policy issues.

Political parties: Channel integration, cash and co-option

During the past decade, different elections have seen specific new media channels (sub-media) highlighted as areas of specific innovation and public attention. The late 1990s and early 2000s saw a focus on the deployment of campaign websites (Gibson 2002), the 2007 election was notable for the use of YouTube and social networking services (Chen 2008), and the 2010 election saw considerable attention devoted to the role of micro-blogging service Twitter (Macnamara and Kenning 2011). While often useful tools in positioning (branding) parties and candidates through association with technical sophistication and capability, these innovations tended to remain peripheral to campaign strategy in terms of both presentation and organisational management (Gibson and Cantijoch 2011: 8–9).

The 2013 election is distinct from this pattern in that the use of a wide range of online channels by the established parliamentary parties was undertaken using integrated multi-channelling. Multi-channelling in this context is defined as 'the use of more than one channel or medium to manage customers in the way that is consistent and coordinated across all the channels or media used' (Hobbs *et al.* 2003: 316). This approach is synergistic: maximising the benefits of individual sub-media through combining their strengths and mitigating weaknesses. While this has been seen in previous elections (particularly the use of email and SMS messaging to drive key audiences like journalists to webpages), in 2013 a wider range of channels were employed, including email, search and display advertising, and social media.[1] The sources of this change result from the significance parties are placing on new media as primary campaigning tools, and their willingness to engage in pro-active learning from a range of sources.

Getting serious about new media

In lead-up to the 2013 campaign, the Australian Labor Party (ALP), Liberal Party of Australia (Liberals) and Australian Greens (Greens) displayed a far more disciplined and instrumental approach to the management of new media communications. This is reflected in decisions to increase levels of expenditure on online advertising, systems acquisition and staff, to reduce the visibility of candidates through discouraging their use of some channels (the Liberal Party; Wright 2012), as well as increasing the organisational importance of new media managers within the core campaign team (personal interviews: Skye Laris,

---

1   The term 'social media' is generally used to describe services like Twitter, Facebook and blogs (though see Kaplan and Haenlein 2010 for a more complex definition).

ALP Director of Digital Communications, Organising and Campaigns, 23 July 2013; Rosanne Bersten, Australian Greens National Digital Communications Coordinator, 2 August 2013).

While social media channels have been used to a degree in previous campaigns (although with a strong preference towards more 'top-down' communications methods by the major parties; Grant *et al*. 2010), the 2013 campaign saw these parties become much more active in these areas (Loughnane 2013). There was recognition of the considerable benefits social media channels can bring in linking political communication with audience action. In addition, while uncertainty has tended to encourage isomorphism of application in previous elections, the ends-directed nature of planning for the 2013 campaign saw considerable divergence in the way the parties deployed new media. This is evident in the different use of 'push' channels by the two major parties: the ALP making greater use of targeted email, while the Liberals used more targeted advertising on Facebook. Additionally, the ALP tended to focus on the figure of the leader (and through him, downplay the party), while the Liberals highlighted the party over the leader (see the arguments of Strangio and Walter in Chapter 3, this volume). In this context, Kevin Rudd's continual use of 'selfie' photographs with members of the public contrasts with the Liberals' use of the party brand and promotion of the new Liberal 'team' over highly personalised messaging.

Each of these parties benefited considerably from a more managerial approach, avoiding the use of 'gimmicks' that might have been employed under previous management approaches (such as phone apps that have unproven value in spite of rapid smartphone adoption; see Sadauskas 2013), preferring instead strategies based on clear cost-benefit terms. Overall, the Liberals won both the election and the 'visibility war', outperforming their rivals in driving traffic to their website through both search engines and via social media channels. As in previous years, the Greens have a higher online visibility than their primary vote would suggest (Grant *et al*. 2008), reflecting the tendency for Greens supporters to be correlated with attributes associated with higher levels of internet uptake and intensity of use (education, urban living). Following Small's (2008) observation of the Canadian electoral context, minor parties may be able to have an online presence equivalent to that of the established parties, but this does not automatically lead to heightened levels of visibility; constituency and strategy is critical in overcoming the structural advantages of parties of government.

The strong new media performance of the Liberals is illustrated in Table 1: the Liberals were more effective in driving traffic to their site than the ALP.[2] Significantly, they were able to achieve this at lower cost in search engine advertising than the ALP, and to attract more than three times the rate of referrals via social media sources. The Liberals also used online video more effectively and were far more visible on Facebook. While Kevin Rudd was able to dominate visibility on Twitter due to his established presence on the channel with large numbers of followers, the comparatively smaller population of this avenue (2.5 million Australian users compared with Facebook's 11.5 million; Frank Media 2013) is a considerable weakness in reaching voters and encouraging message distribution through their social networks, even if its popularity among journalists gives it greater inter-media agenda-setting potential (Messner and Garrison 2009: 394). This agenda-setting effect—moving messages from Twitter to mainstream (news organisations) and alternative media (blogs, social media discussions)—has its limitations, however. Rudd's 'selfies', while popular with a younger audience and a useful micro-targeting tactic, could not be controlled in the open context of Twitter and quickly became the subject of some ridicule. Targeted messaging of this type, therefore, is far better employed in social networking services like Facebook, with higher pass-along, but lower visibility to and pick-up by, mainstream media organisations.[3]

Table 1: Comparative party website performance, election 2013

	liberal.org.au	alp.org.au	Ifabbottwinsyoulose.com.au(ALP)	greens.org.au	palmerunited.com	nationals.org.au
Australian site rank (popularity)	1,844th	2,323rd	4,475th	2,726th	6,172nd	29,543rd
Visitors Aug 1–Sept 7	505,000	330,000	120,000	260,000	95,000	26,000
% referral from search engine—July–Sept	39.8%	48.2%	51.9%	35.9%	52.3%	-
% of search result paid	13.9%	23.7%	0.0%	0.5%	0.0%	-
% referral from social media	16.2%	4.8%	4%	13.1%	12.7%	-
Source:						
Facebook	49.7%	72.8%	67.9%	88.7%	98.2%	-
Twitter	6.6%	20.7%	11.7%	6.1%	1.8%	-
Reddit	0.1%	6.2%	20.5%	4.7%	0.0%	-
YouTube	43.8%	0.4%	0.0%	0.3%	0.0%	-

Source: Compiled from SimilarWeb data.

---

2   Unlike in previous national elections, the Liberal's main negative website 'Rudd Facts' was part of their main party domain (www.liberal.org.au/ruddfacts). Traditionally, the parties have distanced their negative/attack sites from their main campaigning sites with separate domains and non-party branding.

3   The general exception to this tending to be 'gaffes'.

Raising campaign money through new media

While professionalisation of management and implementation had clear performance advantages in enhancing the visibility of the established parties, the 2013 election campaign is also instructive in regard to parties learning from campaign experience in other countries and co-opting the strategic repertoires of civil society organisations. The ALP was quite active in recruiting temporary and permanent personnel with experience in international new media campaigning, and experience with the Online Social Movement Organisation (OSMO) *GetUp!* (Personal interview: Skye Laris, 23 July 2013). The Greens were also very active in drawing on lessons from OSMOs, domestic and international (Personal interview: Rosanne Bersten, 2 August 2013).

The types of lessons drawn ranged from simple engagement strategies (such as providing ready-made 'activist identity' Facebook profile icons on issues like animal rights and same-sex marriage) to more complex ideas about voter engagement, mobilisation and motivation. In the latter area, the Liberal Party and the ALP were particularly interested in developing their 'big data' database analytics capacity for the targeting of direct email, following successes in micro-targeting in the United States (Loughnane 2013). Labor and the Greens were invested in 'commitment curve' models of voter engagement that involve working supporters through an increasingly steep set of requests with corresponding feedback and rewards (see Chen 2014).

These rewards included access to information 'first', direct messaging showing the impact of funds provided, and the incorporation of individual narratives in a process of political 'storytelling', adopted directly from the OSMOs (Vromen and Coleman 2013). Pertinent examples of this approach were 'Kevin calls Michelle to say thanks for her $5 donation' campaign message (about 'Michelle from Bundaberg's' journey from swinging voter to donor out of concern for the implications of an Abbott-led Government; posted 8 August 2013) and Tanya Plibersek's 'Let's clear the air' cigarette plain packing email that linked ALP policy achievements with tobacco industry donations to the Liberal Party (issued 1 August 2013). Similarly, the Greens' 'not in my name' email campaign around asylum seekers was extremely effective in quickly raising money to purchase print media advertising. The Greens have reported that email, rather than other social media, represented the strongest driver for donations (raising 75 per cent of donations; Bersten 2013).

The impact of these types of methods demonstrated considerable benefits to the parties. The ALP, through the use of highly customised, targeted direct email and commitment curve strategies, was able to raise $800,000 in small-unit donations during the campaign (Snow 2013), while the Greens' website raised over $600,000. This is significant, as the ALP suffered considerable problems in fundraising prior to the return of Rudd to the leadership, as its chance of electoral success was perceived as so limited. Overall, therefore, the established parties demonstrated a capacity to enhance both their visibility and strategic capacity during the campaign using their more focused and pragmatic approaches to new media. This compared favourably to parties without these strategies, as was illustrated in Table 1.

Political journalism 2.0: Innovation without impact?

The Australian news industry has been under considerable economic pressure during the past decade. This is largely due to increased competition for attention and advertising resulting from the expansion of media channels. As established media organisations have begun to substantially reduce their editorial and journalistic workforces in response (Flew and Swift 2013: 195),[4] the threat of 'churnalism' has been seen as inevitable (Martin and Dwyer 2012). In this case, 'churnalism' has a range of dimensions, including:

- greater use of newswire reports between media (decreasing diversity of content);
- lower editorial standards (decreasing accuracy and parsimony);
- increasing susceptibility to information subsidy (public relations and 'spin'); and,
- a simultaneous deskilling (loss of journalistic specialisations) and upskilling (multi-media journalism, single-person crews, etc.) within the industry.

Because of these implications for practice, the comparative power of media organisations relative to their sources appears to have declined. This has re-established the relevance of Hall *et al.*'s (1979: 58) argument that political and party elites (leaders, campaign managers) are more likely to act as 'primary definers' of issues and topics because of their structurally-privileged position relative to alternative sources of interpretative frames. The extent to which this can be seen in the Australian electoral context has relevance for our understanding of the democratic impacts of the political economy of new media. Significantly, as journalists and political elites attempt to exert mutual influence without acquiring dependency (Tiffen 1990), changes in media practice also point to attempts by journalists to free themselves of dependency upon political

---

4   In the lead-up to the 2013 campaign, the Australian media landscape saw these problems, with up to 30 per cent of staff in News Limited and Fairfax's metropolitan operations laid off in 2012–13.

5. New Media in the Electoral Context

elites as primary definers. In the context of the 2013 campaign, we can explore this by looking at the way mainstream news media employed social media, and innovations in the practice of conventional reporting.

Social media, media 'events' and elites

The integration of social media into journalistic practice has been ongoing for many years (O'Donnell *et al*. 2013:16). The reasons for this are varied, but include generational change, personal branding, market sensing, and new forms of elite interaction performed in public (Chen 2013). In the 2013 election campaign, the use of social media as part of journalistic practice was highly visible, as illustrated in Figure 1.[5]

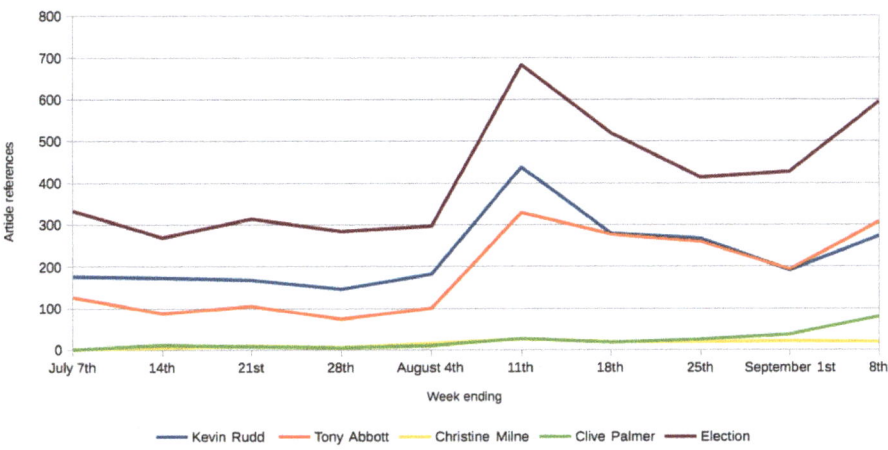

Figure 1: References to social media in political journalism, 2013

Source: Factiva.

This figure, a subset of all print coverage, shows a number of tendencies. First, journalists are selective in the material they import from social media. Thus, Kevin Rudd's tendency to dominate Twitter discussion is not automatically reflected in reporting. While Rudd entered the election with a higher word association with social media than Abbott, the focusing of election coverage on the two leaders quickly reduced this advantage. This also reflects the medium's decreasing novelty, which has reduced the type of strategic meta-coverage that would have previously given Rudd an advantage over Abbott.

---

5   Based on a search against leaders names and 'Election' and the terms 'twitter', 'tweet', 'facebook', and 'social media'.

Second, the significant use of social media by minor party leaders receives considerably less media coverage than the two 'parties of government'. This continues to re-affirm Goot's (2009) findings that internet news coverage is narrower than conventional reporting, particularly in its under-reporting of minor parties relative to their vote share. This is a counter-balance to the visibility advantages the Greens have online, and further demonstrates the media logic behind their considerable investment in online channels over many years.

Third, discussion of the political content of social media is not wholly driven by party campaigns, but is now being employed as independent content: journalists are increasingly reporting on events through the lens of social media discussions about them. This has become easier as a range of tools have emerged for tracking trends online, but the focus remains on those social media with the most open publishing platforms, particularly Twitter. Two examples of this are the coverage of popular responses to Tony Abbott's remarks about a candidate having 'sex appeal', leading to the story becoming a top trending topic (#sexappeal; AFP 2013), and the response to Kevin Rudd's defence of his same-sex marriage position in the final leaders' debate (Knox 2013). Overall, this supports Livingston and Bennett's (2003) hypothesis that the shift towards reporting live events (associated with the constant news cycle and continual publishing) may broaden the source base for journalism.

New news organisations and practices

The 2013 election campaign saw the emergence of some news organisations with novel (for Australia) business models. Examples include the entry of the *Guardian Australia* (a non-profit trust) into the Australian market, situating itself to the left of the Fairfax editorial position, as well as the maturation of the non-profit, university-sponsored site *The Conversation*. During the election period, each performed quite well relative to established media organisations (Table 2) given their comparatively small operating budgets. In addition to these developments, Fairfax extended its paywall model from the *Australian Financial Review* to its other online properties in mid 2013.

Table 2: Comparative news organisation website performance, August 2013

Website	Type	Australian site rank (popularity)	August page visits
ninemsn.com.au	Commercial	12th	28,000,000
abc.net.au	Public	21st	14,700,000
news.com.au	Commercial	40th	12,700,000
smh.com.au	Commercial	41st	11,700,000
theage.com.au	Commercial	50th	8,100,000
heraldsun.com.au	Commercial	63rd	6,200,000
theaustralian.com.au	Commercial	177th	3,300,000
theguardian.co.uk/au	Independent trust	n/a	3,879,200
dailytelegraph.com.au	Commercial	133rd	3,000,000
crikey.com.au	Commercial	430th	930,000
theconversation.edu.au (.com/au)	Non-profit, university	748th	930,000
politifact.com.au	Commercial start-up	24,884th	130,000
newmatilda.com	Non-profit	11,664th	40,000
insidestory.org.au	University	25,439th	25,000
2013electionwatch.com.au	University	33,879th	9,000

Source: Compiled from SimilarWeb data.

While attempts at 'independent' news media websites are not new, one significant new journalistic endeavour during the 2013 campaign was the introduction of branded 'fact-checking' journalism. This idea was imported to Australia from the United States, both in spirit (the ABC set up its internal fact-checking organisation with an increase in funding from the Labor Government; *The Conversation* had a dedicated fact-checking unit for the election) and as a direct licensed version of the original *Politifact* organisation.[6] The latter maintained its own site, but syndicated its content to the Fairfax group and the Seven Network (Holmes 2013). As in the US, the visibility of these assessments was quite high in the media organisations that employed them.

An interesting facet of these fact-checking units is not simply their evaluation of political claims as truthful or false, but also in the way these evaluations are presented as evidence-based, with substantiation of claims made. This represents a significant counter to concerns about the decline of journalism into 'churnalism' with limited attention given to complex policy issues and technical points (Phillips 2011). It also contradicts concerns regarding the development of a more assertive style of journalism that moves away from the traditional focus on perceived 'balance' through the provision of equal time to alternative positions.

---

6   *Crikey* also started a small fact-checking theme, producing 13 assessments from April 2013 (Knott 2013).

While there is little evidence of any direct impact of these groups on the conduct of elites during the election (Kevin Rudd, for example, persisted in using a figure of $70 million in Coalition cuts after it had been declared false), they mark a response by some media organisations to perceptions that they lack rigour (and therein legitimacy). Moreover, due to marketplace logics, these developments appear to continue into the period of government. As the production and reproduction of news content proliferates between established, emerging, and amateur websites, these types of activities allow rebranding and product differentiation. And, as with the expanded use of polling, fact-checking services permit the spontaneous generation of news on demand by media organisations (therein regularising their production processes), and extending coverage of issues with new angles and interpretations.

Overall, it appears that news organisations are embracing new forms of journalistic practice that move away from their dependency on political elites as 'talking heads'. Media organisations also invested more time in collecting and developing data of electoral behaviour and performance during the campaign. This often took the form of data collection (such as the ABC's *Vote Compass*), data visualisations, maps and interactive explainers. News Limited produced a poll aggregator (the 'Poll Pulse'), while the *Australian Financial Review* provided a range of visualisations from electoral explainers to leaders' movement maps at its established data journalism sub-domain (www.data.afr.com). These types of initiatives show how established organisations are employing increasingly rich forms of multi-media to present data in interactive and manipulable forms.

Conclusion

The 2013 federal election was not a competitive race. But the campaign did demonstrate a considerable range of technical and methodological innovation in Australia's political and media landscape that made it a more interesting event than the 2010 election. While the victory of the Coalition will encourage attention to its use of social media and strong cross-channel integration strategies, the effectiveness of small unit fundraising and storytelling strategies by the ALP is also likely to garner considerable attention from party tacticians. Overall, the 2013 campaign shows how quickly and comprehensively the established parties are able to co-opt the technologies and tactics of the online social movement organisations when they see organisational advantage in doing so. This clearly demonstrates the structural and economic advantages of the major parties in the Australian political system, but also the enduring explanatory value of the normalisation hypothesis in broad terms. (For a good example of the significant, but atypical role of new media in equalising competitiveness at the local level, see the arguments of Costar and Curtin in this volume.) The lessons for the news media are less clear, but the range of new journalistic practices deployed for the 2013 election demonstrates how media organisations are moving beyond reactive strategies associated with downsizing and withdrawal, to examining new ways to engage media audiences and produce higher quality output.

References

Agence France-Presse (AFP). 2013. 'Australia's Abbott in "sex appeal" blunder'. *Capital News*, 13 August: <www.capitalfm.co.ke/news/2013/08/australias-abbott-in-sex-appeal-blunder/>.

Bersten, Rosanne. 2013. 'Digital and Social Media: 2013 Federal Election Analysis', 16 November.

Chen, Peter John. 2005. 'The new media: E-lection 2004?' In Marian Simms and John Warhurst (eds), *Mortgage Nation: the 2004 Australian Election*, Perth: API Network.

Chen, Peter John. 2008. 'Australian political parties' use of Youtube 2007'. *Southern Review: Communication, Politics and Culture* 41(1): 114–41.

Chen, Peter John. 2012. 'The new media and the campaign'. In Marian Simms and John Wanna (eds), *Julia 2010: The caretaker election*, Canberra: ANU E-Press.

Chen, Peter John. 2013. *Australian Politics in a Digital Age*. Canberra: ANU E-Press.

Chen, Peter John and Walsh, Lucas. 2010. 'e-lection 2007? Political competition online'. *Australian Cultural History* 28(1): 47–54.

Chen, Peter John. 2014. 'The virtual party on the ground'. In Anika Gauja, Narelle Miraglotta and Rodney Smith (eds), *Resilient and Defiant: Reflections on Contemporary Party Organisations*, Melbourne: Monash University Press, in-press.

Flew, Terry and Swift, Adam. 2013. 'Regulating journalists? The Finkelstein Review, the Convergence Review, and news media regulation in Australia'. *Journal of Applied Journalism and Media Studies* 2(1): 181–99.

Frank Media. 2013. *Social Media Statistics Australia—April 2013*, viewed 15 January 2014: <frankmedia.com.au/2013/05/01/social-media-statistics-australia-april-2013/>.

Gibson, Rachel. 2002. 'Virtual campaigning: Australian parties and the impact of the internet'. *Australian Journal of Political Science* 37(1): 99–130.

Gibson, Rachel and Cantijoch, Marta. 2011. 'Comparing online elections in Australia and the UK: Did 2010 finally produce "the" internet election?' *Communication, Politics & Culture* 44(2): 4–17.

Gibson, Rachel and McAllister, Ian. 2011. *A net gain? Web 2.0 campaigning in the Australian 2010 election*. Paper prepared for presentation at the 2011 Annual Meeting of the American Political Science Association, Seattle.

Gibson, Rachel and Ward, Stephen. 2003. 'Letting the daylight in? Australian state parties and the WWW'. In Rachel Gibson, Paul Nixon and Stephen Ward (eds), *Net Gain? Political Parties and the Internet*. London, UK: Routledge.

Goot, Murray. 2009. 'Is the news on the internet different? Leaders, frontbenchers and other candidates in the 2007 Australian election'. *Australian Journal of Political Science* 43(1): 99–110.

Grant, Will, Moon, Brenda, and Grant, Janie. 2010. 'Digital dialogue? Australian politicians' use of the social network tool twitter'. *Australian Journal of Political Science* 45(4): 579–604.

Hall, Stuart, Critcher, Chas, Jefferson, Tony, Clarke, John, and Roberts, Brian. 1979. *Policing the Crisis: Mugging, the State and Law and Order*. London, UK: Macmillan.

Hobbs, Matt, Khaleeli, Mahnaz, and Stone, Merlin. 2003. 'Multi-channel customer management'. In Neil Woodward, Merlin Stone and Bryan Foss (eds), *Customer Management Scorecard: Managing CRM for Profit*, London, UK: Kogan Page.

Holmes, Jonathan. 2013. 'Truth trivial in an election: now there's a fact'. *The Sydney Morning Herald*, 21 August, viewed 15 January 2014: <www.smh.com.au/federal-politics/federal-election-2013/truth-trivial-in-an-election-now-theres-a-fact-20130820-2s92b.html>.

Kaplan, Andreas and Haenlein, Michael. 2010. 'Users of the world, unite! The challenges and opportunities of Social Media'. *Business Horizons* 53(1): 59–68.

Knott, Matthew. 2013. 'Fact off: ABC and Fray's PolitiFact dig into pollies' spin'. *Crikey*, 29 April, viewed 1 October 2013: <www.crikey.com.au/2013/04/29/fact-off-abc-and-frays-politifact-dig-into-pollies-spin>, accessed: 1/10/13.

Knox, David. 2013. 'Kevin Rudd defends gay marriage position. "It is how people are built"'. *TV Tonight*, 3 September, viewed 15 January 2014: <www.tvtonight.com.au/2013/09/kevin-rudd-defends-gay-marriage-position-it-is-how-people-are-built.html>.

Livingston, Stephen and Bennett, W Lance. 2003. 'Gatekeeping, indexing, and live-event news: Is technology altering the construction of news?'. *Political Communication* 20: 363–80.

Loughnane, Brian. 2013. 'Address to the National Press Club'. Canberra, 23 October, viewed 26 October 2013: <lpaweb-static.s3.amazonaws.com/Brian%20Loughnane%20-%20National%20Press%20Club%20Address%20-%2023%20October%202013.pdf>.

Macnamara, Jim and Kenning, Gail. 2011. 'E-electioneering 2010: Trends in social media use in Australian political communication'. *Media International Australia* 139: 7–22.

Martin, Fiona and Dwyer, Tim. 2012. 'Churnalism on the rise as news sites fill up with shared content and wire copy'. *The Conversation,* 25 June, viewed 15 January 2014: <theconversation.com/churnalism-on-the-rise-as-news-sites-fill-up-with-shared-content-and-wire-copy-7859>.

Messner, Marcus and Garrison, Bruce. 2009. 'Internet communication'. In Don Stacks and Michael Salwen (eds), *An Integrated Approach to Communication Theory and Research*, 2nd edn, New York: Routledge.

O'Donnell, Penny, McKnight, David and Este, Jonathan. 2012. *Journalism at the Speed of Bytes: Australian Newspapers in the 21st Century*. Sydney: Media, Entertainment and Arts Alliance.

Phillips, Angela. 2011. 'Transparency and the new ethics of journalism'. In Bob Franklin (ed.), *The Future of Journalism*, London: Routledge.

Sadauskas, Andrew. 2013. '57% of Australians have smartphones, adoption rates outpace the US and Europe'. *Smart Company*, 17 May, viewed 15 January 2014: <www.smartcompany.com.au/information-technology/049727-57-of-australians-have-smartphones-adoption-rates-outpace-the-us-and-europe.html>.

Small, Tamara. 2008. 'Equal access, unequal success: Major and minor Canadian parties on the net'. *Party Politics* 14: 51–70.

Snow, Deborah. 2013. 'How Kevin Rudd's 2013 election campaign imploded'. *The Sydney Morning Herald*, 9 September, viewed 15 January 2014: <www.smh.com.au/federal-politics/federal-election-2013/how-kevin-rudds-2013-election-campaign-imploded-20130908-2teb1.html>.

Tiffen, Rodney. 1990. *News and Power*. Sydney: Allen & Unwin.

Vromen, Ariadne and Coleman, William. 2013. 'Online campaigning organizations and storytelling strategies: GetUp! in Australia'. *Policy and Internet* 5(1): 70–100.

Wright, Jessica. 2012. 'Liberal gag twits'. *The Sydney Morning Herald*, 9 December, viewed 15 January 2014: <www.smh.com.au/technology/technology-news/liberals-gag-twits-20121208-2b284.html>.

6. Campaign Advertising and Communication Strategies in the Election of 2013

Sally Young

For 40 years, Australia's major political parties have prioritised television and viewed it as the pre-eminent medium for communicating with voters during an election. As Gough Whitlam's speechwriter, Graham Freudenberg (2000: 122), observed first-hand, the 1969 election was 'the last campaign that wasn't tailored mainly to TV'. From 1972 onwards, the parties have focused both their 'paid media' strategies (commercial advertising) and their 'free media' (media management) activities upon TV (Young 2011: 126–45). But in 2013, with fragmenting media audiences diminishing television's impact and audience reach, the major parties took a multi-faceted approach. While TV ads were still the major component of their communication strategies, these were supplemented by other forms of communication including both digital and one-to-one methods. This was a campaign notable for the parties' use of information gleaned from market research and new methods of detailed data analysis, their reliance upon professionalised campaign operatives and their increased use of targeting and micro-targeting approaches to reach strategically important voters.

Advertising and campaign spending

In a less than promising start for Labor, planning for the Party's advertising strategy was disrupted when its relationship with its original advertising agent, Mark Collis, broke down around March 2013. Labor then assembled a new team comprising Essential Media Communications (the progressive polling and campaigning group responsible for the Australian Council of Trade Union's 2007 *Your Rights at Work* campaign) and advertising agent Dee Madigan. In a blaze of publicity, Labor also brought in international expertise in digital media in the form of Obama campaign veterans. These included British social media strategist Matthew McGregor (dubbed 'Obama's digital attack dog') and Tom McMahon, the former executive director of the Democratic National Committee. Reportedly without consulting central campaign headquarters, Kevin Rudd also brought back Neil Lawrence from the *Kevin07* campaign to develop the slogan 'A New Way' and the accompanying advertisement which suggested an initial 'positive' focus that later gave way to more standard negative campaign techniques.

As befits a conservative party, the Liberal Party stuck with its longstanding in-house team of market researchers and strategists, Mark Textor and the Crosby Textor group, along with advertising agent Mark Pearson who had worked for the Liberals since the 1996 campaign. And, as befits a party that was widely expected to win, the Liberal advertising campaign played it safe and relied upon traditional challenger messages which highlighted disunity and inconsistency in the government and promoted the need for change.

Campaign spending patterns reveal important information about the campaign priorities and strategies of the parties but, unfortunately, accurately determining election advertising spending is extraordinarily difficult in Australia. Despite the generous public funding provided for Australian election campaigns, political parties are not required to disclose how they spend their funds during federal elections. Other countries—including the United Kingdom—have much stronger disclosure and political finance reporting requirements. In Australia, there is a troubling lack of transparency and accountability by comparison (Young and Tham 2006; Ewing, Rowbottom and Tham 2012). As a result, we have to rely upon estimates of party spending, particularly from commercial agents monitoring advertisement buying in the political domain, known in the industry as 'ad buy monitors'. These estimates can vary significantly.

Before the election, there had been estimates in media outlets that the two major parties would spend $20–25 million each. There were even estimates during the campaign that they would spend a record amount of up to $90 million (e.g. Shanahan 2013). But after the election, in one of the more comprehensive estimates of spending, advertising monitoring group ebiquity suggested the two parties spent a combined total of just under $11 million across TV, radio and print with the Liberal Party spending $6.75 million compared to $4.04 million for Labor (for the period 5 August to 6 September 2013) (*Campaign Brief* 2013). In contrast, global measurement company Nielsen reported that the two parties spent a total of $18.5 million with at least $11 million spent by the Liberals and $7.5 million by the ALP throughout the campaign on multiple types of advertising including broadcast, print, out-door and direct mail (Nielsen 2013; Aqx 2013). According to Nielsen, the Liberal Party spent more than $4 million in just the last week of the campaign alone compared to Labor's spending of $1.5 million in that last week.

So, whether the two parties' combined total spending was as low as $11 million (a figure that a senior campaign strategist for one of the major parties refuted as being far too low) or, more likely, over $18.5 million (as reported by Nielsen), their overall spending did still seem to be less than anticipated and less than is usual. For the 2010 election, the two parties reportedly spent around $27 million (combined) on TV advertising alone, up from around $24 million in 2004 (Young 2005: 103; see also Young 2004: 41). Estimates of spending in 2013 therefore seem relatively low.

One clear indicator that the major parties did feel they were short of cash in 2013 was their thwarted attempt earlier in the year to increase public funding for campaigns through legislation. That deal would have delivered around $20 million a year to all parties and elected independents over three years for 'administrative purposes', but it was dropped after a public backlash. The attempt to boost public funding arose because the parties have faced increasingly lean times in terms of private fundraising. Between the 1998 and 2010 elections, the total pool of private donations going to the ALP and the Liberal Party shrank from $76 million to $61 million (Tham and Anderson 2013). But it may also be that, with the result seemingly a foregone conclusion, neither party was willing to spend up big or go into debt. This was especially true for Labor which, as the clear underdog, probably had fewer private donations and perhaps judged that it was wiser to conserve some funds for a future campaign with better prospects.

Although the campaign advertising spending estimates provided by different monitoring companies varied, they did contain some similar conclusions. Of the two major parties, the Liberals outspent Labor during the campaign by at least double—or even by four to one according to some reports—in the crucial final few days before the electronic blackout (*Campaign Brief* 2013; Jackson 2013; Nielsen 2013). Liberal Party resources seem to have been especially focused upon the last two weeks of the campaign.

Another important point of agreement was the evidence that the two major parties had new competition during the 2013 election. According to ebiquity, billionaire Clive Palmer's Palmer United Party almost rivalled Labor's total spending and, on both the Nielsen and ebiquity figures, Palmer definitely outspent Labor during the last week (*Campaign Brief* 2013; Nielsen 2013). But, again demonstrating the confusion and misinformation that inadequate disclosure provisions in Australia cause, while Palmer reportedly spent $3.02 million on advertising during the election (*Campaign Brief* 2013), others suggested he spent 'about $12 million' (Hurst 2013). Palmer himself suggested his party spent between $10–12 million during the campaign (AAP 2013; for further discussion and analysis of Clive Palmer's party in the 2013 election, see Chapter 17 by Tom King).

Both the ebiquity and Nielsen reports on spending show that the other major new player in 2013 was a third party interest group rather than a political party. The Australian Salary Packaging Association reportedly spent over $1.4 million on advertising during the election to lobby against Labor's proposed changes to the fringe benefits tax on car leases (Nielsen 2013; *Campaign Brief* 2013). Close behind in spending was the pro-mining Australian Petroleum Production and Exploration Association, the leading lobby group for the oil and gas industry, which reportedly spent $1.2 million on ads during the election (*Campaign Brief* 2013). By comparison, the Greens were reported to have spent about half that of the Australian Salary Packaging Association (*Campaign Brief* 2013). The Greens focused particularly on the seat of Melbourne in what may have been the biggest expenditure in a single seat.

The Australian Chamber of Commerce and Industry also launched an advertising campaign to promote issues important to small business called 'Small Business Too Big To Ignore'. Other older (non-party) advertisers included the ACTU and *GetUp!* which both spent over $500,000 during the 2013 campaign (*Campaign Brief* 2013). The ACTU started advertising in June 2013 under the banner 'Australian Unions. Join. For a Better Life'. The ACTU argued this was about issues broader than just the election but others viewed the advertising as designed to support Labor's re-election. Combined spending by major unions—including the ACTU but also the Australian Education Union, the National Union of Workers, the Construction, Forestry, Mining and Energy Union, and the National Tertiary Education Union—exceeded $1.5 million (*Campaign Brief* 2013).

The high spending in 2013 by third party groups trying to influence election outcomes and party policy is the continuation of a tradition in recent years in Australia which has seen advertising become a dominant method of political discourse. This is not confined to elections. Businesses ran various expensive campaigns against Labor government policy between 2007 and 2010 including campaigns against the mining tax, carbon pricing, cigarette plain packaging and gambling reforms. Nor is the advertising confined to parties and interest groups.

Governments have also run expensive campaigns—at taxpayer expense—to either promote or defend themselves and their policies. This trend accelerated in the 2000s with the Howard government's advertising on the Goods and Services Tax (*Unchain My Heart*) and later its *WorkChoices* policy (Young 2007), and continued under the Rudd and Gillard governments so that it is now impossible to examine (political) election advertising without also considering pre-election, and even caretaker period, government advertising.

Indeed, one of the controversies that erupted during the 2013 election was the Labor government's use of government advertising during the caretaker election period. The Labor government continued an advertising campaign about its new asylum seeker deal with Papua New Guinea that included full-page newspaper ads stating, 'If you come here by boat without a visa—YOU WON'T BE SETTLED

IN AUSTRALIA' and warning that asylum seekers were 'buying a ticket for another country'. These ads ran heavily in domestic newspapers, radio and TV from July and into the campaign proper. This provoked controversy, as it had during previous elections, about caretaker conventions and the potential misuse of government advertising for partisan purposes just before, or even during, an election.[1] During the election period in 2004, for example, the Howard government ran 'Help protect Australia from terrorism' ads on TV, radio and in newspapers that Labor at the time criticised as unreasonable and as creating a potential political advantage during the election (Young 2005: 104).

This is an extension of another familiar pattern since the 2000s; namely that of sudden surges in incumbent spending on government advertising in the lead up to an election (Grant 2003–04). The Howard government, in its final year, reportedly spent $254 million (Lewis 2013b). In 2013, Labor government advertising spending surged in the three months before the election with advertising campaigns on asylum seeker policy, the National Broadband Network (NBN), the Gonski education reforms, household assistance and the National Disability Insurance Scheme (NDIS). Estimates suggested that spending on federal government advertising surged by 50 per cent in April 2013 alone, including over $50 million spent in the four months before the election (*West Australian* 2013; Coyne 2013; Priest and Anderson 2013).

Aside from the pre-election and caretaker period government advertising campaigns, there were two other interesting political advertising controversies in 2013. After the electronic advertising blackout was enforced at midnight on the Wednesday before polling day, viewers continued to see Palmer-themed commercials for the Palmer Coolum Resort. Palmer spokespeople argued these were not political and therefore did not breach the blackout rules (Hurst 2013). Raising some very different issues (less about rule enforcement than about media censorship), a *GetUp!* advertisement critical of Rupert Murdoch and News Corporation's anti-Labor campaign in its newspapers (especially the *Daily Telegraph* and the *Courier-Mail*) was dropped by Channel Nine even though it was approved for broadcast by Free TV Australia. Channels Seven and Ten also refused to run the ads.

---

[1] Liberal Senator George Brandis said the ads were 'nothing but political advertisements designed to promote the policies and the propaganda of the Labor Party' (Owens 2013). Tony Abbott called it a 'gross misuse' of public funds (Lewis 2013a). Other critics also suggested the ads seemed designed to reach voters in Australia rather than people overseas contemplating a boat voyage to Australia. Independent Senator Nick Xenophon also complained that Labor was breaching caretaker conventions. The Auditor-General, Ian McPhee, wrote back to say that the caretaker conventions gave the Government latitude regarding advertising campaigns, and noted in any case that the conventions are not legally binding (McPhee 2013).

'Old' media, technology and communications: TV, radio, print, direct mail, door-knocking and phone banks

Television advertisements still constituted the biggest single expenditure for the major parties and were the central focus of their advertising and communications plans, as has been the case since the 1970s. However, a range of newer methods of communications were also put to use and traditional methods of face-to-face communication, print and telephones also experienced something of a resurgence as the parties took a mixed approach to their communications.

The Liberal Party's use of printed material to promote its *Real Solutions Plan* was a key to its communications strategy (as Nicholas Reece explains in Chapter 7). Distribution of five million copies of what is, for political mail, a very dense booklet, was a significant investment in print. The Liberals appear to have spent nearly three times as much on direct mail as Labor did (Aqx 2013). On the Labor side, greater investment was made in metropolitan radio advertising and on using American-style telephone banks for cold calling. Labor made over one million calls to voters in marginal seats using volunteers as well as MPs and candidates (ALP 2013). This was reportedly a more than ten-fold increase on the number of people Labor called in 2010 (Kenny 2013). Aside from 'live' phone calls, 'robocalls' were also a feature of the 2013 campaign, although they are used much less extensively in Australia than in the United States (in Australia, the 2004 election was reported to represent the peak of robocalling). 'Live' calls are considered far more effective. Unlike commercial entities, political parties are exempt from respecting the requirements of the Do Not Call register which allows people to be put on a list of those who do not wish to receive marketing phone calls.

In 2013, the parties made use of a variety of techniques because, as audiences fragment, so too do the communications strategies of the parties and different media are used for different purposes. For example, although it receives vastly less advertising spending than TV, radio is still a useful medium because, as infrastructure fails to keep up with population growth, more people spend more time in their cars during long commutes and more regular traffic jams. Door-knocking is also an important part of on-the-ground campaigns as a way of achieving the sort of one-on-one interaction that Labor's phone calls were aiming for (Mills 2014: 201–2). Among the more publicised examples of this was the Coalition candidate Michael Feneley in Kingsford Smith who reportedly door-knocked 18,000 houses and Michelle Rowland's volunteers who reportedly door-knocked 50,000 houses in Greenway.

Even the return to 'traditional' campaigning methods such as mail and doorknocking seen in 2013 were, unlike bygone eras, underpinned by sophisticated databases and the use of increasingly refined data mining on voters and data analysis techniques to target particular voters or groups.

'New' communications: Online, digital and social media

Data has long been important in Australian election campaigns (van Onselen and Errington 2004) and the parties have built up extensive databases on voters since the 1980s. But the degree of sophistication involved in collecting and using that data is advancing rapidly. In 2013, Labor employed individuals and firms specialising in the use of algorithms that can sort voters into useful categories (including predictions of their voting intentions) to help the Party target campaign resources toward the right electorates, suburbs and even streets (O'Malley and Johnson 2013). Such individuals and techniques are especially associated with US campaigns, and the use of 'big data' to 'micro-target voters' was discussed by Labor's (and Obama's) digital strategist Matthew McGregor in a 2012 article (Faust and McGregor 2012).

The 2013 campaign also saw continued experimentation with digital ads, including ads on social media sites, pop-up ads on online news sites and—especially after the Wednesday midnight blackout which halts political advertising on TV and radio—ads on YouTube and Facebook. Labor designed an elaborate spoof campaign for a fake product that it launched through a central website, Facebook marketing and YouTube videos. The fake product was 'Abbott's Internet' to be 'sold' on the streets of Prague, New York, Singapore and Bucharest. The punchline was that 'Abbott's Internet' was slow, wouldn't be delivered until 2019 and by then would already be out of date. Labor also fed the advertisement for the fake internet provider through its alternative social media presence which had minimal Labor branding, and which was used for more off-beat (and often more negative) messages.

After the election, both major parties were quick to claim digital media superiority. Labor claimed to have harnessed over 230,000 email addresses (compared to only 30,000 in 2010), sent over three million emails to supporters and raised funds of over $700,000 through nearly 10,000 online donors (ALP 2013). Meanwhile, the Liberal Party claimed after the election to have comprehensively outperformed Labor in social media, pointing to its website visitor numbers, Facebook page 'likes', the reach of its targeted Sharing app, growth in its leaders' Twitter followers and views on its YouTube channel as evidence (Loughnane 2013; see also Chapter 5 by Peter John Chen).

As anyone who signed up to a major party's email list can attest, the parties sent frequent email messages during the campaign. Mostly these were soliciting donations but many also communicated specific campaign messages. Even these emails were part of a sophisticated technological operation behind the scenes. The computers that sent the emails were also monitoring responses and learning from them in order to fine-tune the messages in each email. This meant that, after months of testing, emails could be directed very specifically and with carefully designed scripts. These processes continued to evolve throughout the campaign.

Advertising priorities and messages

The strength and consistency of the Coalition's lead prior to the election meant the Liberal Party's ads could focus on reinforcing pre-existing perceptions. The conservatives could also run predominantly as a buoyant challenger and fated victor in the mould of the Whitlam Labor 'It's Time' campaign in 1972. One sign of this was the way the Liberals focused on positive ads. Federal Director Brian Loughnane (2013) argued after the election that more than 70 per cent of their advertising was positive and that figure was supported by independent research by ebiquity. Conversely—and with a glaring inconsistency with Rudd's 'new way' positive message at the beginning of the campaign—three-quarters of Labor's advertising was negative (*Campaign Brief* 2013).

Of all the election ads running in 2013, it is telling that the single most broadcast TV advertisement of the campaign appears to have been Palmer's 'Revolution' advertisement (*Campaign Brief* 2013). It showed Palmer talking to camera saying, 'We want to give you money back. $2,500 … off your tax bill so that you can spend the money. You can decide what your family needs. Not the government'; and promising 'more jobs' and 'more growth'. Palmer's extraordinary level of advertising expenditure for a minor party was widely credited with building crucial name recognition and his party's unexpected success viewed as a demonstration of the influence of both money and advertising in Australian politics.

Yet, at the same time as a billionaire candidate was using his personal resources to underwrite the biggest minor party campaign in Australian political history, at the other end of the spectrum, Cathy McGowan was running as an independent in Indi and using 'crowd funding' pitches via *Chip In* and social media to raise money for advertising and campaigning. McGowan (2013) reported raising $117,000 from over 1,000 different donors (see Jennifer Curtin and Brian Costar's analysis in Chapter 16).

For the Coalition and Labor, their most shown ads (which they presumably, therefore, had judged to be their most effective) were the Liberal Party's 'Captain Chaos' and 'Our Plan' ads and, for Labor, its 'You Lose' ad. The Liberal's 'Captain Chaos' advertisement targeted Kevin Rudd's handling of financial management and asylum seeker policies as a 'Ruddy mess'. It showed multiple images of Rudd's face on screen including stills from the infamous leaked out-takes of him as foreign minister swearing in frustration. The 'Captain Chaos' advertisement ended with the line 'All this chaos in just 31 days. Imagine three more years of Labor failure'. The Liberal's 'Our Plan' advertisement referenced the Party's published booklet and showed Tony Abbott promising that:

> Our Plan will deliver two million more jobs over the next decade and better services for you and your family ... lower taxes and lower debt and stronger borders where the boats are stopped.

Labor's most shown advertisement was 'If Abbott wins, you lose'. It showed concerned-looking ordinary Australians standing in spotlights being relegated to the dark when the lights are successively turned out on them as the serious-sounding voiceover makes claims about how Abbott's plans will affect people.[2] Light is a classic political metaphor. Indeed, the Liberal's 1975 campaign slogan was 'Turn on the lights' after what they characterised as the 'three dark years' of Labor's Whitlam Government (Penniman 1977: 204–8; Young 2004: 120–2). But the notion of families being struck down is also common in political advertising. In 1993, the Liberal Party made a memorable and controversial advertisement that showed ordinary people as targets, being viewed through the cross hairs of a gun and struck down by Labor's 'mismanagement' and failure to stop high unemployment rates (Young 2004: 270). Labor had its own series of ads in 1998 showing family photos with the faces crossed out by a black marker as the voiceover explained how the Howard Government had adversely affected them.

Conclusion

Both Brian Loughnane and George Wright identified the 2013 campaign as different to its predecessors. Loughnane (2013) argued the Liberal's success showed that negativity is not the only way to campaign. But Rudd's adviser, Bruce Hawker (2013), countered that the Liberals did not need to run a negative

---

2   *The Conversation* 'fact-checked' this advertisement as part of its series of fact-checks. The ABC, Fairfax and Peter Fray's *PolitiFact Australia* also ran fact checks during the campaign and all four outfits concentrated mostly on fact-checking statements and claims rather than political ads. These 'fact-checks' were a new part of the media landscape of Australian elections but have been widely used in the US where there are also specific 'Ad Watches'. American broadcasters began in 1992 to broadcast 'Ad Watches' that critique political ads and interrogate their claims (Hall Jamieson and Cappella 1997). These ads are broadcast on the same medium as the original ads, giving them much broader reach. We have yet to see these on commercial TV in Australia.

campaign in 2013 because the Murdoch press ran it for them (see Wayne Errington's chapter). In terms of campaign methods, Wright (2013) argued that the 2013 campaigns were a further step into a third generation of campaigning based not on mass advertising alone or demographic targeting but on 'direct, and individual, one-on-one conversation and voter engagement, and the micro-targeting of information and messages to individuals'. For campaign observers, including political scientists and journalists, this poses a challenge because there is an increasing need to see things that are beyond our immediate sight and that are difficult to access or evaluate using traditional methods of analysis.

To get a full picture of how the parties communicate with voters now requires examining not only modes of communication which are highly visible or easily accessible—such as TV ads, list emails or Facebook posts—but also some new methods of gaining access to, and making sense of, the vast array of individualised messages that the parties communicate through letters, phone calls and conversations with hundreds of thousands of individual voters. We must be able to analyse both the macro and micro campaigns that occur throughout Australia during a campaign. At the macro level, we especially need a full picture of campaign spending. At present, the lack of clear information about spending is impairing our understanding and the need for better disclosure is becoming more pressing as wealthy individuals, corporate interests and other third party groups become more substantial and overt players in elections.

References

Australian Associated Press (AAP). 2013. 'Clive Palmer says questions about his spending are a political witch-hunt'. *The Australian*, 7 November: <www.theaustralian.com.au/national-affairs/clive-palmer-says-questions-about-his-spending-are-a-political-witch-hunt/story-fn59niix-1226754711424>.

Australian Labor Party (ALP). 2013. 'The million person campaign: A report to members'. Emailed report sent by George Wright to ALP email list recipients, 12 September.

Aqx. 2013. 'Standard report'. *ABC News*, viewed 15 January 2014: <www.abc.net.au/news/2013-09-20/ad-spending-claims-pure-campaign-spin/4966426>.

Campaign Brief. 2013. 'Liberal Party beats Labor Party in campaign advertising stakes and at the polls—ebiquity'. 9 September, viewed 15 January 2014: <www.campaignbrief.com/2013/09/the-liberal-party-beats-labor.html>.

Coyne, Brendan. 2013. 'Government spending pushes ad market to record July'. *Ad News*, 15 August.

Ewing, Keith, Rowbottom, Jacob and Tham, Joo-Cheong. 2011. *The Funding of Political Parties: Where Now?* New York: Routledge.

Faust, Patrick and McGregor, Matthew. 2012. '2012 from an international perspective'. *Huffington Post*, 10 December, viewed 15 January 2014: <www.huffingtonpost.com/patrick-faust/2012-from-an-internationa_b_2272801.html>.

Freudenberg, Graham. 2000. Recorded interview with Graham Freudenberg AM, Interviewer: John Farquharson. Oral History Section, Canberra, National Library of Australia (CTRC 3994).

Grant, Richard. 2003–04. *Research note no.62 2003–04: Federal government advertising*. Canberra: Parliamentary Library, Parliament of Australia.

Hall Jamieson, Kathleen and Cappella, Joseph N. 1997. 'Setting the record straight: Do ad watches help or hurt?' *The Harvard International Journal of Press/Politics* 2(1): 13–22.

Hawker, Bruce. 2013. *The Rudd Rebellion: The Campaign to Save Labor*. Melbourne: Melbourne University Publishing.

Hurst, Daniel. 2013. 'Palmer party denies resort ads breached TV blackout'. *The Sydney Morning Herald*, 11 September.

Jackson, Sally. 2013. 'Big-spending Libs left Labor for dead on advertising'. *The Australian*, 9 September: 28.

Kenny, Mark. 2013. 'Big call: Labor hits the phone'. *The Sydney Morning Herald*, 27 August.

Lewis, Steve. 2013a. 'Abbott sinks boot into Labor over litz of refugee boat ads'. *Courier-Mail*, 30 July: 2.

Lewis, Steve. 2013b. 'Anger at Labor's ad spend of $65m'. *Cairns Post*, 22 July: 6.

Loughnane, Brian. 2013. 'The 2013 Federal Election: Address to the National Press Club'. Canberra, 23 October.

Mills, Stephen. 2014. *The Professionals: Strategy, Money and the Rise of the Political Campaigner in Australia*. Melbourne: Black Inc.

McGowan, Cathy. 2013. 'The story', *Cathy McGowan* [official website], viewed 15 January 2014: <www.cathymcgowan.com.au/the_story>.

McPhee, Ian. 2013. 'Letter to Senator Nick Xenophon'. 14 August, viewed 15 January 2014: <www.anao.gov.au/Whats-New/ANAO-News/~/media/6FC30264813E4B64BE1E5C86CC206940.PDF>.

Nielsen. 2013. 'Press release: Australians jump online for last minute election news'. 21 October: <www.nielsen.com/content/dam/corporate/au/en/press/2013/nielsen-media-release-online-results-for-September-21.10.13.pdf>.

O'Malley, Nick and Johnson, Chris. 2013. 'How Barack Obama is changing the face of Australian political campaigns'. *The Sydney Morning Herald*, 4 August.

Owens, Jared. 2013. 'New leg of "unlawful" boat ads launched'. *The Australian*, 10 August: 9.

Penniman, Howard R. 1977. *Australia at the Polls: The National Elections of 1975*. Washington, D.C.: American Institute for Public Policy Research.

Priest, Marcus and Anderson, Fleur. 2013. 'Handouts galore as $725m set aside'. *Australian Financial Review*, 16 May: 9.

Shanahan, Dennis. 2013. 'Libs call off TV blitz to focus spending on final stretch'. *The Australian*, 22 August: 6.

Tham, Joo-Cheong and Anderson, Malcolm. 2013. Raw data based upon political party returns to the AEC and collated by Tham and Anderson, provided to the author in correspondence, 26 November.

van Onselen, Peter and Errington, Wayne. 2004. 'Electoral databases: Big brother or democracy unbound?' *Australian Journal of Political Science* 39(2): 349–66.

West Australian. 2013. 'Election ads to top $70m'. *The West Australian*, 24 May: 2.

Wright, George. 2013. 'Address to the National Press Club'. Canberra, 29 October, viewed 15 January 2014: <d3n8a8pro7vhmx.cloudfront.net/australianlaborparty/pages/1890/attachments/original/1383017072/George_Wright__Address_to_NPC_Transcript.pdf>.

Young, Sally. 2004. *The Persuaders: Inside the Hidden Machine of Political Advertising*. Melbourne: Pluto Press.

Young, Sally. 2005. 'Political advertising: Hey big spender!' In Marian Simms and John Warhurst (eds), *Mortgage Nation: The 2004 Australian Election*. Perth: API Network.

Young, Sally. 2007. 'A history of government advertising in Australia'. In Sally Young (ed.), Government Communication in Australia. Melbourne: Cambridge University Press.

Young, Sally. 2011. *How Australia Decides: Election Reporting and the Media*. Melbourne: Cambridge University Press.

Young, Sally and Tham, Joo-Cheong. 2006. *Political Finance in Australia: A Skewed and Secret System*. Canberra: Democratic Audit of Australia, The Australian National University.

7. Making Policy and Winning Votes: Election promises and political strategies in the 2013 campaign

Nicholas Reece

This chapter examines the intersection of public policy and politics in the 2013 federal election campaign. More than any other point in the political cycle, election campaigns are a time in which candidates and political parties release a large amount of new policy in the hope that it will win them increased public support. The candidates and the parties also attack the policies and policy record of their opponents to decrease support for their competitors. Political parties release policy they claim will benefit the nation. But, the parties also use policies in a highly strategic way to enhance their campaign and outmanoeuvre their opponents.

Election studies have shown the growing importance of election policies and issues in deciding the outcome of elections (Dalton 2000; McAllister 2011). Long-term factors such as social background and socio-economic status do not have the same level of influence on a person's voting behaviour as they once did (McAllister 2011). The electorate has also become more fragmented, without the relatively homogeneous personal networks and social structures of previous eras. These factors have helped cause a decline in partisanship. As a consequence the political environment is now one in which voting patterns are far more volatile. Shorter-term influences on the vote, such as parties' policy positions and preferences, performance evaluation and leaders' public profiles, have emerged to fill the gap left by the decline of longer-term influences (Dalton 2000).

The 2013 Australian federal election illustrates how political parties have adapted to the greater importance of policy and issue voting and to broader changes in the electorate. At least symbolically, this was demonstrated by the Liberal Party which produced five million copies of its policy manifesto and distributed it to households across Australia. It has been several decades since a policy document—albeit a glossy 16-page summary version—has been produced and distributed on this scale.

This chapter will show that the major political parties have become more sophisticated in their development and strategic use of policy. Methods include the engagement of market research teams to assist with the positioning and public presentation of policies. The parties have become highly tactical in their use of policy to achieve political objectives such as the wedging of an opposition party, targeting specific voter groups or keeping the media focus on a desired policy area. Many policies announced during the 2013 election were the product of a lengthy development process, while other policies were 'made up on the run' to meet a pressing political objective. For different reasons, there were a significant number of policies that were drafted by Labor and the Liberals but never released publicly. The major parties have also adopted the practice of 'gaming' the policy costing process that was established under the *Charter of Budget Honesty* in 1998 such that the process is no longer meeting its objectives.

The chapter first provides an overview of the policy development process used by the Liberal and Labor parties in the 2013 campaign, including the formal approval process and the adoption of *ad hoc*, spur-of-the-moment announcements and the attendant controversies over policy costings. It then identifies the salient issues of the campaign as identified by voters through surveys such as *Vote Compass*, and catalogues the major policies announced by the parties in the election. Thirdly, it examines the ways in which the parties used policies to achieve political strategic objectives during the campaign.

This chapter is based on interviews with senior campaign figures in the Labor and Liberal parties as well as the author's personal experience as a campaign director and coordinator of the policy development process for a major political party in previous Australian elections. The study is confined to the ALP and Coalition (Liberal and National) parties and does not examine the policies and strategies of the Greens and other minor parties.

The policy development process behind the 2013 campaigns

Both the Liberal and Labor parties have a highly developed process for drafting and approving election policies. Notwithstanding party rules requiring varying degrees of consultation with party members, the policy development process has become highly centralised. This reflects the pressure of media and campaign management and the specialised nature of policy making in certain fields. The parties have become highly reliant on market research and data analytics to identify groups of party supporters and persuadable voters (Penn 2007; Hawker 2013). Using this information, a plan is developed to try and build a winning coalition of supporters.

Policy development in the Coalition parties

Senior shadow minister Andrew Robb led the policy development process for the Liberal Party as the chairman of the Coalition Policy Development Committee. This was essentially a three-year process that commenced with a review of the Coalition's policies after the 2010 election. Robb is a former federal director of the Liberal Party and was a federal campaign manager for the 1993 and 1996 campaigns. Joe Hockey and Andrew Robb also oversaw a costings process for the Opposition. This involved a process of internal scrutiny, consultation with stakeholders, assessment by the Parliamentary Budget Office (PBO) and a panel of review by three 'eminent experts in public finance and administration' comprising former top bureaucrat Peter Shergold, economist Geoff Carmody and former Queensland auditor-general Len Scanlan.

Liberal Federal Director, Brian Loughnane, and market research and political strategy firm Crosby Textor, led by Mark Textor, provided input on framing the election contest, the overarching narrative for the campaign, testing of TV ads and marketing materials, demographic analysis of target voter groups and a list of target seats for the Liberal campaign. Crosby Textor also provided market research feedback on various ALP policy positions and the policy positions and options for the Coalition. Textor had been Liberal Party campaign pollster for six federal campaigns from 1996 to 2010.

The Coalition's strategy was *not* simply to run a negative commentary on six years of Labor Government, but also to demonstrate that it was 'time for real change' (Textor 2013). Key policies such as abolishing the carbon tax, introducing the paid parental leave (PPL) scheme and direct action on the environment were symbols of change. The Liberals' policy program was presented as 'carefully managed change' not as a radical new agenda. This fitted with the broader strategy to present the Coalition as a 'safe' alternative to the incumbent Labor Government. The Coalition claimed it would be a government that was 'grown up' and run by 'adults' and committed to being 'a government of no surprises' that would 'under-promise and over-deliver'.

One of the distinctive features of the 2010 election was the way in which state results swung in different directions. In 2013, the Liberals hoped to win additional seats in Victoria, South Australia, Tasmania and New South Wales. These states had held out against the national swing against Labor in 2010. The Liberals also wanted to reverse the female voting imbalance that had worked against the Party in 2010. Both major parties continued to target young families. Typically, this implies a household with children in school, where Dad has a trade qualification or works in an administrative white-collar role and Mum works part-time. This young family has an above average level of mortgage stress, faces cost of living pressures and uses a car as the principal mode of transport.

Policy development in the Australian Labor Party

The ALP election policy development process ran for approximately nine months leading up to the September election. Senior minister in the Gillard and Rudd governments, Jenny Macklin, chaired an Election Expenditure Review Committee. Following the leadership change from Gillard to Rudd in June 2013 there were significant ministerial and staff changes and much of this process fell into abeyance. National Secretary of the ALP, George Wright, revealed that of the 150 staff slated to work in the Party's national campaign headquarters, 110 resigned following the change of leadership (Wright 2013).

As a consequence of these changes many of the policies that were released by Labor during the campaign did not go through a rigorous governance arrangement. Some of the most high profile included the establishment of a special economic zone in the north of Australia; the policy to move the Australian Navy from Sydney's Garden Island facility to Brisbane; and Rudd's call for a tightening of foreign investment rules in the guise of 'economic nationalism' (Hawker 2013).

Rudd relied on a number of key campaign advisors. The ALP's National Secretary George Wright, the campaign firm Essential Media Communications (EMC), John Utting from polling firm UMR, and Tony Mitchelmore, provided research input on framing the election contest, the overarching narrative for the campaign, demographic analysis of target voter groups and a list of target seats. Late in the campaign preparation process, advertising executive Neil Lawrence was commissioned to prepare the ALP launch advertisement and the campaign slogan 'A New Way'. This was not done in consultation with the ALP's national secretariat nor with EMC who produced other advertisements and messaging for the campaign such as the 'If he wins you lose' attack advertisements against Tony Abbott.

Labor's market research told it that ALP in-fighting and lack of discipline had made the Party unworthy of re-election in many voters' eyes. On the policy front, the steady increase in asylum seeker arrivals by boat was costing the ALP support amongst key target voter groups. Slower growth in the economy and deficit budgets had made people uncertain about the economic future. For the ALP, the target voter groups in 2013 were those who had deserted Labor since the 2010 election, followed by those they had lost at the 2010 election itself. Some of the key demographics of these groups included men with trade qualifications, Queenslanders, Western Australians and Tasmanians. Like the Coalition, Labor was also chasing the young families that comprise a large portion of the marginal electorates in outer suburban and regional Australia.

The election policy costing process

The establishment of the statutory *Charter of Budget Honesty* in 1998 and the Parliamentary Budget Office (PBO) in 2012 were intended to bring a new level of transparency and honesty to the costing of election promises. Despite these reforms, the process for costing and disclosing the budget impact of policies descended into high farce in the 2013 Australian election as the major parties discovered how to game the system.

The Coalition took advantage of the new resources available to it through the PBO and submitted more than 200 policy commitments for costing. However, the Coalition did not submit a single policy to Treasury and the Department of Finance and Regulation for costing during the caretaker period. As outlined earlier, the Coalition instead used its own panel of review comprising three 'eminent experts in public finance and administration'. The Coalition released over 700 pages of policy documents for the 2013 campaign but only released the associated policy cost and budget impact two days before the election. These did not include an independent costing for three of its biggest financial commitments: the NBN, its Direct Action Plan on climate change, and its asylum seeker and border security measures.

Labor submitted its policy commitments through the Treasury and Finance process and released them progressively throughout the campaign. Labor tried to make a virtue of doing this while attacking the Coalition for not participating. However, Labor got into trouble when it submitted a series of initiatives for costing that it had no intention of pursuing itself but thought the Coalition might. This was not part of a policy development process but an election tactic to expose the Opposition for an alleged 'budget black hole'. But the tactic backfired when Treasury and Finance issued statements saying Labor had misrepresented their findings.

Issues and policies of the 2013 campaign

From one election to another the issues that are of highest priority to voters change. The political parties monitor changes in issue salience and shape their policy offerings and marketing campaigns accordingly. Set out in Table 1 is an issue salience list from the 2013 election.

The issues in 2013

In 2013, the University of Melbourne, University of Sydney and the ABC in cooperation with political scientists at the University of Toronto developed *Vote Compass* for the Australian election. *Vote Compass* was an online educational tool to help voters understand where they stand on the issues compared to the parties. The survey was completed voluntarily 1.4 million times. This sample was then adjusted using the ABS census and other data sets to produce an estimate of voter attitudes (*Vote Compass* 2013a).

Table 1: Issue salience in the 2013 election

Issue	Per cent mention
Economy	28
Asylum seekers	13
Health and hospitals	10
Climate change	9
Education	9
Broadband	7
Taxation	3

Source: *Vote Compass*. Respondents were asked: 'Which issue is most important to you personally in this election campaign?'

As a useful point of comparison the Australian Electoral Study produced the following results on issue salience amongst a sample of voters in the 2010 election.

Table 2: Issue salience in the 2010 election[1]

Issue	Per cent mention
Health and Medicare	23
Management of the economy	21
Education	13
Global warming	8
Interest rates	7
Taxation	7
Refugees and asylum seekers	6

Source: *Australian Electoral Study 2010*. Respondents were asked: 'Still thinking of these 12 issues, which of these issues has been most important to you and your family during the election campaign?'

A comparison of the 2013 and 2010 results shows some significant changes amongst the issue priorities of voters. The economy was a significantly more

---

1 At the time of publication the results for the AES 2013 had not been released.

7. Making Policy and Winning Votes

important issue to voters in 2013 compared to 2010 as well as being far more important relative to other issues in 2013. Asylum seeker and refugee policy was the second most important issue in 2013 while it was only seventh in 2010. Health and education issues both slipped in importance compared to 2010.

The issues on which an election is fought are a key consideration for the parties in formulating their campaign strategy. This is because different parties are seen as being best able to handle certain issues. In general, debates about health and education will deliver more benefits to centre-left parties like the Labor Party. Debates about border security, taxation and to a lesser extent the economy benefit centre-right parties like the Coalition (McAllister 2011). This is part of the 'brand essence' of these parties. The changes in the issue landscape between 2010 and 2013 benefited the Coalition at the expense of Labor as the issues which the Coalition was seen as being best able to handle had greater salience for voters than in 2010.

The major policies announced in 2013

Set out below are the major policy announcements made by the major parties during the campaign. This list has been determined using a mixed methodology that takes into account the following factors: a review of all the policy documents released; the campaign launch speech by the party leaders; media mentions of specific policies; the level of expenditure committed to a policy initiative; and policies which featured in party advertising.

The major policies announced by Tony Abbott and the Coalition

- Scrap the carbon tax and abolish the Clean Energy Finance Corporation;
- 'Stop the boats' through 'Operation Sovereign Borders', including boat buy-backs and towing back the boats;
- Abolish the mining tax;
- $17 billion in budget savings including a reduction of 12,000 public servants;
- Build the roads of the 21st century: the WestConnex in Sydney, the East West Link in Melbourne, the Gateway Upgrade in Brisbane, the North South Road in Adelaide and the Swan Bypass in Perth;
- Cut the company tax rate by 1.5 per cent;
- Cut red tape by $1 billion a year;
- Move the workplace relations pendulum 'back to the sensible centre': restore the Australian Building and Construction Commission (ABCC), introduce new penalties for 'dodgy' union officials;
- Reinstate the fringe benefits tax exemption on company cars that are salary packaged at a cost of $1.8 billion;

- Build a National Broadband Network (NBN) that is slower but cheaper;
- Introduce a standing Green Army, growing to some 15,000 individuals;
- Deliver on the National Disability Insurance Scheme (NDIS);
- Abolish the School Kids Bonus;
- Abolish the low-income super offset funded by the mining tax;
- Delay the Superannuation Guarantee Levy increase;
- Stop the scheduled increase in the humanitarian migrant intake;
- Support the 'Gonski funding reforms' for three years;
- A Paid Parental Leave (PPL) scheme, paid to working women at their actual wage up to $150,000;
- Index eligibility thresholds for the Commonwealth Seniors Health Card;
- Commit an additional $200 million to dementia research;
- Give apprentices access to a $20,000 loan, similar to that enjoyed by university students;
- A more functional Federation where the states are sovereign in their own sphere;
- Public schools and hospitals will have local boards and more autonomy;
- By the end of the first term, the budget will be on track to a believable surplus;
- Within a decade, the budget surplus will be one per cent of GDP, defence spending will be two per cent of GDP, and each year government will compromise a progressively smaller percentage of the national economy;
- Restore the Private Health Insurance Rebate within a decade; and,
- Recognise indigenous people in the Constitution, and Tony Abbott as prime minister will spend a week a year in a remote indigenous community.

The major policies announced by Kevin Rudd and the ALP

- Abolish the carbon tax by bringing forward an Emissions Trading Scheme (ETS) by one year;
- The 'PNG solution' to provide offshore processing and settlement for irregular maritime arrivals in Papua New Guinea;
- Reform of the ALP, including direct election of the Party leader;
- Introduce legislation in the first 100 days to support same-sex marriage;
- Build an NBN using the best broadband technologies;
- The Northern Australia Plan including a special tax zone in Australia's north;
- Maintain Australia's low debt and deficit levels;
- The Small Business Tax Boost: an upfront tax deduction on the purchase of new equipment;

- All projects worth $300 million or more to adopt Australian Industry Participation Plans;
- Increase the 'Tools for Your Trade' payment to apprentices to $6,000;
- Require state governments to maintain and grow their funding of TAFE; failing this, a Commonwealth takeover of the TAFE sector;
- A new Jobs, Training and Apprenticeships Guarantee (JTAG) and a new institution called Jobs and Training Australia to bring together the employment services and training systems;
- Implement the Better Schools Plan with $15 billion of additional investment;
- Build the health and hospital system for the future with an additional $19 billion investment;
- Build a Clean Energy Future and keep the Clean Energy Finance Corporation;
- Maintain the School Kids Bonus;
- Keep the *FairWork Australia* industrial relations system to protect penalty rates and overtime;
- Keep the current Paid Paternity Leave scheme based on the minimum wage;
- Relocate the naval base at Garden Island in Sydney to northern Australia;
- Reject any review of the GST; and,
- Reject the alleged $70 billion in cuts to be made by the Opposition.

Those policies the public never got to see

One of the great unknowns and imponderables of the 2013 federal election is the slate of policies that the public never got to see. Interviews for this chapter have confirmed that much of the policy work that was done by ministers and senior advisers in the Gillard Government in the months leading up to the June leadership change were not adopted by new prime minister Kevin Rudd. Meanwhile, the Coalition did not release many of the policies it had drafted because it had a commanding lead in the polls and opted for a small target strategy. This involved holding back policy so as to avoid attack from their opponents on policy detail. The tight fiscal environment also significantly curtailed the more ambitious policy ideas of both major parties.

The tactical use of policy to deliver campaign strategy

Most election policies announced by political parties involve a calculated combination of good policy and good politics. This section focuses on the *political* objectives of policies developed for the campaign rather than their policy objectives. This process may be thought of as something like a chess game in which each side moves its pieces—in this case, policies—to achieve a strategic campaign objective. While there is scholarly consensus about the increased importance of policy and issue voting in modern election campaigns, much less is understood about the way political parties use policies in a tactical way to achieve their broader campaign strategy. The following section helps fill this knowledge gap by outlining how election policies were used by the major parties during the 2013 election to deliver on political campaign objectives.

Demonstrate a vision for the future

One of the key ingredients for electoral success is to demonstrate a vision for the future. This is usually done by outlining a narrative of what the future looks like, supported by the policies that 'build the bridge' toward it. One of the more interesting ways the Coalition did this was through the publication of its 52-page *Real Solutions Plan* in early 2013. Over five million copies of a 16-page condensed version were circulated to households across Australia. Coalition strategists knew that the document would not be widely read. But they believed that its presence in millions of households sent a strong message about the Coalition having a plan for the future and being ready for government. The print distribution was also supplemented by electronic advertising promoting the Plan from early 2013 through to mid-2013 (Loughnane 2013). For the Coalition, the plan to 'build the roads of the 21st century' was also a key policy to help achieve this objective.

One of the shortcomings of Labor's campaign was its failure to build an agenda for the future. Labor's policies to tackle climate change and build the NBN had been central to its 'future vision' since 2007. However, by the 2013 campaign these policies had become tarnished by implementation challenges and political debate. The Northern Australia Plan was part of a future vision but attracted significant media scepticism, especially as Labor had earlier severely criticised a similar set of proposals emanating from the Coalition. The campaign launch contained some very significant new initiatives on training and apprenticeships but these came too late to have a major impact.

Policy as values and policy to characterise the leader

For well over a decade, conservative and progressive American academics and campaign consultants have been highlighting the importance of 'values' in framing political issues (Lakoff 2004; 2006; Luntz 2007). Accordingly, policy is marketed to the public not just in terms of its underlying benefit to society but also as a way of communicating the values and character of the party and its leader.

Tony Abbott's promise to spend one week a year as prime minister in a remote indigenous community was used to promote his commitment to addressing Indigenous issues and his personal empathy for those facing disadvantage. The Coalition also worked to keep the carbon tax policy debate on the agenda during the election campaign. This debate in fact helped the Coalition in other debates about economics and cost of living, both of which were critical issues amongst target voters. The carbon tax debate also fuelled a values debate about broken promises and trust. This is because Julia Gillard and Labor were viewed by many as having broken a promise not to introduce a carbon tax.

For Labor, Kevin Rudd's reforms to the ALP helped meet the political objective of improving the tarnished brand of the Party. It also demonstrated Rudd's strength as leader and allowed him to talk about his values, including 'sticking up for the little guy' and giving ordinary people a say.

Policy to win support from targeted constituencies

Democratically elected politicians have always searched for policies that they believe will win over certain constituencies. However, recent advances in data analysis have allowed many of these policy decisions to be data-driven and to reflect micro-targeting approaches. The Coalition's policy to suspend fishing restrictions around marine national parks was a direct play to fishing groups and Australia's five million recreational fishers. The Coalition also released an Economic Growth Plan for Tasmania. Tasmania was the only state to be the beneficiary of such a plan. It is also the state where the Coalition did not win a single House of Representative seat in 2010 and stood to make significant electoral gains in 2013. The Coalition's very generous PPL scheme attracted criticism from Labor and others. However, the Coalition was happy to have this debate as the PPL was a key policy offer to working mums, a key voter group with which the Coalition had underperformed in 2010.

Labor's policy on gay marriage helped portray Rudd as a modern leader and to mobilise the Party's activist base which is critical for its campaign volunteer efforts. Kevin Rudd's policy of bringing forward a floating carbon price by one year and portraying this as 'axing the tax' was aimed squarely at ALP voters who had abandoned the Party since the last election. Both parties offered significant inducements to trade apprentices, well-known as an important target voter group in elections. The Coalition offered apprentices a $20,000 HECS-type loan while Labor offered a $6,000 grant for tools.

Policy to move the election debate onto preferred territory

As previously outlined, defining the issue territory on which an election is fought is a key campaign strategy for the parties and each party attempts to move the debate onto issues where it is seen to have an advantage over its competitors. For the Coalition, the incremental announcement of border security policies—such as Operation Sovereign Borders, the boats buy-back scheme and the 'tow back of boats'—was part of a strategy to keep the debate in an area it is seen as being best able to manage. For Labor the centrepiece policy of its campaign launch was a series of major announcements on TAFE education and training, including the possible takeover of the TAFE sector by the Commonwealth. This was an attempt to move the policy debate to an issue that voters believe the ALP handles best.

Policy to keep the election debate off the opponent's territory

Just as parties use policy to move the public debate to their issues they also use it to stop debate in a policy area that is their opponent's strong point. The 2013 election provides several examples of this tactic. Labor's policy to support off-shore processing and the settlement of asylum seekers in PNG was aimed at shutting down debate on an issue that was seen as a Coalition strength. The Coalition's decision to adopt Labor's Better Schools funding agreement with the states, support DisabilityCare, amend its NBN plans to be more like Labor's and to declare *WorkChoices* dead were all aimed at shutting down political debate on issues that were viewed as Labor strengths.

Policy to 'wedge' the opponent

A wedge issue is one that is divisive or controversial and can split a population or political group. Political campaigns use a wedge policy to exploit tension within a targeted population. The objective is to divide the Opposition, create the impression of disunity, and drive the defection of supporters who are in the minority on that issue.

The debate on asylum seeker policy is a wedge issue *par excellence* for the ALP. A *Vote Compass* survey of 375,000 voters undertaken during the election campaign revealed that 48 per cent of Labor supporters disagreed with the Party's policy that asylum seekers who arrive by boat should not be allowed to settle in Australia, while 40 per cent of Labor voters agreed with the policy. In contrast, Coalition and Green voters were much more firmly locked in behind their parties' policy positions (*Vote Compass* 2013b).

For the Coalition, an example of a wedge issue was the mining tax with the Liberal Party proposing to abolish the tax. A *Vote Compass* survey during the campaign showed that only 19 per cent of Liberal voters wanted the miners to pay less tax while 38 per cent wanted them to pay more and 43 per cent wanted them to pay the same (*Vote Compass* 2013c). Interestingly, the ALP did not pursue this policy during the election campaign. This was in part due to concerns about implementation problems with the tax and the risk of losing support in Western Australia and regional Queensland.

Conclusion

The 2013 election highlights the very strategic way in which political parties use policies to enhance their campaign and outmanoeuvre their opponents. The major political parties have become more sophisticated in the development and marketing of their policies. This includes the engagement of market research teams to assist with the positioning and public presentation of policies. The major parties have worked out how to game the policy costing process established under the *Charter of Budget Honesty* in 1998 and supplemented by the establishment of the PBO in 2012. This occurs to such an extent that the system now falls well short of meeting its stated legislative objectives. Even with the increased complexity of the policy development process, the 2013 election still included the release of policies that were 'made up on the run' to meet a pressing political objective. For different reasons, there were also a significant number of policies drafted by the major parties that were never released publicly.

Changes in issue salience between 2010 and 2013 worked to the Coalition's advantage. The Coalition was seen as being best able to handle issues that had risen in importance, such as the economy and asylum seekers. Meanwhile issues that were seen as a traditional strength of Labor, such as health and education, decreased in importance. Both the Liberal and Labor parties released a significant volume of policy during the 2013 campaign, with the key policies listed in this chapter. Both parties attempted to use policy in a tactical way to achieve certain campaign objectives.

References

Dalton, James. 2000. 'Citizen Attitudes and Political Behaviour'. *Comparative Political Studies* 33(6/7): 912–40.

Green, Donald P and Gerber, Alan S. 2003. 'Under provision of Experiments in Political Science'. *Annals of the American Academy of Political and Social Science* 589: 93–112.

Hawker, Bruce. 2013. *The Rudd Rebellion: The Campaign to Save Labor*. Melbourne: Melbourne University Publishing.

Issenberg, Sasha. 2012. *The Victory Lab*. New York: Crown.

Lakoff, George. 2004. *Don't Think of an Elephant*. Hartford: Chelsea Green Publishing.

Loughnane, Brian. 2013. 'Address to the National Press Club'. Canberra, 23 October, viewed 26 October 2013: <lpaweb-static.s3.amazonaws.com/Brian%20Loughnane%20-%20National%20Press%20Club%20Address%20-%2023%20October%202013.pdf>.

Luntz, Frank. 2007. *Words that Work*. New York: Hyperion.

McAllister, Ian. 2011. *The Australian Voter: 50 years of change*. Sydney: UNSW.

McAllister, Ian, Bean, Clive, Gibson, Rachel Kay and Pietsch, Juliet. 2011. *Australian Election Study, 2010*. Canberra: Australian Data Archive, ANU.

O'Malley, Nick and Johnson, Chris. 2013. 'How Barack Obama is changing the face of Australian political campaigns'. *The Sydney Morning Herald*, 4 August.

Penn, Mark. 2007. *Microtrends: The small forces behind tomorrow's big changes*. New York: Twelve.

Plouffe, David. 2009. *The Audacity to Win*. New York: Viking.

Textor, Mark. 2013. 'Why Tony Abbott won Australia's trust'. *Australian Financial Review*, 23 September.

Vote Compass. 2013a. 'Vote Compass Methodology'. Viewed 15 January 2014: <australia.votecompass.com/assets/media/site/pdfs/VoteCompassMethodology.pdf>.

Vote Compass. 2013b. 'Kevin Rudd's Asylum Seeker Policy Divides the Labor Faithful'. *ABC News*, 21 August, viewed 15 January 2014: <www.abc.net.au/news/2013-08-21/asylum-seekers-vote-compass-boats-immigration/4899914>.

Vote Compass. 2013c. 'The Most Important Issues to Voters'. *ABC News*, 9 August, viewed 15 January 2014: <www.abc.net.au/news/2013-08-09/vote-compass-data-results-important-issues/4872896>.

Wright, George. 2013. 'Address to the National Press Club'. Canberra, 29 October, viewed 15 January 2014: <d3n8a8pro7vhmx.cloudfront.net/australianlaborparty/pages/1890/attachments/original/1383017072/George_Wright__Address_to_NPC_Transcript.pdf>.

8. How the Pollsters Called the Horse Race: Changing polling technologies, cost pressures, and the concentration on the two-party-preferred

Murray Goot

For students of public opinion polls—more particularly, students of the pollsters' attempts to monitor voting intentions and predict election outcomes—three features of the 2013 campaign stood out and, in assessing the performance of the polls, it is on these features that this chapter will dwell: the substantial increase in the number of polling organisations involved as new pollsters sought to publicise their skills to potential clients; the spread of 'robo' polls, a development that allowed the press to recover its pre-eminent position as the sponsor of pre-election polls; and the proliferation of polling technologies as pollsters grappled with the challenges posed by voters shifting from landlines to mobile phones and the internet. Shaping this changing landscape were not only the availability to pollsters of newer, cheaper technologies, but also the cost pressures faced by the press, and the increasing focus in the media on the two-party-preferred vote—a way of framing the race that reduces everything that matters to a single number and with it the risks involved in calling the result.

No fewer than nine firms produced estimates of how the race was going and/or of the final result; in 2010 the corresponding figure was six. Eight firms produced estimates of the vote nationwide, five also produced estimates of the votes in a number of the marginal seats, while the ninth (JWS Research) restricted itself to estimating the outcomes in some of the marginals. Three of the firms were long-established (Newspoll, Nielsen, and Roy Morgan Research), three had been conducting election polls for much shorter periods (Galaxy, Essential Research, and JWS), and three were new to election polling (AMR, Lonergan Research, and ReachTEL). As the last of the companies operating out of the smaller states was sidelined—this time the Patterson Research Group, which had polled for *The West Australian* at federal elections since 1990 and for *The Canberra Times* since 2007, was not asked to poll for any newspaper—two of the newer companies along the eastern seaboard spread their reach: Galaxy, which for the first time serviced all News Corp's metropolitan tabloids, and ReachTEL, which polled not only for *News 7* (something it had done since March 2010), but also for Fairfax Media, the *Mercury*, and the Launceston *Examiner*. In-house polling also disappeared with *The Advertiser*'s polling in South Australia being taken over by Galaxy. As usual, the polls focused on the election for the House of Representatives; only Lonergan offered any sort of guide to the race for the Senate.

A second feature was the nature of the technology used to monitor the distribution of party support in the most marginal of seats that were polled. Instead of staying with CATI (Computer Assisted Telephone Interviewing), newspapers hired firms that ran 'robo-polls'—telephone polls based on Interactive Voice Recognition software where respondents listen to pre-recorded questions and then key-in their answers (Goot 2014). Four of the five firms hired to run marginal seat polls—Galaxy, JWS, Lonergan, and ReachTEL—used 'robos'; in 2010 only JWS had used this technology. The switch to 'robos' represented a big cost saving for newspapers under severe financial pressure from declining revenues. In the marginals, only Newspoll stuck with CATI. The low cost of 'robos' even enticed one of the television networks, *News 7*, to run short polls. Newspapers, however, continued to commission national polls that used CATI—Newspoll, commissioned by *The Australian*; Galaxy, commissioned by News Ltd to service its metropolitan mastheads; and Nielsen, for Fairfax Media (*Age*, *Sydney Morning Herald*, and *Australian Financial Review*). As usual television stations added to the drama of election night by commissioning election-day polls (Newspoll for News Ltd's Sky News) or exit polls (Galaxy for Channel 9; Roy Morgan for Channel 10).

The shift to 'robo-polls' also shifted the balance of initiative in the generation of poll data for public consumption away from polls paid for by market researchers—a feature of the 2010 election (Goot 2012: 91)—back to polls commissioned by the press. JWS conducted a round of marginal seat polls for the *Australian Financial Review*, Lonergan did some polling for the *Guardian Australia* online, and ReachTEL ran marginal seats polls for Fairfax, the *Mercury* and the Launceston *Examiner*. Galaxy, Newspoll, and Nielsen maintained their relationship with News Ltd and the Fairfax press. Four companies paid their own way: AMR, Essential and Morgan (all of which conducted national polls), and JWS (which polled in the marginals). Compared to 2010, four independent pollsters represented an increase of one, but in relative terms four was a decrease. Morgan posted the results of its polling on its website, and distributed the results to some 12,000 email addresses as well as to newspapers and television stations. Essential published its results online via *Crikey* and distributed them to 1,000 email addresses, including numerous media outlets. JWS published all its findings online, regardless of whether they had been commissioned by the press or paid for by JWS.

A third feature was the range of the data gathering techniques that pollsters deployed. As well as variety across the industry, the campaign was marked by the use of an increasing range of technologies within particular firms. Morgan used SMS for its exit poll but during the campaign it used mixed modes—varying combinations involving face-to-face interviews, landlines, text messaging, and questionnaires posted online. Galaxy used telephone interviewers for its national polls, face-to-face interviews for its exit poll, and—to remain commercially competitive—'robo-polls' in the marginals. Newspoll, which ran a day-of-the-election poll in selected marginals, used CATI throughout; together with Nielsen it stuck to the technology it knew best, a technology it continued to trust and one the newspaper it serviced was prepared to pay for. Essential ran its polling online. JWS, Lonergan, and ReachTEL ran 'robos' in marginal seats through landlines. Lonergan switched to mobiles for its final 'robo'—the only poll it conducted nationwide.

Almost all the polls came very close to predicting the national two-party-preferred. Even if we allow for the fact that their estimates, as it turned out, were based on a mistaken understanding that preferences would split in much the same way as they had done in 2010, the polls did much better than their long-term average. Inevitably, of course, there was an order of merit. For the most part, however, only someone who knew nothing about sampling variance would attach much importance to the differences. Nonetheless, the polls generally over-estimated Labor's share of the two-party-preferred, something they have done for a number of elections.

While commentators were happy with the polls' performance in predicting the national outcome, some expressed concerns about the reliability of the polls—particularly the 'robo-polls'—in individual seats where results at odds with the national polls had raised unnecessary hopes or unjustified alarm. This was especially true in relation to the Prime Minister's seat of Griffith. Closer examination suggests that the performance of the 'robos' in the marginals was not significantly worse than the performance of the polls that used CATI, with most polls suffering from small sample sizes, the worst errors coming from polls of all descriptions taken early in the campaign.

Less impressive than the polls' estimates of the two-party-preferred were their estimates of first preferences. Noteworthy, too, was the relatively poor performance of polls that sampled mobiles, polls conducted on the day of the election, and polls that attempted to estimate the outcome in the Senate.

Predicting the house vote nationwide

For once, the question of whether the national polls had got it right—even the question of which of them had done best—did not loom large in the post-election wash-up. There seemed to be general agreement that most of these polls had got it right. At the end of the night, Simon Jackman, whose comments on the polls appeared regularly in the *Guardian Australia* online, thought the national polls had 'fared pretty well', especially if one allowed for a further shift towards the Coalition once the pre-poll and postal votes were counted (Jackman 2013). On the Monday following the election (9 September), William Bowe anticipated that a drift to the Coalition in late counting would bring the results into line with his *BludgerTrack* poll, built by aggregating the national polls (Bowe 2013a). In *Crikey*, Matthew Knott also noted that 'most of the big pollsters appear to have performed well' (Knott 2013).

In each of these assessments the measure of accuracy was the polls' approximation to the national two-party-preferred—not, as is the case everywhere else in the world, the average error in estimating the parties' first preferences or the gap between the first preferences for the government and the first preferences for the opposition. The two-party-preferred is relatively easy to approximate especially when many pollsters are attempting to do it. The leaking of party polls suggesting Labor was headed for a resounding defeat may have helped as well. Judgments about how well the polls had done were certainly helped by the fact that none of the pollsters dared to predict the two-party-preferred to the first decimal place—as Newspoll had done in 2010. Such a practice is likely to end in tears or in the pursuit of something even more absurd—that is, predictions accurate to the second decimal point, an attempt to ratchet-up the competition trialled by Morgan in 2010 (Goot 2012: 88). Assessments of the polls in the *Poll Bludger* and *Crikey* were based on how the polls had performed nationally, not on how well they had predicted the outcomes in marginal seats; only the *Guardian Australia* alluded to that. Assessments were also restricted to how well the polls had estimated the vote for the House of Representatives; their performance in relation to the Senate was ignored.

Usually, several polling organisations claim to have produced the most accurate poll. This time there was only one. Roy Morgan Research, which entered three horses in the race—its penultimate pre-election day poll, its final pre-election day poll, and an SMS exit poll—declared its exit poll the winner. In a statement issued on 9 September, Morgan claimed 'The Roy Morgan–Channel 10 SMS Exit Morgan Poll' proved 'the most accurate measure of the voting intentions of Australian electors' (Roy Morgan Research 2013a). At that stage of the count, Morgan's two-party-preferred was just 0.1 percentage points outside the Australian Electoral Commission's (AEC) figures. 'In addition', Morgan claimed, it had produced 'the only poll to show the surge in support for the Palmer United Party' (this wasn't true) and to have predicted that Clive Palmer 'could' win the seat of Fairfax, something Morgan had done shortly before the election but without furnishing any figures (Roy Morgan Research 2013a). John Stirton from Nielsen—one of the few polling firms not to have polled in single seats—

noted how poorly the polls had fared in individual seats where the polling, he insisted, had 'often' been 'out of whack with reality'; of the 55 polls conducted in single seats Labor 'should have been in front on 25', he said, not just the 12 in which the AEC had them leading at the close of counting (Allard 2013).

Not all the newspapers commented on the polls, notwithstanding that all had published polls and almost all, at some stage, had commissioned them; only one metropolitan daily, *The West Australian*, failed to commission any polling. In the *Australian Financial Review*, Edmund Tadros (2013) overcame his reluctance to pass judgment—'polling', he intoned, 'is not predictive'—to declare Morgan 'the most accurate of the pre-election polls', followed by Galaxy, ReachTEL, and Newspoll. Least accurate was Lonergan's 'robo-poll' conducted via mobiles. In the marginals, he argued, 'robo-pollster' JWS published by the *Financial Review* had 'performed the best, picking the eventual winner in more than 80 per cent of the seats it surveyed'. While another robo-pollster, ReachTEL, would also 'be pleased with its performance', Tadros suggested Newspoll's efforts in the marginal seats were '[l]ess successful' with fewer than 70 per cent of its polls foreshadowing the eventual winner. The record of the Galaxy poll in marginal seats passed without mention. At the *Daily Telegraph*, which had published the Galaxy poll and whose stable mate *The Australian* had published Newspoll, the editor-at-large saw things quite differently. 'In the battle of the polls', John Lehmann declared, 'Galaxy and Newspoll dominated' (Lehmann 2013). Here the marginal seat polling of both Galaxy and Newspoll passed without mention. In the *Age*, which had published the Nielsen poll, Tom Allard (2013) noted, with a sense of *schadenfreude*, that 'a slew of polls of individual electorates' had 'suggested a diabolical outcome for Labor, including Mr Rudd losing his seat of Griffith and a wipeout in western Sydney'. Allard singled out the *Australian*, relying on Newspoll, for predicting that 'Labor would lose between 12 and 16 seats in NSW and between four and six in Queensland'. About the performance of ReachTEL, commissioned by the *Age* to poll four Victorian marginals, he said nothing, notwithstanding that ReachTEL had substantially over-estimated (Melbourne) or under-estimated (Corangamite) Labor's first preference vote in two of the four.

All three commentators focused on the pre-election polls; the Morgan exit poll, the Galaxy exit poll, and the election day Newspoll did not rate a mention. In arriving at the percentages of hits and misses none of the three commentators attempted to calibrate degrees of difficulty. Only Lehmann cast an eye over the first preferences. If he judged Galaxy's performance best against the two-party-preferred, he judged Newspoll 'the most accurate in primary votes'. He discounted Morgan, which had done better on the two-party vote than Galaxy, because it 'was the least accurate of the major polls on primary votes'. Nielsen, he noted, had 'overstated The Greens primary vote' (Lehmann 2013).

Written shortly after the election, and well before the counting of the 'declaration votes'—absentee and postal votes, of which there were estimated to be over 3.5 million—these judgments of the polls' performance were premature at best, exercises in corporate propaganda at worst. Day-after-the-election judgments, written by journalists against tight schedules and with incomplete data, usually are.

Judged against the final two-party-preferred nationwide—53.5 per cent for the Coalition, 46.5 for Labor—almost all the pre-election estimates were remarkably close. Leaving aside the last-minute Lonergan poll, the spread across the other seven polls was just 2 percentage points, with the Coalition expected to win between 52 and 54 per cent of the two-party vote (Table 1). For two of the three CATI polls—Nielsen (which had provided pre-election estimates of the two-party-preferred since 1993), and Galaxy (which had done so since 2004) —the results were their best ever. For the third, Newspoll, the size of its error was half its 20-year average (Goot 2012: 95).

Nonetheless, the polls generally over-estimated Labor's two-party-preferred. While two polls had the Coalition winning 54 per cent of the two-party-preferred, five polls had the Coalition winning 53 per cent or less—the Lonergan poll, with a 50.8 per cent estimate, undershot the mark by a sizeable margin (Table 1). Had the pollsters allocated preferences on the basis of how they were going to be distributed in 2013 rather than on the basis of how they *were* distributed in 2010—the typical though not universal approach adopted by the various polling companies—the estimate of the Coalition's two-party-preferred, according to Bowe (2013b), would have been 1 percentage point less. In other words, the polls might have over-estimated Labor's two-party-preferred by an even bigger margin. Moreover, almost every poll might have over-estimated it. Based on this finding, Bowe argues against Morgan's claim to have estimated the two-party-preferred accurately. However, Morgan stands out precisely for having allocated preferences according to how respondents said they would allocate them (53.5:46.5). Indeed, Morgan openly disparaged other pollsters for assuming preferences would be allocated according to the 2010 pattern; on Morgan's own data this would have produced a two-party-preferred of 54.5 to 45.5 (Roy Morgan Research 2013b). Nielsen calculated the likely distribution (54:46) if preferences were allocated according to the 2010 pattern; it also recorded, though it didn't report, how respondents said they would allocate them (53:47—Nielsen 2013). Both the Morgan and unpublished Nielsen figures tell the same story—a story that Bowe's arithmetic would subsequently confirm.

Table 1: Final pre-election day polls for the House of Representatives election, 7 September 2013

Poll	Method	Date	Days before election	LNP*	ALP	Greens	PUP	KAP	Oth/Ind	DK	N	2PP# (LNP)
Nielsen	CATI	4–5 Sept	2	(43/3) 46	33	11	4	1	2/2 (4)	[na]	(1431)	54
Newspoll	CATI	3–5 Sept	2	46	33	9	na	na	(12)	[3]	(2511)	54‡
Galaxy	CATI	2–4 Sept	3	45	35	9	5	na	(6)	[6]	(1503)	53
Morgan	Multi	4–6 Sept	1	44	31.5	10.5	6.5	1	(6.5)	[1.5]	(4937)	53.5
Essential	Online	1–4 Sept	3	43	35	10	na	na	(12)	[na]	(1035)	52
AMR	Online	30 Aug–2 Sept	5	44	34	10	na	na	(12)	[12]	(1101)	53
Lonergan	Mobile	5 Sept	2	42	34	14	na	na	(10)	[-]	(862)	50.8
ReachTEL	IVR	5 Sept	2	(40.4/3.1) 43.5	33.7	10.2	7.0	1.1	(4.6)	[na]	(3512)	53
Election (AEC)		7 Sept		(40.9/4.6) 45.6	33.4	8.7	5.5	1.0	4.5/1.4 (5.9)			53.5

na: not available

*Proportions in brackets indicate Liberal (National Party) support where separately reported. Liberal vote includes the Liberal Party, and Liberal National Party (Qld); National Party vote includes the Nationals and Country Liberal Party (Northern Territory).

#Based on the distribution of minor party preferences at the 2010 election (Essential), except for Morgan, which based its result on how respondents said they would vote.

‡Excludes Northern Territory.

Source: Nielsen: www.nielsen.com.au/opinion-polls-2/opinion-polls-2/; Galaxy: www.galaxyresearch.com.au/polling/; Roy Morgan: www.roymorgan.com/findings/5169-morgan-poll-federal-election-2013-201309061457; ReachTEL: www.reachtel.com.au/blog/7-news-national-poll-5september13; Guardian Australia (for Lonergan): www.theguardian.com/world/2013/sep/06/two-party-preferred-vote-narrows; AMR: twitter.com/amr_australia; and, final election results (AEC): www.aec.gov.au/Elections/Federal_Elections/2013/.

The tendency of the polls to over-estimate Labor's two-party-preferred charted a familiar pattern. In 2010, six of the seven polls under-estimated the Coalition's share of the two-party-preferred (Goot 2012: 91). In 2007, four of the six polls under-estimated it (Goot 2009: 125), and in 2004 four out of the six polls did so (Goot 2005: 60). Before that the pattern was more mixed. Historically, the tendency to over-estimate Labor's two-party-preferred has been a feature of some polling organisations more than others, of Morgan in particular and more recently of Essential. Given the proliferation of polling organisations and approaches to polling in recent years, the study of 'house effects', first undertaken in 2004 by Jackman (2005), needs to be updated.

Meanwhile, a comparison of first preferences tells a less flattering story about the accuracy of the polls. If we compare the polls' estimates of the votes for the ALP, Coalition, Greens, and Others with the votes actually recorded the median error was roughly three times as large (1.4 percentage points) as the two-party-preferred error (0.4 percentage points). Every poll, including Morgan, over-estimated the vote for the Greens. Few polls, Morgan among them, under-estimated the Labor vote (Table 1). Compared with the polls' order of merit on the two-party-preferred, the order of merit on first preferences looks quite different. The poll that scored best was Newspoll (average error 0.4), followed by AMR and Galaxy (1.0), Nielsen and ReachTEL (1.1), Essential (1.5), and Morgan (1.7), with Lonergan (3.0) a distant last.

We get a slightly different story if instead of looking at the estimates that *every* poll generated we look at the estimates that *each* poll generated—some polls having estimated separate results for the Liberal and National parties, or disaggregated the results for the Palmer United Party and/or Katter's Australia Party. Of the three polls that disaggregated their estimates, Morgan (average error 1.1 percentage points) and ReachTEL (1.0) did better on this measure, while Nielsen (1.4) did worse. The under-estimate of the National Party vote, as regular as it is predictable, may be a special case (see Aitkin 1982: 188–90)—few of the pollsters even reported it.

Exit polls

'I know of few things more pointless', Mark Textor, the Liberal Party's pollster, tweeted on the last day of the campaign, than '[e]xit polls on votes'. 'Wait a few hours', he advised, 'seriously' (Textor 2013). For someone wanting to know the outcome of the election and nothing more, the truth of Textor's remarks could hardly be gainsaid. However, exit polls on election day are not much different from polls conducted in the last days of the campaign: they are undertaken not just to satisfy the public's interest in knowing the outcome of the election ahead of the official results but also in the hope of demonstrating the abilities of pollsters to forecast the results. These twin objectives—satisfying public curiosity and promoting the profile of particular firms—ahead of official announcements also characterise estimates by private bodies of inflation, unemployment, and likely movements in interest rates.

Of the two exit polls released on the day, Morgan's was the only one that relied on respondents' texting their decision after they had voted. It had the biggest sample, and almost certainly the best geographical spread. Preliminary figures had gone to air on Channel 10 at around 1 pm AEST and were updated every two hours. Galaxy conducted an exit poll, face-to-face, for Nine News with half the number of respondents Morgan mustered. Its interviewing was confined to just 27 polling booths across Australia, in metropolitan and non-metropolitan areas, covering 'marginal seats, reasonably safe seats and very safe seats' (pers. comm.). Its results were tweeted at 5.51 pm (YouDecide9 2013). Crosby/Textor also conducted an exit poll for the Australian Petroleum Production and Exploration Association with 400 respondents drawn from 20 seats in New South Wales and eight seats in Queensland. The poll was designed to measure the impact of particular issues rather than to forecast the outcome, and no results were released on the night (Tasker 2013).

In addition to the exit polls, Newspoll conducted a Day of the Election poll across Labor marginals in New South Wales (10 seats) and in Queensland (eight seats), drawing as many respondents from the Prime Minister's seat of Griffith as it did from all the other Queensland seats combined. Newspoll had polled all 18 seats for *The Australian* during the campaign. The results went to air on *Sky News* at 4 pm (AAP 2013), two hours before the polls closed in eastern Australia and five hours before the polls closed in Western Australia.

Morgan's poll, once the final figures were in, was not quite as accurate a measure of the two-party-preferred as its final pre-election poll turned out to be. Nonetheless, it did very well—off by just 0.5 percentage points. Galaxy, off by 1 percentage point, was less accurate. Newspoll, by contrast, did not do well. Matching its figures to the final figures in the seats in which it polled reveals an error of 3.5 percentage points—easily the biggest error among any of the polls, including the Lonergan mobile poll conducted just before the election (Table 2).

Table 2: Exit and election day polls, House of Representatives, 7 September 2013

Poll	Method	Type	Population	LNP	ALP	Greens	PUP	KAP	Oth/Ind	N	2PP# (LNP)
Newspoll	CATI	Ordinary	NSW & Qld marginals*	45	36	8	na	na	11	(1501)	53.0
Galaxy	Face-to-face	Exit	National**	47	33	9	5	1.0	5	(3220)	54.5
Morgan	SMS	Exit	National	43.5	33.0	11.0	5.0	na	7.5	(6215)	53.0
Election			National	45.6	33.4	8.7	5.5	1.0	5.9		49.5
											53.5

na: not available

#Based on the distribution of minor party preferences at the 2010 election, except for Morgan, which based its result on how respondents said they would vote.

*Kingsford Smith, Dobell, Parramatta, Page, Eden-Monaro, Reid, Banks, Lindsay, Robertson, Greenway (NSW; n = 500); Oxley, Rankin, Blair, Capricornia, Lilley, Petrie, Moreton (Qld; n = 501); Griffith (Qld; n = 500).

**Interviews outside 27 polling booths drawn from all state capitals and from non-capital city areas, incorporating 'marginal seats, reasonably safe seats and very safe seats'.

Source: Business Spectator (Newspoll): //www.businessspectator.com.au/news/2013/9/7/election/exit-poll-tips-coalition-landslide (viewed 10 September 2013); #YouDecide9 (Galaxy): @YouDecide9, 7 September 2013 (viewed 10 September 2013); Roy Morgan: www.roymorgan.com/findings/5170-morgan-federal-election-exit-polls-201309070155 (viewed 5 October 2013); and final election results (AEC): www.aec.gov.au/Elections/Federal_Elections/2013/.

Again, things look different if instead of focusing on the two-party-preferred we look at the estimates that the polls generated for the individual parties. On this measure, Galaxy with an average error of 0.6 percentage points for five parties (plus Others) eclipsed Morgan whose average error was 1.2 percentage points for four parties (plus Others). But the worst poll was Newspoll with an average error of 3.6 percentage points for the three parties (plus Others). Newspoll's main sources of error were the Labor vote, which it under-estimated by a massive 6.7 percentage points, and the vote for the minor parties, which it over-estimated by 4.3 percentage points. The errors were similar in both News South Wales and Queensland.

Marginal seats

Polling in marginal seats started early, involved an unprecedented number of firms, and was dominated—measured by their number if not by their impact—by 'robos'. Galaxy polled in 20 seats, ReachTEL in 14, JWS in 13, and Lonergan in four; all used 'robos'. Newspoll, the only firm to use CATI, polled in 32 seats. With one exception (ReachTEL, which polled twice in Bass), no firm polled any seat more than once. On election day, Morgan came out with predictions for every seat in the country. These were based on questionnaires administered by CATI, via SMS, and online.

Some 25 polls were conducted in the first or second weeks of the campaign, 19 in week three, and 21 in week four (two straddling week three), and just one in week five. Focusing their efforts on the first two weeks helped the companies least well-known—JWS, Lonergan, and ReachTEL—become talking points. Concentrating on weeks three and four meant Galaxy and Newspoll did their most intensive polling as interest in the election built. With relatively few seats (18 of the 55) attracting the attention of more than one pollster—or, more to the point, the interest of more than one client—it was difficult for pollsters to ponder their results in the light of other polls and to contemplate whether, as a result, they might adjust them. By not polling individual seats in the last week—again, based on decisions made mostly by newspapers and television stations not by the pollsters—the polling companies could avail themselves of the defence, if their polls erred, of 'a late swing'.

The seat most frequently polled was Griffith (Queensland). Held by Kevin Rudd by what should have been a reasonably safe margin (8.5 percentage points two-party-preferred), Griffith attracted five polling organisations. ReachTEL (5 August) noted an anti-Labor swing of 4 percentage points two-party-preferred early in the campaign when Labor was looking not just to hold on to the seats it already held but to win additional seats in Queensland. Lonergan (21 August) and Newspoll (21–22 August) caused an even greater stir by suggesting that Rudd was actually trailing his Coalition opponent and former Australian Medical Association president Bill Glasson, 48:52, the two-party-preferred reported by both polls. Galaxy (29 August) had Rudd back where ReachTEL had him. JWS (30 August) had Rudd doing almost as well as in 2010.

The results of the polls, especially those in Griffith, generated controversy. Much of it centred on the deployment of 'robos'. How did the 'robos' fare? While most of the seats went the way these polls pointed, about one in five did not. Of the 20 seats polled by Galaxy, two (Werriwa and Greenway in New South Wales) didn't fall as Galaxy suggested they might, while another two (Barton in New South Wales, and Hindmarsh in South Australia) were lost despite the figures suggesting Labor might hang on to them. Two of the 13 seats polled by ReachTEL (McMahon and Kingsford Smith in New South Wales) didn't fall as it suggested they might. And three of the 13 seats polled by JWS (McMahon; McEwen in Victoria; Lilley in Queensland) were retained by Labor, not lost as the JWS polls suggested might happen. With Rudd holding on in Griffith, one of the four Lonergan polls also proved a poor bet.

Even where the 'robos' successfully picked the winner, their estimates were sometimes out substantially. As well as pointing to the likelihood of Labor losing two seats it actually retained, Galaxy either under-estimated (Blair) or over-estimated (La Trobe and Perth) Labor's two-party-preferred by 3 percentage points or more. The ReachTEL figures proved even less reliable. In addition to suggesting that Labor would lose two seats that did not change hands, it under-estimated Labor's two-party support by at least 3 percentage points in Blaxland and Bennelong (NSW), as well as in Braddon, Franklin and Lyons (Tasmania). JWS under-estimated Labor's two-party vote in Lindsay (NSW), Aston (Victoria) and Forde (Qld) by 4 to 6 percentage points, while over-estimating it in Griffith. Lonergan, which did not calculate a two-party-preferred except in Griffith, over-estimated the Liberal or LNP first preferences in both Lindsay and Forde by 13 percentage points. What polling didn't detect in seats like these was the late surge in support for minor parties.

Newspoll doesn't appear to have done any better. It did well in Forde, but in Griffith it under-estimated Labor's two-party-preferred by nearly 5 percentage points. In Lyne, where Newspoll did not calculate a two-candidate-preferred (National versus Independent), it under-estimated Labor's first preference vote by 5 percentage points, and in New England it over-estimated Labor's vote by 12 percentage points. These were its only single seat reports. Most of the seats Newspoll surveyed were in clusters and reported as a group. Across the three Victorian seats it polled, the average two-party vote Newspoll reported turned out to be very close to the final figure. Across two groups of Queensland seats—a group of seven held by Labor, and a group of eight held by the LNP—Labor's two-party-preferred was 3 or 4 percentage points greater than Newspoll's estimate. In its cluster of five western Sydney seats, Newspoll under-estimated Labor's two-party-preferred by nearly 7 percentage points, though in what the *Australian* called Labor's 'coastal' seats—five seats stretching from Page in the north of New South Wales to Eden-Monaro in the south of the state—its under-estimate was a more respectable 2 percentage points.

Regardless of mode—'robo' or CATI—sample sizes in individual seats were generally modest. Galaxy recorded between 548 and 660 interviews per seat (an average of 577); JWS between 482 and 757 (an average of 589); and ReachTEL between 541 and 860 (an average of 631). Newspoll, in its single-seat polls, interviewed between 500 and 504 voters; in three of its cluster polls (polls across three, five or seven seats) it conducted 800 interviews, while in its other polls it conducted either 1,106 interviews (five seats) or 1,832 interviews (eight seats). Only with Lonergan, which recorded between 958 and 1,160 interviews per seat (an average of 1,031), were the numbers markedly better. The contrast with the final national polls is striking. Nationally, Lonergan (n = 862) sampled fewer than 1,000 voters; Essential (n = 1,305), AMR (n = 1,101), Nielsen (n = 1,431), and Galaxy (n = 1,503) sampled more than 1,000; Newspoll (n = 2,511), ReachTEL (n = 3,512) and Morgan (n = 4,937) sampled many more (see Table 1). The media drew little, if any, attention to what small or large samples implied about the reliability of the results.

Typically, it was in New South Wales where the 'robos' were widest of the mark. This was true of: JWS, which polled there as well as in Victoria and Queensland; ReachTEL, which polled in all these states as well as in Tasmania; and Galaxy, which polled in every state except Tasmania. One reason why the New South Wales results were wider of the mark than polls elsewhere is that in New South Wales they were taken relatively early. There, the last of the JWS and ReachTEL polls were conducted in week two and the last of the Galaxy polls in week three of the five-week campaign. For Newspoll, the worst single set of seats was also in New South Wales. Overall, however, there wasn't much to choose between Newspoll's performance in New South Wales and its performance in Queensland. In both states, Labor did distinctly better in its marginal seats than Newspoll had suggested.

In addition to reporting its results, Morgan released a set of seat-by-seat *predictions*. These it derived from its final (mixed-mode) sample of 4,937 respondents—a sample that yielded, on average, just 33 respondents per seat. Morgan's predictions proved less than perfect. In New South Wales, two of the seats predicted to be Liberal–National Party gains (Greenway and Parramatta) failed to change hands, while three of the seats Morgan tipped Labor to hold (Barton, Eden-Monaro and Page) did change hands. In Victoria, the Liberals lost Indi, a seat Morgan expected the party to hold. In Queensland, the LNP did not take Blair, Lilley or Moreton from Labor, each of which Morgan predicted would fall; Morgan did not foresee the fall of Fairfax notwithstanding its post-election boast about being 'the only poll ... to predict Clive Palmer could win the seat'. In South Australia, Morgan thought Labor would hold Hindmarsh but it didn't. In Tasmania, Morgan had Labor holding Bass, Braddon, and Lyons—all of which were lost to the Liberals. And in the Northern Territory, Morgan had the Coalition winning Lingiari, a seat where Labor held on (Roy Morgan Research 2013c).

After the election, the fact that none of the polls, 'robo' or otherwise, paraded their prowess at measuring the vote in individual seats should have come as no surprise. Fortunately for its reputation, none of the post-election commentary registered Morgan's predictions let alone the sample sizes on which they were based.

The senate

In 'horse race' journalism, the Senate finishes a very long last. The political race that stops the nation is the race for the House of Representatives, the race to win government, and the race to be prime minister. Polling for the Senate requires large samples in every state. As with polls in marginal seats, respondents need to be given a list of the parties that are running, or at least a list of the parties that are likely to be in contention. This time, the proliferation of parties made the mechanics of polling for the Senate harder than ever. Notwithstanding this, and the difficulty of calling the last two of the six places in most states, one pollster had a go—not accidentally, perhaps, the one with no previous experience of this most hazardous of undertakings.

In its final poll, conducted via mobiles on 5 September, Lonergan included a question on the Senate vote. The results: 40 per cent for the Coalition, 29 per cent for Labor, and 16 per cent for the Greens, with eight per cent for other parties. Lonergan's figures didn't add up to 100, presumably because the proportion 'undecided' was left out. If we exclude the 'undecided' and redistribute the percentages, the Coalition was on 43 per cent, Labor on 31 per cent, the Greens on 17 per cent, with 'others' on 9 per cent. None of Lonergan's figures were disaggregated by state; with a sample size of just 862 any such division would have been foolish. The results came hedged with a warning. The 'actual Senate vote', Lonergan cautioned, 'has tended to differ from the self-reported voting intention figures in polling, possibly because it is very difficult to convey the complexity of a Senate voting form over the telephone' (Taylor 2013).

The Lonergan poll proved less accurate than any other poll conducted during the campaign. Although its estimate of the Labor vote was close to the mark, it over-estimated the Coalition vote by over 5 percentage points, and the Greens by more than 8 percentage points. There was a corresponding under-estimate of the vote for 'others' of nearly 15 percentage points. The average error for the Coalition, Labor, the Greens and others exceeded 7 percentage points.

Essential had ventured into this territory in January and February, building a sample of sufficient size over a number of weeks to enable it say something about Senate support in each of the states, except Tasmania (Bowe 2013c). The sort of figures generated by this poll helped support early views about the likely Senate outcome with speculation about the prospects of the Shooters and Fishers as well as the Christian Democratic Party in New South Wales, the possibility of another Democratic Labour Party senator from Victoria, the strength of Katter's Australia Party in Queensland, and how well Nick Xenophon might do in South Australia. Outside of Western Australia, micro parties did not yet loom as any kind of possibility, and the Palmer United Party (PUP) had yet to emerge.

When Gary Morgan predicted, four days before the election, that PUP 'may take a spot in the Senate', he appears to have been relying on polling data for the House not the Senate. He was also focusing on Queensland where his polling had the PUP, on average, doing twice as well as anywhere else (Roy Morgan Research 2013a). Like everyone else, Morgan under-estimated the party's performance. The PUP didn't only win a Senate seat in Queensland—it also won a seat each in Tasmania and Western Australia, where Palmer's candidate Zhenya Wang won a Senate seat after an appeal to the Court of Disputed Returns (High Court) resulted in an April 2014 re-election.

Conclusion

The proliferation of polls, and the rise of 'robos', are related. So, too, are the proliferation of polls and the availability of respondents online. Compared to the cost and speed of face-to-face polls, or even CATI, 'robos' have obvious appeal not least to newspapers wanting to sponsor polls but finding the funds to do so increasingly difficult to come by. This is especially true where the data newspapers—and television stations—mainly want, or the only data they can afford are data on voting intentions (Goot 2013).

To have the performance of the polls judged against the two-party-preferred rather than the average error per party is a further incentive to the proliferation of polls since the risk of getting the result of the two-party-preferred wrong—not in the sense of calling the wrong winner but in the sense of under-estimating or over-estimating the winner's margin—is less than the chances of error in estimating the vote for a number of individual parties. It was clear half-way through the campaign that the Government was destined to fall; no fewer than three-quarters of those polled by Nielsen (Kenny 2013), Newspoll (2013) and ReachTEL (2013) in the last week of the campaign knew this. Since 1972 no government had changed hands with less than 52.7 per cent of the two-party-preferred, so no well-informed observer should have expected a two-party-preferred for the Coalition of less than about 53 per cent.

'Robo-polling' by landline, polling *via* SMS, and polling online also attracted market researchers who lacked media sponsors but wanted to take advantage of the media coverage election polling inevitably generates. Even without a media sponsor, relationships are easily institutionalised: the polls produced by Essential were written up and promoted in the Monday editions of *Crikey*; JWS's findings were exclusive to the *Australian Financial Review* even when the paper hadn't paid for them. Pollsters judged to have done well are more likely to generate business opportunities beyond the media than those judged to have done poorly, regardless of whether the media simply reported their polls or commissioned them. Since market research firms depend much more heavily on non-media clients than on media clients, publicity is important.

Anxieties within the industry about the possibility of the polls falling foul of voters who had shifted from landlines to mobiles proved unwarranted. Far from doing badly the traditional CATI polls—Nielsen, Newspoll, and Galaxy—did well. Measured against the two-party-preferred their median error was well inside the long-term (post-1993) median, which in 2010 stood at 1.8 percentage points. Even the average error per party, which was greater than the error on the two-party-preferred, provided no grounds for thinking that the performance of the polls had been affected by the increasing difficulty of reaching respondents who had switched to mobiles—the young, in particular. The relatively poor performance of the final Lonergan poll, conducted via mobiles, will have provided added reassurance. For those who stuck with CATI, the application of standard weighting procedures seems to have done the trick. Anxieties may have been allayed. However, with the rapid growth in the proportion of voters who can only be contacted by mobiles or online, these anxieties will not have been laid aside.

Where the polls ran into most trouble was in marginal seats. For the most part this was a matter of the polls being taken too soon, especially in New South Wales and Queensland, because votes for minor parties or 'flash' parties are more likely to crystallise later in the campaign. It also had to do with the size of samples—in the Morgan case, spectacularly so. Importantly, it was not because of the 'robos'—the records of Newspoll and Morgan, with their very different techniques, were not markedly different (see also Bowe 2013b).

The pollsters' lack of transparency remains a problem. This is most obvious in relation to Galaxy, with its use of mixed modes, and Morgan, which compounded the mystery surrounding its use of mixed modes by using its final poll to predict the outcomes in every seat. But the question of transparency transcends issues around modes or how they are combined. What is more remarkable is the similarity of all the two-party-preferred results. Either this is a case of all roads leading to Rome, with different ways of getting there making little difference, or it is a case of pollsters looking over their shoulders to see what their rivals are doing—the 'late mover's advantage' (Goot 2009: 128) or 'herding', as Nate Silver (2012) has called it. While this may be one of the legacies of the campaign which calls for further investigation, it is unlikely that pollsters would allow an investigation of this kind to get very far.

Acknowledgements

For their assistance in providing data or clarifying their practices, I am grateful to Chris Pyra and Rebecca Tilly of AMR, Peter Lewis of Essential Media Communications, David Briggs of Galaxy Research, John Scales of JMS Research, Chris Lonergan of Lonergan Research, John Stirton of Nielsen, Martin O'Shannessy of Newspoll, James Stewart of ReachTEL, and Vaishali Nagaratnam of Roy Morgan Research. Thanks, too, to Samuel Paske of Enterprise Marketing and Research Services (EMRS), Richard Herr, and Keith Patterson of the Patterson Research Group.

References

AAP. 2013. 'Exit poll tips coalition landslide'. *Business Spectator*, 7 September, viewed 13 January 2014: <www.businessspectator.com.au/news/2013/9/7/election/exit-poll-tips-coalition-landslide>.

Aitkin, Don. 1982. *Stability and Change in Australian Politics*. 2nd edn. Canberra: Australian National University Press.

Allard, Tom. 2013. 'Two states key to Coalition victory'. *The Age*, 9 September: 6.

Bowe, William. 2013a. 'Random observations'. *Crikey*, 10 September, viewed 13 January 2014: <blogs.crikey.com.au/pollbludger/2013/09/10/random-observations/>.

Bowe, William. 2013b. 'The verdict is in on pollsters: Coalition bias, electorate polls fail'. *Crikey*, 2 December, viewed 13 January 2014: <www.crikey.com.au/2013/12/02/the-verdict-is-in-on-pollsters-coalition-bias-electorate-polls-fail/>.

Bowe, William. 2013c. 'Senate race: polling shows challenge to Greens power'. *Crikey*, 20 February, viewed 13 January 2014: <www.crikey.com.au/2013/02/20/senate-race-polling-shows-challenge-to-greens-power/>.

Goot, Murray. 2005. 'The polls: Labor, Liberal or too close to call?'. In Marian Simms and John Warhurst (eds), *Mortgage Nation: The 2004 Australian Elections*, Perth: API Network and Curtin University of Technology Press.

Goot, Murray. 2009. 'Getting it wrong while getting it right: the polls, the press and the 2007 Australian election'. *Australian Cultural History* 27(2): 115–33.

Goot, Murray. 2012. 'To the second decimal point: how the polls vied to predict the national vote, monitor the marginals and second-guess the Senate'. In Marian Simms and John Wanna (eds), *Julia 2010: The Caretaker Election*, Canberra: ANU E-Press.

Goot, Murray. 2014. 'The rise of the robo: media polls in a digital age'. In *Essays 2014: Politics*, North Melbourne: Australian Scholarly Publishing.

Jackman, Simon. 2005. 'Pooling the polls over an election campaign'. *Australian Journal of Political Science* 40: 499–517.

Jackman, Simon. 2013. 'Election 2013: how did the polls perform?'. *Guardian Australia*, 8 September, viewed 13 January 2014: <www.theguardian.com/world/the-swing/2013/sep/08/election-2013-polls-performance-australia>.

Kenny, Mark. 2013. 'Abbott to sweep aside Labor'. *Sydney Morning Herald*, 6 September.

Knott, Matthew. 2013. 'Election poll war: landline lives as mobiles fall flat'. *Crikey*, 9 September, viewed 13 January 2014: <www.crikey.com.au/2013/09/09/election-poll-war-landline-lives-as-mobiles-fall-flat/>.

Lehmann, John. 2013'.Galaxy on the money with polls'. *Daily Telegraph*, 9 September.

Newspoll. 2013. Poll. 3–5 September, viewed 13 January 2014: <polling.Newspoll.com.au.tmp.anchor.net.au/image_uploads/130922%20Final%20Election%20Poll.pdf>.

Nielsen, 2013. 'Federal poll report', 6 September.

ReachTEL. 2013. '7 News—National Poll—5th September 2013', viewed 13 January 2014: <www.ReachTEL.com.au/blog/7-news-national-poll-5september13>.

Roy Morgan Research. 2013a. 'Roy Morgan–Channel 10 SMS Exit Morgan Poll most accurate on 2PP'. 9 September, viewed 15 January 2014: <www.royMorgan.com/findings/5173-federal-election-2013-accuracy-201309090137>.

Roy Morgan Research. 2013b. 'LNP set to win federal election and over 90 seats. High vote for Palmer Party (6.5% in Queensland), helps the L-NP vote'. 6 September, viewed 15 January 2014: <www.royMorgan.com/findings/5169-Morgan-poll-federal-election-2013-201309061457>.

Roy Morgan Research. 2013c. 'Roy Morgan–Channel 10 Exit Poll—1pm'. NewsMaker.com, 8 September, viewed 15 January 2014: <www.newsmaker.com.au/news/27511/roy-Morganchannel-10-exit-poll-1pm#.UlpKvBA5Ns4>.

Silver, Nate. 2012. 'Pollsters may be herding'. *Votamatic*, viewed 13 January 2014: <votamatic.org/pollsters-may-be-herding/>.

Tadros, Edmund. 2013. 'Robots ring changes in election polling'. *Australian Financial Review*, 9 September: 12.

Tasker, Sarah-Jane. 2013. 'Exit poll shows as protests all hot air'. *The Australian*, 11 September.

Taylor, Lenore. 2013. 'Labor gains ground on Coalition, says new mobile-only poll'. *Guardian Australia*, 6 September, viewed 13 January 2014: <www.theguardian.com/world/2013/sep/06/two-party-preferred-vote-narrows>.

Textor, Mark. 2013. 'Exit polls on vote. I know of few things more pointless. Wait a few hours. Seriously'. Twitter post, 6 September, viewed 28 September 2013: @markatextor.

YouDecide9. 2013. 'JUST IN: The Coalition has reached the required number of seats to declare victory'. Twitter post, 7 September: @YouDecide9, <twitter.com/YouDecide9/status/376302903213817856/photo/1>.

9. All That Glitters: Betting markets and the 2013 Australian federal election

Simon Jackman

Political betting markets featured prominently in pre-election prognostication, perhaps more so ahead of the 2013 election than in any other recent Australian election. Major newspapers such as the *Australian* and the *Australian Financial Review* frequently reported on the state of the national betting markets, offering daily updates after the election date was announced. I routinely referenced the betting markets in weekly columns I was penning for the *Guardian Australia*.[1]

The attention garnered by political betting markets is a relatively recent development. To be sure, political betting has been around for a long time in Australia; the survey by Rhode and Strumpf (2013) cites evidence of person-to-person wagering on colonial elections through to newspaper reports of relatively large wagers being placed on the 1949 federal election. This is despite the fact that gambling on federal elections has been illegal for most of the history of the Commonwealth. 'Wagering on the result of any election' remained on the list of electoral offences[2] until extensive amendments were made to the *Commonwealth Electoral Act* in 1983.

Political betting has since come out of the shadows. The rise of online bookmaking is a large part of the story, increasing the accessibility and visibility of political betting markets (and many other betting markets), relative to pre-internet forms of wagering.

Not coincidentally, the intellectual respectability of political betting markets has grown in recent decades, reflecting a broader interest in prediction markets as forecasting tools in a wide array of domains; see, for example, the survey in Wolfers and Zitzewitz (2004). In election betting markets, wagers are being placed over discrete events. For instance, which party will form government after the election, or which party or candidate will win a particular House of Representatives seat. Under the assumption that the markets are efficient,

---

1   For example, Jackman 2013a.
2   For example, section 182, *Commonwealth Electoral Act* 1902; section 170, *Commonwealth Electoral Act*, 1918.

market-clearing prices reflect an aggregation of the probabilities agents assign to these discrete events; information that changes agents' probabilistic beliefs is reflected in price movements (see, e.g. Wolfers and Zitzewitz 2006).

The consensus among social scientists, political commentators and the public is that political betting markets produce reasonably accurate forecasts of election outcomes. In the specific case of Australian elections, Wolfers and Leigh (2002) made a persuasive case for the predictive power of political betting markets, contrasting the predictions of: (1) opinion polls; (2) statistical models analysing the long-run relationship between macro-economic conditions and election outcomes; and (3) the prices offered by the betting markets ahead of the 2001 federal election. Leigh and Wolfers (2006) considered predictions of the 2004 federal election, concluding that national polls varied too much—both across polling houses and over time—to be 'particularly useful' as forecasts, or at least relative to the 'useful' forecasting performance and 'more reasonable' degree of volatility exhibited by political betting markets.

Critics contend that while betting markets may produce good forecasts of election outcomes, this is largely because they are reacting to the polls. In this view, the predictive power of the betting markets is due to the fact that they incorporate the information in polls. Indeed, the polls are not nearly as poor a predictor of election outcomes as Leigh and Wolfers might have us believe, at least not when aggregated across survey/polling houses, temporally smoothed, and when corrections for house effects are applied; see, for instance, my poll-averaging model (Jackman 2005; Jackman 2009: Chapter 9) and the work of other poll-aggregators such as William Bowe.[3]

It is worth noting that in their 2006 paper, Leigh and Wolfers did not suggest nor demonstrate that the betting markets ignored the polls. Although they did not explicitly test that betting markets react nearly instantaneously to changes in the polls, Leigh and Wolfers found no lag in the reaction of the 2004 *Betfair* market to changes in the polls[4]—inviting the conclusion that the *Betfair* market reacted nearly instantaneously—and that the *Centrebet* market adjusted to polling information with a slight delay (2006: 332 Panel D, Table 3). Leigh and Wolfers also pointed to the rapid reaction of the betting markets to important campaign events in 2004 (2006: 331, Figure 2). On the other hand, Leigh and Wolfers do imply that the polls have a limited effect on the betting markets. If we are to accept their conclusion that betting markets provide 'useful' forecasts of election outcomes, but that polls are not 'particularly useful', then the betting markets must be reasonably independent of the polls.

---

3 Bowe publishes his model at the popular blog *Pollbludger*, hosted by *Crikey!*: <www.crikey.com.au>.
4 Changes in the *Betfair* prices appear to be linearly independent of these lagged changes in the polls, where 'recent' is defined as changes in the polls between one and eight days ago, two and nine days ago, and three to 10 days ago. Therefore, any reaction in the *Betfair* market to the polls happens instantaneously or with a longer lag.

Whatever one's view of the efficient markets hypothesis (the assumption that markets process relevant information efficiently), it seems implausible that betting markets would ignore polling information or that polls are of no forecasting value whatsoever. It further seems implausible that today's betting prices always anticipate tomorrow's poll results. Poll results may contain new information. It would be astonishing if markets failed to react to that information. Accordingly, it isn't especially interesting to ask *if* the betting markets react to the polls, but *how much* and *under what conditions*.

The national 'party to form government' betting market, 2011–13

Starting on 1 July 2011, I gathered data on the prices in the election betting market offered by two of Australia's largest online internet bookmakers, *Centrebet* and *Sportsbet*. Prices were offered on the 'party to form government' after the next election: Labor or the Coalition. I used computer programs to store the prices offered on the websites of these bookmakers every hour. There is a small amount of missing data due to occasional computer and/or network outages, as well as some brief periods of political drama when bookmakers took their markets offline.[5] The resulting hourly time series commences at 5 pm, 1 July 2011 (for *Centrebet*; at 6 pm, 5 July 2011 for *Sportsbet*) and ceases at 9 pm on election night, 7 September 2013, Sydney time.

Both *Centrebet* and *Sportsbet* quote decimal odds, the value of a successful one-dollar wager, bounded from below at 1.0. Higher-priced wagers reflect beliefs that the corresponding event is less likely to occur. It is straightforward to convert the price offered for a particular outcome into the implied probability of the event occurring. If event A is priced at p and event $\sim A$ at q ($p, q > 1$), then the implied probability of event A occurring is $(1/p)/(1/p + 1/q)$. For instance, wagers on flips of fair coins (e.g. the coin toss ahead of a cricket match) are often priced at about 1.95 even though 2.00 would seem the fair price of a 50–50 proposition. Note that $1/1.95 + 1/1.95 > 1$, with the excess over one the source of the bookmaker's profit (the 'over-round' or 'vigorish'). Accordingly, the inverse prices ($1/p$, $1/q$ etc) cannot be considered probabilities until divided by the sum of the inverse prices, ensuring that the resulting implied probabilities sum to one over the set of outcomes, effectively factoring out the bookmaker's profit.

---

5 Of the possible 19,181 hourly observations over this period, I have 18,754 hourly observations from *Centrebet* (2.2 per cent missing) and 17,990 hourly observations from *Sportsbet* (6.2 per cent missing). The longest sequence of missing data in the *Centrebet* series is a one-week gap in October 2011; I am also missing *Sportsbet* data for the same period. For the *Sportsbet* data the longest span of missing data is between 23 February 2013 and 21 March 2013. These gaps in the data series seem to pose no threat to the validity of the analyses presented below.

I convert the quoted prices to an implied probability of a Labor win (henceforth 'IPW'), which I multiply by 100 for convenience of presentation. For instance, through June 2012, *Sportsbet* offered prices of 7.00 on a Labor win and 1.10 on a Coalition win, implying a $(1/7)/(1/7 + 1/1.1) = 13.5$ per cent probability of a Labor win.

Figure 1 displays the hourly time series of ALP IPWs from *Centrebet* and *Sportsbet*, from 1 July 2011 to the 2013 election. The two markets generally track together, with *Centrebet*'s prices exhibiting more volatility than *Sportsbet*. At no point over the 26 months spanned by these data did market prices reflect a belief that Labor was more likely to win the election than the Coalition. The shortest Labor price and longest Coalition price in these data occurs at the very start of the series. On 5 July 2011, *Sportsbet* was offering Labor at 2.55 and the Coalition at 1.50, corresponding to a 37 per cent IPW. Labor's price generally eased over the remainder of the term, save for some recoveries in late 2011 and late 2012 and in the immediate aftermath of Rudd's return to the leadership in 2013. Considerable volatility is apparent on the afternoon of 21 March 2013, when it was widely believed that Rudd would challenge for the Labor leadership (he did not); Labor's IPW (using *Centrebet*'s prices) jumped from 19.6 per cent to 26 per cent before returning to 19.6 per cent and falling to 15 per cent by the evening of 22 March 2013.

Rudd's eventual return on 26 June 2013 saw Labor's IPW jump from 15.5 per cent (*Centrebet*) and 13.3 per cent (*Sportsbet*) at 1 pm that afternoon to 21.3 per cent at 8 pm (*Centrebet*) and 20.8 per cent at 6 pm (*Sportsbet*). Labor's price recovered further in the weeks ahead, reaching 2013 peaks with ALP IPWs of 34.9 per cent and 33.1 per cent at *Centrebet* and *Sportsbet*, respectively, on 16 July 2013. Election betting firmly favoured the Coalition throughout August 2013. Labor's price blew out at both betting agencies over the campaign proper, with *Sportsbet* paying out its Coalition wagers on 29 August 2013, nine days ahead of the election.[6] By 1 September, Labor was at 16 to the Coalition's 1.01 at *Centrebet* (IPW of 5.9 per cent) and 12.50 to 1.02 (IPW of 7.5 per cent) at *Sportsbet*. *Centrebet*'s market closed as the polls opened on election day, with Labor at 14.00 to the Coalition's 1.02 (6.7 per cent IPW). *Sportsbet* kept its market open throughout election day, with Labor's price easing from 12.00 to 41.00 and the IPW falling from 7.9 per cent to 2.4 per cent.

In short, the Coalition was always firm favourite to win the 2013 election. In this sense the betting markets 'got it right' and well ahead of the election.

---

6 Maher (2013). The announcement by *Sportsbet* appears at: <http://www.*Sportsbet*.com.au/blog/home/*Sportsbet*-pays-out-early-on-coalition-to-win-2013-election>.

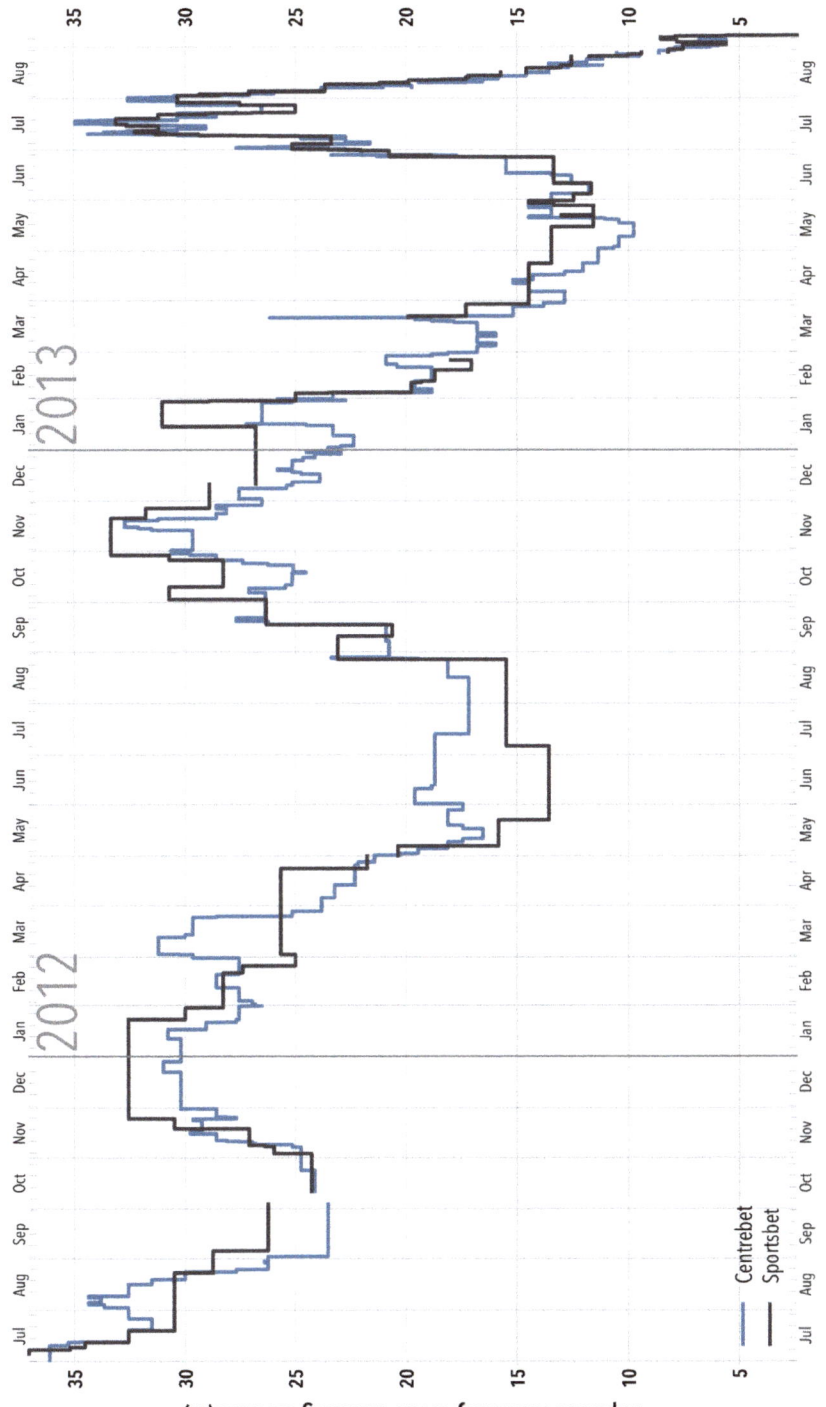

Figure 1: Hourly time series, ALP implied probability of winning, *Centrebet* and *Sportsbet*, 1 July 2011 to 7 September 2013. Breaks correspond to periods of missing data.

Source: Author's research.

Large betting market movements coincide with polling 'news'

I also gathered data on national opinion polls fielded in the 2010–13 parliamentary term. I recorded poll results, sample sizes and field dates, but also the 'release date' of each poll, the date at which the poll's results were published or otherwise released to the public and thus the earliest time at which we might expect to see any reaction to the polling information in the betting markets.

Figure 2 displays the eight largest daily changes[7] in the betting markets in descending order of magnitude. Each panel shows the trajectory of ALP IPW over a 72-hour period bracketing a day of especially large market movement. To the right of each panel I note recent polling information (changes in major polls' estimates of Labor's share of two-party-preferred voting intentions, henceforth ALP TPP) or political events coinciding with or immediately preceding the corresponding time period. As noted earlier, election day itself saw a large movement in IPW at *Sportsbet*—the largest in any 24-hour period in my data—but is excluded from this set of 'largest daily changes'.

These data clearly indicate that the markets are responding to the polls. Putting election day aside, the single biggest movement in IPW occurred on Tuesday, 9 July 2013. That day the *Australian* published a Newspoll result of ALP TPP at 50 per cent, up from 49 per cent in the Newspoll published the previous week; the poll also showed Rudd vastly outperforming Abbott as 'preferred prime minister'. This was Labor's best Newspoll result since October 2012 and further confirmed the recovery in Labor's poll numbers following Rudd's return. Social media reported the result late on Monday evening, 8 July, and the Newspoll result dominated Tuesday's political news. Both *Centrebet* and *Sportsbet* swung towards Labor overnight and through the day: Labor's price moved from 4.15 to 3.10 at *Centrebet* (the ALP IPW moving from 22.7 per cent to 30.3 per cent) and from 4.00 to 3.20 at *Sportsbet* (23.3 per cent to 29.4 per cent). Labor's gains continued the next day, if less dramatically: Labor reached 2.75 at *Centrebet* and ended the day at 2.80 (33.6 per cent), and reached 3.00 at *Sportsbet* (31.4 per cent).

---

7   I group the hourly data into 9 pm to 9 pm, 24-hour periods (Sydney time), since newspaper websites, other media (e.g. the ABC's *Lateline*) and social media often disseminate poll results late in the evening prior to their 'official' release.

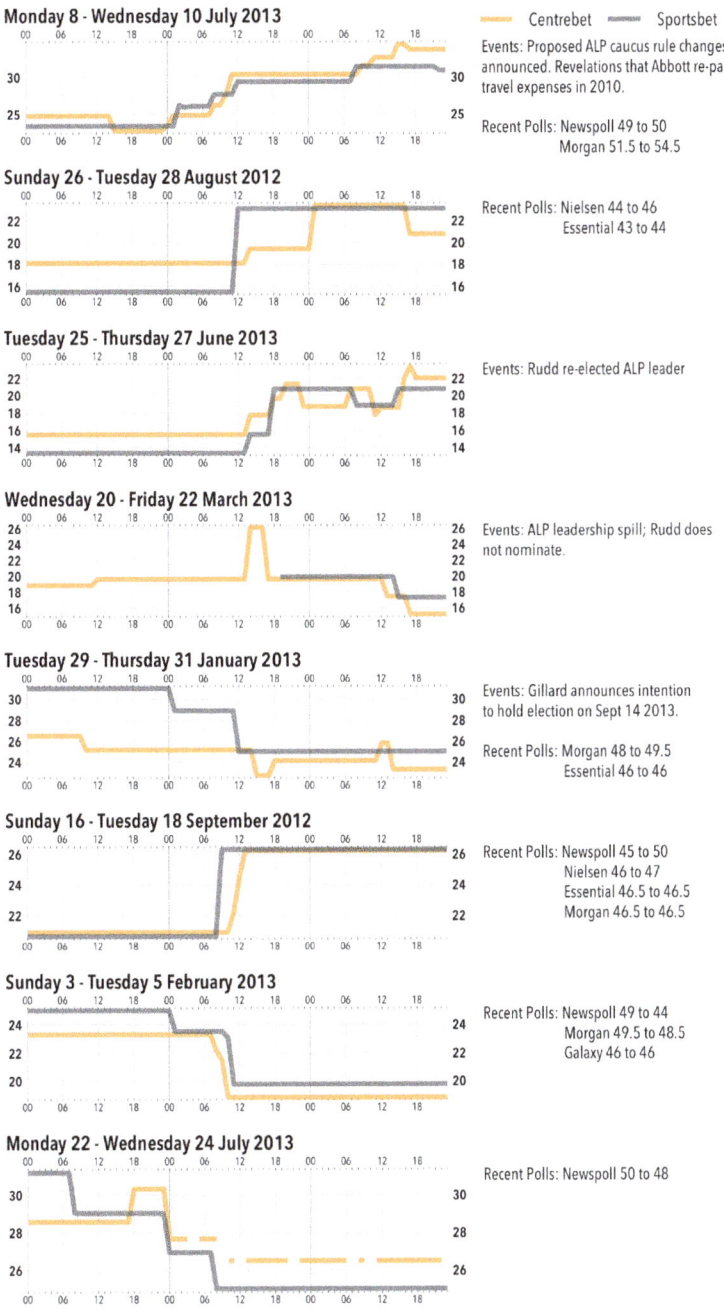

Figure 2: Eight largest daily movements in the political betting markets. Breaks correspond to periods of missing data.

Note: Each panel shows a 72-hour history of ALP IPW at *Centrebet* and *Sportsbet*, bracketing a 24-hour period of large movement. Text to the right of each panel lists recent poll movements or political events.

Source: Author's research.

Political events might have had something to do with this large movement. The biggest political news of Monday 8 July was the announcement of proposed changes to Labor's leadership selection procedures (see *PM* 2013). Around the same time, mainstream media reported that Abbott had repaid the Commonwealth in 2010 for 'incorrectly claimed travel expenses'; Abbott's handling of questions about the revelations on Tuesday 9 July became part of the story (Jabour 2013; Black 2013; Wilson 2013).[8] Newspoll was not the only big political story on 9 July, but it largely trumped the travel expenses revelations and the ALP's proposed rule changes, leading most reports of the 'day in politics' (see *Lateline* 2013).

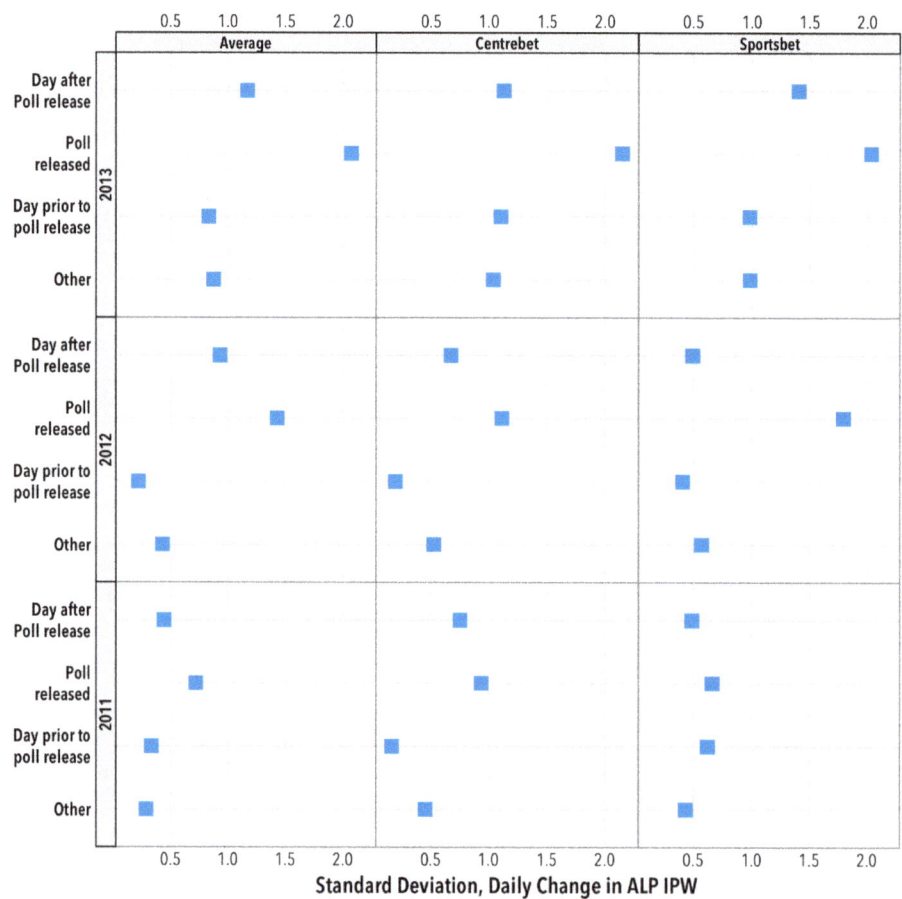

Figure 3: Standard deviation of daily change in ALP IPW, by betting agency, year and type of day

Source: Author's research.

---

8 The 'citizen-journalism' website *No Fibs* broke the news on 6 July; see Kingston 2013.

Political events are clearly responsible for some of the large day-on-day changes in the betting markets: Rudd's return on 26 June 2013 (third panel of Figure 2), the ALP leadership spill on 21 March 2013, in which Rudd did not nominate (fourth panel) and Gillard's 30 January 2013 announcement of her intention to hold the election on 14 September (fifth panel). The volatility in the betting market—and improvement in Labor's odds—induced by Rudd's return on 26 June continued into the next day. But polls clearly appear to be driving large market movements too, and in the anticipated directions. In addition to the substantial market movements around 9 July 2013 (first panel), seemingly due to a favourable Newspoll for Labor, poll movements appear to be the cause of the other large market changes shown in Figure 2. In each case, the polls led, or were especially prominent, in the day's political news.[9] For this particular set of large day-on-day changes in the betting markets, poll movements appear to be at least as large a driver of market movements as political events.

Analysis of the complete data further suggests that betting markets are largely reacting to the polls. In Figure 3, I graph the standard deviation of the daily change in Labor's IPW by four types of day (the day after a poll release, the day of a poll release, the day before a poll release and all other days, looking at poll releases by Newspoll, Nielsen and Galaxy), subsetting the data by betting agency and year.[10] There is more volatility in the betting markets on the day a poll is released—and even on the following day—than on other days. In 2013, poll releases saw movements in ALP IPW with a standard deviation of just over 2 percentage points, more than twice the volatility on days prior to a poll release or on 'other' days. Volatility in the betting markets following a poll release is more pronounced in the election year than in 2012 or 2011. The differences in betting market volatility by the four 'day types' displayed in the nine panels in Figure 3 are overwhelmingly statistically significant[11] with the sole exception of the 2011 *Sportsbet* volatilities in the lower right panel ($p = 0.22$).

Regression analysis further supports these findings. I fit a model similar to that fit by Leigh and Wolfers (2006: Table 3), regressing the daily 9 pm ALP IPW on its lagged value, plus a term capturing change in the polls—on the day of a poll release, this variable is equal to the change in the poll relative to the last poll released by that survey house and equals zero on all other days.

---

9   On Monday, 27 August 2012 (Panel 2 of Figure 2), the Nielsen poll was the second story on the ABC's *AM* (2012a) radio program. On Monday, 17 September 2012 (Panel 6), see *AM*'s (2012b and 2012c) two lead stories on 17 September 2012. On Monday, 4 February 2013 (Panel 7), *AM* (2013a) led with 'Parliamentary year kicks off with Cabinet reshuffle and poor polls for Labor'. The arrival of a royal baby and asylum seeker policy pushed a polling story ('Polling boost for Rudd on boats, but dips on PM preference') to fourth slot on *AM* on Tuesday, 23 July 2013 (bottom panel of Figure 2; see *AM* 2013b).
10 If, for instance, Nielsen released a poll the day after a Newspoll was released, then both days are classified as a 'poll release' day.
11 The greatest p value is .02, from Fligner-Killeen tests of the null hypothesis that the variances of daily change in ALP IPW are constant across the four 'day types'; this non-parametric test is described in Conover, Johnson and Johnson (1981).

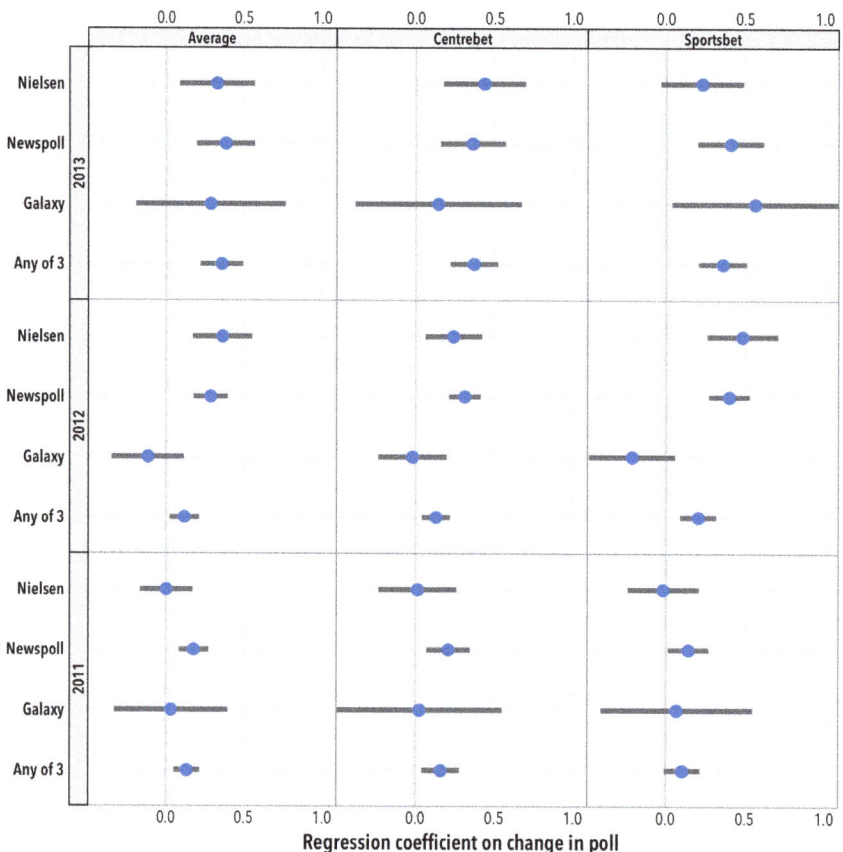

Figure 4: Regression coefficients on change in poll and 95 per cent confidence intervals, regression of daily ALP IPW on lagged ALP IPW (measured at 9 pm Sydney time) and change in a given poll's estimate of ALP TPP, by betting agency, year and polling house

Source: Author's research.

In Figure 4, I plot the estimated coefficients of the 'poll change' variable along with 95 per cent confidence intervals, with the analysis restricted to examining the effects of changes in Newspoll, Nielsen and Galaxy (or any of the three) on *Centrebet*, *Sportsbet* and their average, in each of 2011, 2012 and 2013, producing a total of 36 regressions. The vast majority of the coefficients in Figure 4 are positive and distinguishable from zero at conventional levels of statistical significance. The responsiveness of the betting markets to the polls tends to be larger in 2013 than in earlier years. Across the nine panels in Figure 4, the Newspoll coefficient is always positive, around 0.35 to 0.40; that is, a 1 per cent improvement in Newspoll's estimate of ALP TPP is associated with a 'same day' 0.35 to 0.40 percentage point boost in ALP IPW. Coefficients with broadly similar magnitudes are obtained for Nielsen polls in 2013 and 2012. Galaxy produces fewer polls than Newspoll or Nielsen, and so the responsiveness of the betting market to this pollster is estimated with far less precision. Nonetheless it seems that a statistically significant shift in any of these polls, say, a three-point change in ALP TPP, would shock ALP IPW by about one to 1.2 percentage points.

These 'near-instantaneous' effects do not seem especially large, but keep in mind that: (a) most of the variation in ALP IPW is in a 15-point band (15 per cent to 30 per cent) in the 2011–13 period (see Figure 1); (b) ALP IPW is either a random walk or close to it (the coefficient on lagged ALP IPW is indistinguishable from one), implying that the betting markets' responses to the polls (or anything else, for that matter) are permanent; and (c) the simple regression analysis here assumes all poll changes in ALP TPP have constant effects on the betting markets irrespective of the level of ALP TPP (the effect of ALP TPP going from 43 to 44 is constrained to be the same as the effect of a change from 49 to 50) or proximity to the election. Indeed, close to the election, a series of relatively stable yet lop-sided poll results ought to produce a trend in the betting markets, which is precisely what we observe in August and September of 2013 (see Figure 1).

Betting markets and poll averages

Participants in betting markets can do better than rely on changes in a single poll. Different polls might be given different weight by different people, implying that the market is responding to an average of the polls. The markets might even be responding directly to poll averages of the sort produced by William Bowe or myself.

To investigate this possibility, I utilise the poll average I developed while writing for *Guardian Australia* ahead of the 2013 election. My model-based poll average estimates daily levels of ALP TPP, relying not just on Newspoll, Nielsen and Galaxy (as in the analysis above), but also incorporating national polls by Essential, Morgan, AMR, ReachTEL and Lonergan. In forming the daily poll average I treat the operative 'date' of the poll as its 'release' or 'publication' date (rather than the field dates of the poll), so as to better assess the timing of any betting market reactions to the poll. In this way the daily poll average reflects polling information released up through (and including) that particular day. Technical details appear in earlier work (Jackman 2005, 2009 and 2013a), including a discussion of how the model generates TPP estimates on days without poll releases and corrects for 'house effects' (biases specific to each polling house).

Table 1: Regression analysis of average of *Centrebet*'s and *Sportsbet*'s ALP IPW, measured daily (9 pm, Sydney time), 14 January 2013 to election day (7 September 2013)

	M1	M2	M3	M4	M5	M6	M7
Intercept	0.035	-0.034	-0.003	-0.281	0.070	-0.232	-0.197
	(0.225)	(0.210)	(0.206)	(0.438)	(0.200)	(0.419)	(0.419)
y_{t-1}	0.992	0.995	0.993	1.00	0.989	0.997	0.996
	(0.012)	(0.011)	(0.011)	(0.015)	(0.010)	(0.014)	(0.014)
Δ Polls$_t$			0.840	1.60	0.825	1.74	1.80
			(0.237)	(0.475)	(0.227)	(0.454)	(0.456)
50 - Polls$_{t-1}$				0.032		0.035	0.032
				(0.045)		(0.043)	(0.043)
Δ Polls$_t$ ×				-0.214		-0.259	-0.262
(50 - Polls$_{t-1}$)				(0.112)		(0.108)	(0.108)
Δ Polls$_{t-1}$					0.845	0.910	1.43
					(0.228)	(0.227)	(0.455)
Δ Polls$_{t-1}$ ×							-0.142
(50 - Polls$_{t-2}$)							(0.108)
June 26, 2013		6.73	6.72	6.68	6.62	6.57	6.61
		(1.12)	(1.10)	(1.09)	(1.05)	(1.04)	(1.04)
r²	0.968	0.972	0.973	0.974	0.976	0.976	0.977
$\hat{\sigma}$	1.20	1.12	1.09	1.09	1.05	1.04	1.04
AIC	87.7	55.8	46.0	45.8	27.4	24.8	25.0
BIC	94.7	66.2	59.9	66.6	44.7	49.1	52.7

Cell entries are least squares regression coefficients; standard errors in parentheses. $T = 237$. The regressor 'Polls' is the model-based poll average discussed in the text; 'June 26, 2013' is a dummy variable for that day (Rudd's return as prime minister).

Note: Cell entries are least squares regression coefficients; standard errors in parentheses. $T = 237$. The regressor 'Polls' is the model-based poll average discussed in the text; 'June 26, 2013' is a dummy variable for that day (Rudd's return as prime minister).

Source: Author's research.

Regression analysis reported in Table 1 confirms that betting markets are quite responsive to an average of the polls, at least in 2013. The dependent variable in this analysis is the average of the *Centrebet* and *Sportsbet* ALP IPW, measured at 9 pm Sydney time each day, from 14 January 2013 until the election. The resulting series displays the random walk property observed in the analyses reported above, with the coefficient on the lagged dependent variable indistinguishable from one in all the models reported in Table 1. The large jump in ALP IPW associated with Rudd's return as prime minister on 26 June is captured with a dummy variable in models M2 through M7. Daily changes in the poll average generate betting market movements. Model M3 finds the effect of a 1 percentage point movement in ALP TPP produces a 'same day' change of about 0.84 points in ALP IPW, an effect roughly twice as large as the coefficients shown in Figure 4.

But this is only half the story. In model M4, change in the poll average is interacted with the lagged level of the poll average, differenced from 50 per cent ALP TPP. When Labor polls at levels suggesting a close election (say, 50 per cent TPP), a 1 percentage point change in the poll average has a large 'same day' effect, shifting ALP IPW by about 1.6 points. When Labor is polling poorly, say, at 44 per cent TPP, the betting markets pay little heed to a 1 percentage point movement: model M4 estimates the 'same day' effect in this case to be $1.60 - 0.214 \times 6 = 0.316$. This is entirely sensible. Movement in the poll average close to 50 per cent TPP ought to shape beliefs as to whether Labor will win the election more than the same movement at uncompetitive levels of TPP.

Models M5 through M7 indicate that the effects of changes in the polls on the betting markets are not instantaneous, but are absorbed over at least a two-day window, consistent with the considerable volatility in the betting markets on the day after polls are released presented in Figure 3. Model M6 repeats the interactive specification of M4, including the lagged change in the poll average, with model M7 interacting the lagged change with the second lag of the level of the poll average.[12] Again, we see larger poll effects on ALP IPW when Labor is polling close to 50 per cent TPP. Using the estimates from model M7, a one-day, one-point rise/fall in the poll average starting from 50 per cent TPP would see ALP IPW rise/fall by 1.80 points today, and a further 1.43 points tomorrow, for a total, two-day, short-run effect of 3.23 points ($t = 4.74$). Note again that the random walk nature of the ALP IPW series means that these estimated effects are permanent. These short-run effects are much smaller when Labor is polling at uncompetitive levels; using the estimates from model M7, the same one-point change in the poll average—but starting from a baseline of 44 per cent ALP

---

12 The AIC model selection criterion points to M6 or M7 as the preferred models, although the BIC criterion—placing a higher premium on parsimony—suggests M5 (no interactions) as the preferred model.

TPP—is estimated to produce a 1.80 - 0.262 × 6 = 0.228 point movement in ALP IPW today, and a further 1.43 - 0.142 × 6 = 0.578 point movement tomorrow; neither of these short-run changes are distinguishable from zero at conventional levels of statistical significance ($t = 0.67$ and 1.68, respectively), although the total short-run, two-day effect of 0.806 points on ALP IPW has $t = 1.79$.

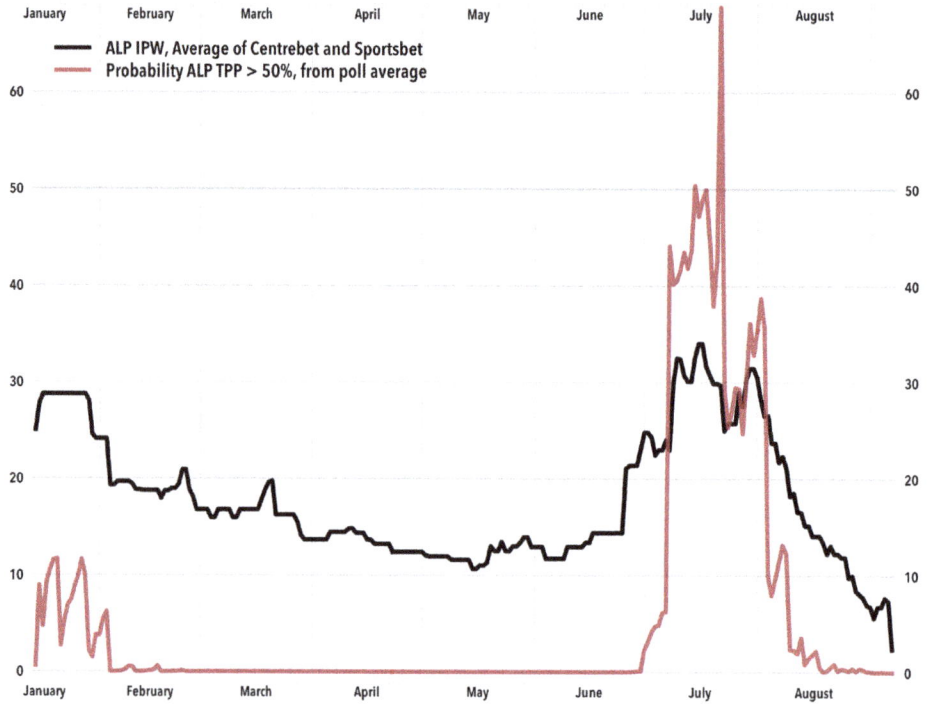

Figure 5: Daily time series, ALP IPW (average of *Centrebet* and *Sportsbet*, 9 pm Sydney time) and probability that ALP TPP exceeds 50 per cent based on poll average, 14 January 2013 to 7 September 2013

Source: Author's research.

Finally, in Figure 5, I compare two implied probabilities of Labor victory over 2013: the black line displays ALP IPW from an average of *Centrebet* and *Sportsbet*; the red line is the estimated probability that ALP TPP lies above 50 per cent, given the poll average used above (and uncertainty around the poll average on a given day).[13] The markets always saw the Coalition as firm favourites. But with the exception of one or two days in July 2013, averaging the polls also generated the same conclusion, but with much greater confidence.

---

13 The 50 per cent TPP threshold probably results in an over-estimate of Labor's chances of winning; Labor probably needed a little more than 50 per cent TPP nationally to be able to form government.

By late July the polls were again confidently indicating a Coalition win. The poll average IPW fell below 10 per cent in early August, some two to three weeks before the betting markets reached the same level of confidence. The polls appear to lead the betting markets in the 'race to the bottom' on the right-hand side of Figure 5. By 10 August, the poll average IPW had fallen back to virtually zero, where it had been for most of 2013. *Sportsbet* conceded as much on 29 August, paying out its wagers on the Coalition.

Conclusion

Poll movements shape the betting markets, especially as the election draws close, and especially when the polls suggest the election might be closer than previously thought. Newspoll and Nielsen seem especially important 'market movers', probably due to their long-standing brand power and their association with newspapers in multiple media markets. Betting markets react quickly to changes in the polls, but not instantaneously. Poll movements take at least 48 hours to be digested by the betting markets, suggesting that secondary media reports of the polls are important (e.g. evening TV news reports of poll results from that morning's newspapers).

Polls and betting markets ask distinct questions: asking someone *who they would vote for 'if an election were to be held this weekend'* is not the same as asking *who they think will win the next election*. As the election draws closer, the hypothetical nature of the vote intention survey response fades. The betting markets pay more attention to the polls, particularly if the polls indicate the election is close. In a lop-sided election like 2013, we can expect that betting markets will react to little or no change in the polls, 'catching up' with the polls in the final week of the campaign. That is, we should not be surprised to see political betting markets reacting to polls. Rather, we should expect a somewhat subtle interplay between the two, as shown in the analyses I have presented here.

References

AM. 2012a. 'Nielsen poll encouraging for Govt, but Oppn well ahead'. Radio program transcript, ABC, Sydney, 27 August, viewed 28 January 2014: <www.abc.net.au/am/content/2012/s3576302.htm>.

AM. 2012b. 'New polls give lift to ALP and Prime Minister'. Radio program transcript, ABC, Sydney, 17 September, viewed 28 January 2014: <www.abc.net.au/am/content/2012/s3591213.htm>.

AM. 2012c. 'Opinion polls confirm lift for Labor and PM'. Radio program transcript, ABC, Sydney, 17 September, viewed 28 January 2014: <www.abc.net.au/am/content/2012/s3591293.htm>.

AM. 2013a. 'Parliamentary year kicks off with Cabinet reshuffle and poor polls for Labor'. Radio program transcript, ABC, Sydney, 4 February, viewed 28 January 2014: <www.abc.net.au/am/content/2013/s3682200.htm>.

AM. 2013b. 'Polling boost for Rudd on boats, but dips on PM preference'. Radio program transcript, ABC, Sydney, 23 July, viewed 28 January 2014: <www.abc.net.au/am/content/2013/s3808721.htm>.

Black, Simon. 2013. 'Opposition leader Tony Abbott sparks storm on Twitter after telling Bridie Jabour to "calm down"'. *Daily Telegraph*, 9 July, viewed 28 January 2014: <www.dailytelegraph.com.au/news/nsw/opposition-leader-tony-abbott-sparks-storm-on-twitter-after-telling-bridie-jabour-to-calm-down/story-fni0cx12-1226676460305>.

Conover, William J, Johnson, Mark E and Johnson, Myrle M. 1981. 'A comparative study of tests for homogeneity of variances, with applications to the outer continental shelf bidding data'. *Technometrics* 23: 351–61.

Jabour, Bridie. 2013. 'Tony Abbott denies wrongly claiming expenses from 2009 book tour'. *Guardian Australia*, 8 July, viewed 28 January 2014: <www.theguardian.com/world/2013/jul/08/tony-abbott-book-tour-expenses>.

Jackman, Simon. 2005. 'Pooling the Polls Over an Election Campaign'. *Australian Journal of Political Science* 40(4): 499–517.

Jackman, Simon. 2009. *Bayesian Analysis for the Social Sciences*. New York: Wiley.

Jackman, Simon. 2013a. 'Election 2013: betting markets suggest Labor will win just 50 seats'. *Guardian Australia*, 6 September, viewed 28 January 2014: <www.theguardian.com/world/the-swing/2013/sep/06/election-2013-betting-markets-suggest-labor-will-win-just-50-seats>.

Jackman, Simon. 2013b. 'Election 2013: average the averages and it looks like 1996'. *Guardian Australia,* 4 September, viewed 28 January 2014: <www.theguardian.com/world/the-swing/2013/sep/04/election-2013-polling-like-1996>.

Kingston, Margo. 2013. 'EXCLUSIVE: Abbott forced to repay $9,400 he charged taxpayers to promote his book'. *No Fibs* [blog], 6 July, viewed 24 February 2014: <nofibs.com.au/2013/07/06/exclusive-abbott-forced-to-repay-taxpayers-9400-he-charged-taxpayers-to-promote-his-book/>.

Lateline. 2013. 'Rudd's popularity soars'. Television program transcript, ABC, Sydney, 9 July, viewed 28 January 2014: <www.abc.net.au/lateline/content/2013/s3799592.htm>.

Leigh, Andrew and Wolfers, Justin. 2006. 'Competing Approaches to Forecasting Elections: Economic Models, Opinion Polling and Prediction Markets'. *Economic Record* 82(258): 325–40.

Maher, Sid. 2013. 'Election race still tight, Tony Abbott insists, despite *Sportsbet* payout'. *Australian*, 29 August, viewed 28 January 2014: <www.theaustralian.com.au/national-affairs/election-2013/election-race-still-tight-tony-abbott-insists/story-fn9qr68y-1226706624356#>.

PM. 2013. 'Rudd proposing radical changes to ALP rules'. Radio program transcript, ABC, Sydney, 8 July, viewed 28 January 2014: <www.abc.net.au/pm/content/2013/s3798547.htm>.

Rhode, Paul W and Strumpf, Koleman. 2013. 'The Long History of Political Betting Markets: An International Perspective'. In Leighton Vaughan Williams and Donald S Siegel (eds), *The Oxford Handbook of the Economics of Gambling*, New York: Oxford University Press.

Wilson, Lauren. 2013. 'Abbott takes swipe at PM over expenses "dirt"'. *The Australian*, 10 July, viewed 28 January 2014: <www.theaustralian.com.au/national-affairs/abbott-takes-swipe-at-pm-over-expenses-dirt/story-fn59niix-1226676740115#>.

Wolfers, Justin and Leigh, Andrew. 2002. 'Three Tools for Forecasting Federal Elections: Lessons from 2001'. *Australian Journal of Political Science* 37(2): 223–40.

Wolfers, Justin and Zitzewitz, Eric. 2004. 'Prediction Markets'. *Journal of Economic Perspectives* 18(2): 107–26.

Wolfers, Justin and Zitzewitz, Eric. 2006. 'Interpreting prediction market prices as probabilities'. NBER Working Paper No. 12200, National Bureau of Economic Research, May, viewed 28 January 2014: <www.nber.org/papers/w12200>.

10. Nearly All About Kevin: The election as drawn by Australian cartoonists

Haydon Manning and Robert Phiddian

In her account of the Danish cartoon furore of 2005, Klausen (2009: 6) notes that 'political cartoons tell a story or make a comment on current events', and 'use exaggerated physiognomic features to make a statement about the fundamental nature of a person or thing'. On the subject of 'person', it is our contention that the cartoons of the 2013 election broadly mirrored the wider campaign, particularly in focusing on the nature and antics of Prime Minister Rudd and less on those of his challenger, Tony Abbott.

To all dispassionate spectators, 2013 was an election where a change of government was all but guaranteed, but the newly reminted PM clearly believed that a miracle resurrection of Labor's fortunes was possible. As Peter Hartcher (2013), a regular media confidant of Rudd, wrote after the election: 'He did not insist that he would challenge only if election victory were guaranteed; he told his most senior supporters that he was prepared to run if Labor had a 30 per cent chance of winning the election'. Whether or not this was a realistic possibility, the cartoonists (in their role as instant graphic historians in the wide range of capital city and regional newspapers surveyed for this chapter) duly told the story that Rudd tried and failed to make the running while Abbott mostly succeeded in playing the disciplined small target. So in relation to the lower house contest the cartoonists generally told an accurate if unsurprising story centred on personalities.

However, the Senate contest was far more open and unpredictable than that of the House of Representatives. A plethora of minor and micro parties, all keen to 'harvest' preferences, saw Senate ballot papers expanding to the size of a small tablecloth. Most voters were quite happy to sign away control of the flows of preferences by voting 'above the line', even though the consequences will be with us for six years.

Hence, a more perceptive comment on the election is David Pope's prescient cartoon on the eventual make-up of the Senate that anticipated the most remarkable 'thing' to emerge from the election. It also represents one of the earliest calls for reform of how the Senate vote is orchestrated and counted (see Green's chapter). The child's comment to his bemused father about remembering 'the inflatable Fielding' is particularly poignant as it reminds us that in the 2004

Senate election in Victoria, Family First Party candidate Stephen Fielding, with the benefit of ALP preference support, was elected on a primary vote of merely 1.8 per cent. However, compared to Ricky Muir's 2013 success in Victoria from 0.51 per cent on the initial count, Fielding's vote begins to look like a solid sort of mandate!

Figure 1

Source: David Pope, *The Canberra Times*, 20 August 2013.

Cartoons considered for this study appeared in the online websites of the major capital city daily newspapers and also *The Australian* and the *Australian Financial Review*. The focus was on editorial page cartoons and front page 'pocket cartoons'. Over the six weeks of the campaign 383 cartoons were filed for showing to an audience of colleagues and students. Assessing audience response and subsequent conversation regarding the insight and comic impact of the collection informed our selection, but equally the task of chronicling the key machinations of campaign 2013 influenced our selection.

The 'licence to mock'

Colin Seymour-Ure (2001) explains that the cartoonists' use of caricature and pithy comment is essentially about making two types of observations regarding those who govern—or seek to govern—us. The first is an essential definition or interpretation, as in: 'this is what the prime minister is really like'. The second and stronger type in terms of the cartoonists' armoury is a bolt of criticism, such as: 'he is a fool'. The two-part process is neatly illustrated by Jon Kudelka's take on Rudd's growing obsession with 'selfie' photos:

Figure 2

Source: Jon Kudelka, *The Australian*, 31 August 2013.

The 'selfie' on the nightly news became almost as closely associated with Rudd as the cigar was with Churchill, so many commentators and voters came to conclude he had a strong streak of narcissism. The 'mirror, mirror on the wall' reference to the vain queen in Snow White precisely reflects this view, absurdly confirmed by an earlier act of unusual publicity from the PM. In early July, Rudd posted an Instagram photo of himself having cut his face while shaving—this quickly 'went viral'. While many thought this pursuit of celebrity culture unbecoming in a national leader and others point to it engaging with younger voters (Leys 2013), there is no question that it was a gift to cartoonists and other satirists.

The cartoon is thus 'an editorial in pictures' (Seymour-Ure 2001: 335), meaning the better cartoonists earn 'a wary kind of respect' (Seymour-Ure 2003: 230). They employ the satirist's arsenal of ridicule, parody, metaphor and archetype, as outlined by scholars such as Gombrich (1978), Press (1981), Seymour-Ure (1997; 2001; 2003), Condren (2012) and Phiddian (2013). As Elizabeth El Refaie (2008: 184–5) explains, the:

political cartoon constitutes a very specific genre, with its own history, distinctive styles, conventions and communicative purposes [and while] not always humorous, they do generally contain an element of irony or at least something incongruous or surprising.

Consequently, Australian art critic and curator Joan Kerr points out that political cartoons derive not from the 'maleness, whiteness or gloominess' of the cartoonist but rather from their capacity to 'show us as we are, warts and all—indeed, warts above all—in ways that we all understand and appreciate' (Kerr 1999: 78). Importantly, they are assured a daily audience—which now includes the ease of online access and forwarding on to friends—numbering in the hundreds of thousands. Though newspapers may have a troubled business model in the world of new media, cartoons and their descendants in visual satire are enjoying a healthy period of development.

It is clear from surveying the cartoonists' view at each election since 1996, that they take the 'citizens' perspective' on the policy sales campaign and leaders' efforts to scare voters into jumping at policy shadows. A common theme found in election cartoons is impatience at the debasement of national political life by the political classes at a time that should be a celebration of democracy. The following cartoons by Cathy Wilcox, John Spooner and Pat Campbell express the cartoonists' and the voters' varying levels of anger and contempt.

Figure 3

Source: Cathy Wilcox, *The Sydney Morning Herald*, 1 September 2013.

10. Nearly All About Kevin

Figure 4

Source: John Spooner, *The Age*, 29 August 2013.

Figure 5

Source: Pat Campbell, *The Canberra Times*, 26 August 2013.

With their mixture of vivid images and succinct words, political cartoons provide graphic islands in a sea—or perhaps we should say 'swamp'—of election campaign analysis. The point is, 'cartoonists draw on timely topics that have already been established in the mainstream media', and while they 'speak of the world in hyper-figurative terms, political cartoons are but one mode of opinion news discourse that enables the public to actively classify, organise and interpret what they see and experience in meaningful ways' (Greenberg 2002: 195).

It was noted at the beginning of this chapter that cartoonists tend to highlight issues of personality. Our main observation about the cartoonists' perspective on the 2013 campaign is that they viewed it as 'nearly all about Kevin'. The majority of cartoons focused on Rudd's campaign whereas Abbott escaped the satirists' close scrutiny. Perhaps Abbott's relentless work of demolishing Labor's credibility, abetted hugely by Labor's internal dysfunction, had blunted the cartoonists who, like the majority of voters, were transfixed by Labor's bitter internal divisions rather than the opposition's credentials. For those who hoped there would at least be some sort of contest, the realistic question was whether Rudd might campaign as he did in 2007 and 'save some of the furniture' or whether Labor was headed for a thrashing like those recently experienced by its New South Wales and Queensland branches. We begin by looking at the leaders' campaigns, starting with Abbott to test the proposition that little mud stuck to him. We then turn to what the cartoonists observed about some key issues, the minor parties, the Murdoch press and finally the result. Here too, the focus on personality remained a key theme, with Rupert Murdoch, Bob Katter and Clive Palmer being obvious additional targets for the cartoonists' tools of caricature and pithy comment.

Abbott's script: 'Sex appeal', sexism and softening the caricature

Labor had long sought to demonise Tony Abbott with some apparent success, as his 'net satisfaction rating' measured in Newspoll travelled deeply in the negative zone throughout his time as opposition leader; in fact worse than for most opposition leaders. However, as is usually the case, it improved once the campaign started (Brent 2013). Given the electorate's hostility to the ALP government, the main thing Abbott needed to do was avoid gaffes that might expose him to Labor's attack upon his Catholic conservatism and supposedly old fashioned and 'sexist' views of women. The cartoons (being sensitive gaffe-detectors) show that he largely succeeded in this by making only a few mistakes that, crucially, didn't 'stick' as major impressions on public consciousness. For instance, Alan Moir's cartoon points to Abbott having surprised commentators, and arguably his own colleagues, by his disciplined approach and dogged capacity to stay 'on message'.

Figure 6

Source: Alan Moir, *The Sydney Morning Herald*, 12 August 2013.

As Pamela Williams observes, his campaign rested on the fact that he 'was disciplined, focused and operating comfortably in a framework where everyone had their eye on the same goal working from a unified script' (Williams 2013). The cartoon also alludes to a moment in the 2010 campaign when Julia Gillard announced that she would become the 'real Julia' rather than an overly stage-managed leader. Cartoonists are quick to pick any lack of authenticity, and with leaders so much in the hands of campaign professionals and their daily messaging, Moir is also suggesting, almost sympathetically, how frustrating it must be to be so scripted. Long-time readers of Moir's cartoons (and much of the Fairfax press) will realise, however, that the tiny bit of sympathy is much outweighed by fear that the real Tony will come out after the election as an authoritarian muscle-man.

Early in the campaign's second week Abbott went off-script with a couple of gaffes, neither particularly serious, which featured across old and new media for a couple of days and offered Labor hope that more would follow. The first saw him misconstrue the English language while the other provoked debate over whether he was steeped in sexist views of women. Addressing the party faithful at the Liberals' campaign launch in the seat of Deakin, he took aim at Rudd's one-man-band approach to governing. Unfortunately a slip of the tongue, or perhaps a leap of logic, had him say, 'No-one, however smart, however well-educated, however experienced, is the suppository of all wisdom, and I believe that we will be a much better government because we have a very strong team'. Of course he meant to say 'repository' and for his trouble within half an hour someone inaugurated a Twitter hashtag *#suppository* accompanied by photoshopped images with suppository-inspired captions ('know your enema', 'squeezing out a policy', etc). It trended quickly as a tweet and featured in the nightly news bulletins. The phrase featured in a number of cartoons and in other comic modes but it did no lasting damage, partly because it was merely an isolated slip of the tongue (so people could identify with Abbott) and perhaps also because it worked as a joke that confirmed a low public assessment of the wisdom of politicians.

Later in the day, while campaigning in the Western Sydney seat of Lindsay, Abbott made a potentially more dangerous slip. A journalist asked him how Liberal candidate Fiona Scott compared with former Liberal MP Jackie Kelly, an innocuous question which solicited this response: 'They're young, feisty, I think I can probably say have a bit of sex appeal and they're just very connected with the local area'. In the charged atmosphere since Julia Gillard's 'misogyny' speech of October 2012, this clearly risked fuelling the view that Abbott was sexist. Cartoonists and politicians waded in.

Figure 7

Source: Ron Tandberg, *The Age*, 14 August 2013.

Figure 8

Source: Sean Leahy, *Courier-Mail*, 14 August 2013.

Rudd described the comment as 'odd', while Labor frontbencher Kim Carr seized upon it saying, 'He's pathetic, he really is pathetic … Sometimes we should think Tony Abbott really hasn't crawled out of the 1950s'. Coalition women like New South Wales minister Pru Goward, a former sex discrimination commissioner, leapt to his defence. His own daughter, who was standing behind him at the time and was heard to gasp, later described her father's statement as a 'daggy dad moment'. Savaging Abbott as 'superficial and sexist', Greens leader Christine Milne asked, 'Why didn't he talk about professionalism or policy or intellect?' (Ireland and Swan 2013).

Abbott's 'sex appeal' gaffe highlighted the only real question mark over the Coalition's campaign, namely Abbott's 'problem with women'. Certainly the problem didn't derail his campaign—as his opponent had just defeated the nation's first female prime minister in a bloody party-room ballot, there was a limit on how far the argument could be pressed—but the Coalition campaign made clear and obvious moves to neutralise the risk. Whether it was planned months before the campaign we do not know, but the Liberals' campaign launch was very much directed at debunking the view that there was ever a problem. Two of Abbott's daughters, Frances and Bridget, introduced him to the party faithful, and their tightly scripted words sought to dispel any notion that their father was sexist, let alone a misogynist. The imagery was analogous to

Obama's campaign style (Joye 2013) as it celebrated these alpha women's efforts to convince voters, who may have harboured doubts about their father's values, to reconsider.

Figure 9: Tony Abbott with wife Margaret and daughters Bridget and Frances at the Coalition's campaign launch in Brisbane

Source: *Herald Sun*. Picture: Jay Town.

TV bulletins and front pages led with his daughters, driving home the message Liberal HQ desired with phrases like these from his daughters' script: 'I've seen my Dad with people from all walks of life—young, old, rich, poor, gay, straight, the frail, the fit, indigenous and migrant, and he treats every single one of them with equal respect'; and, 'My dad looks out for everyone and I know he will look out for you'. Toward the end of the campaign Abbott appeared on the Nine Network's show *Big Brother*, where, sitting alongside his daughters, he urged contestants to vote for him because he was the one with the 'not bad looking daughters'. David Rowe presents the Liberal campaign's use of the daughters as an insult to voter intelligence in this memorably grotesque image.

It seems likely that this issue was never going to change many minds. Those who thought Abbott sexist were already opposed to him and in the 'old Australia' where much of the 'rusted-on' Liberal vote resides, such attitudes were seen as fairly reasonable. The following cartoon from Mark Knight may imply this, but it may also suggest that Abbott would be uncomfortable with a gender role reversal in which he was sexually objectified, with an older unappealing geriatric commenting on the sex appeal of the younger man.

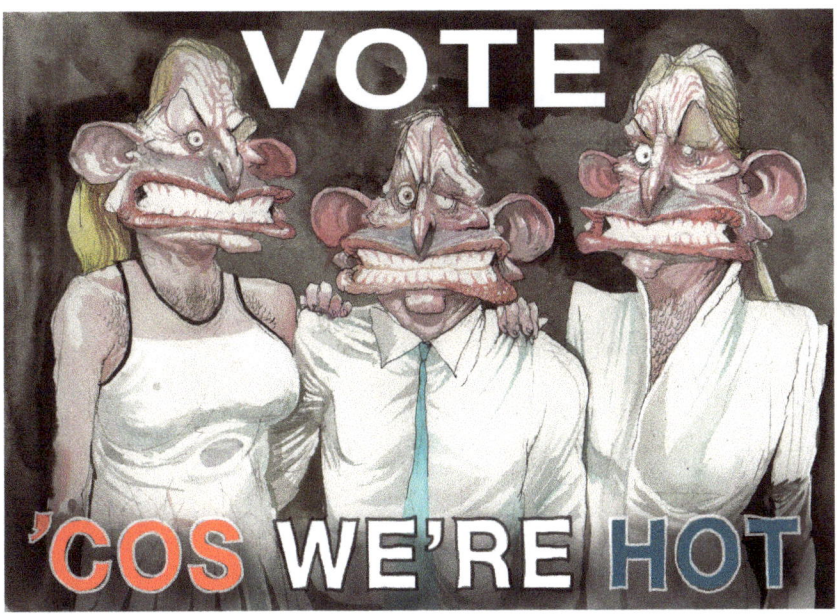

Figure 10

Source: David Rowe, *Australian Financial Review*, 5 September 2013.

Figure 11

Source: Mark Knight, *Herald Sun*, 15 August 2013.

As Knight's further cartoon on Abbott's personally championed paid parental leave scheme suggests, several constituencies were prepared to avert their gaze from problems in his profile simply in order to get rid of the other mob:

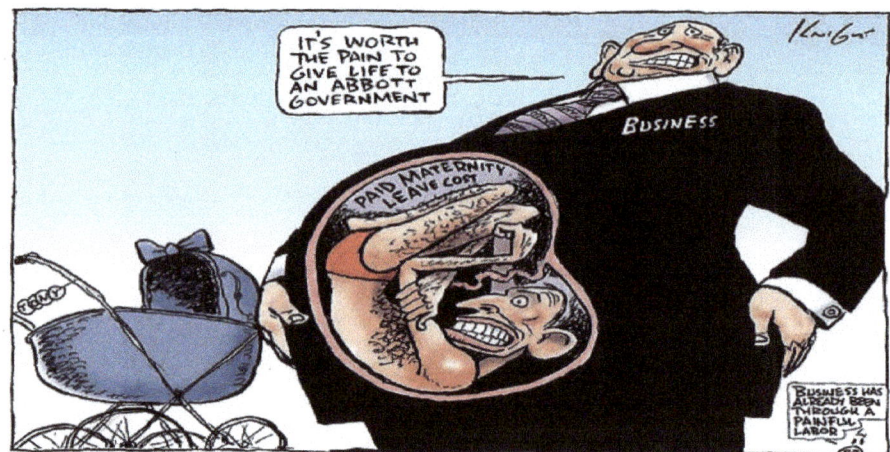

Figure 12

Source: Mark Knight, *Herald Sun*, 19 August 2013.

Rudd's chaotic burnout

Labor's principal aim in this campaign was realistically about damage control and how Kevin Rudd, who had campaigned so brilliantly in 2007, could deliver a respectable loss. In the inner group travelling with the restored PM, there was more optimism about a possible victory and this tension between realists and dreamers caused mounting trouble as the campaign wore on. The Gillard government's last months saw Labor's primary vote in the polls sink so low that a generation of future Labor leaders faced defeat, and being reduced to only 30 seats in the next parliament seemed a serious possibility (Wright 2013). Labor began 2013 with some hope, but the rot set in once the aborted leadership challenge unfolded in March. This cartoon captures well the farcical events when former leader Simon Crean backed Rudd to challenge, only to find him unwilling to front. Gillard was tactically devastating and then ruthless in victory to the former ministers represented here decapitated on pikes.

Then, in June, Rudd won the party room ballot and felt redeemed. Shockingly close to an election, the Labor campaign required reinvention and new staff as many Gillard supporters departed. Much would depend on Rudd's capacity to present a focused and disciplined campaign, but he had few policy successes to tout and a millstone of critique from within Labor ranks. With crude headlines in the Murdoch press calling for Labor's demise, Rudd complained of bias, and Bill Leak, who in 2007 characterised Rudd as the youthful and hopeful

Tintin, now presented a far harsher view of the resurrected prime minister as a grotesque and vengeful Narcissus obsessed with his own image or a Dorian Gray keeping his true nature hidden from public view.

Figure 13

Source: Mark Knight, *Herald Sun*, 23 March 2013.

Figure 14

Source: Bill Leak, *The Australian*, 8 August 2013.

Leak was clearly the most critical of the cartoonists, with most of his cartoons aimed at lampooning what he saw as Rudd's dysfunction and propensity to narcissism, but other cartoonists also drew upon these themes. Upon returning to the prime ministership Rudd promised a 'New Way' and 'New Politics' and when that was exposed as hollow he sought to demonise his opponent with images of a government likely to embrace austerity and raise the GST. Leak suggests voters would smell the rat when Rudd did a set piece media stunt with a jar of Vegemite arguing its price would increase under Abbott's secret plan to increase the GST.

Figure 15

Source: Bill Leak, *The Australian*, 12 August 2013.

When Labor turned to former Queensland premier Peter Beattie to run in the Liberal-held marginal seat of Forde, the sense of an ill-considered campaign began to fester. Political recycling rarely gains traction and David Rowe's caricature of Beattie catches him poised between success and failure, either as a cane toad about to derail Abbott's campaign or caught in the headlights of his cruise to victory. Ultimately voters were not impressed and, after an initial flurry of excitement, little was heard from Beattie as his chances sunk.

Why did Rudd's campaign appear so chaotic? Charitable opinion might argue Rudd had little time to prepare a campaign based on his policy priorities, plus he needed to distance himself from the Gillard legacy and the stench of chaos and corruption in state ALP branches, especially New South Wales where Alan Moir focuses this powerful cartoon:

Figure 16

Source: David Rowe, *Australian Financial Review*, 9 August 2013.

Figure 17

Source: Alan Moir, *The Sydney Morning Herald*, 3 September 2013.

Little wonder nothing seemed to work and, by the end of August, Leak depicted an embattled Rudd sinking in a sea of sharks, sending up increasingly desperate thought bubbles.

Figure 18

Source: Bill Leak, *Australian*, 31 August 2013.

Policies were announced without the Melbourne-based campaign office being prepared, let alone the stakeholders involved. Leak's cartoon certainly reflects what leading members of the commentariat wrote post-election (Bramston 2013; Snow 2013; Williams 2013) and is best highlighted by two clear examples of policy by thought bubble: the northern Australia lower tax zone and the proposed movement of naval forces from Sydney Harbour to Queensland.

The headline-grabbing policy of 'Growing the North' with special tax concessions for businesses in the Northern Territory lacked detail and, worse, it was basically the same as a policy Abbott had announced in June that Labor had criticised when Gillard was leader. It quickly fell flat and Mark Knight depicts Rudd strolling into the jaws of a dilemma holding little more than a lamp for guidance:.

Williams (2013) succinctly observes that, 'Proposals such as a changed economic zone for the Northern Territory had no resonance in the general campaign message and instead became the subject of ridicule'. Rayner and Wanna (Chapter 1) point to the Coalition's effort to portray Rudd as unelectable due to his 'manic edge':

> One of the Coalition's cut-through campaign messages of 2013 which tagged Kevin Rudd as 'Captain Chaos' had its genesis in this earlier period, when it seemed as though the energy and enthusiasm of 2007 had acquired a more manic edge.

Figure 19

Source: Mark Knight, *Herald Sun*, 17 August 2013.

Cartoonists picked up on this aspect as illustrated by Warren Brown's pointed critique of the planning behind the proposed transfer of naval forces:

Figure 20

Source: Warren Brown, *Daily Telegraph*, 29 August 2013.

While Rudd's first week of campaigning went well and he performed marginally better than Abbott in the three leaders' debates, there remained throughout a 'curious sense that Rudd was performing as an opposition leader rather than an incumbent PM, complaining about the Coalition and (fruitlessly) demanding that Abbott answer his questions'. Abbott seemed always in control and Rudd forever keen to try and scare voters with what Abbott might do in government. All this played to the 'Captain Chaos' stereotype that Rudd's opponents within the ALP had done so much to propagate, and the cartoonists helped this impression gel in the minds of voters. Rudd's final days on the campaign trail seemed little more than endless crowds of young Labor recruits taking 'selfies' with Kevin. Mark Knight turned this into an election eve cartoon that encapsulates much about the man who caused, over the previous three years, so much electoral damage to his party.

Figure 21

Source: Mark Knight, *Herald Sun*, 6 September 2013.

Jon Kudelka sums up the entire resurrection experiment almost wistfully. Rudd was an Icarus whose wings had melted in the heat of the Labor party room in 2010. Now they were melting again in the heat of the 2013 election. At no point had the promise of 2007 been fulfilled.

Late in the campaign, Labor's gamble in changing leaders yet again was unravelling with little evidence of the 'New Way' Rudd had promised at the campaign's outset. All he had left in the end was the claim that he had done it all to save Labor from a catastrophically deep defeat.

10. Nearly All About Kevin

Figure 22

Source: Jon Kudelka, *The Australian*, 3 September 2013.

Key issues and minor parties

Asylum seekers were an issue in the 2013 campaign but for the cartoonists they presented a much more confusing issue than they had in previous elections, especially the 'Tampa election' of 2001. At that time both leaders, Howard and Beazley, took a tough line but the cartoonists took the moral high ground and produced some searing satire (Manning and Phiddian 2002). Twelve years later the issue had become more complex as deaths at sea mounted and the people smugglers seemed untouchable. Labor's harsh deterrents to 'boat people' mirrored the Coalition's policies and only the Greens remained steadfast with their assertion that such policies were 'cruel' and 'immoral'. The closest we came to a cartoon with the force of 2001 is Wilcox's effort to chastise two devoutly Christian leaders on what she sees as a range of hypocrisies. But even this pales against what we have viewed in the past and the decline in the Greens vote is possibly also an indication that this issue is no longer straightforward for those with a 'bleeding heart'.

Figure 23

Source: Cathy Wilcox, *The Sydney Morning Herald*, 2 September 2013.

The elephant in the election campaign room is often the question of where the money to pay for promises is coming from. This was an even bigger issue than usual because there was so much squabbling and mutual accusations of hypocrisy. Sean Leahy ponders the matter after the final leaders' debate:

Figure 24

Source: Sean Leahy, *Courier-Mail*, 23 August 2013.

As is now customary, it was only in the dying days of the campaign that the opposition released its calculations and by that point the issue was no longer a potential vote changer. Had Labor managed to earn a reputation for fiscal coherence in six years of government this may have played out differently, but voters and cartoonists seem not to have felt there was much between the parties on probity.

From the start of the campaign, the Murdoch press presented a level of hostility toward Labor that surprised some, including Kevin Rudd himself (Williams 2013). This is covered in Errington's chapter so we will not analyse it here; the point is that cartoonists working outside of the News Limited newspapers certainly took the opportunity to comment. Peter Broelman amuses readers with a sense of history when he parodies the 'Mongolian Octopus' image first drawn by cartoonist Phil May for the *Bulletin Magazine* in 1886. May's image was racist and aimed at warning Australians of the 'Asian Peril' with the Octopus's arms carrying slogans such as 'Fan-Tan', 'Opium', 'Small Pox' and 'Cheap Labour'. Broelman's grisly Rupert Murdoch acts as a warning to voters to beware his newspapers' propaganda power, something the social activist organisation *GetUp!* also commented on in a crude but funny sketch/commercial. They sought to pay for wide public exposure on commercial television but found the networks reluctant to accept their money. ABC TV's program *Media Watch* (2013) gave it an airing and YouTube also ensured it received wider circulation.

Figure 25

Source: Peter Broelman, Fairfax Syndication and APN regional press, 15 August 2013.

With so much voter disaffection, the minor parties became a haven for disaffected voters and one big man with a gift for comedy played a particularly big role. Queensland-based billionaire mining magnate and resort owner Clive Palmer blasted himself into Election 2013 with unprecedented campaign spending—possibly as high as $12 million—and big boasts when interviewed on current affairs shows that he would win Fairfax in Queensland and at least two Senate places in Queensland, Tasmania and Victoria as well as at least one New South Wales Senator (Kelly 2013). Palmer was a figure of fun in cartoons and on the commercial television program *Wednesday Night Fever*,[1] but he used this notoriety cleverly to garner free publicity on morning infotainment television programs and even in a sketch he scripted, sending himself up on national television.[2] Clearly, he was underestimated by the political commentators and in this cartoon by Bill Leak, but neither can be particularly blamed for never has an Australian spent so much money or hyperbole in pursuit of elected office.

Figure 26

Source: Bill Leak, *The Australian*, 6 September 2013.

Katter's Australia Party (KAP) was the immediate victim of the Palmer United Party's emergence on the right wing of national politics. Party founder and member for Kennedy, Bob Katter is renowned for wearing a large hat and had been the consummate anti-politician of Australian politics. A large part of the story of the failure of KAP to become a force lies in Palmer's money and talent for

---

1 <www.youtube.com/watch?v=-_j34T5WNiE>.
2 <www.youtube.com/watch?v=chrIvuLS0Mg>.

populism, but a cartoon by Sean Leahy focuses on a sneaky political deal that may have tarnished Katter's image as an honest broker. Katter struck a deal to exchange preferences with Labor in a host of marginal seats in return for Labor's support in the Senate—Labor placed KAP ahead of all other parties. Katter tried to keep the preference decision 'secret' but this ended when an outraged KAP candidate, Paul Hunter, informed local media (Scott 2013). Sean Leahy very early in the campaign gave weight to the rumours that he was talking to Labor.

Figure 27

Source: Sean Leahy, *Courier-Mail*, 13 August 2013.

Katter was returned in Kennedy but his primary vote declined by 17 per cent, arguably in large part due to his efforts to do a 'secret deal' with Labor and because Palmer's candidate kept Katter's out of the Senate.

Victor and vanquished

When Tony Abbott defeated Malcolm Turnbull for the Liberal leadership in December 2009 by a solitary vote few considered him a genuine contender; he was just another prime ministerial hopeful likely to be replaced after Labor secured its second term. Labor MPs and most of the political commentariat believed him simply unelectable; the less charitable dubbed him the 'Mad Monk'. If Kevin Rudd had demonstrated the emotional intelligence required to lead a fairly united cabinet, Abbott's time as leader would likely have been short. To the surprise of many, Abbott managed to unite his party by relentlessly attacking Labor's 'faceless men' as a reflection of the party's dying organisational culture. Discipline became his calling card and he was constantly the recipient of chaotic leadership and policy making from a Labor Party that mistook activity for achievement. His rare feat was to undo three Labor prime ministers due to his relentless focus on their frailties. While at least three cartoonists represented his long march to victory with an image of red budgie smugglers flying over Parliament House, we think Matt Golding's neat depiction of his triumph rewards more careful attention. Abbott had repeatedly said winning office from opposition was akin to climbing Everest; and here he is standing on a defeated sphinx-like Rudd in the Himalayas.

Figure 28

Source: Matt Golding, *The Age*, 8 September 2013.

Rudd's concerted effort to persuade voters that the Coalition had a secret agenda of 'cuts, cuts, cuts, cuts and more cuts' ultimately failed to resonate because, as Leak suggests, Abbott had already cut away his credibility. The irony is that over four years Abbott was arguably the most negative opposition leader in national political history. Yet when the election of 2013 finally arrived, the job of opposition was done and he was able to campaign on a more positive note by promising voters 'a grown-up government'. On the other hand, Rudd could only counter this picture with an overtly negative scare campaign; for frankly there really was relatively little good to say about the previous three years of Labor government and what positives there were, he was not responsible for! Here he is as Monty Python's Black Knight with 'just a scratch'—a fitting requiem for *Kevin13*.

Figure 29

Source: Bill Leak, *The Australian*, 7 September 2013.

References

Bramston, Troy. 2013. 'Captain Chaos major pain for ground control'. *The Australian*, 9 September, viewed 9 September 2013: <www.theaustralian.com.au/national-affairs/election-2013/captain-chaos-major-pain-for-ground-control/story-fn9qr68y-1226714852806>.

Brent, Peter, 2013. 'Opposition leader Newspoll net satisfaction graphs'. *The Australian, Mumble*, 21 August, viewed 21 August 2013: <blogs.theaustralian.news.com.au/mumble/index.php/theaustralian/comments/opposition_leader_newspoll_net_satisfaction_graphs/>.

Condren, Conal. 2012. 'Satire and definition'. *Humor* 25: 375–99.

El Refaie, Elisabeth. 2009. 'Multiliteracies: how readers interpret political cartoons'. *Visual Communication* 8(2): 181–205.

Gombrich, Ernst. 1978. *Meditations on a Hobby Horse*. Oxford: Phaidon Press.

Greenberg, Josh. 2002. 'Framing and temporality in political cartoons: A critical analysis of visual news discourse'. *Canadian Review of Sociology and Anthropology* 39 (2): 181–98.

Hartcher, Peter. 2013. 'Collapse: how it all ended in tears'. *Canberra Times*. 20 November, viewed 26 November 2013: <www.canberratimes.com.au/interactive/2013/meltdown/ >.

Hawker, Bruce. 2013. *The Rudd Rebellion: The Campaign to Save Labor*. Melbourne: Melbourne University Press.

Ireland, Judith and Jonathan Swan. 2013. 'Young, feisty and with sex appeal'. *The Sydney Morning Herald*, 13 August, viewed 13 August 2013: <www.smh.com.au/federal-politics/federal-election-2013/young-feisty-and-with-sex-appeal-abbott-talks-up-candidate-20130813-2ru0b.html>.

Joye, Paula. 2013. 'Tony's Daughters are Dressing to Win'. *The Sydney Morning Herald*, 1 September, viewed 1 September 2013: <www.smh.com.au/lifestyle/fashion/tonys-daughters-are-dressing-to-win-20130831-2sx0v.html>.

Kelly, Joe. 2013. 'Clive Palmer setting himself up for major fall'. *The Australian*, 12 August, viewed 12 August 2013: <www.theaustralian.com.au/national-affairs/clive-palmer-setting-himself-up-for-major-fall/story-fn59niix-1226695164061>.

Kerr, Joan. 1999. *Artists and Cartoonists In Black and White*. Sydney: Southwood Press.

Klausen, Jytte. 2009. *The Cartoons That Shook the World*. New Haven: Yale University Press.

Leys, Nick. 2013. 'Kevin Rudd—selfie-obsessed PM misses the mark'. *The Australian*, 10 August, viewed 10 August 2013: <www.theaustralian.com.au/media/kevin-rudd-selfie-obsessed-pm-misses-the-mark/story-e6frg996-1226694575617>.

Manning, Haydon and Phiddian, Robert. 2002. 'Two men and some boats: the cartoonists in 2001'. In Marian Simms and John Warhurst (eds), *The Centenary Election,* St Lucia: University of Queensland Press.

Media Watch. 2013. 'The ad that didn't get up'. Television program, ABC Television, 9 September, viewed 13 January 2014: <www.abc.net.au/mediawatch/transcripts/s3844762.htm>.

Phiddian, Robert. 2013. 'Satire and the limits of literary theories'. *Critical Quarterly* 55: 44–58.

Press, Charles. 1981. *The Political Cartoon*. Rutherford: Fairleigh Dickinson University Press.

Scott, Steven. 2013. 'Katter Candidate Paul Hunter in revolt over preference deal with Labor in Forde'. *Courier-Mail*, 21 August, viewed 20 November 2013: <www.couriermail.com.au/news/queensland/katter-candidate-paul-hunter-in-revolt-over-preference-deal-with-labor-in-forde/story-fnihsrf2-1226700937030>.

Seymour-Ure, Colin. 1997. 'Drawn and quartered: how wide a world for the political cartoon?'. *The Hocken Lecture 1996, The Hocken Library & The New Zealand Cartoon Archive Trust*. Dunedin: Printing Department, University of Otago.

Seymour-Ure, Colin. 2001. 'What Future for the British Political Cartoon?'. *Journalism Studies* 2(3): 333–55.

Seymour-Ure, Colin. 2003. *Prime Ministers and the Media, Issues of Power and Control*. Oxford: Blackwell.

Snow, Deborah. 2013. 'How Kevin Rudd's 2013 election campaign imploded'. *The Sydney Morning Herald*, 9 September, viewed 9 September 2013: <www.smh.com.au/federal-politics/federal-election-2013/how-kevin-rudds-2013-election-campaign-imploded-20130908-2teb1.html>.

Williams, Pamela. 2013. 'How Kevin Rudd's campaign unravelled'. *Australian Financial Review*, 9 September, viewed 9 September 2013: <www.afr.com/p/national/how_kevin_rudd_campaign_unravelled_MUATc7semL7gLrK69U2OvN>.

Wright, George. 2013. 'Address to the National Press Club'. Canberra, 29 October, viewed 15 January 2014: <d3n8a8pro7vhmx.cloudfront.net/australianlaborparty/pages/1890/attachments/original/1383017072/George_Wright__Address_to_NPC_Transcript.pdf>.

Part 3. Party Perspectives

11. The Liberal Campaign in the 2013 Federal Election

Brian Loughnane

On Saturday 7 September 2013 the Liberal and National Coalition won a decisive majority, the Labor Party recorded its lowest primary vote in over 100 years and the Greens had their worst Senate vote in three elections. The Coalition's success was driven by the support of the Australian people for our Plan to build a strong prosperous economy and a safe, secure Australia. It was the result of strong leadership by Tony Abbott, supported by his colleagues, and a clear strategy which was implemented with discipline and professionalism over two terms of parliament.

Under Tony Abbott's leadership, in the past two elections, the Coalition won a net 31 seats from Labor and achieved a 6.2 per cent nationwide two-party-preferred swing. At the 2013 election the Coalition had swings towards it in every state and territory—ranging from 1.1 per cent in the Northern Territory to 9.4 per cent in Tasmania. At the electorate level, the Coalition won a majority of the primary vote in 51 seats.[1] In contrast, Labor only won seven seats with a majority of the primary vote.

Table 1: Primary vote at 2007 and 2013 federal elections

Primary vote	2007	2013	Change
Labor	43.38%	33.38%	-10.00%
Coalition	42.09%	45.55%	+3.46%
Greens	7.79%	8.65%	+0.86%
Others	6.74%	12.42%	+5.68%

Source: Australian Electoral Commission.

Laying the foundations for victory

In simple terms, the seats which decided this election were those that did not swing to the Coalition in 2010. We laid the base in 2010 and built on it in 2013. The strategy which drove this momentum was built on a positive plan for Australia's future and an experienced, stable team, led by Tony Abbott, who

---

[1] Includes three-cornered contests where the combined Liberal and National primary vote exceeded 50 per cent.

emerged over the four years prior to the election as the only true and authentic national leader. It was supplemented by strong local candidates, with good community credentials, who were supported and resourced by the Liberal and National parties.

The foundations for the Coalition's success in 2013 were paradoxically set in our defeat in 2007 and the period immediately afterwards. The party's ability to contain its losses in 2007 provided a strong base on which we could rebuild. This was due to the economic and social achievements and the competence and stability of the Howard Government. The party, although defeated, retained very important and salient strengths in the eyes of the community. This helped minimise our loss in 2007 and ensured we had a strong parliamentary platform on which to rebuild.

Table 2: Number of seats won by Labor and the Coalition at the 2007 and 2013 federal elections

Seats won	2007	2013
Labor	83 seats	55 seats
Coalition	65 seats	90 seats

Source: Australian Electoral Commission.

Going into opposition, our expectation was that the new Rudd Government would operate in a manner not dissimilar to the Hawke and Keating governments. It quickly became clear this was not the case and that the Rudd Government was drifting and—as I explained in my National Press Club speech after the 2010 election[2]—quickly provided political opportunities for the Coalition. Despite the challenges, we achieved a remarkable result at the 2010 election for a first term opposition, resulting in the Coalition winning more seats than Labor, but a hung parliament.

After the 2010 election the Coalition went through the process of discussion with the Greens and independents because we believed securing a stable parliament was in the national interest. However, we did not expect that the crossbench was seriously considering supporting a minority Coalition government, and we were not prepared to concede key values and principles with which the Coalition is closely identified.

---

[2] See also my chapter in Simms and Wanna (2012).

Labor's politicking

Labor by contrast appeared willing to pay any price—and ultimately did. This was most obvious in the deal Labor signed with Bob Brown and the Greens. Labor did not need to do that deal and, if the party had any core integrity, it would not have. What would have happened if Labor had refused to enter a formal pact with the Greens? Does anyone seriously believe the Greens would have voted on the floor of the parliament to support an Abbott Coalition government? The deal with the Greens was a sign of Labor's weakness, not of its strength, and it meant the Labor Government was unnecessarily compromised from the start.

The most apparent manifestation of this was in Labor's decision to break its clear commitment to the Australian people not to introduce a carbon tax. Labor did not need to do this because the Greens ultimately would have continued to support them on the floor of the House. But Labor's strategic weakness, coupled with its own internal ideological confusion, resulted in the unnecessary and poorly thought through carbon tax.

Many of the senior Labor figures during this period were clearly more skilled at politics than governing. A hung parliament therefore, at one level, played to their strengths. Julia Gillard was not a strong leader in the sense of having a vision for our country or even a clear policy agenda. But her strength was tactical. She was prime minister because she could command a majority of votes in the Labor caucus and a working majority on the floor of the House. She faced real and significant threats to both majorities. Almost all of the history of the Gillard period can be simply explained by the compromises and deals she needed to make to maintain her position. Her priority was survival *today*, rather than building a track record of achievement and ultimately a case for re-election. Practically nothing was off the agenda, resulting in policy confusion, significant maladministration and grubby unethical deals. Nothing was ever as it seemed and Australians came to believe they were never getting the full story from Labor.

Our research showed growing community concern at what was happening in Canberra and a sense of drift developing from the lack of leadership that was impacting on business and consumer confidence. Labor was all politics and no policy.

Australians became increasingly concerned at the lack of budget management and in particular the growing debt and deficit. Every few months Labor chopped and changed its approach to these issues and had no credible comprehensive strategy to deal with them. The community knew this and was deeply worried by it. Labor seemed more concerned with the *politics* of the surplus (or lack thereof) than actually developing a path to achieving one.

The same was the case with border security. Labor decided immediately after the 2007 election to change the successful Howard Government border security policy. It did so, not because of any policy failure, but because of internal political pressure within Labor. Having made the change it was unable to return to the proven Howard policies and spent the subsequent six years with a series of compromised positions which the people smugglers interpreted as a sign of weakness.

Driving much of this was the unresolved leadership issue within Labor. All Australians knew Labor was a divided camp and that Julia Gillard was a compromised leader. Kevin Rudd was actively making mischief—and everyone knew it. This reached a crescendo when Rudd resigned from cabinet and launched his first direct challenge. The character assessments given by numerous Labor figures about Kevin Rudd, while not surprising Australians, removed any pretence of a united government focused on the concerns of the community. Taken together, Labor's behaviour during the hung parliament created a picture in the public's mind of chaos, instability and dysfunction.

But at the outset of the 43rd parliament the Coalition was not to know just how bad Labor would become. We had to assume they would govern competently with the real possibility of an early election. We therefore spent considerable time after the 2010 election reviewing our situation and from that developed a comprehensive strategy which drove our approach over the subsequent three years. We determined we needed to build community support for our policies and our team, not just wait and assume Labor would fail. This decision became the foundation of our strategy.

The Liberal Party campaign: A positive alternative

The Coalition retained very strong policy credibility in the public's mind, built on the legacy of the Howard Government and the policies we took to the 2010 election. At a time of policy drift and compromised leadership, the strength and clarity of Tony Abbott and his senior colleagues were a strong foundation for the Coalition to build on.

After the 2010 election, Tony Abbott and the senior leadership team began a major outreach program, travelling to all parts of Australia, listening and assessing our policy direction. A major policy review, conducted by a group chaired by Andrew Robb, produced the detailed, fully-costed policies we took to the election. Tony Abbott himself, in the three years leading up to the 2013 election, conducted over 50 community forums.

From this process Tony Abbott began making a series of major speeches, expanding on the policy priorities and direction of the Coalition. We published the most important of these speeches at the end of 2012 in a volume titled *A Strong Australia* (Abbott 2012). The Coalition's policies were practical and addressed directly the key challenges facing Australia. They were designed to drive economic growth in a way which is achievable and affordable.

Political commentary on elections has a tendency to dwell on negative campaigning and consequently often misses significant changes that are occurring. The focus of successful campaigns around the world over the past decade has increasingly been on the positive rather than the negative. To emphasise our positive alternative was a key strategic decision the Coalition leadership took early on in our campaign preparations and it drove much of what we did. But because of the chaos in the Labor Party much of the commentary missed this important development.

A key step in our campaign was the launch at the start of 2013 of our *Real Solutions Plan*, which set out the Coalition's values, priorities and direction. The book's launch was supplemented by television advertising across Australia in late January 2013 and was an important step in building the Coalition's credibility as an alternative government.

Figure 1: Front cover of Our Plan: Real Solutions for all Australians

Source: Liberal Party of Australia.

We continued to advertise during the first half of the year, almost entirely on our positive *Real Solutions Plan*. The *Plan* was one of the most comprehensive documents ever produced by an opposition and provided a clear policy direction for our MPs, candidates and supporters. In addition, over five million copies of a 16-page condensed version were circulated to households across Australia.

By the start of 2013 the Coalition parties had also preselected candidates in most key seats. The calibre of these candidates was particularly strong and most had been actively campaigning in their local communities for at least 12 months by the time of the election. The swing to the Coalition in the 17 seats gained from Labor on 7 September was over 6 per cent compared to the national swing of 3.6 per cent, confirming the strength of our candidates against popular, entrenched Labor incumbents—an important contribution to our overall success. The party invested significant resources over the three years to the election supporting our candidates with experienced on-the-ground campaigners and improved systems and technology, including social media and micro-targeting.

Table 3: 2013 federal election, House of Representatives—swings to the Coalition in the 17 seats gained from Labor

Seat	State	TPP	Swing
Banks	NSW	51.83	+3.28
Barton	NSW	50.31	+7.17
Bass	Tas	54.04	+10.78
Braddon	Tas	52.56	+10.04
Capricornia	Qld	50.77	+4.45
Corangamite	Vic	53.94	+4.22
Deakin	Vic	53.18	+3.78
Dobell	NSW	50.68	+5.75
Eden-Monaro	NSW	50.61	+4.85
Hindmarsh	SA	51.89	+7.97
La Trobe	Vic	54.01	+5.67
Lindsay	NSW	52.99	+4.11
Lyons	Tas	51.22	+13.51
Page	NSW	52.52	+6.71
Petrie	Qld	50.53	+3.04
Reid	NSW	50.85	+3.53
Robertson	NSW	53.00	+4.00
Average			+6.05

Source: Australian Electoral Commission.

A critical step in building our positive alternative was Tony Abbott's 2013 Budget-In-Reply speech. It set out a clear positive alternative to Labor and was an important moment in the community accepting him as an alternative prime minister, rather than simply leader of the Opposition.

Our response to Labor's leadership change

As part of our campaign planning, we had assumed that Julia Gillard might be replaced as Labor leader, most likely by Kevin Rudd, and possibly at short notice. We were, however, conscious of the reluctance of Labor to return to Rudd and had also prepared in the event somebody else became Labor leader.

We were therefore ready when Kevin Rudd returned. We quickly made the critical decision not to significantly alter our strategy. In my view, leadership was just one element of the serious problems responsible for Labor's weakened position. We thought a change of leader might result in a short bounce of support, but unless Labor addressed their underlying challenges, nothing would change fundamentally. We were conscious of Kevin Rudd's skill as a message manipulator and closely monitored developments and calibrated our strategy accordingly. Nevertheless, at no stage did we move from our emphasis on presenting a clear, strong and credible positive alternative. By the start of the formal campaign we were confident our strategic settings were correct and that Kevin Rudd's return had not changed the fundamentals of the election.

Put simply, Labor's change to Rudd in the lead up to the election did not work. In our private polling Rudd declined quickly, ending with a worse 'net favourability' and 'preferred prime minister rating' than Julia Gillard before the change. By the start of the campaign Rudd's lead over Tony Abbott as preferred prime minister was neutralised and he never regained the lead. This, in my view, helped explain why Labor retreated to such a negative, defensive campaign as it became more desperate.

Other strategic elements of the campaign

The campaign was important in determining the final result. As in every election, a contest can be won or lost during the campaign period. Tony Abbott and his senior colleagues began the campaign with a series of positive initiatives directly relevant to ordinary Australians. This allowed us to maintain and build on the momentum we had developed before the campaign. Australians were embarrassed by Labor's chaos and were looking closely at the Coalition. The focus of the Coalition's campaign was therefore almost entirely on our positive

Plan to improve our country. More than 70 per cent of our advertising was based on this positive alternative. Australians did not want to vote against a bad government. They wanted to embrace and support a positive alternative which would make a real difference to their lives. Figures 2 and 3 indicate this message.

Figure 2: Liberal television advertisement promoting *Our Plan*

Source: Liberal Party of Australia.

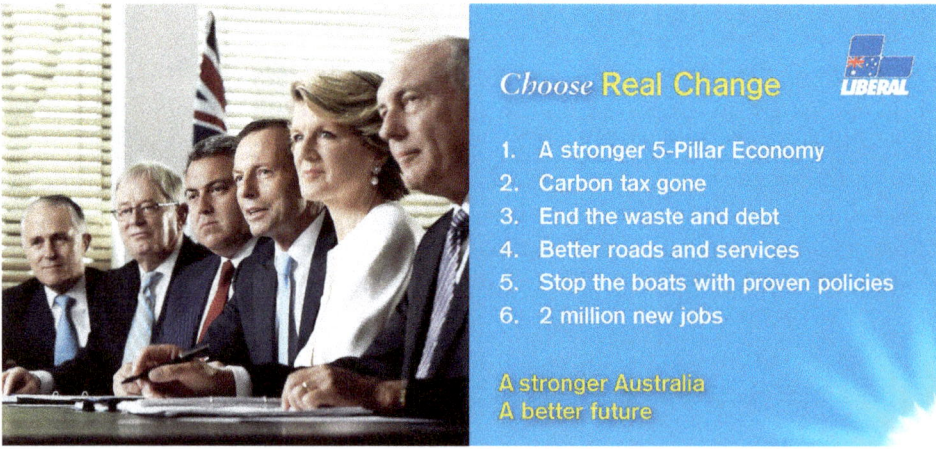

Figure 3: Back page of Liberal Party how-to-vote cards

Source: Liberal Party of Australia.

For most of the last term of Parliament, Labor attempted to make something of the costings of Coalition policies. We determined early on to have a comprehensive detailed process run by respected independent experts. We were confident our modest policy announcements and savings were affordable and in line with our commitments to responsible budget management. Once again Labor's addiction to politics, rather than sensible policy and analysis, led them to overplay their hand. At no point during the last parliament was there any credibility to Labor's claims. Joe Hockey and Andrew Robb oversaw a rigorous, detailed process that gave us great confidence in the viability of the policies we announced. The Coalition's costings process set a new standard for opposition and, given Labor's emphasis on its importance, the Australian people expect Labor in opposition to at least match the exacting standard for costings set by us. The costings process, and Labor's failed attacks on it during the campaign, further strengthened the Coalition as a credible alternative in the minds of the public and great credit goes to Joe Hockey for the important responsibility he shouldered during the campaign.

The Coalition team was a vital element of our campaign over the past three years. Labor was clearly split and most of its best people were refusing to serve. The stability of our shadow ministry for the whole of the last term contrasted dramatically with the revolving door of Labor ministers in key portfolios and was an important factor in our success.

Our research confirmed our policy positions were much more closely aligned to the concerns of the community than Labor's. Economic management, broadly defined—including taxes, debt, the deficit, jobs and cost of living for families—was by far the most significant issue. Border security and immigration was also an issue of significance. Our post-election research confirmed issues and policies were more important than ever. Issues were a primary focus for 36 per cent of the electorate in this election, an increase of 8 per cent on the 2010 election in the key seats.

The Liberal brand is significantly stronger than either Labor or the Greens and has strengthened over the past five years. According to our research we were seen to 'run a strong campaign with a clear message', and to have a large lead over Labor on 'positive plans and goals for the future'. Not surprisingly, we also had a very strong lead on the important indicator of being able to 'provide strong, stable government after the election'.

Conclusion

So in summary, while Labor's internal crisis provided opportunity for the Coalition, it was not inevitable that we would win the election. The community wanted something to vote *for* not just *against*. The Coalition's positive *Real*

Solutions Plan, strong leadership, united team and outstanding candidates, together with a clear strategy that was followed throughout the last term with great discipline, drew strong community support.

It is why the Coalition won the election rather than Labor lost it.

Appendix

Federal election 2013: key facts

- The average two-party-preferred swing in the 17 seats that the Coalition won from Labor was over 6 per cent—close to double the national average (3.6 per cent).
- The Coalition has won more seats than Labor in six of the last seven federal elections (1996, 1998, 2001, 2004, 2010 and 2013).
- In 2013, Labor received its lowest primary vote since 1903 (lowest in over 100 years).
- Labor has had a swing against it in four of the five last federal elections (2001, 2004, 2010 and 2013).
- Labor's primary vote under Rudd in 2013 was 10 per cent lower than it was under Rudd in 2007.
- The Coalition received 1,571,453 more primary votes than Labor (Coalition: 5,882,881 vs Labor: 4,311,365).
- The Coalition won 51 seats with a majority of the primary vote; Labor only won seven seats with the majority of the primary vote.
- Labor received its worst Senate result since the Senate was expanded in 1984.
- The Greens Senate vote of 8.6 per cent is the lowest since 2004 (7.7 per cent in 2004); their vote halved in Tasmania (16.8 per cent in 2010 vs 8.3 per cent in 2013).
- The Coalition has achieved more than 50 per cent of the two-party-preferred in four of the last seven elections, but has won more seats than Labor in six of the last seven elections.
- During the campaign, the Liberal Party website had 980,000 unique visitors, compared to 556,000 unique visitors to the ALP website.
- On the Friday before polling day, the Liberal website had 106,000 unique visitors compared to just 56,000 unique visitors to the Labor website.
- Tony Abbott's Facebook page 'likes' grew during the campaign by over 550 per cent, to achieve 258,830 'likes' compared to Kevin Rudd's 127,476 'likes'.

- The Liberal Party's Facebook page had more than 200,000 'likes', compared to just 165,000 for Labor.
- The engagement rate for Tony Abbott's Facebook page was three times that of Kevin Rudd's page.
- During the campaign, the Liberal Party released the first 'targeted sharing' app ever developed in Australia, which used Facebook data to personalise a video—and then ask that person to ask their friends to vote for the Coalition. This targeted sharing app reached 7.5 million Australians on Facebook.
- The number of Tony Abbott's Twitter followers grew by 28 per cent compared to one per cent for Kevin Rudd during the campaign.
- The Liberal Party's YouTube channel received 1.2 million views during the election compared to less than 300,000 for the ALP channel.
- The most popular video on the Liberal Party channel has received over 432,000 views compared to Labor's most watched video with 109,000 views.

References

Abbott, Tony. 2012. *A Strong Australia: The values, directions and policy priorities of the next Coalition government*. Canberra: Liberal Party of Australia. Available online from the website of the Liberal Party of Australia, viewed 18 March 2014: <shared.liberal.org.au/Share/eBooks/StrongAustralia.pdf>.

Abbott, Tony. 2013. 'Budget Reply'. Parliament House, Canberra, 16 May. Transcript available online from the website of the Liberal Party of Australia, 16 May, viewed 18 March 2014: <www.liberal.org.au/latest-news/2013/05/16/tony-abbott-budget-reply-parliament-house-canberra>.

Liberal Party of Australia. 2013. *Real Solutions for all Australians*. Canberra: Liberal Party of Australia. Available online from the website of the Liberal Party of Australia, viewed 18 March 2014: <lpa.webcontent.s3.amazonaws.com/realsolutions/LPA%20Policy%20Booklet%20210x210_pages.pdf>.

Loughnane, Brian. 2010. 'Address to the National Press Club'. Canberra, 10 November. Transcript available at *Australianpolitics.com*, 'Brian Loughnane analyses Result of 2010 Federal Election', 10 November, viewed 18 March 2014: <australianpolitics.com/2010/11/10/brian-loughnane-national-press-club-address.html>.

Loughnane, Brian. 2012. 'The 2010 Federal Election: The Liberal Party'. In Marian Simms and John Wanna (eds), *Julia 2010: The caretaker election*. Canberra: ANU E-Press.

12. The Labor Party Campaign and Aftermath

George Wright

Disunity versus discipline

Labor did not so much lose the election as lose government. In Australian football terms, we had put the Liberals 10 goals ahead when the year started. Labor's defeat in 2013 had been determined years earlier as we persisted with a jaw-dropping lack of unity and seemingly endless infighting. It is remarkable that, amid all of that, we advanced literally hundreds of legislative reforms. However, very few of those were noticed by the public as a result of the number of news stories on our disunity. Even though Kevin Rudd's opponents went silently after he resumed the leadership in June 2013, the years of infighting and undermining had left Labor in an unwinnable position.

The policy changes, the legislation passed, and the reforms delivered counted for very little against an overwhelming perception of disunity. All the Coalition had to do to win was hold their nerve when we inevitably made a comeback, as we did when Kevin Rudd resumed the Labor leadership. The crucial thing that the Coalition had in spades, and ruthlessly drove home their advantage with, was the biggest thing Labor's team lacked: discipline.

> Any observer of politics would observe that really where the problems for the Labor Party started was when we removed a first-term prime minister [Kevin Rudd in 2010]. Whatever the details of our incapacity to get over that, the truth is that we never did.

Figure 1: Extract from George Wright's responses to questions following his address to the National Press Club, 29 October 2013

Source: *Australianpolitics.com*—<australianpolitics.com/2013/10/29/george-wright-alp-federal-election-analysis.html>.

History will not remember the Coalition's campaign as brilliant, but it *should* be remembered as brilliantly disciplined. From their captain to their most junior backbencher they played like a team, and it worked. That meant the Liberals could align and manage their leader to the needs of their party's campaign strategy. They kept Opposition Leader Tony Abbott under tight control and resisted pressure to release detailed policies and costings until after the voters had already made up their minds.

The Coalition's research would have been telling them the same thing that ours was telling us: Mr Abbott was neither all that respected nor all that liked. The Liberal's determination to keep the focus off Tony Abbott and on Labor was executed with absolute precision. Yet despite all their campaign successes, and the ridiculously large target Labor presented, it should not be forgotten that the Coalition's primary vote at the 2013 election improved by only 1.8 per cent—the lowest increase to the winning party on a change of government since the early 1940s.

Labor now stands to be a more competitive opposition than it was able to be in the first terms after the defeat of both the Whitlam (1975–77) and the Hawke/Keating governments (1996–98). If the Liberals lose the number of seats at the next election that they lost to Kim Beazley in 1998 their majority will have been wiped out in one term. A one-term Abbott Government is possible with the unity and discipline Bill Shorten and the Labor team are showing. That would not be the case if our defeat had been more comprehensive.

Australians voted against the disunity and infighting of a Labor government which appeared more interested in itself than in the Australian people. Having changed leaders just weeks out from the likely election date, our campaign had to be the inverse of the one the Liberals undertook. It had to emphasise Kevin Rudd and his strengths and work the party's strategy into making the most of these, not the other way around. To do anything else would have been implausible.

Pulling off a 'Dunkirk'

For the party to install a new leader in such drawn out and dramatic circumstances meant our leader was always going to be in the spotlight. Prime Minister Kevin Rudd had earned the right—or perhaps accepted a duty—to campaign on his strategy.

Quite obviously, given the election outcome, we could not pull off the impossible victory. But by changing leaders back to Kevin Rudd, Labor did cauterise its potential losses. In the second quarter of 2013, our polling was telling us Labor was looking at being reduced to as few as 30 seats in the House of Representatives. Western Sydney looked like it would become a Liberal heartland. Queensland, Western Australia and South Australia all risked being reduced to a single Labor seat each, and we fully expected that Tasmania and the Northern Territory would return no Labor seats at all.

Eventually, we ended up holding 55 seats—six more than we held in 1996 and 19 more than we won in 1975. This was a solid loss and a bitter disappointment, but Labor did succeed in salvaging a team capable of being a strong opposition and a credible alternative government. As one commentator wrote, we pulled off a 'Dunkirk' evacuation—suffering a major defeat, but managing to escape with our army intact. We live to fight another day.

> … I briefed the leader on the polling, and the leadership team. I didn't shop it round, I didn't leak it, I didn't do all of those things that have poisoned the Labor Party in the way that it deals with these things in recent years. I will not lead a national secretariat that indulges in that sort of stuff. I think that's the wrong thing for Labor, the wrong people, the wrong thing for the parliamentary party and I just won't have any truck with it. But of course I did brief the leadership on the state of the polling.
>
> … I think there was a period when Kevin Rudd came back when there was a prospect of us achieving a highly unlikely victory at the election. He made a difference, he did make a difference. Yes he did. He campaigned extremely hard during the 2013 campaign. He threw everything that he had at it. He did make a difference and the change of leadership did make a difference. [In] the period immediately following him returning to the leadership, there was a very, very significant improvement in our numbers, and our numbers in the seats that we would need to be competitive in and win to win the election. We weren't able to sustain that to the line …

Figure 2: Extract from George Wright's responses to questions following his address to the National Press Club, 29 October 2013

Source: *Australianpolitics.com*.

As Bill Shorten's new frontbench proves, Labor's Generation X MPs have saved their seats and that means Labor has good grounds for future optimism. Not only have we retained experienced parliamentarians like Jenny Macklin and Wayne Swan, we also gained a new generation of high calibre MPs like Claire O'Neill, Jim Chalmers, Pat Conroy and Tim Watts.

A new direction in campaigning

So, why did we not suffer a greater loss? There is no doubt that the change to Labor's leadership was important, but there were other reasons beyond the leadership change which contributed to stemming our losses. At an organisational level we started work on strengthening our party's finances, reinvigorating our campaign capacity and working on the democracy deficit that has frustrated many of our members and put a strain on our grassroots connection with the community. On all of these objectives we still have much work to do, but we have made progress.

Over the past two years we have re-organised our finances and fundraising and eliminated a decade's worth of operating debt. That put us in a position to be able to invest earlier in our on-the-ground campaigning and in our relationship with the Labor community. Importantly, we have started to re-tool the way we engage with our members and supporters and how we campaign. Labor has started building a stronger, more inclusive and effective campaigning machine that will positively contribute to our competitiveness in future elections.

From here we intend to take Labor into a new third generation of large scale political campaigning. Unlike the two previous generations—which relied first almost exclusively on mass advertising, then second on demographic targeting—this third generation relies more heavily on direct and individual, one-on-one conversations and voter engagement, and the micro-targeting of information and messages to individuals. It requires better-trained, organised and resourced campaigners and supporters at every level of the party—and it will only work if we are truly willing to invite our supporters into our party and our campaigns. This type of campaigning requires widely accessible resources and many thousands of volunteers—but has a target audience of one.

A year out from the 2013 campaign we significantly increased the resources dedicated to digital and good old fashioned face-to-face campaigning. In the hands of good local members, trained local organisers and their campaign teams, this investment, I believe, made a material difference in a score of seats across the country.

Since 2011 we have increased by more than 10 times the size of our campaigning email list of potential volunteers and donors. Back then, our most popular online material was attracting around 50,000 views—in 2013 we were achieving as many as three million. We increased the amount of campaign funds raised from small donors by more than 13 times. Small online donors now contribute more than twice the campaign funds to federal Labor than any individual union or corporate contributor. This will have a significant and positive impact on our party into the future, and we will keep building on it.

More than 12 months out from the 2013 election Labor also placed 40 full-time national organisers into the field across our most contested electorates. Their task was to build large volunteer networks which made more direct and face-to-face contact with voters than we ever have before. As just one example of this, the number of volunteer and candidate one-on-one phone calls to voters in our campaigns increased more than 12-fold between the 2010 and 2013 election campaigns.

> In terms of who was running the campaign, I was campaign director and I take complete responsibility for it. It was a unique set of circumstances. So for example, in May we had a full trial of the campaign headquarters … 150 people in the campaign headquarters in their roles, doing their jobs, set, ready to go. Two weeks out from the election we had to replace 110 of those people because of the change of leadership and the impact that had on people's interest and willingness to participate in the campaign. So there were massive logistical issues and strategy issues that we had to deal with in a very tight timeframe.
>
> Was it a perfectly run, well-oiled machine campaign? No it wasn't. No it was not. Did we hold it together? I think we did. Did we fight to the line? I think we did. Did we leave Labor in a position from which it can rebuild and did Kevin leave Labor in a position from which it can rebuild? I think he did.
>
> None of that is a criticism of Julia Gillard at all, for whom I have the greatest and deepest respect. I think history will be much, much kinder to Julia Gillard than contemporary politics has been. But politics is hard and it is unfair, and I think both Kevin and Julia would agree with that.

Figure 3: Extract from George Wright's responses to questions following his address to the National Press Club, 29 October 2013

Source: *Australianpolitics.com*.

None of this, of course, won us the election, but it did help Labor hold seats. In Parramatta, Julie Owens and her team knocked on more than 10,000 doors. In Greenway, Michelle Rowland's volunteers made phone contact with more than 50,000 households. In McEwen, Rob Mitchell's team of volunteer tele-campaigners made thousands of calls right up until midday on 7 September—Rob won his seat by 380 votes. In the New South Wales seat of Kingsford Smith and Adelaide (SA) we held our ground against the tide. In Morton and Blair in Queensland, and in Fowler (New South Wales), we had swings to us.

The leadership ballot which followed the election was a great success and a recent survey shows it was one supported by more than 90 per cent of our members and supporters. In the past two years as National Secretary I have overseen the conduct of three national ballots of all ALP members—for the party president, for membership of Labor's new National Policy Forum and most recently for the election of Labor's leader. The participation of Labor members in the direct election of our leader was an outrageous success. More than 4,500 new members joined the Labor Party since our 7 September election defeat.

This process delivered Bill Shorten the most solid platform that any Labor opposition leader anywhere in the country has had for a long, long time. It has been a shot in the arm for Labor and we must embrace it, build on it and drive it forward. These are the green shoots of a bigger, stronger and better Labor Party starting to come through. Labor lost the 2013 election, but we are in good shape to rebuild and wage an even stronger campaign next time. We continue to strengthen the party's financial resources, to improve the effectiveness of our local and national campaigning and to democratise the operation of our party. This is not an idealistic position or words we think we ought to say, it is a pragmatic reality—our supporters and members demand it of us and we cannot hope to win without them.

The Rudd–Gillard legacy and Labor's vision for the future

So what is the real significance of the 2013 election? The Rudd and Gillard governments kept Australia out of a world recession and struck out in new directions crucial to the future of our nation. Improving our schools, building a world class national broadband network (NBN), creating a modern early learning infrastructure, tackling climate change, extending the principles of Medicare to disability, greater equality for women, and many other things. The forward march of this Labor agenda may have been temporarily halted because the government failed to manage its time in office successfully, but that agenda has not yet fully played itself out.

There is an optimistic parallel here with the years 1975 to 1983. When the Whitlam Government was defeated, it was not so much because of its program of reform but because of its management of reform. The things Whitlam introduced could not be consolidated without better political management, but they could not be stopped either. It was replaced by a government, led by Malcolm Fraser, which knew what it was against, but not what it was for. Labor under a new generation was able to get its act together sufficiently quickly to take advantage of the lack of purpose in Fraser's administration and the deterioration that inevitably resulted.

The circumstances of Labor's 2013 loss of government do not necessarily forebode a long time in opposition. If Labor can learn the necessary lessons, it can be back in government sooner than many think. The 2013 election may have been dominated by voters' distaste for Labor's instability—and the politics of the recent past. But it did not resolve the big questions voters really want answered about the future:

- *Where is Australia headed?*
- *Where will our economy and community be in five, 10 and 20 years from now?*
- *Where will the jobs of the future come from beyond the China mining boom?*
- *Will I, or my kids, ever be able to afford to buy our own home?*
- *Will our education, health, broadband, roads and transport services help my family and my community get ahead—or will they leave me behind?*

At the 2013 election, the Liberals won the past, but they did not win the future. This remains the greatest opportunity for Bill Shorten and Labor in opposition.

The progressive achievements, issues and programs on which Labor set its course during the Rudd and Gillard years won't be buried by the political rubble that era also created, or by the current Coalition Government. Tackling climate change, justice for people living with a disability, needs-based education funding, world-class broadband, equitable access to university, properly funded retirement incomes, fair workplace rights, balancing the demands of jobs and the environment; these issues will not be kicked off the national agenda. We must never walk away from them because they are our mandate. They speak to who we are and who we represent—and it is still only Labor that can truly progress them.

> For Labor to be successful, we must be a party that has broad appeal and a broad representation. We can't 'narrow-cast' in the way that the Greens do, or some of the other parties do. We are a party of government. And if you look at our history, I believe when we have been successful there has always been some coalition that we have been able to form between the more socially conservative working class and the more 'liberal' sort of better-heeled classes … in any victory we've ever had, we've had to have both.
>
> The Liberals have been expert at cleaving part of that more socially conservative, more traditional, Labor base away from us. I think it's what they built a lot of their success during the Howard era on and I think they're hoping that they will equally build their success in this era on that. But I don't believe that the issues that have caused that cleave for us over the past few years are as deep as the ones that caused that cleave during the Howard years. I don't think they are on as solid ground. I think they always do something about inner city 'trendies'—well, it used to be something different, it used to be 'elites' or something. They'd always have something about characterising us as alienated from our working class base.
>
> But I think that is a challenge Labor always has to struggle with. It's a struggle the Liberals always have to struggle with, to some extent, between basically the party of big business interests—where they've said to big business, 'On this occasion, you will decide what the government spends money on and what it doesn't spend money on'—and having to get the support of more traditional working class voters. So both parties are in this field and competing, and you know, we win some, we lose some. But I don't think any of these things are permanent. I don't think there's any permanent drift in the Labor Party that means that we can't win those voters.

Figure 4: Extract from George Wright's responses to questions following his address to the National Press Club, 29 October 2013

Source: *Australianpolitics.com*.

13. The 2013 Federal Election: The Greens campaign

Andrew Bartlett

For a political party with a relatively short history, all elections can seem historic. However, the 2013 federal election was ground-breaking for the Greens in both positive and negative ways. For those who closely follow the fortunes of minor or 'third' parties, there were some noteworthy firsts.

The 2013 election saw a minor party (excluding the National/Country Party) retain a lower house seat for the first time, with Adam Bandt holding on to the seat of Melbourne with a swing of more than 7 per cent towards the Greens, taking his primary vote to 42.62 per cent. Senators Peter Whish-Wilson (Tasmania) and Sarah Hanson-Young (South Australia) were returned and Janet Rice was elected from Victoria. While Scott Ludlam was also deemed to be re-elected following the recount of the Western Australian Senate vote, this entire Senate contest was subsequently voided by a High Court judge sitting as the Court of Disputed Returns. Ultimately, Ludlam was successful again at the re-running of the Western Australian Senate contest and the Greens now hold 10 Senate seats. This is not only the Greens' highest ever number of seats held, but the highest ever for any minor party, beating the nine seats the Democrats held following the 1998 federal election. Measuring political success by that base indicator—representation in parliament—in 2013 the Greens did well, at the very least holding their ground in an electoral environment far less favourable than that faced three years earlier.

New leadership for the Greens

It was widely noted that this was the first election for the Australian Greens without former senator Bob Brown as parliamentary leader,[1] a position he had held since first entering the Senate in 1996. Christine Milne became only the second parliamentary leader of the Greens and Adam Bandt became the deputy leader. Many commentators saw this as a major test for the party and for Christine Milne with her different style of leadership. Bob Brown's retirement

---

1   There had been Senators for the Western Australian Greens from the late 1980s to 1998, but at that time the Western Australian Greens were structurally separate from the national Greens party.

from Parliament in June 2012 led to many predictions that this would see the Greens follow the same path to extinction that had befallen the Australian Democrats, increasing the expectations and pressure on Christine Milne.

However, this supposed parallel was always an overly simplistic and factually flawed one. When Don Chipp—the Democrats founder and in that respect quasi-equivalent to Bob Brown—retired in 1986, also being succeeded by the party's first female leader, the same predictions of extinction were made. Yet history shows that at Janine Haines' first election as leader in 1987, the Democrats managed to retain the same number of Senate seats and went on to achieve their highest ever vote at the following election in 1990. Christine Milne has now passed the same test, with the Greens managing to hold the lower house seat as well as winning one extra seat in the Senate.

Background context: Comparing the 2007 and 2010 elections

Most commentators have focused their observations not so much on the 2013 outcome in terms of seats for the Greens, but on the swing suffered by the party. Nationally, the Greens vote fell from 11.76 per cent in the House of Representatives and 13.1 per cent in the Senate to 8.65 per cent in both Houses. No state or territory was immune from the swing away from the Greens, but the size was varied across the country—with the smallest in New South Wales and the largest in Tasmania.

The 2010 election was a high point in the Greens' electoral history. It was the first time any minor party had won a Senate seat in every state, and the Greens managed a historic breakthrough with Adam Bandt's election in the House of Representatives seat of Melbourne. The Greens' primary vote had been steadily increasing at each election since 1996, but jumped significantly in 2010. The successes of 2010 meant that the Greens were able to support the ALP to form a minority government. This meant that positive outcomes and key Greens policies were achieved. The first steps for Denticare were made, the Parliamentary Budget Office was established, and of course the Clean Energy package, including carbon pricing and the establishment of the Clean Energy Finance Corporation.

The Coalition's successful demonisation of the carbon tax and the difficult political circumstances created by the Greens' perceived association with an unpopular Labor Party meant that a decrease in vote share was expected. However, the size of the decline in the Senate vote in some states was concerning for the party.

Table 1: Green vote by state, 2007, 2010 and 2013

State Totals	2013 % House of Reps	2010 % H of R	Swing	Swing as a % of vote	2007 % H of R	2007 to 2013 swing	2013 Senate	2010 % Senate	Swing	Swing as a % of vote	2013 Senate premium	2007 % H of R	2007 to 2013 swing
ACT	13.37	19.20	-5.83	-30.36	13.20	0.21	19.27	22.92	-3.02	-13.18	5.90	21.47	-2.18
NSW	7.92	10.24	-2.32	-22.66	7.88	0.04	7.79	10.69	-3.03	-28.34	-0.13	8.43	-0.64
NT	7.89	12.97	-5.08	-39.17	8.05	-0.16	8.67	13.55	-4.88	-36.01	0.78	8.82	-0.15
Qld	6.20	10.92	-4.72	-43.22	5.63	0.57	6.04	12.76	-6.97	-54.62	-0.16	7.32	-1.28
SA	8.25	11.98	-3.73	-31.14	6.95	1.30	7.09	13.30	-6.40	-48.12	-1.16	6.49	0.60
Tas	8.32	16.82	-8.50	-50.54	13.50	-5.18	11.66	20.27	-8.73	-43.07	3.34	18.13	-6.47
Vic	10.71	12.66	-1.95	-15.40	8.17	2.54	10.84	14.64	-3.90	-26.64	0.13	10.08	0.76
WA	9.72	13.13	-3.41	-25.97	8.93	0.79	9.49	13.96	-4.63	-33.17	-0.23	9.30	0.19
National	8.65	11.76	-3.16	-26.87	7.79	0.81	8.65	13.11	-4.46	-35.09	-0.00	9.04	-0.39

Source: Australian Greens.

Table 2: Green vote in the House of Representatives, 2013—highest vote

Electorate	Gender	2013 %	2010 %	Swing	Swing as a % of vote	2007 %	2007 to 2013 swing	State and Demographic	Enrolment
Melbourne	m	42.62	36.17	6.45	17.00	22.80	19.82	Vic inner metropolitan	97,277
Batman	f	25.96	23.48	2.48	10.56	17.17	8.79	Vic inner metropolitan	100,456
Grayndler	m	22.90	25.90	-3.00	-11.58	18.70	4.20	NSW inner metropolitan	97,203
Wills	m	21.19	20.60	0.59	2.86	13.82	7.37	Vic inner metropolitan	63,060
Melbourne Ports	f	20.04	20.66	-0.62	-3.00	15.03	5.01	Vic inner metropolitan	100,075
Richmond	f	17.34	16.15	1.19	7.37	14.93	2.41	NSW rural	94,247
Sydney	f	17.30	23.75	-6.45	-27.16	20.71	-3.41	NSW inner metropolitan	99,999
Gellibrand	m	16.49	15.35	1.14	7.43	9.38	7.11	Vic inner metropolitan	94,121
Kooyong	f	16.14	18.48	-2.34	-12.66	11.82	4.32	Vic inner metropolitan	97,046
Higgins	m	15.87	17.9	-2.03	-11.34	10.75	5.12	Vic inner metropolitan	101,202
Goldstein	f	15.85	16.21	-0.36	-2.22	10.37	5.48	Vic inner metropolitan	102,115
Warringah	m	15.40	16.34	-0.94	-5.75	12.53	2.87	NSW inner metropolitan	95,370
Curtin	f	15.19	17.72	-2.53	-14.28	13.45	1.74	WA inner metropolitan	106,303
North Sydney	f	15.14	15.53	-0.39	-2.51	9.21	5.93	NSW inner metropolitan	97,113
Wentworth	m	14.78	17.44	-2.66	-15.25	14.96	-0.18	NSW inner metropolitan	88,324
Ryan	m	14.33	18.96	-4.63	-24.42	9.43	4.90	Qld outer metropolitan	100,943
Brisbane	f	14.15	21.28	-7.13	-33.51	11.80	2.35	Qld inner metropolitan	137,895
Mackellar	m	14.14	16.77	-2.63	-15.68	11.72	2.42	NSW outer metropolitan	102,327
Mayo	m	13.95	16.97	-3.02	-17.80	10.96	2.99	SA rural	65,856
Fraser	m	13.90	19.84	-5.94	-29.94	13.38	0.52	ACT inner metropolitan	94,112
Jagajaga	m	12.85	14.95	-2.10	-14.05	10.25	2.60	Vic inner metropolitan	98,484
Bradfield	f	12.73	16.34	-3.61	-22.09	11.26	1.47	NSW inner metropolitan	103,012
Canberra	f	12.49	18.56	-6.07	-32.70	12.95	-0.46	ACT inner metropolitan	102,918
Cowper	f	12.22	9.09	3.13	34.43	11.04	1.18	NSW rural	100,280
Franklin	f	12.13	20.87	-8.74	-41.88	14.44	-2.31	Tas outer metropolitan	102,768

Electorate	Gender	2013 %	2010 %	Swing	Swing as a % of vote	2007 %	2007 to 2013 swing	State and Demographic	Enrolment
Newcastle	f	11.81	15.47	-3.66	-23.66	10.01	1.80	NSW provincial	95,395
Fremantle	m	11.78	17.65	-5.87	-33.26	14.57	-2.79	WA inner metropolitan	103,393
Corangamite	m	11.71	11.43	0.28	2.45	7.97	3.74	Vic provincial	93,264
Boothby	m	11.67	13.24	-1.57	-11.86	10.22	1.45	SA outer metropolitan	97,787
Cunningham	f	11.49	15.12	-3.63	-24.01	14.63	-3.14	NSW outer metropolitan	95,317
Swan	m	11.38	11.81	-0.43	-3.64	10.13	1.25	WA inner metropolitan	105,317
Stirling	m	11.18	12.90	-1.72	-13.33	7.56	3.62	WA inner, metropolitan	94,919
Pearce	f	11.08	13.24	-2.16	-16.31	8.59	2.49	WA outer metropolitan	109,262

Source: Australian Greens. Table shows seats where the Greens captured 11 per cent or more of the vote.

Table 3: Green vote in the House of Representatives—seats with largest swing against the Greens

Electorate	Gender	2013 %	2010 %	Swing	Swing as a % of vote	2007 %	2007 to 2013 swing	State and demographic	Enrolment
Denison	f	7.84	18.98	-11.10	-58.69	18.60	-10.76	Tas inner metropolitan	100668
Fairfax	m	8.30	18.00	-9.70	-53.89	8.53	-0.23	Qld rural	100431
Werriwa	m	3.25	12.70	-9.45	-74.41	3.79	-0.54	NSW outer metropolitan	105149
Franklin	f	12.13	20.87	-8.74	-41.88	14.44	-2.31	Tas outer metropolitan	102768
Lyons	f	8.22	16.75	-8.53	-50.93	11.17	-2.95	Tas rural	97292
Fisher	m	7.57	15.84	-8.27	-52.21	5.61	1.96	Qld rural	102122
Forde	f	4.16	12.22	-8.06	-65.96	4.80	-0.64	Qld outer metropolitan	101819
Bass	f	7.76	15.58	-7.82	-50.19	15.27	-7.51	Tas provincial	97915
Brand	f	7.27	14.74	-7.47	-50.68	8.60	-1.33	WA outer metropolitan	96145
Brisbane	f	14.15	21.28	-7.13	-33.51	11.80	2.35	Qld inner metropolitan	137895
Blair	f	4.24	11.06	-6.82	-61.66	3.92	0.32	Qld provincial	96752
Braddon	f	5.14	11.96	-6.82	-57.02	8.14	-3.00	Tas rural	102815
Port Adelaide	m	8.44	15.11	-6.67	-44.14	8.76	-0.32	SA inner metropolitan	93894
Calwell	f	5.20	11.86	-6.66	-56.16	4.36	0.84	Vic rural	105512

Electorate	Gender	2013 %	2010 %	Swing	Swing as a % of vote	2007 %	2007 to 2013 swing	State and demographic	Enrolment
Wright	f	5.35	11.95	-6.60	-55.23		5.35	Qld rural	102333
Throsby	m	5.37	11.93	-6.56	-54.99	9.08	-3.71	NSW outer metropolitan	91563
Sydney	f	17.30	23.75	-6.45	-27.16	20.71	-3.41	NSW inner metropolitan	99999
Oxley	m	5.37	11.79	-6.42	-54.45	5.13	0.24	Qld outer metropolitan	97275
Wakefield	f	5.07	11.30	-6.23	-55.13	4.13	0.94	SA rural	73859
Canberra	f	12.49	18.56	-6.07	-32.70	12.95	-0.46	ACT inner metropolitan	102918
Indi	f	3.40	9.45	-6.05	-64.02	7.58	-4.18	Vic rural	95691

Source: Australian Greens. Table shows seats with swings against the Greens of 6 percentage points or more.

Greens strategists recognised early that given the different circumstances of the 2013 election, a repeat of or an increase on the success of 2010 was highly unlikely. Instead, the 2007 federal election was used as the party's benchmark, partly to ensure realistic expectations and, at least with respect to South Australia, because Nick Xenophon was also due for re-election in this cycle. When Kevin Rudd resumed leadership of the ALP, this became further justification to use 2007 as a benchmark to measure our performance.

Compared to 2007 the Greens' House of Representative vote continued its upward trend. Ninety-four out of 150 seats did better in 2013 compared to 2007. However, due in no small part to the continuing proliferation of micro and single-issue parties, the Senate vote declined below trend.

Table 4: Green vote in the House of Representatives—largest swings to and against the Greens, 2007 v 2013

Electorate	Gender	2013 %	2010 %	Swing	Swing as a % of vote	2007 %	**2007 to 2013 swing**	State and demographic	Enrolment
Melbourne	m	42.32	36.17	6.15	17.00	22.80	**19.52**	Vic inner metropolitan	97277
Batman	f	25.96	23.48	2.48	10.56	17.17	**8.79**	Vic inner metropolitan	100456
Wills	m	21.19	20.60	0.59	2.86	13.82	**7.37**	Vic inner metropolitan	63060
Gellibrand	m	16.49	15.35	1.14	7.43	9.38	**7.11**	Vic inner metropolitan	94121
Durack	m	6.97	9.25	-2.28	-24.65		**6.97**	WA rural	94735
North Sydney	f	15.14	15.53	-0.39	-2.51	9.21	**5.93**	NSW inner metropolitan	97113

Electorate	Gender	2013 %	2010 %	Swing	Swing as a % of vote	2007 %	2007 to 2013 swing	State and demographic	Enrolment
Goldstein	f	15.85	16.21	-0.36	-2.22	10.37	5.48	Vic inner metropolitan	102115
Wright	f	5.35	11.95	-6.60	-55.23		5.35	Qld rural	102333
Higgins	m	15.87	17.90	-2.03	-11.34	10.75	5.12	Vic inner metropolitan	101202
Melbourne Ports	f	20.04	20.66	-0.62	-3.00	15.03	5.01	Vic inner metropolitan	100075
Braddon	f	5.14	11.96	-6.82	-57.02	8.14	-3.00	Tas rural	102815
Cunningham	f	11.49	15.12	-3.63	-24.01	14.63	-3.14	NSW outer metropolitan	95317
Sydney	f	17.30	23.75	-6.45	-27.16	20.71	-3.41	NSW inner metropolitan	99999
Blaxland	m	2.86	6.26	-3.40	-54.31	6.46	-3.60	NSW inner metropolitan	72194
Throsby	m	5.37	11.93	-6.56	-54.99	9.08	-3.71	NSW outer metropolitan	91563
Indi	f	3.40	9.45	-6.05	-64.02	7.58	-4.18	Vic rural	95691
Bass	f	7.76	15.58	-7.82	-50.19	15.27	-7.51	Tas provincial	97915
Denison	f	7.84	18.98	-11.10	-58.69	18.6	-10.76	Tas inner metropolitan	100668

Source: Australian Greens. Table shows seats with swings of 5 per cent or more towards the Greens, and seats with swings of 3 per cent or more against the Greens.

The Greens in 2010 had benefitted in part from voters protesting against having to vote for the ALP or the Coalition. In 2013, there were many more choices in this regard. The cashed-up Palmer United Party, Katter's Australia Party, the Wikileaks Party and the Pirate Party, along with an explosion of other micro and single-issue parties, gave voters more choice than ever before. The voters took up this choice—the vote for the ALP and Coalition fell from 81.55 per cent in 2010 to 78.93 per cent in 2013 in the House and from 73.76 per cent to 67.83 per cent in the Senate. Both of these figures are record lows for the combined ALP–Coalition vote at a federal election (Green 2013). The fact that nearly one in three voters supported minor parties and independents ahead of Labor and the Coalition in the Senate is a significant outcome that has not received a great deal of attention. The long-standing upward trend in voting away from Labor and the Coalition, particularly in the Senate, has fully recovered from the slump generated by the Democrats' protracted death throes across the 2004 and 2007 elections.

However, this time around the Greens were not so much the beneficiary of the decline of the major party vote. Some post-election analysis conducted internally by the Greens suggests that a significant number of voters switched their 'protest' vote from the Greens to the Palmer United Party, whose TV advertising spend came close to matching that of the major parties in the final weeks of the campaign.

The Greens campaign

The re-election of Adam Bandt was established as a major goal of the Greens 2013 election strategy a long way in advance. The Melbourne campaign was organised very early on and modelled in part on the '08 and '12 Obama campaigns, although obviously on a much smaller scale. Using tailored messaging and theming, the Greens dominated the local Melbourne outdoor advertising space and backed this up with a very intensive and systematic door-knocking campaign over a prolonged period. Despite regular favourable opinion polling, many commentators seemed to have difficulty accepting the strength of the Greens campaign in this area. In the end, Adam Bandt achieved a primary vote of 42.62 per cent with a 7.03 per cent swing. This is the fourth highest primary vote percentage for a Greens candidate contesting a federal single seat electorate anywhere in the world (see Global Greens n.d.[2]). As perhaps one indication of Adam Bandt's personal vote compared to the generic level of support for the Greens, Bandt's House of Representatives vote was 7.18 per cent higher than the votes cast by Melbourne voters for the Greens in the Senate.

The greater embrace of social media campaigning by all the main parties was another key development in 2013 and the Greens were at the forefront in this area. Many Greens candidates had higher social media profiles than their major party opponents. Christine Milne live tweeted the leaders' debates to ensure that more than two voices were heard, as Bob Brown had done in 2010. Senator Scott Ludlam and Adam Bandt used 'Ask Me Anything' forums on Reddit to reach new audiences. The Greens Food Policy was launched via Google Hangout on Air—the first major policy to be launched on social media in Australia.

Election 2013 was the Greens most successful election fundraising effort to date. While still dwarfed by the efforts of the ALP and Coalition, the Greens received substantially more in donations compared with 2010. A number of trade unions again publicly backed the Greens stance on industrial relations and opposition to university funding cuts. There was also a large focus on email and micro donations, based on techniques developed by the Obama campaign. This fundraising success occurred despite the absence of the record million dollar individual donation that was given in the 2010 election.

---

2   Note that at time of writing, this site had not been updated to include Bandt's 2013 result.

Shifts and patterns in the Greens' vote

One of the developments from the 2013 election was something of a shift in the Greens 'heartland' from Tasmania to Victoria. Senator Peter Whish-Wilson filled Bob Brown's casual Senate vacancy in 2012. While Whish-Wilson has brought a stronger business and economics background to the Greens, there was an 8.61 per cent Senate vote swing against the Greens in Tasmania. Peter Whish-Wilson was comfortably returned as a Senator, but the swing against the party was bigger in Tasmania than in the other states and territories. Denison and Franklin also recorded the biggest and fourth biggest negative swings in House of Representatives seats.

It is reasonable to hypothesise that this was partly due to the absence of Bob Brown's considerable personal following, along with some local blowback from the Greens being seen as aligned with the not so popular local state Labor Government. Having said that, both the polls prior to the Tasmanian election and the actual outcome in March 2014 indicated a much greater decline in the local Labor vote than in support levels for the Greens.

Victoria, on the other hand, saw the smallest House of Representatives state-wide swing against the Greens, and it joined Tasmania, South Australia and Western Australia as states with two Green senators. Additionally, the Greens came second on primary votes in Batman (repeated from 2010) and in Wills—both seats adjoin the seat of Melbourne. With Adam Bandt's re-election, Victoria is now the strongest state federally for the Greens in terms of seats held and percentage of the House of Representatives vote.

Overall, the Greens only recorded a positive swing in 12 of the 150 House of Representative seats—six each in New South Wales and Victoria. Ninety-four seats recorded a positive swing compared to the vote in 2007. But extrapolating the Senate vote across the House of Representatives' electorates the number of seats in which a positive swing occurred was 53.

Post-election research suggested that around one in four voters decided who they would be voting for in the final month, with as much as 16 per cent indicating they had not decided until the final week or even polling day itself. There is also a growing portion of the electorate not identifying themselves as being aligned significantly with any party.

The Greens' growing profile and influence in Australian politics

The Greens long-standing efforts to demonstrate strength across a wide range of issues is being recognised by a growing proportion of the electorate. A roughly equivalent number of people gave 'stopping Tony Abbott getting absolute power' and climate change or the environment in general as their most important reason for voting Greens. Other issues such as a more caring society, marriage equality and refugees also were primary influences on the vote of many who supported the Greens. The ideal of having a more caring society was a key message for the Greens, and post-election research suggested that this was having some impact, with the Greens about on a par with the two larger parties in this regard. Not surprisingly, the issues with greatest cut-through for the Greens were environment-related ones. However, the Greens efforts in promoting issues aimed at assisting people meet their basic needs did not have the same impact in the election context.

One aspect to which the Greens paid considerable attention in election planning was the goal of ensuring all policies released for the election were fully costed. The Parliamentary Budget Office is a valuable new accountability mechanism which was set up following the 2010 federal election as part of the arrangement the Greens struck with Julia Gillard as she was pulling together support for a minority ALP government. The Greens parliamentary wing, using the resources of the PBO, put significant effort into developing a fully costed policy platform—another first in the party's history. This move most likely did not shift a lot of votes this time around, despite the stark contrast with the lack of costing released by the Coalition in the election lead-up. However, the Greens' costing initiatives were commented on by a number of print commentators, and this helped stymie the attacks that were likely to have appeared on this front and which had been a characteristic of the 2010 election.

This focus on showing economic accountability and credibility is a long-term goal for the Greens. This policy area is one remaining area where voters are most likely to have doubts about the Greens, and demonstrating credentials in this area is something which will be consistently pursued. Post-election research conducted by the Greens suggested that economic issues such as jobs, debt and cost of living were the vote-deciding issue for around a third of voters.

In looking at the topics where the Greens gained most media coverage during the election period proper, data indicates that preferences was most common, followed by asylum seekers, carbon tax, mining, and paid parental leave. In a pleasing sign for the future, the topic of policy costings was also one where the Greens did gain regular coverage—greater than the number of mentions in the context of the contest for Melbourne.

The Greens still have work to do in increasing public awareness about the party's policy achievements. Gains such as the establishment of the Parliamentary Budget Office, the initiation of Denticare (another feature of the Greens' agreement with Julia Gillard after the 2010 poll), the exploration of high-speed rail and, even to a degree, the Greens' role in bringing about the *Clean Energy Act*, are not as widely recognised as the party would like. But an ever increasing information base about which ways are most effective at reaching the electorate should assist in improving that situation.

The high level of media attention on the Greens in the context of stories about preferences was in large part due to the coverage of the Liberal Party's announcement that it would be putting the Greens last, or close to last, on how-to-vote cards and in its Senate preference allocations. The determination of the Liberals to do this saw them place the Greens lower in Senate above-the-line preferences in some states than a number of extremist and racist parties such as Australia First, Rise Up Australia, the Citizens Electoral Council and One Nation. Nevertheless, this action by the Liberal Party makes it even more significant that Adam Bandt managed to retain his House of Representatives seat, with a minimal swing against him in two-party-preferred terms.

Conclusion

In the context of the 2013 election, delivering a change of government, with a new Greens leader with only a little over a year in the saddle and an increase in populist candidates from other parties, the Greens can be considered to have done quite well. Notwithstanding the decline in their primary vote from 2010, the return of Adam Bandt, the retention of three Senators plus the election of a new Senator in Victoria, mean the Greens can continue to look positively towards the future. Whilst the party still faces significant challenges in its overarching goal of building its primary vote to a level that can further challenge the century-long stranglehold that Labor and the Coalition have had over Australia's political system, there are strong foundations which will assuredly see the Greens soon become unchallenged on almost any measure as the most successful third party in Australian political history.

References

Global Greens. n.d. 'Greens Elected in Federal Single Seat Elections'. Viewed 28 February 2014: <www.globalgreens.org/officeholders/elected-federal-single-seat>.

Green, Antony. 2013. 'Record Vote for Minor Parties at 2013 Federal Election'. *Antony Green's Election Blog*, 19 November, viewed 11 March 2014: <blogs.abc.net.au/antonygreen/2013/11/record-vote-for-minor-parties-at-2013-federal-election.html>.

Part 4. Regional Variations in Voting Trends

14. The Electoral Geography of the 2013 Election: Voting patterns in the states and regions for the Lower House

Dean Jaensch with Narelle Miragliotta and Rae Wear[1]

Analyses of Australian federal elections at the sub-national level are traditionally organised on the bases of the various individual states and territories. Such data provides a summary of party support and swings, and allows comparative analyses—but may mask significant differences in the patterns of party support within and across the state and territory borders. This chapter first provides a summary of the electoral contests in the states for the House of Representatives where government is decided, and then offers a detailed analysis of the election in Australia's main regions using electoral clusters. The chapter does not cover the electoral geography of the Senate vote.

The elections fought in the states

In January 2013, when Julia Gillard announced the 'longest campaign' in Australian history, the Labor Party appeared to be in a dire situation. Given that it had governed in a minority situation then for over two years, it could not afford to lose even one seat if it wished to retain government, and had to win seats from the Coalition if it wished to hold government in its own right. The national polls suggested either outcome would be an uphill battle.

At the start of 2013, Labor's primary vote was below its 2010 support in each of the five mainland states. The swing against Labor was least in Western Australia, but in the other states the slump was around minus 4 to 5 per cent, enough to send the Labor Party into the oblivion of opposition.

Eight months later, the swings were confirmed in the September 2013 election, with Labor suffering primary swings often well in excess of the pollsters' predictions. Labor suffered heavy primary swings in the states of Victoria

---

[1] We acknowledge invaluable assistance in the preparation of this chapter from Antony Green, John Wanna, and Nick Economou.

and Tasmania and, to a lesser extent, in South Australia. Despite the fears of the party that there could be a big loss in New South Wales, there was only a comparatively small swing of -2.8 per cent.

The format of the following table will be followed in the remainder of this chapter. It contains a summary of the primary vote, swing, and two-party vote for the Labor Party, the primary and two-party votes for the Coalition, as well as the primary support for the Greens, all in percentages of the votes cast.

Table 1: 2013 election results — patterns of party support, states and territories

	NSW	Vic	Qld	WA	SA	Tas	NT	ACT
ALP primary	34.50	34.80	29.80	28.80	35.70	34.80	37.40	42.90
ALP swing	-2.80	-8.00	-3.80	-2.40	-5.00	-9.20	-0.50	-2.10
ALP two-party	45.65	50.20	43.00	41.70	47.60	51.20	49.65	59.90
Coalition primary	47.30	42.70	45.70	51.20	44.90	40.30	41.70	34.60
Coalition two-party	54.35	49.80	57.00	58.30	52.40	48.80	50.35	40.10
Green primary	7.90	10.80	6.20	9.70	8.30	8.30	7.90	13.40

Source: Australian Electoral Commission (2013).

Labor lost 17 seats to the Coalition: eight in New South Wales, three in each of Victoria and Tasmania, two in Queensland, and one in South Australia. The other jurisdictions remained unchanged.

The political contexts of the states

The second section of this chapter focuses on regions, campaigns and policy foci in the states, and clusters of electorates which cross state boundaries and significantly different political environments. This section provides a summary of the electoral contexts of the states.

New South Wales

Electing 48 of the 150 seats in the House of Representatives made New South Wales crucial to both Labor and the Coalition. In 2013, to have any hope of retaining government, Labor needed to hold all of its New South Wales seats (26 held after the 2010 election). But to achieve this, it had to reverse the trend for the support of New South Wales Labor to lag behind its national vote.

In January 2013, Labor in New South Wales appeared in no shape to be a real contender in the election. It had been massacred in the state election in 2010, winning a meagre 25.6 per cent of the first preference votes, 35.8 per cent of the two-party votes, and was left with only 20 of the 93 seats in the Legislative Assembly. The fear that this landslide against Labor would be repeated was the prime reason the Labor Right faction(s) supported the change to Kevin Rudd in June 2013.

New South Wales Labor had been dysfunctional while in government and had infamously conducted a leadership rotisserie, involving four leaders over three years from 2008–11 (Premiers Morris Iemma, Nathan Rees, and Kristina Keneally and finally Opposition Leader John Robertson). In opposition after 2010 the party continued to be beset by problems: 'racked by voting anger at infrastructure deficiencies, ministerial scandals, and acrimonious internal conflict over privatisation of power' (Thompson and Robinson 2012: 173). Labor also feared that the continuing revelations of corruption in the Independent Commission Against Corruption (ICAC) hearings would seriously impinge on the federal election.

A January–March 2013 Newspoll reinforced a gloomy picture for Labor in New South Wales: the party was likely to receive only 33 per cent of the primary votes and 46 per cent of the two-party vote. An April–June Newspoll showed a further slump in Labor's primary support to 30 per cent. In two August Newspolls, one month before the election and following the reinstatement of Prime Minister Kevin Rudd, Labor's primary support recovered slightly, to 34 per cent, but the Coalition was comfortably ahead with a primary vote of 51 per cent.

One potential problem for Labor was the attitudes of residents of the western Sydney suburbs, the former site of 'Howard's battlers' after 1996, which had returned to federal Labor from 2004. Both Gillard and Rudd recognised this and gave the area close attention. Two focused Newspolls in August, only days out from the election, emphasised Labor's problem. One poll, in the western suburbs key seats of Parramatta, Reid, Banks, Lindsay and Greenway, found Labor on 34 per cent of the primary vote and the Coalition sitting on 52 per cent. The second, a mixed bag of Labor marginal seats—Dobell, Robertson, Kingsford-Smith, Page and Eden-Monaro—produced a similar result: Labor 36 per cent, Coalition 48 per cent. These patterns suggested that the Coalition would not only hold its non-metropolitan seats, but it had the potential to erode Labor's seats in Sydney. It meant that Labor would have to look elsewhere to have any hope of retaining government.

The election confirmed the polls. A swing of -2.8 per cent saw Labor lose eight marginal seats to the Coalition: Banks, Barton, Dobell, Eden-Monaro, Lindsay, Page, Reid, and Robertson.

Victoria

Victoria was for many years the 'jewel in the Liberal crown' but in the 1990s became a Labor stronghold. In the 1998 election, Labor won 53.5 per cent of the two-party vote and, with the exception of 49 per cent in 2004, maintained this level of support. In the 2010 federal election, Labor won the Victorian seats of McEwen and La Trobe from the Liberal Party, the only seats lost by the Coalition across Australia. Labor's primary vote in Victoria was 5 percentage points higher than its national vote, while the Liberal Party was 5 percentage points below.

In 2013, Victoria offered Labor an opportunity to overcome its potential losses in New South Wales. But the polls told a different story. A January–March Newspoll had Labor on 37 per cent of primary votes to the Coalition's 44 per cent. The April–June Newspoll showed a major slump in Labor's primary support to 29 per cent, with the Coalition on 46 per cent. At the state level, however, the Coalition Government had seen its one-seat majority disappear when one member decided to become an independent, and began a bitter war against the Liberal Speaker, Ken Smith. State Liberal politics descended into turmoil and an almost complete breakdown, reinforcing Labor's hopes of a positive effect on its 2013 chances.

The August Newspolls showed a narrowing of party fortunes: Coalition 39 per cent of primary votes, Labor 37 per cent. This was an encouraging trend for Labor, which even had the possibility of winning seats in Victoria to overcome any losses in New South Wales. But one week before the election, a Newspoll conducted in three key marginal electorates, La Trobe, Deakin, and Corangamite, provided evidence that Labor was in trouble where it mattered. The Labor Party was on 34 per cent of the primary vote, the Coalition 47 per cent. Further, Labor continued to face a strong challenge from the Left. The Green vote had increased from 7.5 per cent in 2004 to 8.2, and 13 per cent in the August poll. In 2010, the electorate of Melbourne saw Adam Bandt become the first Green member of the House of Representatives to win at a general election. Labor was forced to fight the 2013 election on two flanks.

In the election, Labor suffered a primary swing against it of -8.0 per cent, but Green preferences enabled it to achieve a two-party vote of 50.2 per cent. Despite the dire predictions from the polls, Labor lost only three seats to the Coalition: Corangamite, Deakin and La Trobe; but significantly failed to win back Melbourne from the Greens despite the Liberal Party directing its preferences to Labor ahead of Bandt. The Liberals only gained two seats net as they lost the rural seat of Indi with sitting member Sophie Mirabella defeated by the Independent Cathy McGowan (see Chapter 16).

Queensland

'Queensland is a large, diverse, decentralised state with distinctive political geography and culture.' It is also a state with distinctive patterns of party support. Over the past few decades, it has been the case that 'Queenslanders have long been more reluctant than the rest of the nation to embrace federal Labor' (Ward 2012: 217). But Labor needed to do well in this northern state, as Queensland was crucial for Labor to balance its expected losses elsewhere. In early 2013, at the beginning of the campaign, it faced real problems. A similarly catastrophic result as occurred in New South Wales for Labor in the 2012 state election resulted in Labor's primary vote plummeting to 26.7 per cent, and the party was reduced to only seven of the 89 seats. Federal Labor was hoping that the 'Newman effect' would improve its outlook through voters' reactions to the financial cutbacks, the personal style of the premier, and the government's internal problems of transparency and accountability.

However the polls showed a bleak picture. A Newspoll in January–March showed federal Labor with a primary vote of 30 per cent, to 49 per cent for the Coalition's Liberal National Party (LNP). Over the next six months, the picture remained gloomy for the ALP. The return of 'I'm Kevin Rudd from Queensland' to the prime ministership was crucial for any hopes to reverse the trend. It did to a degree, with the August Newspoll showing Labor with 37 per cent of the primary vote to 46 per cent for the LNP. But this was not enough. On polling data, the ALP would be left holding two or three seats at the most and, two weeks before polling day, there were even suggestions that Rudd would lose his own seat.

In the final week before the election, Newspoll conducted a survey in seven marginal seats: Blair, Lilley, Moreton, Oxley, Petrie, Rankin and Capricornia. The overall primary votes were Labor 38 per cent, Coalition 42 per cent, and Greens 8 per cent. This suggested that these marginal Labor seats could go either way. But a further Newspoll in the key marginal seats of Brisbane, Forde, Longman, Herbert, Dawson, Bonner, Flynn, and Fisher produced an overall party support of Labor 32 per cent, LNP 54 per cent, and Greens 10 per cent.

The political battle was fought over the issue of which leader could exert the greater influence. Kevin Rudd campaigned as a local 'Queenslander', and Labor's hope was that his leadership would produce a better result than a potential loss of all seats under Gillard. On the other hand, the policies of LNP Premier Campbell Newman, involving savage cuts in almost every government area, had the potential to wash over to the federal context, especially once Tony Abbott made statements regarding cuts to the public service. But in the final analysis, it appeared that federal Labor was depressing Queensland Labor more than the state LNP was boosting Labor, and Queenslanders seemed to have 'got over' the cuts made by the Newman LNP Government (Wear 2013).

Two other complicating factors emerged. Queensland's maverick sitting member Bob Katter announced he was leading a charge across Australia to win seats for Katter's Australian Party. Meanwhile, Queenslander Clive Palmer announced a full team of candidates for his newly created Palmer United Party. Katter's intervention had the potential to damage the LNP; the possible effects of Palmer's intervention were less clear.

The electoral geography of Queensland also provided more hope for the LNP than for Labor. Of the nine electorates in the rural and provincial city areas, seven were held by the LNP, one (Capricornia) by Labor, and one by Katter. There was no real prospect of Labor increasing its representation in those seats. Of the 13 electorates in the metropolitan area, the LNP held eight to Labor's five. That was the key arena for Labor, not only for the Queensland result. As in Victoria, Labor had to at least hold all of its Queensland seats, and hope to increase its representation, to balance what was expected in New South Wales. In the event, Labor lost Capricornia and Petrie, and Palmer narrowly won Fairfax from the LNP.

Western Australia

The 2010 federal election had 'affirmed Western Australia's recent status as a conservative heartland state and one of the ALP's most unforgiving electorates' (Miragliotta and Sharman 2012: 231). For 30 years, Labor's share of the vote in federal elections had been lower than its performance at the state level, and had been declining. One long-term factor was the west's traditional animosity towards Canberra, regardless of party politics, but especially pronounced under a Labor federal government. The 2013 context was dominated by the perceived effects of the Gillard mining tax, and a potent argument from the WA Premier, Colin Barnett, that the state was being sold out under the GST distribution.

The 2010 election had left Labor with only three of the 15 seats. Further, Labor's primary vote of only 31.2 per cent was the lowest of any state or territory, and it had to depend on Green preferences to hold Brand, Fremantle and Perth. The polls during 2013 showed Labor's support continuing to decline. Over three Newspolls during 2013, Labor's primary support was 31, 25 and 30 per cent, with the Coalition holding an absolute majority on 50, 55 and 52 per cent.

A focused Newspoll in March emphasised the bleak picture for Labor. In the metropolitan area, the Liberal Party held a primary vote advantage over Labor of 50 to 35 per cent. In the rural areas, the margin was 66 to 24 per cent. Faced with a potential wipeout, Labor put all of its resources into attempting to save its three seats. It succeeded, despite the fact that Labor's state-wide two-party vote was the lowest in Australia, at 41.7 per cent. The campaign for marginal seats succeeded to the point where there was even a slight increase in Labor's primary vote in Fremantle. The only seat change was O'Connor, which, with the retirement of the Nationals' Tony Crook, shifted back to the Liberals in a three-cornered contest.

South Australia

South Australia did not promise to be important in the 2013 election. Of its 11 seats in the House of Representatives, five were held by the Liberal Party, and six by Labor. Three seats were marginal, all Liberal-held. But, given the evidence from the polls, Sturt, Boothby and Grey were likely to be retained.

The 2010 state election had seen massive swings against the Rann Labor Government, with swings of double figures recorded in the safe seats held by Rann ministers. However Rann was returned on the basis of an intense campaign, in key Labor marginals. The replacement of Rann by Jay Weatherill was a deliberate attempt to excise the Rann legacy and his style, and rebuild support in the metropolitan area. But under Weatherill, Labor faced a depressed economy, critically ill public finances, a depleted treasury, high unemployment—the second worst in the country after Tasmania—and a generally sullen electorate. The decision by BHP Billiton to postpone its Roxby Downs expansion, and the constant talk of the closure of the Holden car manufacturing plant, did not help Labor's standing; nor did the decision of Standard and Poors to reduce the state's rating from AA+ to AA.

In three Newspolls in 2013, Labor primary support was 32, 30 and 32 per cent, with the Liberal Party on 41, 44 and 46 per cent. This was not encouraging for Labor, but there was a buffer in its favour. All of its five seats were held by solid margins, and would be difficult for the Liberal Party to pick off. In the final analysis, Labor lost its most marginal seat Hindmarsh to the Liberal Party, with a two-party swing of 8 per cent.

Tasmania

The island state contains five electorates: Bass (based on Launceston), Denison and Franklin (Hobart), and two rural electorates—Braddon and Lyons. In the 2007 election, Labor won all five seats in the House of Representatives and in 2010 Labor retained four of the five, with independent Andrew Wilkie winning

Denison. This result prompted one analyst to comment that: 'The Liberal Party in Tasmania is at a crossroads over its capacity to attract both the voting public and candidates who can connect with the constituency' (McCall 2012: 208).

But neither Labor nor the Greens were in good odour in Tasmanian politics. The Labor–Green coalition Government, formed after the 2010 state election, had not succeeded in revitalising the state. The economy was the worst-performing of the states, with the highest unemployment level and little investment, while being increasingly dependent on federal largesse.

Labor's slim chances rested on the Greens continuing their meteoric rise in support: increasing from 9.9 per cent in the 2004 federal election to 13.5 per cent in 2007, and 16.8 per cent in 2010. The hope was that the Greens could pick up solid proportions of primary votes and feed them through to Labor. But a poll by Enterprise Marketing and Research Services on state voting intentions just prior to the 2013 election showed Labor with a primary vote of 23 per cent, Liberal 44 per cent, and Greens 12 per cent, with 17 per cent undecided.

After the 2013 election, it appears that the Liberal Party has moved past the crossroads McCall described by winning Bass, Braddon and Lyons. The Labor Party was reduced to only one seat, Franklin, where the primary swing against Labor was only 2.9 per cent, compared to the state-wide swing of 9.2 per cent. Andrew Wilkie was returned in Denison, with a swing in his favour of 16.8 per cent. The results indicated that Labor now had the problem of evaporating support especially in rural areas: a 9 per cent first-preference swing against Labor in Bass, -11.1 percent in Braddon, -11 per cent in Denison, and -12.1 per cent in Lyons. Overall, Labor suffered a state-wide two-party swing of -11.3 per cent, while the Greens lost more than half of their 2010 vote, falling from 16.8 to 8.3 per cent.

Northern Territory

The Northern Territory is a unique region. It had a population of 231,331 at the 2011 census, of which 26.8 per cent were Aboriginal or Torres Strait Islanders. There are two electorates in the territory. Solomon covers the city of Darwin and the satellite city of Palmerston. It was created in 2001, and was won by the Country Liberal Party (CLP) in 2001, 2004 and 2010, and by Labor in 2007. Lingiari comprises the remainder of the territory, including the Christmas and Cocos Islands. Forty-three per cent of Lingiari's population are Aboriginal and Torres Strait Islanders. This makes it unique in Australia. Labor has held the seat from its formation in 2001 on the back of very strong support from Indigenous voters. Until the 2013 election, Labor's Indigenous constituency had easily overcome solid support for the CLP in Alice Springs and Katherine. This hegemony was tested in the 2010 federal election when Labor only narrowly retained Lingiari, surviving a swing of -13.9 per cent against the incumbent, Warren Snowden, even though the CLP's vote was almost unchanged, with a swing against it of only -0.4 per cent.

The 2012 election for the territory Assembly produced a result that was a surprise to everyone. Since the first Assembly election in 1974, the outback electorates, which define Lingiari, had been the heartland of the Labor Party. For the first time since 1974, when Labor won no seats, the Aboriginal voters swung heavily to the CLP, which won five of the seven seats.

The CLP had hopes that the seat of Lingiari would repeat this swing at the 2013 federal election, partly through the support and efforts of two Aboriginal women members of the Assembly. Bess Price is a highly respected elder, who has been outspoken in favour of the federal intervention in the Aboriginal communities. Alison Anderson had won her seat of Macdonnell in 2008 as a Labor member, and was re-elected in 2012 as a CLP member. Both were highly respected in Aboriginal communities, and were expected to bolster the CLP vote.

However, serious instability in the CLP Government, which included the removal of Alison Anderson from her ministerial position, along with a lack of achievement by the CLP to produce what it had promised for the outback communities, resulted in the Labor Party narrowly holding onto the seat of Lingiari with a two-party swing of -2.82 against the sitting member. The CLP also narrowly retained Solomon.

Australian Capital Territory

The Australian Capital Territory is essentially the city-state of Canberra. Both of its electorates are Labor heartlands, with strong support from the overwhelmingly dominant component of the population—the Australian public service. The Labor Party has never been under any real threat. In the past five federal elections, the two-party Labor vote has fluctuated between a low of 61.1 per cent in 2001 to 63.4 per cent in 2007. Given fears over public service cuts, there was little doubt that such results would be repeated, and in 2013, the electorates of Canberra and Fraser produced a two-party vote of 57.0 per cent and 62.6 per cent respectively.

A regional analysis

The most obvious regional division in Australia is between the metropolitan and non-metropolitan areas. The rural electorates are almost exclusively the province of the Coalition, shared between the Liberal and National parties. The metropolitan areas have traditionally been the arena for a two-party contest between Labor and Liberal parties but, in recent elections, the Greens have intervened. The 2013 election result again demonstrated this regional division.

Table 2: Patterns of party support, metropolitan and non-metropolitan

	Metropolitan	Non-metropolitan
Labor primary	36.20	29.40
Labor swing	-4.00	-5.40
Labor two-party	49.40	42.40
Coalition primary	43.90	47.80
Green primary	10.00	6.80

Source: Australian Electoral Commission (2013).

Of 63 electorates in the non-metropolitan region, Labor held 23 in the run-up to the 2013 election; it retained only five. In the metropolitan region, Labor held 49 seats prior to the election; it retained 39.

This division between metropolitan and non-metropolitan regions masks important sub-regions, which have differing socio-economic characteristics and different patterns of party support. To extend and refine the analysis, the focus will be on clusters of similar electorates across Australia, defined by the Australian Electoral Commission (AEC). There are:

- *Rural cluster*: divisions without a majority of enrolment in major provincial cities (43 divisions in 2013);
- *Provincial cluster*: divisions with a majority of enrolment in major provincial cities (20 divisions);
- *Inner metropolitan cluster*: located in a capital city, and comprising well-established, built-up suburbs (44 divisions); and the
- *Outer metropolitan cluster*: located in capital cities and containing areas of more recent urban expansion (43 divisions).

Our regional analysis is based on these clusters of electorates in the six states. The Northern Territory, with two electorates, can be regarded as a region in its own right, defined especially by the fact that its population includes over 25 per cent Aboriginal people, and the lack of a sizeable metropolitan area. The Australian Capital Territory, essentially the city of Canberra, also has a unique socio-economic structure.

In terms of numbers of seats, the key to winning elections in Australia, except in the case of a very tight election, as in 2010 which resulted in a hung parliament, are the metropolitan areas. Of the 150 electorates in this analysis, 87 are in the metropolitan areas.

Table 3: Patterns of party support by clusters

	Inner metro	Outer metro	Provincial	Rural	Total
Labor primary	35.70	36.80	35.50	26.00	33.40
Labor swing	-3.10	-4.20	-6.60	-5.00	-4.60
Labor two-party	48.20	48.10	48.60	40.20	46.60
Coalition primary	43.40	44.10	44.30	48.40	45.60
Green primary	12.10	7.30	7.40	6.80	8.70

Source: Australian Electoral Commission (2013).

The most obvious aspect in this data is the relatively low variations of patterns of voting across the first three subsets. The rural cluster is the sole outlier, as would be expected, and showed by far the lowest Labor vote and the highest support for the Coalition. This cluster is the heartland of the Liberal and National parties. Yet, the patterns across the metropolitan and provincial clusters were remarkably similar on three indices: Labor primary and two-party vote, and Coalition primary vote. This looks, at first sight, to offer support for a thesis of a relatively uniform vote and swing. But the relative similarity was the result of significantly different primary swings. The swing against Labor in the provincial cluster was significantly higher than in the two metropolitan clusters. The Green vote was significantly higher in the inner metropolitan cluster. These differences are explored below.

The rural cluster

This cluster comprises 43 electorates across the six states. New South Wales (14 electorates), Victoria (9) and Queensland (10) dominate the cluster, with Western Australia (4), South Australia (3) and Tasmania (2), as well as Lingiari in the Northern Territory.

This cluster is, and always has been, essentially non-Labor territory. For decades, the electoral story of rural Australia was relatively simple: the overwhelming majority of rural seats were won by either Liberal or National candidates. The Coalition agreement under which incumbents of both parties were protected from contests with each other provided a relatively stable outcome. Moreover, the recent formation of the Liberal National Party ended internal coalition conflicts in Queensland, and there is no National Party to contest in Tasmania, and no coalition in South Australia. Outside Queensland, the National Party, holding nine rural seats in New South Wales and Victoria, faces the real potential of contests with the expansive Liberal Party in vacant rural seats, although preference-sharing agreements ensure that the Coalition vote remains relatively stable.

The emergence of new issues particularly relevant to rural areas has produced some tensions: the carbon tax; the mining tax; water supply and security, and coal seam gas developments, international trade and marketing, have the potential to divide the Coalition in the rural areas. More recently, the election context in rural areas has become more complex, with the success of conservative-inclined independents and the formation prior to the election of both Katter's Australian Party (KAP) and the Palmer United Party (PUP). All these developments had the potential to erode Coalition support in rural areas, especially in Queensland where Bob Katter is a formidable incumbent and a former National member.

Table 4: Patterns of party support, rural cluster

	NSW	Vic	Qld	WA	SA	Tas	NT*	Cluster
ALP primary	28.20	24.30	25.20	21.00	27.10	37.20	39.80	26.00
ALP swing	-4.50	-7.70	-6.10	-2.20	-5.80	-9.50	-0.30	-5.00
ALP two-party	40.10	38.80	41.30	35.20	40.10	47.40	53.70	40.20
Coalition primary	51.90	52.80	45.70	60.00	50.00	46.90	38.20	48.40
Green primary	7.20	6.10	5.30	7.80	7.70	8.30	7.80	6.80

*Lingiari. Note that in this and following tables, some sub-clusters contain only a small number of electorates.

Source: Australian Electoral Commission (2013).

Across the rural cluster as a whole, Labor suffered a sizeable mean primary swing against it of -5.0 per cent, with the worst swings in the states of Tasmania (-9.5), Victoria (-7.7) and Queensland (-6.1), but only -2.2 in Western Australia. The Coalition achieved a mean primary swing in its favour of 1.6 per cent. The mean first preference Green vote in the rural cluster was 6.8 per cent, compared to 9.7 per cent in 2010, with the highest support in the electorate of Richmond (NSW) of 17.7 per cent.

The mean primary swing to the Coalition (LNP) was weakest in Queensland, with five of the 10 electorates showing a swing away from the LNP. The main cause was the support won by the PUP and, to a much lesser extent, the KAP (see the chapter by King). The PUP won a total of 13.6 per cent of the primary vote across the cluster, including 26.5 per cent in the electorate of Fairfax. The KAP won 4.7 per cent of the vote across the cluster, although their leader, Bob Katter, suffered a swing of 14.2 per cent to the LNP, and his primary vote was reduced to 29.4 per cent.

The electoral domination by the Coalition parties has come under attack from independents. The 2010 election produced three independents from safe Coalition rural seats, all of whom were formerly National Party members of parliament: Bob Katter in the Queensland electorate of Kennedy; Tony Windsor in New England and Rob Oakeshott in Lyne, both New South Wales rural seats. Windsor and Oakeshott gave their support to the Gillard/Rudd governments, and their retirement from the parliament at the 2013 election pre-empted their almost certain defeat in what were conservative electorates. The Nationals regained both seats. However, the persistence of the independent challenge in these electorates was highlighted in the Victorian rural seat of Indi, where Cathy McGowan ousted the Liberal's Sophie Mirabella who had held the seat since 2001 (see Chapter 16 by Costar and Curtin).

In the 2010 election, the Greens were described as 'harvesting votes and directing preferences in ways that might yet prove difficult for conservative rural MPs' (Woodward and Curtin 2012: 241). In 2013, the harvest was poor. The mean Green primary vote across the 10 rural electorates in Queensland fell from 10 per cent to 5.2 per cent. In the other states, the rural swing against the Greens was more subdued, with six of the rural electorates showing a small swing to the Greens—five in New South Wales.

Labor lost only one rural seat in New South Wales (Eden-Monaro) and two in Tasmania (Braddon and Lyons). Following the election, 34 of the 43 rural electorates are firmly in Coalition control. In a sense, five of the six Labor rural electorates constitute a sub-cluster. Lingiari has been analysed above. The Labor Party retained Richmond and Hunter in New South Wales, Blair in Queensland, McEwen in Victoria, and Wakefield in South Australia. In each of these rural Labor seats, there is a solid industrial/urban component; and in four of the five there was a strong swing against Labor (the exception was Blair with only a -0.5 per cent swing). Hence, the 2013 election reduced all five to marginal status. Across rural Australia there were significant swings against Labor, namely in Hunter (-9.8 per cent), McEwen (-10.2 per cent), Braddon (-11.1 per cent) and Lyons (-12.1 per cent). Queensland produced two rural independents: Bob Katter who was re-elected in Kennedy and Clive Palmer won Fairfax; both seats were previously held by the Nationals.

The patterns of support across the rural cluster imply stability rather than change in 2013. The swings against Labor in the rural cluster suggest that Labor has a difficult task holding its few rural seats. The fact that there was a primary swing against Labor in every rural electorate except Lyne and New England (where the incumbent independents had retired) and a 0.1 per cent swing in O'Connor, suggests that the rural cluster has become even more reinforced as the heartland of non-Labor parties.

The provincial cluster

There are 20 electorates classified as provincial by the AEC, on the basis that a majority of the enrolment is in major provincial cities. Eight are in New South

Wales, seven in Queensland, four in Victoria, and one (Bass) in Tasmania. This cluster is the most diverse in socio-economic terms and there is a significant party division between them. Prior to the election, seven of the eight provincial electorates in New South Wales were held by Labor, as were all four in Victoria, and Bass. Only one of the seven in Queensland was Labor. This contrasting pattern of party support suggests that the differing political contexts in the states had a significant influence on the provincial cities.

The 2013 election saw five provincial seats transferred from Labor to the Coalition, the highest proportion across the four clusters: Dobell and Robertson in New South Wales, both on the central coast; Corangamite in Victoria, including the southern coast but extending to the suburbs of Geelong; Capricornia in Queensland, including suburbs of Rockingham and Mackay; and Bass in Tasmania, centred on Launceston. This result meant that the Coalition now holds all of the provincial seats in Queensland, the sole seat in Tasmania, and four of the 12 provincial seats in New South Wales and Victoria. Further, the swings against Labor have reduced the security of the remaining Labor-held seats to a significant degree.

Labor's loss of the seat of Dobell was an expected outcome: the incumbent Craig Thomson faced charges of fraudulently misusing union funds for personal benefit including for the procurement of prostitutes; he had remained loyal to the Gillard Government but been suspended then expelled from the Labor Party. The replacement Labor candidate then suffered a primary swing against her of -11.2 per cent. All five electorates lost by Labor were all marginal prior to the election, meaning any general swing away from Labor would be enough to see the seat change hands.

Table 5: Patterns of party support, provincial city cluster

	NSW	Vic	Qld	Tas	Cluster
Labor primary	41.30	38.50	27.20	34.70	35.40
Labor swing	-5.30	-8.70	-5.80	-8.80	-6.30
Labor two-party	54.30	52.50	40.00	46.00	51.30
Coalition primary	38.10	40.30	43.00	47.90	41.40
Green primary	8.00	9.50	4.70	7.90	7.20

Source: Australian Electoral Commission (2013).

The Queensland result in the provincial cities was significantly worse for Labor than in New South Wales or Victoria. The mean Labor primary vote was a meagre 27.2 per cent across the seven electorates. The 2013 election produced a clean sweep for the LNP when it won Capricornia from Labor. Further, after the mean swing to the LNP of 5.8 per cent, six of the seven Queensland provincial electorates are now safe for the Coalition, with only Capricornia in a marginal LNP status.

The overall swing against Labor across the cluster was especially marked in Victoria. Three of the four provincial electorates in Victoria, Ballarat, Bendigo and Corio, were previously safe Labor, but the election result reduced this to marginal status. In New South Wales, seven of the eight provincial electorates were held by Labor prior to the election, all but Dobell and Robertson with safe margins. Both these seats were lost to the Liberal Party. Support for the Greens in the provincial cluster was relatively strong in New South Wales, Victoria, and Bass in Tasmania, but significantly weaker in Queensland. The Greens suffered a mean primary swing against them of -3.5 per cent across the cluster.

Provincial electorates, by definition, contain all or part of major provincial cities. In the Victorian case, the four cities can be considered to be closely related to greater Melbourne: Corangamite and Corio in Geelong; Ballarat and Bendigo as major cities. In New South Wales, three of the eight provincial cities (Macquarie, Dobell and Robertson) have all but been absorbed into greater Sydney, while Charlton, Newcastle, Shortland, Cunningham and Throsby are located in the Newcastle and Illawarra areas.

In Queensland, four of the seven provincial cities are not as geographically linked to the capital, as similar seats are in Victoria and New South Wales, but are 'country provincials', namely: Capricornia (Rockhampton), Groom (Toowoomba), Herbert (Townsville), and Hinkler (Bundaberg). These hinterland electorates are closely connected with the rural areas surrounding them, and reflect the political culture of rural Queensland. Three provincial electorates are in the rapidly growing population area between Brisbane and the Gold and Sunshine Coasts. These three are embedded in different socio-economic conditions than in the more 'metropolitan' electorates in Victoria and New South Wales.

The Coalition secured a mean swing of 2.6 per cent in its favour in the four Victorian electorates. The mean swing against Labor was -8.7 per cent, with highs of -10.4 per cent in Bendigo and -9.8 per cent in Ballarat. In New South Wales, there was almost no movement in the mean swing to the Coalition across the eight electorates, with Shortland and Newcastle showing the highest swings (-3.5 and -3.4 per cent respectively). But in Queensland, there was a mean swing of -4.0 per cent against the LNP. This is explained by the involvement of the PUP and, to a lesser extent, the KAP. The mean PUP primary vote over the seven electorates was 12.3 per cent, with the highest in Hinkler, 17.7 per cent. The KAP contested five of the Queensland provincial electorates with a mean primary vote of 4.9 per cent.

On the data examined, it is fair to say that the provincial city electorates better reflect the political contexts of the states than the other clusters. For example, of the 12 NSW and Victorian provincial electorates, Labor holds eight after the election. All seven Queensland provincial electorates are firmly in the hands of the LNP. Overall, this reinforces the impact of location within this sub-cluster. The more 'metropolitan' provincial cities appear to be moving closer to the metropolitan patterns of voting.

Metropolitan areas

Given the rural and provincial clusters offered slim pickings for Labor and, in fact, saw Labor lose seats—it was the metropolitan areas which would decide Labor's fate. A January–March Newspoll indicated that Labor was in trouble in the capital cities: 45 per cent Coalition, 35 per cent Labor. This pattern was repeated in the April–June and August Newspolls. The data suggested that there would be a major swing against Labor in Sydney, especially in the western suburbs; that Adelaide and Melbourne were weakening for Labor; and that Perth may produce a result where Labor lost all of its seats. The implication was that Brisbane had to produce a solid swing to Labor to counteract the losses elsewhere.

Table 6: Patterns of party support, metropolitan areas

	NSW	Vic	Qld	WA	SA	Tas	ACT	NT*	Cluster
ALP primary	35.90	38.20	34.80	30.60	40.70	32.50	42.90	35.40	36.40
ALP swing	-2.00	-8.10	-1.50	-2.60	-4.50	-6.90	-2.10	-0.70	-3.90
ALP two-party	46.30	54.50	47.10	43.30	51.90	57.00	40.10	48.30	49.20
Coalition primary	48.00	39.00	44.80	49.10	41.40	31.10	34.60	44.70	44.30
Green primary	8.40	12.70	7.80	10.20	8.90	10.10	13.40	8.00	10.00

*Solomon.

Source: Australian Electoral Commission (2013).

Western Australia produced the lowest mean primary vote for Labor in the metropolitan areas, and Franklin (Tasmania) the highest. The primary swing against Labor was by far the most pronounced in Victoria.

In New South Wales, with 26 metropolitan seats, 15 were held by Labor, eight of which were marginal. The Labor Party was fearful that the corruption scandals that had led to a landslide in the New South Wales election, and which were continuing, would result in a similar result in the federal election. There were also suggestions that Labor's new, hard-line policy on boat people could have a major effect, especially in the western suburbs of Sydney. Coupled with negative reactions from this region concerning the Rudd proposal for a 'big Australia', this had the potential to produce a backlash against Labor. But the 2013 election saw Labor hold up better than predicted. The New South Wales swing against Labor was merely the second lowest after Queensland, and was only half of the mean swing across the cluster.

The 'ethnic' sub-cluster

As Jupp notes in Chapter 19, there were 14 electorates in Sydney which he labels 'ethnic electorates', containing 25 per cent or more people who used a language other than English at home. All but one (Bennelong) was held by the Labor Party. Nine electorates were in the western suburbs. Of these, three were lost to the Coalition: Banks (-1.9 per cent swing against Labor), Barton (-8.0 per cent) and Reid (-0.9 per cent). In fact, five 'ethnic' electorates showed a swing to Labor: Greenway, Chifley, Grayndler, Blaxland, and Fowler, the last with a two-party swing of 8 per cent. It was evident that the deep concern of the Labor Party that it would lose heavily in Sydney's west was tempered by the small swing against it, despite the loss of ('non-ethnic') Lindsay.

In Melbourne, which had held up for Labor in 2010, there were also suggestions in the polls that Labor support was weakening, and that the Greens would erode Labor support. The former proved to be the case, with a primary swing of -8.1 per cent across the Melbourne metropolitan electorates, although Labor still finished with a two-party vote of 54.5 per cent. The Green vote fell by 1.5 per cent from 2010, but the preference flow to Labor was still decisive. Labor lost only two seats in metropolitan Melbourne (Deakin and La Trobe) both of which were marginal before the election.

The influence of 'ethnic' communities on the metropolitan vote in Sydney and Melbourne showed a significantly different pattern. Of 15 Melbourne-based 'ethnic' electorates, Menzies was retained by the Coalition, and Melbourne itself was retained by the Greens. In the remaining 13, the mean primary vote for Labor was 61 per cent, compared with 53.9 per cent in the Sydney 'ethnic' electorates. A further significant difference between the two 'ethnic' groups was the difference in the Green vote. This reflected the higher proportion of Green support across Melbourne and Victoria as a whole.

Table 7: Patterns of party support, 'ethnic' electorates

	Sydney	Melbourne
Labor primary	45.80	43.10
Labor swing	-0.70	-9.20
Labor two-party	55.10	58.50
Coalition primary	42.30	33.10
Green primary	6.50	12.40

Source: Australian Electoral Commission (2013).

In terms of seats won and lost, the metropolitan areas produced less change than both Labor and the Coalition had predicted. Labor lost eight of the 46 seats it had held: Banks, Barton, Lindsay and Reid in Sydney; Deakin and LaTrobe in Melbourne; Petrie in Queensland, and Hindmarsh in Adelaide. Despite the suggestions in the early polls of 2013, there was no landslide in the metropolitan areas; the swing against Labor was a modest -4.0 per cent.

Nor was there strong evidence of uniformity within the metropolitan cluster. There were different patterns across the state sub-clusters. This is to be expected, as the effects of different state-oriented campaigns, issues and political contexts come into play. The strong swings against Labor in Melbourne, Hobart and Adelaide are prime examples.

The inner metropolitan cluster

This cluster contains 44 electorates across the capital cities. Prior to the election, Labor held 26 of these, with Melbourne held by the Greens and Denison held by independent Andrew Wilkie.

In recent years, these electorates, especially in Sydney and Melbourne, have increasingly become the home for a specific socio-economic group, with a 'concentration of tertiary-educated, human-services-employed, young and affluent voters with social-progressive post-materialist outlooks' (Economou 2012: 184). These have become a heartland for the Greens, and a troubled cluster for the Labor Party. But the result of the 2013 election in the trendy inner-city cluster was a matter of relative stability rather than change. Only four Labor seats were lost to the Coalition, and the mean swing against Labor was -3.1 per cent.

Table 8: Patterns of party support, inner metropolitan cluster

	NSW	Vic	Qld	WA	SA	Tas	ACT	NT*	Cluster
ALP primary	35.80	36.10	36.30	30.50	39.90	24.80	42.90	35.40	35.70
ALP swing	-1.70	-7.80	0.50	-1.40	-4.90	-11.00	-2.10	-0.70	-3.10
ALP two-party	42.30	53.40	49.50	43.40	51.50	45.00	59.90	48.30	48.20
Coalition primary	47.60	38.20	43.80	49.70	42.30	23.20	34.60	44.70	43.40
Green primary	10.40	18.20	10.70	11.90	9.30	7.90	13.40	8.00	12.10

*Solomon.

Source: Australian Electoral Commission (2013).

With the exception of Denison (Hobart) and Perth, Labor's primary vote was remarkably similar across the cluster, with the lowest support in Perth, and (with the exception of Canberra), the highest in Adelaide. But this apparent similarity was a result of significantly different swings. In Brisbane, Sydney and Perth, Labor's primary vote was within 2 percentage points of the 2010 result. The expectation of strong swings against Labor did not eventuate. In Brisbane, there was a small primary vote swing in favour of the Labor Party, a result that was not expected by either side just weeks before the election. The Melbourne sub-cluster produced the strongest swing against Labor, but this did not bolster the Coalition to a significant degree.

The inner metropolitan areas were reinforced as the Green heartland, with a mean primary support across the cluster of 12.1 per cent. But, apart from Melbourne, it was a heartland that eroded significantly in 2013. The Greens lost one-third of their 2010 support in Brisbane, and one-quarter in Perth, Adelaide and Sydney. Melbourne alone was the standout result for the Greens.

The pattern of relative stability was reinforced by the fact that only four of the 44 inner-city seats shifted from Labor to Liberal: Reid, Banks and Barton in Sydney, and Hindmarsh in Adelaide. Despite the predictions of a dire result for Labor, there was no change in party representation in Melbourne, Brisbane and Perth. In Brisbane, Labor held on to its marginal seats in Lilley and Moreton, with a swing to Labor in the latter. In Perth, Labor's marginals, Fremantle and Perth, both recorded a slight swing to Labor. In Adelaide, Labor lost its most marginal seat, Hindmarsh, but retained Adelaide and Port Adelaide.

In Melbourne, with 12 electorates in the inner metropolitan cluster, there were strong swings against Labor in every electorate, a mean of -7.8 per cent, by far the highest in the cluster. But no seats were lost, partly because the largest swings occurred in the safest Labor electorates and, more important, the Green vote held up strongly and fed preferences to Labor. The mean swing against the Greens in Melbourne inner metropolitan area was a miniscule -0.2 per cent. Labor was certainly saved by the Greens.

In the run-up to the election, there were expectations of a strong swing against Labor in Sydney, especially in the western suburbs. Of the 15 electorates in the inner metropolitan cluster of Sydney, six were held by the Liberal Party, five of which were safe: Bradfield, Cook, North Sydney, Warringah and Wentworth. Only one, Bennelong, was marginal. On the other hand, six of the nine Labor seats were marginal: Banks, Barton, Grayndler, Kingsford Smith, Parramatta, and Reid. Twelve of the 15 electorates swung against Labor; whereas Blaxland, Grayndler and Sydney, all safe Labor seats, showed a swing to the Labor Party. Labor lost only three seats: Banks, Barton and Reid—a result that was not expected by either side of politics. The western suburbs did not produce the anti-Labor swing to the extent that Labor feared and the Coalition hoped.

The inner metropolitan cluster showed significant differences in swings: a small swing to the Labor Party in Brisbane; small swings against Labor in Sydney and Perth; a significant swing against Labor in Adelaide, and a very strong swing against Labor in Melbourne. In the single electorate of Denison in Hobart, Labor's primary vote was significantly depressed by support for the independent Andrew Wilkie, and the Perth inner metropolitan electorates produced a significantly lower primary vote. But Sydney, Melbourne Brisbane and Adelaide produced very similar results.

The outer metropolitan cluster

This was the largest cluster, with 43 electorates. Of these, 23 were held by Labor, eight of which were marginal. Ten of the 20 held by the Coalition were marginal. There was potential for considerable change, but despite that fact that there was a primary swing against Labor in every one of the 43 electorates except the Sydney electorates of Chifley (+0.7 increase), Fowler (+7.9) and Greenway (+ 2.2), only four seats moved from Labor to the Coalition: Deakin and La Trobe in Melbourne, Lindsay in Sydney, and Petrie in Brisbane

Table 9: Patterns of party support, outer metropolitan cluster

	NSW	Vic	Qld	WA	SA	Tas	Cluster
ALP primary	37.30	39.90	34.40	30.70	41.90	39.90	36.80
ALP swing	-2.20	-8.80	-2.20	-3.90	-4.00	-2.90	-4.40
ALP two-party	45.70	52.80	46.50	43.10	52.60	55.10	48.10
Coalition primary	47.70	40.00	45.00	47.30	40.00	38.70	44.10
Green primary	5.30	7.30	6.80	8.60	8.30	12.20	12.20

Source: Australian Electoral Commission (2013).

In Sydney, the other five Labor-held seats were safe, and withstood a swing of -2.2 per cent. In Melbourne, the primary swing against Labor of -8.8 per cent was of landslide proportions, but Labor was saved by preferences from the continuing strong vote for the Greens in seats where it mattered. As mentioned, only Deakin and La Trobe were lost to the Liberal Party, both of which were marginal Labor before the election. In the Brisbane sub-cluster Labor held four seats and, with only a muted swing against Labor, was able to retain three, losing only Petrie. In Perth, Brand was saved when there was only a -0.4 per cent swing against Labor.

Perth produced the weakest result for Labor, with Adelaide recording the highest primary vote. In Sydney, Labor continued its hold on the western and south-western suburbs. There were significant differences in the Labor swing. Every Victorian outer metropolitan electorate swung against Labor, with the largest in Lalor (-18.8 per cent) following the retirement of Julia Gillard, Gorton (-12.1 per cent), McEwen (-10.2 per cent), and Scullin (-9.6 per cent). In Melbourne, the primary swing of -8.8 percent against Labor translated to -6.2 per cent on a two-party vote. As in the inner metropolitan cluster, the Green vote held up better in outer metropolitan Melbourne, and saved Labor seats.

Brisbane outer metropolitan electorates were better for Labor than the early polling in 2013 had suggested. Despite the predictions that Brisbane would produce a poor result for Labor, the 10 outer metropolitan electorates in Brisbane produced the lowest primary swing against Labor of the cluster. Despite that, Labor lost Petrie, and now holds only three of the 10 seats. In Sydney, Labor's fears were not realised: the western suburb electorates of Chifley, Fowler and Greenway actually showed a swing to Labor.

In Perth, swings were considerably more variable: -13.7 per cent against Labor in Canning, to only -0.4 per cent in the key Labor electorate of Brand, which Labor retained. In seats, it was a matter of *status quo*. A primary swing of plus 3.9 per cent was not enough for the Liberal Party to win Brand—Labor's only seat in the Perth cluster. In Adelaide, the election mirrored the polls with a swing of -4.0 per cent against Labor. Of the three electorates in the cluster, Boothby was strengthened for the Liberal Party, and Kingston and Makin became weaker for Labor.

The Green vote across the cluster declined from the 2010 level, in all cities, but was most noticeable in Melbourne. The Greens' best results were in Ryan (Brisbane, 14.4 per cent), Mackellar (Sydney, 14.2 per cent), Boothby (Adelaide, 12.0 per cent), and Pearce (Perth, 11.2 per cent).

Explaining regional variability

Examining the regional electoral geography, the 2013 election produced differential results, the highlights of which can be summarised.

New South Wales did not produce the overwhelming anti-Labor landslide that the early polls, and the very public traumas of the state Labor Party, had suggested. However, it was responsible for the loss of eight of the 17 seats that transferred from Labor to the Coalition. To a large extent, the 2013 election was won in New South Wales. Victoria produced a strong primary swing against Labor, but it won a majority of the two-party votes on the basis of Green preferences. Labor was apparently the 'least unpreferred' major party in Victoria. Despite that, Labor lost three seats: Corangamite, Deakin and La Trobe.

Queensland, which had been forecast to be bad news for Labor under Gillard and was a key responsibility for the restored Kevin Rudd, produced only a small swing against Labor losing only Capricornia and Petrie. Western Australia had been predicted to show a strong swing against Labor, with the potential to deliver a complete wipe-out. But there was only a small swing against Labor, and no seats changed hands between the main adversaries (although the ALP did lose a Senate seat to the PUP in Western Australia after the April 2014 re-election).

In South Australia, the election result mirrored the predictions and the state political context: a strong swing against Labor, but the loss of only one seat. Tasmania was the weak state for Labor, with strong swings against Labor, and three of the five seats—Bass, Braddon and Lyons—moving to the Liberal Party. There was no change in the representation from the Australian Capital Territory and the Northern Territory.

The regional analysis was based on clusters of electorates with similar geographic and socio-economic characteristics. A summary of the results of the analysis suggests the efficacy of such an approach. The rural region has a distinct 'anti-establishment' political culture, and the 2013 election produced distinctive patterns of party support. Yet traditional patterns of support for the major parties were retained, although the precise location and context of the states in which they are situated did have some effect (especially with some strong local challenges from PUP and KAP). The major differences in voting patterns across the cluster occurred in the electorates which, while classified as rural, contained a significant and growing urban/industrial component. Examples are Hunter and Richmond in New South Wales, McEwen in Victoria, Blair in Queensland and Wakefield in South Australia. These had characteristics, and patterns of party choice, which more reflected the provincial city cluster than the rural.

The provincial city cluster also showed a strong similarity of patterns of voting, with the exception of the Queensland sub-cluster, all the electorates of which are formed around provincial cities embedded in rural areas, and which, after the Labor loss of Capricornia, is totally 'owned' by the Liberal National Party. In New South Wales, however, Labor retains five of the eight electorates, which is partly explained by the fact that the provincial cities contain elements of greater Sydney, rather than existing within rural areas. In Victoria, two provincial city electorates, Ballarat and Bendigo, have a strong rural influence whereas Corio is embedded in Geelong.

Overall, the metropolitan clusters showed a high degree of similarity in patterns of party support. There were occasional big differences recorded, which can be linked to the influence of a state political context: the high Green vote in Melbourne, the landslide against Labor in Tasmania, the differences between the 'ethnic' sub-clusters in Melbourne and Sydney, and the stable Labor primary vote in Queensland. A comparison of the patterns in the inner, outer, and total metropolitan clusters leaves a clear impression of similarities rather than differences in the primary votes and swings of both parties.

Our conclusion is that there was significantly *more* similarity, even greater uniformity, *within* the regional clusters in the 2013 election, despite the states in which they were situated, than within and between the states themselves. Place rather than party identification may be the main determinant of contemporary voting patterns. The 2016 election will provide further evidence about whether these prevailing patterns remain dominant.

References

Australian Electoral Commission (AEC). 2013. *Election 2013—Virtual Tally Room*. 4 November, viewed 3 February 2014: <results.aec.gov.au/17496/Website/Default.htm>.

Economou, Nick. 2012. 'Victoria'. In Simms and Wanna (eds), *Julia 2010: The caretaker election*, Canberra: ANU E-Press.

McCall, Tony. 2012. 'Tasmania'. In Simms and Wanna (eds), *Julia 2010: The caretaker election*, Canberra: ANU E-Press.

Miragliotta, Narelle and Campbell, Sharman. 2012. 'Western Australia at the Polls: A case of resurgent regionalism', in Simms and Wanna (eds), *Julia 2010: The caretaker election*, Canberra: ANU E-Press.

Miragliotta, Narelle. 2013. 'The View from the West'. Paper presented at workshop, The Australian National University, Canberra, 2–3 November.

Simms, Marian and Wanna, John (eds). 2012. *Julia 2010: The caretaker election*. Canberra: ANU E-Press.

Thompson, Elaine and Robinson, Geoff. 2012. In Simms and Wanna (eds), *Julia 2010: The caretaker election*, Canberra: ANU E-Press.

Ward, Ian. 2012. 'Queensland'. In Simms and Wanna (eds), *Julia 2010: The caretaker election*, Canberra: ANU E-Press.

Wear, Rae. 2013. 'Queensland'. Paper presented at workshop, The Australian National University, Canberra, 2–3 November.

Woodward, Dennis and Curtin, Jennifer. 2012. 'Rural and Regional Australia: The ultimate winners?' In Simms and Wanna (eds), *Julia 2010: The caretaker election*, Canberra: ANU E-Press.

15. Regional Place-Based Identities and Party Strategies at the 2013 Federal Election

Geoff Robinson[1]

During the prime ministership of Julia Gillard themes of place-based identities were prominent in Australian political discourse. At the 2010 federal election Labor's two-party-preferred vote reached historic highs in Victoria, South Australia and Tasmania but fell sharply in Queensland and Western Australia. During the last year of the Gillard Government observers competed to produce more gloomy scenarios of a Labor collapse both in states such as Queensland and Western Australia and ill-defined regions such as 'western Sydney' (Kenny 2013; Shanahan 2012). On election night, 7 September 2013, these predictions were largely unfulfilled. The final result demonstrated a general, rather than regionally specific, estrangement from Labor. The largest swings against Labor were in the states where the Party had performed best in 2010 (see Antony Green's chapter in this volume, Chapter 23).

The 2010 election had been one of firsts: a female prime minister, the near-defeat of a first-term government and an unprecedented vote for the Greens. There were also exceptionally high levels of divergence in electoral behaviour between the states. Across the next three years Australian parties sought to learn the political lessons of 2010. Labor sought to shore up its base against erosion to both the left and right, the Coalition refined their (almost) winning appeal and worked to make Tony Abbott less of the (slight) liability he had been in 2010 (Bean and McAllister 2012: 352). The Greens searched for new constituencies, such as farmers, beyond the urban left they had attracted in 2010. The final result of the 2013 federal election demonstrated that the regionally-based estrangement from Labor apparent in 2010 had become a national disenchantment, but that Labor had some success in defending its base. The Greens found themselves pushed back to their heartland in inner Melbourne while Clive Palmer surfed a wave of political disillusion.

---

1 Thanks are due to participants in the 2013 Election Workshop for comments, to Antony Green for assisting in the location of electoral statistics and to Lisa Hay for editing.

Political regionalism in Australia

This chapter focuses on three lines of regional division in Australian politics: (1) the states and territories; (2) mining and agricultural regions; and (3) the alleged division between 'western Sydney' and inner Melbourne and Sydney. It complements the analysis in other chapters in this volume (see Chapters 14 and 23 by Jaensch, Miragliotta and Wear, and by Green, respectively) by unpacking in more depth the nature of the regional differences that underlie divergent voting patterns. This chapter argues that there are three distinct forms of 'regionalism': social, economic and cultural.

Social regionalism

Social regionalism refers to the fact that the divergent electoral behaviour of different regions is often simply a reflection of their different social composition. Journalistic analyses of regional divergences in Australian politics frequently cite the variant levels of party support in different states as evidence of 'regionalism' (Colebatch 2013a). It is not surprising that Australian states have different levels of party support or that the Greens poll better in inner Melbourne than outer western Sydney. 'Marginal' electorates may be in the suburbs and regions but this does not indicate, contrary to the arguments of some commentators, that there is a distinct 'suburban' or 'regional' identity (Henderson 2013; *The Australian* 2014).

Australia, compared to other federations, is notable for the low level of political divergence between the states and territories. There is no Australian equivalent of Scotland or Alberta, subnational territories in which one side of politics is entirely powerless. Even Western Australia, currently Labor's graveyard, had a state Labor government from 2001 to 2008.

Democratic politics is mostly about a competition by parties to provide voters with the same public goods, even if voters disagree about which goods to prioritise and their evaluation of the competence of different parties to provide them (King *et al*. 2008). The uniformity of political behaviour in Australia exemplifies this principle. In Australian democracy voters mostly want the same public goods, such as rising living standards, national security, defence of borders and high quality government services. Voters do diverge in the weight that they place on particular goods and in their estimate of the competence of different parties to provide them. The Australian colonies entered federation with highly variant party systems and divergent levels of enthusiasm for the project of federation itself (Parker 1949). After 1901, Australian voters demonstrated a uniform preference for the public good of racial exclusion and national development. Class politics stabilised the system, workers in Melbourne and Perth largely valued the same public goods and trusted in Labor to supply them. After 1910, the portion of voters socialised in childhood to identify with one party or the other steadily increased and this added a further element of stability to the system (Aitkin 1982).

Economic regionalism

Economic regionalism describes the fact that the geographical concentration of a particular industry may lead voters in a region to develop a distinct sense of shared economic interest. This pattern first clearly emerged with the rise of the Country Party in the 1920s. Farmers were a small portion of the electorate but the new party drew on an ideology of 'countrymindedness' to convince town residents and many rural workers that they shared common interests with farmers (Aitkin 1985).

The debate about the taxation of the mining industry at the 2010 election revived a modern form of countrymindedness. Many voters in Queensland and Western Australia resented the claims of other states to share in mineral wealth. The number of electors employed in capital-intensive resource industries, such as mining or forestry, is quite small, but voters tend to overestimate their importance as employers and are also prone to accept claims about the dependence on them of other industries (Blainey 2013; Essential Media Communications 2012; Schirmer 2012). This chapter will show that there was a distinct electoral reaction against Labor in mining regions at the 2010 election and that this was maintained in 2013.

Cultural regionalism

A third form of political regionalism, here called *cultural regionalism*, could emerge if significant groups of voters come to question the legitimacy of the state as a provider of public goods. Secessionism is one form of this but the debate about asylum seekers has provided another challenge to state legitimacy. Australian governments have competed to prove their credentials as providers of 'border protection' in recent years. For some voters 'border protection' has a negative value. It is a positional rather than a valence issue. The rhetoric of 'culture wars' is hyperbolic but it does pose the question of whether voters in different regions in Australia have developed radically divergent views about the role of government. In the 1940s, voters in Toorak and Mosman shared similar material aspirations with those of Richmond and Redfern, although they disagreed about how to achieve them. Is it now the case that voters in the 'left-green' and sometimes highly ethnic inner suburbs such as Fitzroy and Marrickville fundamentally diverge in their aspirations from outer suburban locations such as Knox and Penrith?

Kirsten Phillips (2009: 123) has argued:

> The modern state ... can tolerate and 'cultivate' a population which includes even bodies of a 'different race' as long as ordering mechanisms for managing this difference are upheld ... Of key importance is the fact that migrants enter the nation-state under the control and surveillance of that biopolitical state, and can be known, categorised and positioned in the social hierarchy effectively.

The debate about asylum seekers in Australia has challenged the biopolitical state and has destabilised political divisions formed around this state.

The emergence of regionalism in Australia

Economic and cultural regionalism emerge out of a process of social interaction. The holders of power within social networks—those with stocks of social capital—are likely to be able to shape local attitudes. Group interaction reinforces radicalism or conservatism within a locality. The political conservatism of Australian rural areas owes much to the fact that local opinion leaders and community activists are nearly all supporters of the Liberal and National Parties. Strong levels of left party support in mining regions have reflected a similar process (Butler and Stokes 1976: 84–6; Taylor and Johnston 1979: 221–69; Ward and Verrall 1982). As class-based party allegiances weaken, group influences may become more important for voters (Johnston and Pattie 1988). The British Conservatives now poll relatively worse in northern England than they did when it was an industrial heartland (Kellner 2013). A distinct 'northern' political identity has emerged within England that did not exist during the post-war heyday of class politics, perhaps in response to the impact of Thatcherism and deindustrialisation. A distinct social milieu may even attract particular sorts of voters. There is some evidence from Australia and the United States that gays and lesbians may migrate to regions that they regard as more sympathetic (Tam Cho 2013; Davidowitz-Stephens 2013; Mansillo 2013a: 23–8; Sides 2013).

In Australia it is the 'suburbs', in particular 'western Sydney' and the 'inner city', that have dominated recent discussions of political regionalism. In the 1950s and 1960s some cultural commentators attributed Labor's woes to the relocation of working class voters from the tight-knit communities of the inner city to the outer suburbs (Scalmer 1997). This interpretation was challenged by the rise of Gough Whitlam and his appeal to outer suburban voters. Even in 1975 and 1977 Labor held many outer suburban electorates, such as Robertson, which it had first won in 1969 (Forward 1976: 18).

After 1996, regional divergences became a central theme in much Australian political discourse. Initially the focus of commentators was on rural disaffection and the spectre of One Nation, but as the Pauline Hanson phenomenon ebbed the focus turned towards the 'suburbs', in particular 'western Sydney' and most of all the Penrith-based electorate of Lindsay. The proponents of a suburban focus such as Mark Latham sometimes cited the suburbs as evidence of a broader 'middle classing' of the Australian population—an example of what this chapter has defined as *social regionalism*. On other occasions Latham adopted a cultural regionalist approach and cast the suburbs as the base of a distinctive popular conservatism opposed to the social liberalism of the inner city (Latham 2013: 48–51).

Evidence for regionalism

This chapter will now consider the patterns of regional distinctiveness in Australian politics at the 2013 election. This analysis has two components. The first reviews how state-level electoral patterns have changed over time and the extent to which local variations in economic performance may have contributed. The territories are excluded from this analysis due to their small number of electors. The second analysis develops a simple linear regression model that seeks to predict party support from the social characteristics of electorates. The residuals from this model are then examined as possible evidence of regional patterns.

State regional patterns

In the 1970s and early 1980s some radical scholars, such as Humphrey McQueen, predicted that Australia faced an era of regional polarisation between an industrial core of New South Wales, Victoria, Tasmania and South Australia and the periphery of Queensland and Western Australia. The political culture of the core states would remain that of a residual social liberalism but the periphery, McQueen argued, would be dominated by a new and aggressive conservatism (McQueen 1982: 112–6). This prediction was not fulfilled. In the 1980s, Labor committed itself to national economic restructuring under a leader, Bob Hawke, who unlike Whitlam appealed to voters in Queensland and Western Australia. Tasmanian voters reacted against Labor's environmental turn in 1983 but eventually fell in behind the Labor ascendancy by the early 1990s.

The 2010 election seemed to represent the regional realignment that radical scholars of federalism had predicted decades earlier. States with a large mining sector swung strongly against Labor, whilst the south-eastern states reacted against Tony Abbott's aggressive conservatism. In the run-up to the 2013 election some commentators predicted that this regional division would increase and that Labor might lose every seat in Western Australia and Queensland (Coorey 2013). Instead the divergence notably closed. The economic anxiety that had impacted on mining regions in 2010 had now spread nationally.

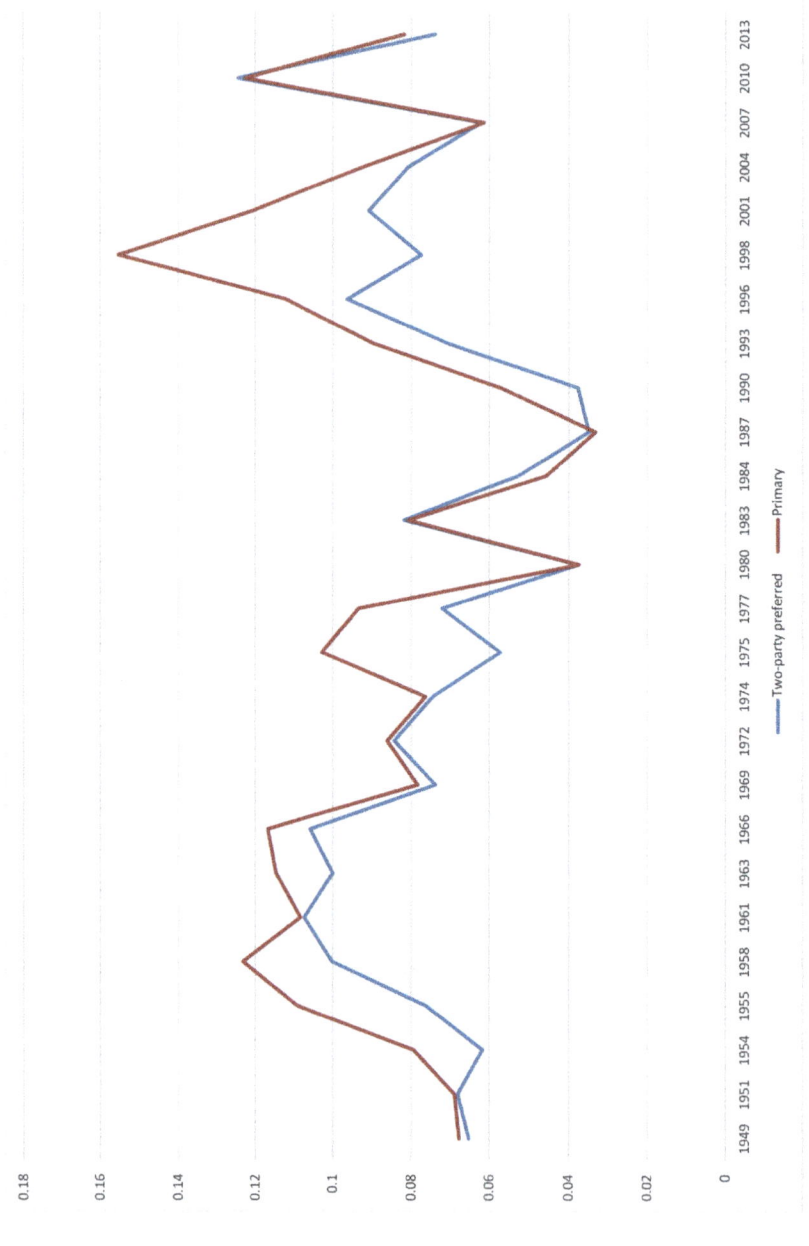

Figure 1: Labor primary and two-party-preferred vote by states—variance 1949–2013

Source: Australian Electoral Commission (2011b and 2013b) and University of Western Australia (2013).

At the state level there is no simple relation between economic performance and political behaviour. Unemployment is an imperfect indicator of state-level economic performance: it excludes discouraged workers and also does not take into account the shift of workers from full to part-time jobs. The relative stability of Australian unemployment during the global financial crisis (GFC) obscured a notable softening in the labour market apparent in withdrawal from the labour market and a fall in working hours. This softening was particularly apparent among blue-collar males. By 2013, less than half of Tasmanian males over 15 were in full-time employment (Cowgill 2013). The heavy swing against Labor at the 2013 federal election in this state probably reflected the strong belief among many Tasmanians voters that at a time of economic uncertainty public policy should support resource industries. It is misleading to extrapolate from the Tasmanian case—as does Tim Colebatch (2013a)—a broader thesis that the state-by-state decline in the Labor vote was largely accounted for by divergences in local economic performance. Overall there was no relation between the decline in male full-time employment by states and the decline in Labor's vote either during the 2010–13 term or across the Rudd–Gillard years as a whole (Australian Bureau of Statistics 2014).

The response of voters to economic trends is dependent on the political environment. At the 1993 federal election unemployed voters were more likely to support Labor, but at the 1996 election they were more likely to support the Coalition (Charnock 1997: 247–9). In 2010, economically anxious voters in Tasmania may have credited federal Labor for its effective response to the GFC but by 2013 they were focused on the welfare of local resource industries, just as Queensland and Western Australian voters had been in 2010.

Electorate level regression analysis

A federal census was conducted in 2006 and 2011. Federal elections were held in 2004, 2007, 2010 and 2013. In 2005, New South Wales and Queensland electoral boundaries were adjusted. In 2008, boundaries were adjusted for Tasmania, Northern Territory and Western Australia. In 2009, boundaries were adjusted in New South Wales and Queensland. Before the 2013 federal election, South Australian and Victorian boundaries were adjusted (Australian Electoral Commission (AEC) 2011a). Electorate-level census data is available for some areas but not combinations of electoral districts and censuses during this period. For some elections the regression analysis in this chapter is based not on the boundaries in place at that election but for the boundaries in place at a later poll for which census data is available. Social data has been matched to electorates using the Australian Bureau of Statistics Tablebuilder.[2]

---

2 Available from <http://www.abs.gov.au/websitedbs/censushome.nsf/home/tablebuilder>.

Table 1: Regression dependent variables

Dependent variables	Census	Definition
2004 ALP		
two-party-preferred	2006	The 2004 Labor two-party-preferred vote applied to the electorate boundaries in place at the 2007 election as estimated by Antony Green (2007). This adjusted two-party vote for the independent electorates of Kennedy and New England is not available so the actual 2004 two-party-preferred vote in these electorates has been used (AEC 2005).
2007 ALP, Coalition and Green primary votes	2006	The 2007 primary vote applied to the electorate boundaries in place at the 2007 election. The Coalition vote includes the total for Liberal and National candidates (AEC 2008).
2007 ALP two-party-preferred	2006	Votes by boundaries in place for 2007 election (AEC 2008).
2007 ALP, Coalition and Green primary votes	2006	Votes by boundaries in place for 2007 election (AEC 2008). The Coalition vote includes the total for Liberal and National candidates.
2010		
ALP two-party-preferred	2011	The 2010 vote applied to the boundaries in place for the 2013 election (Green 2013).
2010 ALP, Coalition and Green primary votes.	2011	The 2010 vote applied to the boundaries in place for the 2013 election. The Coalition vote includes the total for Liberal and National candidates (AEC 2013a).
2013 ALP Two-party-preferred	2011	Votes by boundaries in place for 2013 election (AEC 2013b).
2013 ALP, Coalition, Palmer United and Green primary votes.	2011	Votes by boundaries in place for 2013 election (AEC 2013b). The Coalition vote includes the total for Liberal and National candidates.

Sources: As indicated in table.

Table 2: Regression independent variables

Variable	Type of variable	Definition
Mining	Nominal	An electorate with more than 5 per cent of workforce employed in mining
Agricultural	Nominal	An electorate with more than 5 per cent of workforce employed in agriculture, forestry and fishing
Manufacturing	Interval	Percentage of workforce employed in manufacturing
Tertiary qualifications	Interval	Percentage of population with tertiary qualifications
No religion	Interval	Percentage of population with no religious affiliation
New religions	Interval	Percentage of population with religious affiliation other than Judaism or Christianity

Source: Australian Bureau of Statistics.

These dependent variables have been selected to cover a range of new and old drivers of electoral choice. Religions other than Judaism or Christianity prove a more relevant contemporary measure of cultural diversity than older measures such as country of birth or language used at home. Contemporary conservative discourse has emphasised the importance of Australia's Judeo-Christian antecedents and has argued that this identity has come under challenge from Muslim communities in particular regions such as south-western Sydney (Sheehan 2006).

Table 3: Two-party-preferred Labor vote determinants 2004–13[3]

	2004	2004	2007	2007	2010	2010	2013	2013
	B	Beta	B	Beta	B	Beta	B	Beta
Constant	**19.19**		**27.21**		8.94		9.24	
Agricultural electorate	**-6.26**	**-0.25**	**-6.95**	**-0.28**	**-9.85**	0.32	**-8.80**	**-0.31**
Mining electorate	<u>10.32</u>	0.19	**11.57**	**0.21**	-0.87	-0.02	-0.66	-0.02
Manufacturing	0.68	0.25	**0.91**	**0.34**	1.59	0.46	1.27	0.40
No religion	0.16	0.09	0.05	0.03	**0.44**	**0.25**	0.40	0.25
Non **Judeo-Christian** religion	**0.80**	**0.45**	**0.71**	**0.40**	0.58	0.35	**0.70**	**0.47**
University qualifications	0.08	0.10	0.05	0.06	0.01	0.01	-0.04	-0.49
Public employment	0.72	0.32	0.65	0.29	**0.84**	**0.35**	**0.86**	**0.39**
R-Sq (adj)	0.45		0.47		0.48		0.53	

Source: Australian Bureau of Statistics.

Table 4: Primary Labor vote determinants 2007–13

	2007	2007	2010	2010	2013	2013
	B	Beta	B	Beta	B	Beta
Constant	**22.24**		5.60		6.88	
Agricultural electorate	-8.18	-0.32	-9.72	-0.33	-9.45	**-0.34**
Mining electorate	**13.36**	**0.25**	0.31	0.01	-0.05	0.00
Manufacturing	1.10	0.40	1.78	0.54	1.29	**0.41**
No religion	-0.06	-0.04	0.18	0.11	0.10	0.06
Non Judeo-Christian religion	**0.70**	**0.38**	0.53	0.34	0.73	**0.50**
University qualifications	-0.05	-0.06	-0.07	-0.01	-0.12	-0.16
Public employment	**0.63**	**0.27**	0.76	0.33	0.83	**0.39**
R-Sq (adj)	0.53		0.53		0.62	

Source: Australian Bureau of Statistics.

---

[3] In this table and all subsequent tables, values in bold are significant at 0.01, underlined at 0.05.

The geographical foundations of Labor support are those that would be expected. This pattern demonstrates the persistence of 'countrymindedness', despite the overall decline in agricultural employment and the decline of social capital in rural areas. Strong support persists among both city and country voters for the ideals of countrymindedness and the provision of assistance to farmers (Cockfield and Botterill 2012). The electoral significance of this fact has diminished due to the growth of provincial cities and the urbanisation of coastal regions which have given Labor a stronger foothold outside the capital cities than in previous years (see the preceding chapter by Jaensch, Miragliotta and Wear in this volume). Electorates with a high level of manufacturing employment and those with significant populations of a non-Christian religion remain Labor strongholds. The most notable change in the regional determinants of party support is the collapse in 2010 of Labor's previous significant strength in mining electorates. This reversal was maintained in 2013.

At the 2010 election those states with a higher manufacturing population had rallied to Labor, in contrast to those on the resource-dependent periphery. By 2013, Australian manufacturing was under siege. The high Australian dollar dramatically reduced the competiveness of local industries. Labor had hoped that the mining tax would raise revenues that could assist regions and industries that were under pressure from the high dollar and the general increase in costs associated with the mining boom. The tax came with a heavy political cost but then failed to raise the revenue predicted. Manufacturing remained under pressure (Garnaut 2013: 123, 184). The Coalition challenged Labor in its manufacturing heartlands; it highlighted the alleged impact of the carbon tax on manufacturing, advocated stronger measures against 'dumping' and complained vociferously when in July 2013 the Rudd Government amended the fringe benefits tax on cars (Ferguson and Hannan 2013; Kelly 2013). In April 2013, Labor's primary vote fell sharply at a state by-election in south-eastern Melbourne, an area with a significant manufacturing workforce. This reversal was cited as evidence by some journalists that Labor faced particular challenges in regions with a high manufacturing population (Gordon 2013). During the 2013 election campaign some analysts predicted special difficulties for Labor in electorates, such as Corangamite, situated in regions where the car industry was (or was believed by voters to be) a significant employer (Robinson 2013).

Despite these concerns there was little evidence of a backlash against Labor in manufacturing areas comparable to the backlash it experienced in mining regions. It is an overstatement to suggest, as did one journalist, that the changes to the fringe benefits tax played a large role in the swing against Labor in Victoria and South Australia (Allard 2013).

At the 2010 election, Labor's performance on multicultural and immigration policy, a traditional area of strength, had been clumsy. Julia Gillard distanced

Labor from Kevin Rudd's advocacy of a 'big Australia'. This change of tack sought to respond to the Coalition's effective exploitation of arguments about asylum seekers. This rhetoric, together with candidate selection problems, contributed to sharp declines in Labor's vote in New South Wales ethnic electorates (Thompson and Robinson 2011). After 2010, the Gillard Government responded to this setback. Labor in government tightened its stand against asylum seekers but worked hard to restore the traditional ties between Labor and ethnic communities. In 2012, a Minister of Multicultural Affairs was restored to cabinet for the first time since the government of Paul Keating. Labor in office demonstrated itself marginally more sympathetic to Palestinian aspirations than the Coalition, an orientation some predicted would appeal to Muslim voters in Sydney (Hetherington 2011; Jakubowicz 2013). Rudd's return to the prime ministership probably assisted Labor's appeal to culturally diverse voters. Many electors of Chinese ethnicity had been particularly enthused by Rudd in 2007. It is possible that a married male prime minister may have been more attractive to some socially conservative ethnic voters than an unmarried female one.

In 2010, the Green surge owed something to disillusion among Labor's traditional constituency of public sector human service workers, especially in education. Labor's championing of standardised testing was unpopular among teachers (Fitzsimmons 2010). Many of the policies of the Gillard Government sought to appeal to this constituency. These included the Gonski funding reforms in education, together with the National Disability Insurance Scheme and support for higher pay for community sector workers (Schneiders 2011). The fact that Labor's vote held up in areas of high public employment suggests some success for this strategy.

Table 5: Greens' vote determinants 2007–13

	2007 B	2007 Beta	2010 B	2010 Beta	2013 B	2013 Beta
Constant	0.03		-2.48		-2.42	
Agricultural electorate	-0.99	-0.11	-2.17	-0.17	-1.24	-0.09
Mining electorate	-1.78	0.01	-1.20	-0.08	-0.28	-0.02
Manufacturing	-0.16	-0.17	-0.04	-0.03	-0.14	-0.09
No religion	0.23	0.38	0.38	0.51	0.27	0.34
Non Judeo-Christian religion	0.04	0.06	0.04	0.05	-0.05	-0.07
University qualifications	0.10	0.37	0.14	0.39	0.21	0.55
Public employment	0.07	0.09	0.03	0.03	-0.10	-0.10
R-Sq (adj)	0.51		0.63		0.59	

Source: Australian Bureau of Statistics.

Green support was not simply a 'chip off the left block'. The sectoral economic cleavages that counted against Labor were largely irrelevant. In 2013, new Greens leader Christine Milne had sought to appeal to farmers. The Greens emphasised their opposition to coal-seam gas mining and also criticised the uncompetitive nature of the Australian supermarket sector which they argued had a negative impact on farm produce prices. In response conservatives condemned the Greens as enemies of agriculture. Both these positive and negative appeals had little effect (Milne 2013; Devine 2012). 'Countrymindedness' is a distinctively anti-Labor ideology. As Green support fell from 2007 to 2013 the party found its most loyal supporters in electorates with a high population of university graduates. This may bolster Lindsay Tanner's argument that Green support is a reflection not only of support for particular policy positions but also a manifestation of a broader distaste among the educated for the stunts and gimmickry of contemporary politics (Tanner 2011). Some conservatives identified a regional dichotomy between areas with high proportions of university graduates and the 'real' Australia of the suburbs. For the broader left, as defined by the Labor two-party-preferred vote, this dichotomy did not exist (Davidson 2013).

The pattern for the Coalition was largely the obverse of that for Labor.

Table 6: Coalition vote determinants 2007–13

	2007	2007	2010	2010	2013	2013
	B	Beta	B	Beta	B	Beta
Constant	64.05		78.71		75.20	
Agricultural electorate	5.63	0.22	7.2	0.24	7.77	0.28
Mining electorate	-13.2	-0.25	0.57	0.02	1.29	0.04
Manufacturing	-0.83	-0.31	-1.37	-0.41	-1.05	-0.34
No religion	-0.03	-0.02	-0.32	-0.19	-0.39	-0.25
Non Judeo-Christian religion	-0.71	-0.39	-0.51	-0.32	-0.67	-0.46
University qualifications	-0.07	-0.01	0.04	0.05	0.15	0.21
Public employment	-0.62	-0.27	-0.87	0.38	-0.82	-0.39
R-Sq (adj)	0.38		0.34		0.42	

Source: Australian Bureau of Statistics.

The Palmer United Party (PUP) was not a right-wing version of the Greens. Green support was a distinctive component of the left, but Palmer support was much more amorphous. Palmer United preferences split only very narrowly in favour of the Coalition although its how-to-vote material advised preferences to the Coalition (Brent 2013; Green 2014). PUP was a 'catch-all' party, with the faint qualification that it was less popular in agricultural regions and electorates with a high proportion of university educated voters. The association between PUP support and educational levels has been noted by some observers (Mansillo 2013b). An electorate level analysis, undertaken later in this chapter, demonstrates that there was a strong regional component to its support.

Table 7: Palmer United Party vote determinants 2013

	2013 B	2013 Beta
Constant	19.63	
Agricultural electorate	-1.63	-0.16
Mining electorate	-1.26	-0.10
Manufacturing	-0.39	0.33
No religion	-0.01	-0.01
Non Judeo-Christian	-0.05	-0.09
University qualifications	-0.19	-0.70
Public employment	-0.14	0.17
R-Sq (adj)	0.33	

Source: Australian Bureau of Statistics.

The 2013 election was a much more 'normal' election than 2010; what remained from 2010 was the realignment against Labor in mining regions. The impact of this realignment was significant. The rise of 'countrymindedness' in the 1920s contributed to the conservative inter-war political ascendancy as the Country Party won formerly Labor rural electorates (Rydon 1979: 62). In 2010, the alienation of mining regions cost Labor an overall majority. In 2013, if the 2007 pattern of support for Labor in mining regions had been restored, Labor would have held the central Queensland coal electorates of Flynn, Dawson and Capricornia and probably several electorates in the Perth region.

The other aspect of regionalism highlighted by many observers pitted the 'suburbs'—in particular 'western Sydney'—against the 'inner city'. Implicitly this argument defined the 'suburbs' as formerly Labor-voting outer suburban areas. This would predict that the Labor (and overall left) vote would be notably higher in the 'inner city' but notably lower in the 'suburbs'. An examination of the electorate residuals offers some evidence for the first proposition but none for the second.

Table 8: Largest negative Labor residuals 2004–13

2004 ALP two-party	Residuals	2007 ALP two-party	Residuals	2007 ALP primary	Residuals	2010 ALP two-party	Residuals	2010 ALP primary	Residuals	2013 ALP two-party	Residuals	2013 ALP primary	Residuals
Mitchell	16.7	Curtin	15.1	New England	21.9	Tangney	15.1	Lyne	18.6	Mitchell	15.8	Indi	16.0
Aston	14.8	Murray	14.8	Kennedy	17.5	Mitchell	14.4	New England	14.9	Tangney	14.1	Mitchell	12.3
Murray	14.2	Tangney	14.7	Franklin	14.1	Fowler	13.9	Forrest	13.8	Murray	11.1	Tangney	11.4
Tangney	13.5	Mitchell	13.6	Murray	13.9	Murray	13.9	Fowler	13.5	Berowra	10.1	Denison	11.1
Curtin	13.4	Aston	13.0	Curtin	11.8	Curtin	11.8	Tangney	13.3	Forrest	10.0	Wright	11.0

Source: Australian Bureau of Statistics.

15. Regional Place-Based Identities and Party Strategies at the 2013 Federal Election

Table 9: Largest positive Labor residuals 2004–13

2004 ALP two-party	Residuals	2007 ALP two-party	Residuals	2007 ALP primary	Residuals	2010 ALP two-party	Residuals	2010 ALP primary	Residuals	2013 ALP two-party	Residuals	2013 ALP primary	Residuals
Grayndler	20.4	Grayndler	21.2	Throsby	18.1	Melbourne	25.9	Lalor	19.8	Melbourne	26.1	Sydney	17.8
Throsby	19.2	Throsby	20.7	Fraser	15.4	Lyons	21.0	Hunter	19.7	Grayndler	19.2	Shortland	15.7
Shortland	16.6	Sydney	16.4	Shortland	14.8	Hunter	20.6	Lyons	19.2	Wills	17.5	Hunter	15.2
Lyons	15.9	Fraser	15.7	Grayndler	14.4	Wills	17.1	Shortland	15.7	Batman	17.1	Grayndler	13.6
Fraser	15.8	Batman	15.6	Lalor	12.4	Batman	17.1	Braddon	14.5	Sydney	16.3	Lyons	12.7

Source: Australian Bureau of Statistics.

Labor has always struggled in the affluent suburbs and in farming regions (Forward 1976: 23; Jupp 1982: 30–1). The Labor-held seats where the Party has notably underperformed at recent elections are those where it faced particular local problems of candidate selection, such as Franklin and Fowler. The rural independents took primary votes from Labor.

The electorates in which Labor performed better than the model predicted are largely in two categories. One is inner urban electorates such as Grayndler, which according to the ABC's *Vote Compass* was the most 'left-wing' electorate in Australia (*ABC News* 2013). The second category is Labor's traditional strongholds of the Illawarra and Hunter Valley in New South Wales. Labor's problems in mining regions were less marked in coal producing areas.

Green support has a strong place-based component around 'alternative' communities such as inner Melbourne, part of inner Sydney (in particular the electorate of Grayndler), inner Hobart and the far north coast of New South Wales (Mansillo 2013a: 57–9). In 2007, the Greens benefitted in Bass by virtue of their opposition to the construction of a pulp mill in the area (McCall 2010). There is some evidence of a Melbourne–Sydney dichotomy in Greens support, particularly in 2013. The Greens over-performed the model by 7.1 percentage points in Grayndler, compared to 10.4 in Willis and 13.0 in Batman. In the electorate of Sydney the Greens actually underperformed by 2.5 points. The massive residual for Melbourne reveals that Adam Bandt's victory in the seat of Melbourne reflected more than the demographics of the electorate (Badham 2013; Miragliotta 2013). Bandt's campaign appealed to a particular Melbourne identity—socially progressive, educated and culturally aware.

Table 10: Largest positive Green residuals 2007–13

2007 Green primary		2010 Green primary		2013 Green primary	
Bass	7.4	Melbourne	15.9	Melbourne	24.9
Denison	7.1	Willis	7.4	Batman	13.0
Melbourne	7.0	Lyons	7.3	Willis	10.4
Cunningham	6.9	Batman	7.2	Richmond	7.8
Batman	6.8	Grayndler	7.0	Grayndler	7.1

Source: Australian Bureau of Statistics.

The Greens tend to underperform in ethnic electorates where Labor can rely on traditional allegiances and community ties to bolster its vote (Mansillo 2013a: 28, 60). There is little evidence of a distinctively place-based anti-Green sentiment.

Table 11: Largest negative Green residuals 2007–13

2007		2010		2013	
Bennelong	4.6	Bennelong	7.3	Denison	5.5
Kingston	4.3	Chisholm	5.4	Chisholm	5.2
Herbert	3.9	Lyne	4.1	Bennelong	4.9
Lingiari	3.9	Sturt	4.1	Banks	4.8
Makin	3.4	Parramatta	4.0	Adelaide	4.3

Source: Australian Bureau of Statistics.

The pattern of residuals for the Coalition is largely the obverse of Labor. Like Labor it lost votes to the rural independents in 2007 and 2010, but in 2013 Bob Katter surrendered much of his appeal to Coalition voters. If there is an electorate that incarnates a distinctively Sydney conservatism it is Mitchell not Lindsay.

Table 12: Largest negative Coalition residuals 2007–13

2007	Residuals	2010	Residuals	2013	Residuals
New England	28.7	New England	31.5	Melbourne	28.7
Grayndler	21.4	Kennedy	29.0	Grayndler	18.5
Throsby	18.9	Melbourne	26.9	Willis	18.3
Sydney	16.8	Hunter	19.3	Batman	18.1
Newcastle	16.7	Batman	17.9	Hunter	17.1

Source: Australian Bureau of Statistics.

Table 13: Largest positive Coalition residuals 2007–13

2007	Residuals	2010	Residuals	2013	Residuals
Murray	15.1	Murray	16.8	Mitchell	16.1
Curtin	14.5	Mitchell	16.1	Tangney	13.2
Mitchell	13.7	Tangney	13.9	Forrest	12.4
Aston	13.1	Fowler	13.2	Murray	11.3
Riverina	12.7	Forrest	13.1	Hughes	11.1

Source: Australian Bureau of Statistics.

There is no evidence of a distinctive regional pattern of conservatism in western Sydney contrary to some interpretations (Cater 2013). This absence is compatible with a social rather than cultural regional model. If western Sydney is the mirror of the nation it would be expected to follow the national trend. Voters in western Sydney who switched their vote to the Coalition cited the same concerns as voters elsewhere: Labor disunity and the economy (Carswell 2013). In the Melbourne suburbs Labor in 2010 failed to win Aston, Casey and Dunkley, all of which should have been Labor gains under this model.

Table 14: Western Sydney Labor two-party-preferred residuals 2004–13

	2004	2007	2010	2013
Banks	-0.7	1.0	0.0	-0.2
Blaxland	-5.1	-8.3	-3.4	-3.2
Chifley	8.2	9.0	4.9	7.2
Fowler	-8.9	-10.9	-13.9	-3.2
Greenway	-10.6	-10.3	-5.5	-0.7
Lindsay	0.5	2.9	0.2	0.2
McMahon (Prospect in 2004)	4.4	3.4	3.5	4.7
Parramatta	-4.6	-2.5	-5.0	-7.2
Reid	-6.8	-6.3	-2.3	-3.9
Werriwa	0.7	1.5	-4.3	-5.7

Source: Australian Bureau of Statistics.

Conclusion

The result of the 2010 election appeared to anticipate a major shift in Australian politics: the emergence of a cultural and political polarisation between the states akin to that apparent in the United States. The 2013 election result demonstrated that Australian electoral politics had returned to a more normal pattern. The 2010 result now appeared as the first instalment of a general shift against Labor. During the Rudd–Gillard years Labor lost support across the country, with a particular estrangement in mining regions. There were some signs in the 2013 election of economic regionalism, but little evidence of a distinctively conservative cultural regionalism.

The implications of this regional pattern for the future are unclear. In 2000, Clive Bean argued that although Labor's loss of core support at the 1996 election was disheartening to it as a major party, it had left an easier task for Labor than would have been the case if there had been a general swing against the party. Labor, he argued, could focus on the task of regaining traditional supporters (Bean 2000: 87–8). An alternative argument would be that it is easier for the Labor Party to recover from a general repudiation such as that of 2013. Voters across all regions in 2013 judged Labor harshly for its failure to deliver basic public goods such as economic security and political stability. Kevin Rudd's reforms to the Labor leadership may enable new Opposition Leader Bill Shorten to draw a line under the disunity of the Rudd–Gillard years. Economic uncertainty now counts against an incumbent Coalition government.

References

ABC News. 2013. 'Australia's most left-leaning and right-leaning seats revealed'. 4 September, viewed 18 December 2013: <www.abc.net.au/news/2013-09-04/vote-compass-left-right-electorates/4929064>.

Aitkin, Don. 1982. *Stability and change in Australian politics*. 2nd edn. Canberra: The Australian National University Press.

Aitkin, Don. 1985. '"Countrymindedness": The Spread of an Idea'. *Australian Cultural History* 4: 34–41.

Allard, Tom. 2013. 'Southern discomfort'. *Sydney Morning Herald*, 8 September, viewed 28 January 2014: <www.smh.com.au/federal-politics/federal-election-2013/southern-discomfort-the-states-where-labor-lost-the-election-20130908-2tdi1.html>.

Australian Bureau of Statistics. 2014. *Labour Force Australia*, 13 February, viewed 14 February 2014: <www.abs.gov.au/Ausstats/abs@.nsf/exnote/6202.0>.

Australian Electoral Commission (AEC). 2005. *The Official 2004 Federal Election Results*. Australian Electoral Commission, viewed 1 November 2013: <results.aec.gov.au/12246/results/default.htm>.

AEC. 2008. *The Official 2007 Federal Election Results*. Australian Electoral Commission, viewed 1 November 2013: <results.aec.gov.au/13745/Website/Default.htm>.

AEC. 2011a. *Redistributions*. Australian Electoral Commission, viewed 7 January 2014: <www.aec.gov.au/Electorates/Redistributions/index.htm>.

AEC. 2011b. *House of Representatives—Two Party Preferred Results 1949—Present*. Australian Electoral Commission, viewed 15 January 2014: <www.aec.gov.au/Elections/australian_electoral_history/House_of_Representative_1949_Present.htm>.

AEC. 2013a. *2013 federal election downloads*. Australian Electoral Commission, viewed 5 November 2014: <www.aec.gov.au/Elections/Federal_Elections/2013/downloads.htm>.

AEC. 2013b. *The Official 2013 Federal Election Results*. Australian Electoral Commission, viewed 4 January 2014: <results.aec.gov.au/17496/Website/Default.htm>.

Badham, Van. 2013. 'Adam Bandt's victory in Melbourne is no fluke—and that's worth celebrating'. *Guardian Australia*, 8 September, viewed 29 January 2014: <www.theguardian.com/commentisfree/2013/sep/08/adam-bandt-melbourne-victory>.

Bean, Clive. 2000. 'Who Now Votes Labor?' In John Warhurst and Andrew Parkin (eds), *The Machine: Labor Confronts the Future*. Sydney: Allen & Unwin.

Bean, Clive, and McAllister, Ian. 2012. 'Electoral Behaviour in the 2010 Federal Election'. In Marian Simms and John Wanna (eds), *Julia 2010: The caretaker election*, Canberra: ANU E-Press.

Blainey, Geoff. 2013. 'Mining a rich seam'. *The Age*, 19 October.

Brent, Peter. 2013. 'The 2PP wait is over'. *Mumble*, 29 November, viewed 18 December 2013: <blogs.theaustralian.news.com.au/mumble/index.php/theaustralian/comments/the_wait_is_over>.

Butler, David, and Stokes, Donald. 1976. *Political Change in Britain*. New York: St. Martin's Press.

Carswell, Andrew. 2013. 'Labor's light dims in the west as Sydney seats fall to Coalition'. *Daily Telegraph*, 8 September, viewed 29 January 2014: <www.dailytelegraph.com.au/news/special-features/labor8217s-light-dims-in-the-west-as-sydney-seats-fall-to-coalition/story-fnho52jp-1226714368648>.

Cater, Nick. 2013. 'Labor resists western values'. *The Australian*, 8 November, viewed 29 January 2014: <www.theaustralian.com.au/opinion/columnists/labor-resists-western-values/comments-fnhulhjj-1226700141869>.

Charnock, David. 1997. 'Spatial variations, contextual and social structural influences on voting for the ALP at the 1996 federal election: conclusions from multilevel analyses'. *Australian Journal of Political Science* 32(2): 237–54.

Cockfield, Geoff and Botterill, Linda Courtenay. 2012. 'Signs of Countrymindedness: A Survey of Attitudes to Rural Industries and People'. *Australian Journal of Political Science* 47(4): 609–22.

Colebatch, Tim. 2013a. 'Geography is destiny: states of red and blue'. *Sydney Morning Herald*, 7 December, viewed 29 January 2014: <www.smh.com.au/federal-politics/political-news/geography-is-destiny-states-of-red-and-blue-20131206-2ywri.html>.

Coorey, Phillip. 2013. 'Labor faces annihilation in marginal seats'. *Australian Financial Review*, 28 March, viewed 29 January 2014: <www.afr.com/p/national/labor_faces_annihilation_in_marginal_MRqll2ldnEA2yvStbw4IMM>.

Cowgill, Matt. 2013. 'Low employment in Tasmania: it's not just the seniors'. *We are all dead*, 20 March, viewed 29 November 2013: <mattcowgill.wordpress.com/2013/03/20/low-employment-in-tasmania-its-not-just-the-seniors>.

Davidowitz-Stephens, Seth. 2013. 'How Many American Men Are Gay?' *New York Times*, 7 December, viewed 29 January 2014: <www.nytimes.com/2013/12/08/opinion/sunday/how-many-american-men-are-gay.html?_r=0>.

Davidson, Sinclair. 2013. 'Testing the lucky culture'. *Callataxy Files*, 21 May, viewed 29 January 2014: <catallaxyfiles.com/2013/05/21/testing-the-lucky-culture>.

Devine, Miranda. 2012. ''Greens' country girl Christine Milne no friend of the bush'. *Herald Sun*, 15 February, viewed 29 January 2014: <www.heraldsun.com.au/news/opinion/greens-country-girl-christine-milne-is-no-friend-of-the-bush/story-e6frfhqf-1226326602622>.

Essential Media Communications. 2012. 'Essential Report', 20 August.

Ferguson, John and Hannan, Ewin. 2013. 'Ford blames Kevin Rudd's FBT tax changes for plant shutdowns'. *The Australian*, 23 August, viewed 29 January 2014: <www.theaustralian.com.au/national-affairs/election-2013/ford-blames-kevin-rudds-fbt-tax-changes-for-plant-shutdowns/story-fn9qr68y-1226702474062>.

Fitzsimmons, Hamish. 2010. 'Teachers boycott literacy, numeracy tests'. *ABC Lateline*, 12 April, viewed 14 December 2013: <www.abc.net.au/lateline/content/2010/s2870861.htm>.

Forward, Ann. 1976. *A Geographical Analysis of the Labor Vote in Victoria, 1966–1972*. Melbourne: Department of Geography, Monash University.

Garnaut, Ross. 2013. *Dog Days: Australia After the Boom*. Melbourne: Black Inc.

Gordon, Josh. 2013. 'Federal woes trashing state Labor's brand'. *Sydney Morning Herald*, 2 May, viewed 29 January 2014: <www.smh.com.au/comment/federal-woes-trashing-state-labors-brand-20130501-2it0m.html>.

Green, Antony. 2007. *Antony Green's Election Guide*. ABC—*Australia Votes 2007*, viewed 15 November 2014: <www.abc.net.au/elections/federal/2007/guide/>.

Green, Antony. 2013. 'Electoral Pendulum'. *ABC News*, viewed 17 September 2013: <http://www.abc.net.au/news/federal-election-2013/guide/pendulum>.

Henderson, Gerard. 2013. 'Abbott's anguish: inner-city types in media dislike him'. *Canberra Times*, 3 December, viewed 29 January 2014: <www.canberratimes.com.au/comment/abbotts-anguish-innercity-types-in-media-dislike-him-20131202-2ylyd.html>.

Hetherington, David. 2011. 'Australian Labor re-embraces multiculturalism'. *Policy Network*, 7 March, viewed 10 February 2014: <www.policy-network.net/pno_detail.aspx?ID=3970&title=Australian+Labor+re-embraces+multiculturalism>.

Jakubowicz, Andrew. 2013. 'How Labor won the "ethnic vote" in Western Sydney'. *The Drum*, 18 September, viewed 11 January 2014: <www.abc.net.au/news/2013-09-13/jakubowicz-politics-of-ethnicity/4954660>.

Johnston, Ron J and Pattie, Charles J. 1988. 'People, Attitudes, Milieux and Votes: An Exploration of Voting at the 1983 British General Election'. *Transactions of the Institute of British Geographers* 13(3): 303–23.

Jupp, James. 1982. *Party Politics: Australia 1966–1981*. Melbourne: Cambridge University Press.

Kellner, Peter. 2013. 'Reclaiming the north'. *Prospect*, 17 October, viewed 22 October 2012: <www.prospectmagazine.co.uk/magazine/features/reclaiming-the-north-tories-peter-kellner>.

Kelly, Matthew. 2013. 'Carbon tax destroying confidence: Mirabella'. *Newcastle Herald*, 9 April, viewed 29 January 2014: <www.theherald.com.au/story/1420852/carbon-tax-destroying-confidence-mirabella>.

Kenny, Mark. 2013. 'Labor facing wipeout: poll'. *Sydney Morning Herald*, 2 March, viewed 29 January 2014: <www.smh.com.au/national/labor-facing-wipeout-poll-20130301-2fc6u.html>.

King, Gary, Rosen, Ori, Tanner, Martin and Wagner, Alexander F. 2008. 'Ordinary economic voting behavior in the extraordinary election of Adolf Hitler'. *The Journal of Economic History* 68(04): 951–96.

Latham, Mark. 2013. *Not Dead Yet: What Future for Labor?* Melbourne: Black Inc.

Mansillo, Luke. 2013a. 'Spatial Dimensions of the 2010 Australian Greens Vote: The Gay and Lesbian Effect on Voting'. Honours thesis, The Australian

National University. Available at: <genderinstitute.anu.edu.au/sites/default/files/webform/LJM Luke Mansillo Thesis—Spatial Dimensions of the 2010 Australian Greens Vote THe Gay and Lesbian Effect on Voting_0.pdf>.

Mansillo, Luke. 2013b. 'Palmer United Party: who voted for them?' *Guardian Australia*, 28 October, viewed 29 January 2014: <www.theguardian.com/news/datablog/2013/sep/09/who-voted-for-palmer-united>.

McCall, Tony. 2010. 'Tasmania'. *Australian Cultural History* 28(1): 95–102.

McQueen, Humphrey. 1982. *Gone Tomorrow: Australia in the 80s*. Sydney: Angus & Robertson.

Milne, Christine. 2013. 'Christine launches the Greens' election campaign'. *GreensMPs*, 24 August, viewed 10 February 2014: <christine-milne.greensmps.org.au/content/video/christine-launches-greens-election-campaign>.

Miragliotta, Narelle. 2013. 'Reassessing Melbourne three years'. *The Conversation*, 12 August, viewed 28 October 2013: <http://theconversation.com/reassessing-melbourne-three-years-on-15515>.

Parker, Robert S. 1949. 'Australian Federation: the Influence of Economic Interests and Political Pressures'. In Jennifer Jill Eastwood and Francis Barrymore Smith (eds), 1964, *Historical Studies: Selected Articles*, First Series, Melbourne: Melbourne University Press.

Phillips, Kristen. 2009. 'Immigration Detention, Containment Fantasies and the Gendering of Political Status in Australia'. PhD thesis, Curtin University of Technology. Available at: <espace.library.curtin.edu.au/R?func=dbin-jump-full&local_base=gen01-era02&object_id=129031>.

Robinson, Geoff. 2013. 'Ultra-marginal Corangamite is a mirror of the nation'. *The Conversation*, 6 September, viewed 5 October 2013: <theconversation.com/ultra-marginal-corangamite-is-a-mirror-of-the-nation-16883>.

Rydon, Joan. 1979. 'The Conservative Electoral Ascendancy Between the Wars'. In Cameron Hazlehurst (ed.), *Australian Conservatism: Essays in Twentieth Century Political History*, Canberra: The Australian National University.

Scalmer, Sean. 1997. 'The Affluent Worker or the Divided Party? Explaining the Transformation of the ALP in the 1950s'. *Australian Journal of Political Science* 32(3): 401–18.

Schirmer, Jackie. 2012. 'Still here: why Tasmanian forest industry job figures are misleading'. *The Conversation*, 20 November, viewed 28 October 2013: <theconversation.com/still-here-why-tasmanian-forest-industry-job-figures-are-misleading-10827>.

Schneiders, Ben. 2011. '20% wage boost for low-paid workers'. *The Age*, 10 November, viewed 29 January 2014: <www.theage.com.au/national/20-wage-boost-for-lowpaid-workers-20111110-1n8fq.html>.

Shanahan, Dennis. 2012. 'Even Kevin Rudd at risk in Qld Labor wipeout'. *The Australian*, 2 July, viewed 29 January 2014: <www.theaustralian.com.au/national-affairs/even-kevin-rudd-at-risk-in-qld-labor-wipeout/story-fn59niix-1226413912633#>.

Sheehan, Paul. 2006. 'Ideals become casualties of war'. *Sydney Morning Herald*, 13 August, viewed 29 January 2014: <www.smh.com.au/news/paul-sheehan/ideals-become-casualties-of-war/2006/08/13/1155407666922.html08/13/1155407666922.html>.

Sides, John. 2013. 'Most Americans are not like Antonin Scalia'. *The Monkey Cage*, 18 October, viewed 22 October 2013: <www.washingtonpost.com/blogs/monkey-cage/wp/2013/10/18/most-americans-are-not-like-antonin-scalia>.

Tam Cho, Wendy K. 2013. 'Voter migration is a significant factor in the geographic sorting of the American electorate'. *LSE American Politics & Policy*, 19 November, viewed 5 December 2013: <blogs.lse.ac.uk/usappblog/?p=2457&preview=true>.

Tanner, Lindsay. 2011. *Sideshow: Dumbing Down Democracy*. Melbourne: Scribe.

Taylor, Peter J and Johnston, Ron J. 1979. *Geography of Elections*. London: Croom Helm.

The Australian. 2014. 'Here comes the end of a bad political marriage'. *The Australian*, 10 January, viewed 29 January 2014: <www.theaustralian.com.au/opinion/editorials/here-comes-the-end-of-a-bad-political-marriage/story-e6frg71x-1226798518852>.

Thompson, Elaine and Robinson, Geoff. 2011. 'New South Wales'. In Marian Simms and John Wanna (eds), *Julia 2010: the caretaker election*, Canberra: ANU E-Press.

University of Western Australia. 2013. 'Australian Politics and Elections Database'. *Australian Politics and Elections Database*, viewed 13 October 2013: <elections.uwa.edu.au>.

Ward, Ian and Verrall, Derek. 1982. 'Liberal Ascendancy in the Western District'. In Brian Costar and Colin A Hughes (eds), *Labor to Office: the Victorian State Election 1982*, Melbourne: Drummond.

16. The Contest for Rural Representation: The celebrated contest over Indi and the fate of the independents

Jennifer Curtin and Brian Costar

Over the past decade, independent parliamentarians have become a recurring feature of Australian federal politics (and elsewhere). This has sparked speculation about the extent to which independents represent a permanent challenge to the stability of two-party-dominant systems, both in Australia and internationally.[1] At the state level, independents have regularly held the balance of power and federally, in the Senate, there have been occasions when independents as well as minor parties have shared the title of power broker. Consequently, over the past 20 years there has been occasional scholarly debate over whether the vote for 'other' parties represents a fragmentation of the two-party system and a decline in the strength of party identification as a key determinant of voting behaviour.[2] Yet survey data still tell us that around 80 per cent of voters continue to identify as either Labor or Liberal and such loyalty sets Australia apart from many of its contemporaries (Bean and McAllister 2012). This suggests that independents may indeed be just a passing phase for momentarily disaffected voters.

Yet the historic hung parliament election of 2010 ensured independents took centre stage in a way not seen federally since 1940. Although the percentage of party identifiers remained solid in 2010, with the combined primary vote for the Labor and the Coalition parties at 81 per cent and only 2.5 per cent of voters opting for independents (Brent 2013), support for the latter was sufficiently concentrated in key electorates to return three sitting rural independents (Bob Katter, Rob Oakeshott and Tony Windsor) and elect one other from Tasmania (Andrew Wilkie). These four regional independents, along with the Greens' Adam Bandt and Western Australian Nationals' Tony Crook, were involved in 17 days of government formation negotiations and ultimately became the focus of much opposition and media speculation over the next three years.

So does this mean independents are a passing phase or becoming a new 'tradition' in Australian federal politics? The remainder of this chapter attempts

---

1 For examples of this literature, see: Brancati (2008); Costar and Curtin (2004); Hijino (2013); Rodriques and Brenton (2010); Smith (2006); Weeks (2009 and 2011).
2 These issues have been discussed in more depth in: Bean and Papadakis (1995); Curtin (2004); Moon (1995); Papadakis and Bean (1995).

to answer this question through an analysis of the work of independents in the 43rd parliament (2010–13) and the support they received in the election of 2013. The expectation was that fatigue and disaffection with the perceived instability of a minority government would drive voters to return to the more traditional choices, and the predictable result of an inflated majority for the Liberal–National Coalition. The retirement of Oakeshott and Windsor also fuelled the assumption that independents were unlikely to feature again significantly.

Nevertheless, the Coalition failed to predict one outcome—that of the rural Victorian seat of Indi where voters elected local independent Cathy McGowan over sitting Liberal member Sophie Mirabella. The final section of this chapter offers a detailed review of this result. In some ways Indi was unusual—McGowan is only the third female federal independent[3] and her campaign included a combination of new and traditional strategies that together ensured coverage of a diverse and geographically sizeable rural electorate, appealing to both young and old. Moreover, her win goes against predicted expectations that independents are more likely to stand and potentially be successful when running against a government incumbent rather than a member of the opposition. Conversely, McGowan's success builds on what has become a tradition in Australian politics. Rural constituencies feel forgotten by marginal seat election campaigns run by the major parties, so supporting independents is viewed as a tactical alternative. This rebellious streak amongst otherwise conservative voters, in combination with a general ambivalence about the capacity of major parties to represent local interests, suggests that there will continue to be possibilities for other 'McGowan-like' successes in rural and regional Australia.

The role played by independents and the 43rd parliament

In one sense there was an element of instability in the composition of the 43rd parliament. Although the three incumbent rural and regional independents were a known quantity, the number of parliamentarians who sat on the cross benches fluctuated during this period. West Australian National Tony Crook began his term on the cross benches, separating himself from the federal Nationals and labelling himself an independent representing Western Australian interests. He voted on confidence and supply with the Coalition but also supported the Labor Government on a range of issues. Crook formally joined the federal Nationals in

---

3 Before McGowan's election, both Doris Blackburn in 1946 (Burke) and Pauline Hanson in 1996 (Oxley) had won lower house seats as independents in the federal parliament—although Hanson technically was a disendorsed Liberal candidate (and appeared on the ballot paper as such) and then formed her own One Nation party.

parliament in May 2012, taking the Coalition's seats to 72 compared to Labor's 71. Surprisingly, he did not contest the 2013 poll and O'Connor reverted to the Liberal Party. By contrast, Peter Slipper began the 43rd parliament as the Liberal National Party MP for Fisher but became an independent in September 2011 when he was elected Speaker—a post from which he was forced to resign in September 2012. Craig Thomson also became a nominal independent after a post-scandal exit from the Labor Party in September 2012, while newly elected Tasmanian independent Andrew Wilkie rescinded his guaranteed support for the Government in January 2012.

Despite these fluctuations in cross bench membership, Labor continued to govern, with 561 government bills passed, up from just over 400 in the 42nd parliament (Hawker Britton 2013a). More specifically, over the course of the 43rd parliament there were 491 divisions and, with the support of independents, the Government won the majority in 93.5 per cent of divisions on substantive matters and in 81 per cent of all divisions. There were some amendments to bills but ultimately no government-sponsored bill was defeated on the floor of the House of Representatives (Hawker Britton 2013a).

Percentage support for government bills is a blunt means by which to measure the performance of a government. However, the Gillard Government's capacity to get its legislation passed (in terms of both daily business and more substantive policy changes) also compares well when measured against previous Australian governments since federation. Nick Evershed assigned all Commonwealth of Australia Numbered Acts[4] to a prime minister, political party and parliament based on the date of assent of the Act. He then counted the total Acts for each PM, party and parliament, determined the number of days in office for each PM, and the number of days each parliament and party governed. Using these figures Evershed calculated the rate of Acts per day, which accounted for different lengths of prime ministers' or governments' terms. His results demonstrate that the Gillard Government had the highest rate of passing legislation at 0.495, followed by Bob Hawke at 0.491 (Evershed 2013).

This overarching stability and productivity did not mean the independents acted as Labor 'lackeys'. Individual voting patterns show some variation between the independents across a range of substantive and procedural issues. More generally, Andrew Wilkie voted with the Government in 73 per cent of divisions; Tony Windsor in 75 per cent and Rob Oakeshott in 76 per cent. Although Bob Katter chose not to support Labor formally, he only voted against the Government in 36 per cent of divisions and was conspicuous by his absence (in 37 per cent of divisions). This contrasts with Tony Crook who, while avowedly independent, voted with the Coalition in 88 per cent of divisions (Hawker Britton 2013a).

---

4   <www.austlii.edu.au/au/legis/cth/num_act/>.

However, on Labor's seven key policy areas (carbon pricing, minerals resource rent tax, education and school improvement, national disability insurance, national broadband, aged care and tobacco plain packaging) both Windsor and Oakeshott were solid supporters of the Government's position (Hawker Britton 2013b).

Finally, significant procedural changes were implemented during the 43rd parliament as a result of Oakeshott and Windsor including an annex to their agreement to support a Labor Government. The *Agreement for a Better Parliament: Parliamentary Reform* facilitated an increase in the Selection Committee's referral of private members' bills, the number of questions asked by private members in Question Time, a stronger role for the Speaker in managing Question Time and an increase in time given to private members' business in the House (Parliamentary Library 2013). These procedural changes continue a tradition of Australian independents working to secure good governance and stronger accountability (Costar and Curtin 2004; Smith 2006).

The reforms also enabled independents to take up issues that mattered to their constituents or that had a national focus but were not major party policy. Seventy-six private members' bills were introduced in the House of Representatives, 33 of which were sponsored by the independents. These bills dealt with a range of policy issues; from migration and asylum seekers to environmental protection; from consumer protection and food labelling to restrictions on live animal exports. While only six private members' bills were passed, two of which were initiated by independents (the Auditor-General Amendment Bill and Evidence Amendment Journalists' Privilege Bill), the process of allowing additional debate and consideration has been considered an important institutional change to the workings of the Australian parliament (Parliamentary Library 2013). The valedictory speeches by Oakeshott and Windsor also indicate that the independents saw themselves as having made a substantive contribution to the process of governing and to the institution of parliament (Oakeshott 2013; Windsor 2013).

Election 2013 and the independents

Although threats of no-confidence votes and predictions of instability and policy paralysis abounded, Labor and the independents were able to sustain an amicable and productive relationship in both political and policy terms (Hawker Britton 2013a), and despite Wilkie rescinding his guaranteed support, he supported the majority of the Government's bills during this term

(73 per cent of divisions). Moreover three Budgets were passed and no motions of no-confidence were moved against either the executive or the prime minister (Oakeshott 2013).

Despite this reality, the Coalition parties' campaign strategy in 2013 targeted sitting independents, encouraging voters to see support for independents as a waste of a vote (McKenna and Maher 2013) and linking such support to the risk of continued 'unstable' government (Maher 2013). Nevertheless, throughout the 2013 campaign, Newspoll indicated that a considerable minority of voters continued to show an interest in supporting non-major parties and independents. In the six weeks of the campaign, the primary vote for 'others' stood at 10 per cent on 2 August and hovered around this figure right up to the week of the election (by which time it had increased slightly to 12 per cent) (Newspoll 2013a). In Oakeshott's electorate of Lyne and Windsor's electorate of New England, the support for 'others' stood at 18 and 16 per cent respectively, although ultimately both these electorates were won by the Coalition (Newspoll 2013b). While the actual vote for 'others' nationally (excluding the Palmer United Party and Katter's Australia Party) was much lower than the polls predicted (at around 5.5 per cent), it was sufficiently concentrated in Tasmania and Indi to ensure the re-election of Wilkie and the election of a new independent, Cathy McGowan, in Indi.

However, the former independent Bob Katter did not fare so well in Kennedy. Perhaps because Oakeshott and Windsor were retiring, Katter became a key target of the negative campaigning by the Liberal National Party. 'Katternomics' was ridiculed (Neales 2013) and large advertisements appeared in the *Courier-Mail* urging voters in Kennedy not to vote Katter's Australia Party (KAP). While Katter ultimately held his seat, his micro party won no Senate seats and Katter's majority in Kennedy decreased by 18 points (to 52.2 per cent in two-candidate-preferred terms).

The phenomenon of micro parties became the new 'obsession' in this campaign (see Tom King's Chapter 17), drawing attention towards the Senate and away from any consideration of independents in the House of Representatives election. This reaction is unsurprising. Despite Labor's change in leadership, it was almost a foregone conclusion that the Coalition would win a healthy majority in the House and, if the primary vote was sufficiently high, there was hope this would translate into large wins in the Senate. However, preference deals between micro parties for Senate seats and between independents in the lower house (Wilkie) and the Senate (Xenophon) posed a threat to both major parties. This distraction was to prove most costly to the Coalition. Although they won 90 seats in the House, including a number of previously ALP-held rural and regional seats, 30 per cent of these remain marginal—the same percentage as in 2010 (AEC 2013; Curtin and Woodward 2012).[5] Rural discontent with the Coalition parties was evident in Mallee where the Nationals faced a campaign to 'Make Mallee Marginal' (Ferguson 2013). More significantly, the Liberals inadvertently lost the previously safe seat of Indi, suggesting the idiosyncrasies of the preferential majoritarian electoral system and continuing anti-major-party sentiment in rural Australia can be mobilised effectively by a strong local independent candidate. What follows is a more detailed examination of the case of Indi, in order to shed light on the extent to which this independent win was an aberration or in line with broader electoral expectations about minor parties and independents in Australian and comparative politics.

Paradox or pattern? The result in Indi

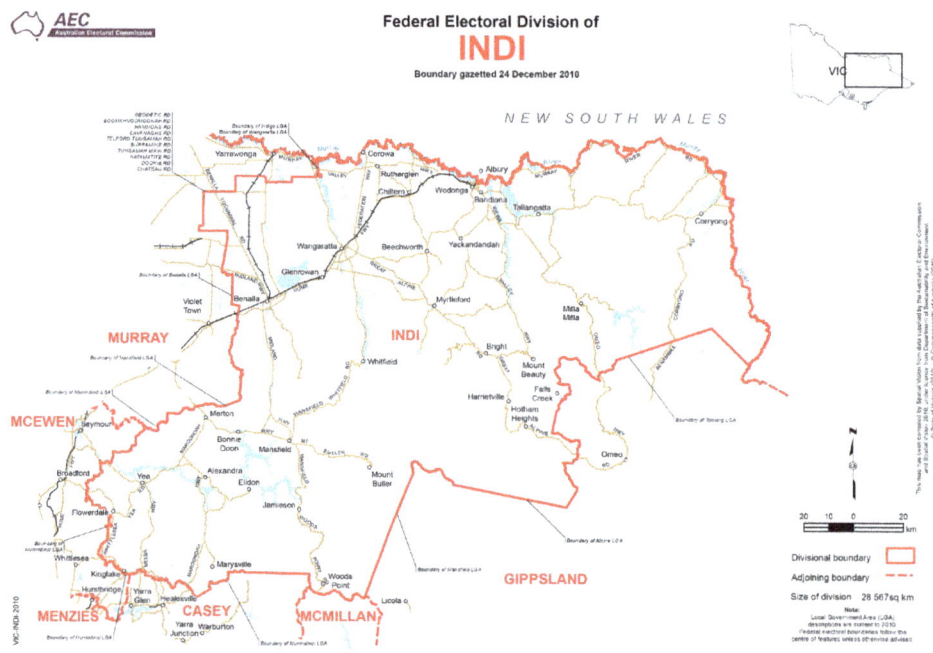

Figure 1: Map of Indi

Source: Australian Electoral Commission.

The Victorian federal division of Indi has been located in the north-east of the state since its creation in 1902 but the 2010 electoral redistribution added nearly 10,000 voters from its south-western neighbour McEwen and the seat now

---

5   We wish to acknowledge the sudden passing of our close friend and colleague Dennis Woodward in 2012. Dennis was a regular election book contributor.

stretches from outer north-western Melbourne to the New South Wales border. While classified as 'rural' by the Australian Electoral Commission (AEC), the division is notable for its diversity. Most of its population resides in the three large towns of Wodonga (30,000), Wangaratta (27,000) and Benalla (14,000), but there are also many smaller towns such as Yea (1,600) and hamlets such as Harrietville (217). The western part of Indi is national park containing the snow resort of Falls Creek and is only lightly populated (AEC 2010).

Indi's industry is more diverse than most rural divisions: 9 per cent of its workforce is employed in agriculture compared to 5 per cent nationally, but 13 per cent is in manufacturing and 7 per cent in accommodation and food services—tourism is a growing sector of the local economy. The increases in employment in the large towns are among professionals and community and personal service workers, with the biggest decline being among labourers. Like so much of regional Australia, it is not particularly wealthy: 26 per cent of families earn $650 or less per week and only 11 per cent earn more than $2,000 per week. Forty-two per cent of its population left school at year 10 or before, with only 21 per cent holding university qualifications.[6]

The division's socio-economic diversity is not reflected in its electoral pedigree and for 105 of its 111-year history it has been held by the conservative parties. From 1937 to 1977 it was in the hands of the Country [National] Party, but long-time sitting member Mac Holten lost the seat to the Liberals' Ewen Cameron in 1977. Cameron was succeeded by Lou Lieberman and his retirement at the 2001 election saw a hotly contested pre-selection ballot and an unlikely winner, Sophie Panopolous, by just one vote. Panopolous was a 31-year-old Melbourne lawyer who had been deeply involved in right-wing politics at the University of Melbourne. She had no prior connection to Indi but, according to one Liberal source, 'She was the star performer of the day by a long way' (Harvey 2010). It was later revealed that she had been able to relocate to Wangaratta to campaign for pre-selection by way of a $100,000 gift from her partner since 1995, former Dean of the Melbourne Law School, Professor Colin Howard (Bachelard 2011). She had come to prominence as an assertive monarchist during the 1999 republican debate and had impressed fellow monarchist Tony Abbott. Panopolous won the 2001 election easily with 40 per cent of the primary and 60 per cent of the two-party-preferred vote. She was then a beneficiary of the 'Latham election' of 2004, winning 62 per cent of the primary vote. Thereafter, her vote share fell by 10 percentage points by 2010 despite the absence of Nationals candidates and the chronic weakness of the local ALP.

As a backbencher Panopolous cultivated a confrontational political persona and has been described as 'one of the Liberal Party's most committed ideological

---

6 These data are drawn from Nelson (2010) and Australian Bureau of Statistics (2011).

warriors' (ABC TV 2013). After supporting Malcolm Turnbull's successful 2008 challenge to Opposition Leader Brendan Nelson she was made Shadow Minister for Early Childhood Education, Childcare, Women and Youth. When Turnbull himself was defeated in the party room by one vote in late 2009, Panopolous (now Mirabella following her 2006 marriage to Greg, a former army officer) was elevated to the job of Spokesperson for Innovation, Industry, Science and Research. This promotion anticipated her joining cabinet should the Coalition win in 2013. Senior shadow ministers often have duties that take them away from their electorates but by 2012 some Indi residents formed the view that Mirabella was focusing too much on her future ministerial career, Liberal Party factional politics and the internal machinations of the increasingly dysfunctional Wangaratta City Council. It was reported that at a meeting of constituents who wished to raise the issues of broadband and mobile black spots, Mirabella told them that 'the people of Indi weren't interested in politics' and that 'there are three issues: cost of living, cost of living, cost of living.' The meeting lasted 11 minutes (Elder 2013).

The constituents who went away disappointed with the local member's response were members of a community organisation established in mid-2012 called *Voice for Indi* (*V4i*) and included the person who was eventually to win the seat, Cathy McGowan AO. *V4i* began by conducting kitchen table conversations around issues local to the area and, by May 2013, 425 people had participated in 53 such conversations (*Voice for Indi* 2013). Initially these meetings were conducted confidentially because of a concern that opposition to the local political elite might attract future retribution in the form of loss of government contracts or removal from local boards (Klose and Haines 2013: 2; V4i Forum 2013). One local Liberal Party official claimed that V4i had started as 'a secret women's group, meeting in a public library. They were carrying on like they were in fear of their lives. It sounded like witchery to me' (Elder 2013).

Nevertheless the organisation flourished, attracted increasing media attention and established an impressive presence online. Eventually a decision was made to enter the electoral fray and support a candidate at the 2013 federal election. Somewhat reluctantly McGowan agreed to be that candidate. She was no political ingénue: her family had lived in the locality for generations; she was a sheep farmer and was active in rural politics as a lobbyist for the National and Victorian Farmers Federations; she had served as a staff member to an earlier Liberal member for Indi and had been a teacher and academic. She was a member of or had easy entrée to a plethora of local organisations. McGowan is difficult to pigeonhole ideologically—she is a Catholic who supports marriage equality, is 'embarrassed' by Australia's asylum seeker policy and believes in climate change. She rejects the description 'conservative' as old politics but supports free trade, strongly advocates for small business and claims her main objective is to re-build the local community and gain for it 'really good infrastructure' (Alcorn 2013; Whinnett 2013). Thus, the contest for Indi was set to be between a sitting member justifiably anticipating a cabinet career and a high profile localist independent.

Over the past two decades hundreds of independents have contested House of Representatives divisions and only a handful have been successful—most of the remainder have not only lost but also forfeited their deposits by failing to win at least 4 per cent of the primary vote. Predicting the likely victory of a first-time independent is a highly imprecise science and McGowan did not emerge as electable until about two weeks before the 7 September polling day. She did, however, have in her favour several factors unusual for independents, the most obvious of which was the existence of hundreds of supporters in *V4i*: her campaign launch in Wodonga on 4 August drew a crowd of 400. By election day, McGowan had 600 registered campaign workers, all of whom had been trained in electioneering techniques and were required to sign a volunteer agreement that committed them to behaving ethically and respectfully—especially to political opponents.

McGowan, in effect, ran a two-tiered campaign: one of the traditional type for regional areas involving extensive door-knocking, leaflet distribution, public and private meetings and phone calls; and a parallel campaign that made extensive use of social media. The second campaign was coordinated by a group of young people—many of whom were the candidate's nieces and nephews (she has 12 siblings)—who were known as 'Indi Expats'. They had been raised locally, had gone to the city for tertiary education, expressed a wish to return but were dissuaded by poor transport and communications infrastructure. They made extensive use of Twitter and Facebook and the cloud-based online software package NationBuilder which enabled the efficient organising of on-the-ground volunteers (Fogarty 2013). This strategy also permitted crowd funding which netted an impressive $120,000 in small donations. Tony Windsor was the only other independent who had managed to raise such a large amount of campaign finance and then only for his last election in 2010 (Klose and Haines 2013). The donations allowed McGowan to engage in extensive advertising and to open campaign offices in four towns. Mirabella and the Liberal Party allegedly spent $500,000 trying to retain the seat.

The Mirabella and McGowan campaigns were vastly different in both content and style. The sitting member essentially channelled the national Coalition campaign into Indi stressing the need to 'turn back the boats' and repeal the carbon and mining taxes. The independent concentrated almost exclusively on the need to upgrade local infrastructure, especially in the areas of transport, telecommunications and health. While McGowan refused to criticise Mirabella personally and forbade her team from doing so, the latter's political aggression both locally and via her regular appearances on the ABC TV show *Q&A* was a major issue in the campaign (Lette 2013: 10). Barnaby Joyce's praising comment that Mirabella 'to be honest' was someone with 'a bit of mongrel' may have been better left unsaid (Kotsios 2013a). Mirabella ran a very traditional campaign via multiple media advertisements, letters, leaflets and 'robo-polling', but hardly used social media at all. She also highlighted a number of visits to the electorate by Joe Hockey, Barnaby Joyce, Malcolm Turnbull and former treasurer Peter Costello.

The McGowan campaign gained prominence by adapting international 'coloured revolutions' techniques and kitted out supporters with bright orange t-shirts. Volunteers were given 'full autonomy and responsibility for activating their part of the electorate' and devised some innovative campaign events (Klose and Haines 2013). For example, one group 'cash mobbed' a florist shop and each purchased $20 worth of flowers which were then donated to local nursing homes to the approval of the local media. Given their electoral inexperience and the free rein given to volunteers, there was an ever-present possibility for the de-railing of the McGowan campaign, though in the end it was remarkably gaffe-free. Mirabella was not to be so fortunate. On the eve of the poll she was required to support the Coalition's promise to abolish the Regional Development Australia Fund which had allocated $5.6 million to projects in Wodonga, Rutherglen, Mount Beauty and Wangaratta—all in Indi (Kotsios 2013b).

The Mirabella campaign also encountered problems with the Liberals' coalition partner, the Nationals. The north-east of Victoria has long been a Nationals stronghold with the majority of the local state electoral districts held by that party. Relations between the Victorian branches of the two parties were tense in 2013 because of the Liberal Party's decision to contest the north-western Victorian seat of Mallee in a three-way contest despite the discouragement of Opposition Leader Abbott (Ferguson 2013). Rumours began to circulate that Nationals branch members in Indi were supporting McGowan's campaign and these gained traction when the former Nationals member for the state seat of Murray Valley, Ken Jasper, publicly endorsed her as did former Liberal Prime Minister Malcolm Fraser (Harris 2013). Senior Nationals figures then unsuccessfully attempted to have Jasper withdraw his support, but no disciplinary action was taken against any member of the Nationals. In his election report to the Liberal Party's state council in December 2013, past president and former Howard Government minister, David Kemp, complained that while Mirabella was supported by the federal and state leaderships of the Nationals, 'there were some Nationals who worked for McGowan' and this cost the Liberal Party the seat (Campbell 2013).

Local government plays a more prominent role in the politics of regional Australia than in the major cities and Mirabella's engagement with the Rural City of Wangaratta Council did not assist her re-election prospects. At the October

2012 council elections only two of the serving seven councillors were returned. Four of the newly elected members constituted a 'team' whose campaigns had been facilitated by one of Mirabella's staff members (Becker 2013). It was later revealed that the member for Indi had written them congratulatory letters in which she accused the former council of running 'a protection racket' and that it was time for 'a clean up' (Johnson 2013). What united the four new councillors was their opposition to Wangaratta City's draft *Rural Land Strategy* that sought to regulate the building of dwellings on farm land (Rural City of Wangaratta 2013). The plan, issued in March 2011, had attracted large protest meetings across the region and was a major issue in the October 2012 election. From its first meeting the new council was riven with conflict with the majority, and Councillor Julian Fidge (a local GP and former army reservist) especially was openly critical of other councillors, the CEO (whom he wished to dismiss) and other senior officers. In March 2013 the Minister for Local Government voiced public concern about the behaviour at the council and required it to renew its code of conduct (Powell 2013a).

This action had little obvious effect and in May 2012 the CEO directed that staff were to have no dealings with Cr Fidge who was also banned from some areas of the council offices (Burke 2013). By May one of the minority councillors had resigned and most of the senior staff were on stress leave. In mid-August a Municipal Association of Victoria (MAV) Councillor Conduct Panel suspended Cr Fidge for two months for bullying behaviour. Describing the panel's procedures as 'corrupt and biased' he appealed the decision to the Victorian Civil and Administrative Tribunal (VCAT) (Johnson 2013; Fidge 2013). On 30 August the CEO and five other senior staff left the council. To this point the council had spent $1.5 million attempting to resolve the disputes (Twomey 2013). In the interim, Minister Powell had commissioned reviews of the council by the Inspector of Municipal Administration and the Local Government Investigations and Compliance Inspectorate. Both were scathing in their criticism of the behaviour of the majority of councillors and the inspector described Cr Fidge as engaging in an 'abuse of process for political point scoring' (Stephenson 2013: 8). On 19 September the state government sacked the Rural City of Wangaratta and appointed administrators (Powell 2013b: 30–3) whereupon Julian Fidge called the minister 'a fascist' (Willingham 2013).

Since Cr Fidge had publicly thanked Mirabella for her support at the height of the conflict—'she has been quietly supportive and encouraging' (Becker 2013)—and acted as one of her scrutineers at the 2013 election count (Kotsios 2013c), it was difficult for her to distance herself from the negative fall-out of the 10-month imbroglio and the external disruption it caused. The inspector's report alluded at length to the impact the council's dysfunctionality had on the economic and other operations of the city (Stephenson 2013b: 8–10). Nevertheless, a month out from polling day Mirabella stated that she 'was absolutely not' worried about losing Indi (Kotsios 2013d). But at the same time her media advisor sent an email to Liberal supporters complaining that they were being 'outgunned by a far more active and enthusiastic campaign team' and urged them to flood the electorate's newspapers with pro-Mirabella letters (Morgan 2013). While the Liberal Party conducted polling and focus groups in Indi, there was no polling by the major companies. A ReachTEL poll in late August recorded Mirabella on 47 per cent of the primary vote and McGowan on 25 per cent (Kotsios 2013e). This was sufficient evidence to make the Liberal Party panic and it poured extra resources and staff into Indi in the last two weeks of the campaign. Also, the theme of the campaign was shifted from positive to negative. Most of the billboards and other signage had Mirabella's photo removed and replaced with slogans denigrating independents such as 'Independents won't stop the boats'. On the eve of polling, Opposition Leader Tony Abbott made personal calls to all local media in support of Mirabella (Johnson 2013). Sportsbet's last odds were Mirabella $1.90, McGowan $1.80, whereas at the start of the campaign the independent had been a 50 to one outsider.

The final Indi outcome had a number of interesting features. Cathy McGowan polled 31.18 per cent of the primary vote (27,763 votes) to Mirabella's 44.68 per cent (39,785 votes) (AEC 2013). However, after the distribution of preferences, McGowan won Indi by 439 votes to become the first female independent to win a regional House seat in Victoria, and Mirabella was the only Coalition casualty of the 2013 election.

The reason for this result is that the independent lifted her primary vote to 50.25 two-candidate-preferred, whereas Mirabella could add only 5.07 per cent to her primary vote through preferences. Historically it is most unusual for a candidate with nearly 45 per cent of the primary vote not to go on to claim the seat (Hughes and Costar 2006: 69). McGowan received strong preference flows from the ALP (89 per cent) and the Greens (88 per cent). While 11 candidates contested the seat, only three of the nine losing contestants officially preferenced Mirabella—Family First, Rise Up Australia and Katter's Australia Party—but she received a majority only from Family First (52 per cent). Indi in 2013 had 103 polling places: McGowan polled well in the large booths in Wodonga, Wangaratta and Benalla, but she was competitive right across the division, except in 11 very small booths. When the Senate count in Indi is examined it shows that 4,471 electors who chose the Coalition team did not vote for Mirabella in the House. As expected, the sitting member won the postal votes by 56.9 per cent to 43.0 per cent. The seat was declared on 19 September but not before a minor counting error when a pile of McGowan's votes was wrongly numbered '1003' when it should have been '2003' (Ferguson 2013). Sophie Mirabella did not challenge the result.

Conclusion

In comparative perspective, Australia's history and contemporary experience of electing independents is unusual. Although independents are most likely to succeed in majoritarian systems with preferential voting in place, it is much less common to find independents working to support governments, to introduce progressive and inclusive policies, and seeking to reform parliamentary process (Brancati 2008; Hijino 2013). The election of independents is also more likely to occur in new democracies where party organisations are still developing and party loyalties less entrenched. Yet in Australia, the election of independents has become an enduring low-level trend over the past three decades despite continued major party loyalty, and in the 43rd parliament it is evident that these representatives laboured to enhance democratic practice. The case of Indi reinforces the argument that independents will often succeed when voters believe political parties have failed to address local and societal interests (Costar and Curtin 2004; Greenberg 1994; Weeks 2011). McGowan's success is also a reminder that majoritarian preferential systems (particularly those with compulsory voting) can facilitate candidate-centred politics that advantages strong independent candidates.

References

Australian Broadcasting Commission (ABC). *Q&A*. Viewed 4 January 2014: <www.abc.net.au/tv/txt/s3016955>. Panelist: Sophie Mirabella.

Australian Bureau of Statistics (ABS). 2011. *Community Profiles of Wodonga, Wangaratta and Benalla*.

Australian Electoral Commission (AEC). 2013. *House of Representatives Results*. AEC, 4 November 2013, viewed 17 July 2014: <results.aec.gov.au/17496/Website/HouseResultsMenu-17496.htm>.

AEC. 2010. *Federal division of Indi*. Map, AEC, viewed 20 January 2014: <www.aec.gov.au/profiles/vic/files/2010/2010-aec-a4-map-vic-indi.pdf>.

Alcorn, Gay. 2013. 'Winds of change may begin with one voice'. *The Age*, 27 September.

Bachelard, Michael. 2011. 'Power, love and money'. *The Age*, 23 September.

Bean, Clive and McAllister, Ian. 2012. 'Electoral Behaviour in the 2010 Australian Federal Election'. In Marian Simms and John Wanna (eds), *Julia 2010: The caretaker election*, Canberra: ANU E-Press.

Bean, Clive and Papadakis, Elim. 1995. 'Minor Paries and Independents—Electoral bases and future prospects'. *Australian Journal of Political Science* 30(1): 111–26.

Becker, Joshua. 2013. 'Cr Julian Fidge grateful for Sophie Mirabella's counsel'. *ABC Radio Goulburn Murray*, 22 August, viewed 20 January 2014: <www.abc.net.au/local/audio/2013/08/22/3831693.htm>.

Bolleyer, Nicole and Weeks, Liam. 2009. 'The puzzle of non-party actors in party democracy: Independents in Ireland'. *Comparative European Politics* 7(3): 299–324.

Brancati, Dawn, 2008, 'Winning Alone: The Electoral Fate of Independent Candidates Worldwide'. *The Journal of Politics* 70(3): 648–62.

Brent, Peter. 2013. 'Mumble Election Tables: Minor party preference flows 2013 federal election in descending order of 2010–2013 change'. *Mumble*, viewed 6 December 2013: <www.mumble.com.au/fedelect13/wall/others/prefstots/Prefflowsbychang10–13.HTM>.

Burke, Steven. 2013. 'You've got mail, Cr Fidge'. *Wangaratta Chronicle*, 24 May.

Campbell, James. 2013. 'Nationals blamed for Liberal loss of Indi'. *Herald Sun*, 1 December.

Costar, Brian and Curtin, Jennifer. 2004. *Rebels with a Cause. Independents in Australian Politics*. Sydney: UNSW Press.

Curtin, Jennifer. 2004. *The Voice and the Vote of the Bush: The representation of rural and regional Australia in the Federal Parliament*. Canberra: Department of Parliamentary Services and the Parliamentary Library.

Curtin, Jennifer and Woodward, Dennis. 2012. 'Rural and Regional Australia: The ultimate winners?'. In Marian Simms and John Wanna (eds), *Julia 2010: The caretaker election*, Canberra: ANU E-Press.

Elder, John. 2013. 'Ironies abound in the battle for Indi'. *The Sydney Morning Herald*, 15 September.

Evershed, Nick. 2013. 'Was Julia Gillard the most productive prime minister in Australia's history?' *Guardian Australia*, 28 June, viewed 21 July 2014: <www.theguardian.com/news/datablog/2013/jun/28/australia-productive-prime-minister>.

Ferguson, John. 2013. 'Indi row "dire" for Mirabella'. *The Australian*, 4 September.

Fidge, Julian. 2013. 'Cr Fidge defends actions, will appeal'. *Wangaratta Chronicle*, 14 August.

Fogarty, Nick. 2013. 'New software helps campaign community organising'. *ABC Radio Goulburn Murray*, 25 July, viewed 20 January 2014: <www.abc.net.au/local/stories/2013/07/25/3810967.htm>.

Greenberg, Stanley B. 1994. *Third Force: Why Independents Turned against Democrats—and How to Win Them Back*. Washington: Democratic Leadership Council.

Harris, Rob. 2013. 'McGowan finds her voice in Indi'. *Weekly Times*, 5 September.

Harvey, Michael. 2010. 'Monarchist about face'. *Herald Sun*, 23 October.

Hawker Britton. 2013a. *How the Independents Voted*. September, viewed 25 October 2013: <www.hawkerbritton.com/hawker-britton-media/federal-act/632/how-the-independents-voted-in-the-house-of-the-43rd-parliament.htm>.

Hawker Britton. 2013b. *Independents' voting record in the House of the 43rd Parliament*. September, viewed 25 October 2013: <www.hawkerbritton.com/hawker-britton-media/federal-act/632/how-the-independents-voted-in-the-house-of-the-43rd-parliament.htm>.

Hijino, Ken Victor L. 2013. 'Liabilities of Partisan Labels: Independents in Japanese Local Elections'. *Social Science Japan Journal* 16(1): 63–85.

Hughes, Colin A and Costar, Brian. 2006. *Limiting Democracy: The Erosion of Electoral Rights in Australia*. Sydney: UNSW Press.

Johnson, David. 2013. 'Pushing The Envelope'. *Border Mail*, 12 February.

Klose, Cambell and Haines, Nick. 2013. 'From little margins, big margins grow'. *The Canberra Times*, 19 October.

Kotsios, Natalie. 2013a. 'Barnaby Joyce backing Sophie Mirabella'. *Border Mail*, 23 August.

Kotsios, Natalie. 2013b. 'Sophie stands by regional cuts'. *Border Mail*, 7 September.

Kotsios, Natalie. 2013c. 'Cathy McGowan wins two cities'. *Border Mail*, 10 September.

Kotsios, Natalie. 2013d. 'Sophie Mirabella 'absolutely not' worried about losing Indi'. *Border Mail*, 8 August.

Kotsios, Natalie. 2013e. 'Battle 'boost' for Sophie'. *Border Mail*, 6 September.

Lette, Kate. 2013. 'Yes She Can', *Weekend Australian Magazine*, 19–20 October.

Maher, Sid. 2013. 'Abbott's plea: don't leave us hanging'. *The Australian*, 6 September.

McKenna, Michael and Maher, Sid. 2013. 'Minor parties waste of your vote: Abbott'. *Weekend Australian*, 7–8 September: 8.

Moon, Jeremy. 1995. 'Minority Government in the Australian States—From Ersatz Majoritarianism to Minoritarianism'. *Australian Journal of Political Science* 30(1): 142–63.

Morgan, Shana. 2013. 'Liberal letters spark storm'. *Wangaratta Chronicle*, 9 August.

Neales, Sue. 2013. 'PM gives Katter Lay of the Land'. *Weekend Australian*, 31 August–1 September.

Nelson, Paul. 2010. *Electoral division rankings: 2006 Census (2009 electoral boundaries)*. Parliament of Australia Research Paper, no. 18, 28 May: 130.

Newspoll. 2013a. *Weekend Australian*, 31 August–1 September.

Newspoll. 2013b. *Weekend Australian*, 7–8 September.

Oakeshott, Rob. 2013. 'Member for Lyne's valedictory address'. *Port News*, 30 June, viewed 10 October 2013: <www.portnews.com.au/story/1606474/member-for-lynes-valedictory-address/>.

Papadakis, Elim, and Bean, Clive. 1995. 'Independents and Minor Parties—The Electoral System'. *Australian Journal of Political Science* 30(1): 97–110.

Parliamentary Library. 2013. *The Hung Parliament: procedural changes in the House of Representatives*. Research Paper 2013–14, 22 November. Canberra: Politics and Public Administration, Parliamentary Library.

Powell, Jeannette. 2013a. 'Wangaratta Council to renew Code of Conduct'. Media Release, 21 March.

Powell, Jeannette. 2013b. 'Local Government (Rural City of Wangaratta) Bill'. Victorian Parliamentary Debates Assembly, 19 September: 30–3.

Rodriques, Mark and Brenton, Scott. 2010. *The age of independence? Independents in Australian parliaments*. Research Paper No. 4. 2010–11. 21 September. Canberra: Parliamentary Library.

Rural City of Wangaratta. 2012. *Rural Land Strategy*: 1–27.

Smith, Rodney. 2006. *Against the Machines: Minor Parties and Independents in New South Wales 1910–2006*. Sydney: Federation Press.

Stephenson, Peter James. 2013. *Report on the Monitoring of the Operations and Governance of Wangaratta Rural City Council*. Melbourne, Victorian Government Printer, September: 1–12.

Twomey, Sharon.2013. 'Dysfunctional Wangaratta council sacked'. *Weekly Times*, 18 September.

Voice for Indi. 2013. 'Kitchen Table Conversations'. *Voice for Indi*, viewed 20 January 2014: <www.voiceforindi.com/report_info>.

Voice for Indi Forum. 2013. Benalla Bowls Club, 9 November.

Weeks, Liam. 2009. 'We Don't Like (to) Party. A Typology of Independents in Irish Political Life, 1922–2007'. *Irish Political Studies* 24(1): 1–27.

Weeks, Liam. 2011. 'Rage Against the Machine: Who is the Independent Voter?' *Irish Political Studies* 26(1): 19–43.

Whinnett, Ellen, 2013. 'Giant Killer'. *Herald Sun*, 14 September.

Willingham, Richard. 2013. 'MP labelled a "fascist" after council axed'. *The Age*, 19 September.

Windsor, Tony. 2013. 'Valedictory Speech'. House of Representatives, Commonwealth of Australia, Canberra, 26 June.

17. The Advent of Two New Micro Parties: The Palmer United Party and Katter's Australia Party

Tom King

This chapter provides an analysis of the performance of the Palmer United Party (PUP) and Katter's Australia Party (KAP) at the 2013 federal election in terms of the number of candidates fielded and the overall results nationally and in each state. The chapter analyses the swings these micro parties received and examines where their votes appeared to come from. This entails analysing which major party or parties had swings against them that saw votes flow to either KAP or PUP. This chapter concludes that Palmer's fledgling party performed far better collectively than the KAP candidates who were led by an experienced sitting federal politician who had secured additional state seats in the Queensland assembly. The analysis suggests that swings to both these micro parties were regionally sensitive and came not from any one party but from a number of other established parties. While the swing varied among electorates, as a general rule the two parties performed better in rural electorates than in urban electorates.

The parties and their leaders

Key (1964: 254ff) has categorised minor parties into three groupings: *secessionist* (parties which form when there is a split in an established party and one section of the party breaks away to form a 'purer' version of the original party); *aggrieved minority* (parties with mainly economic interests but which may have other or even alternative interests; they form because of some resentment regarding these interests); and *doctrinal* (parties which promote a particular doctrine both in and out of season, for example, communist, socialist or neo-nazi parties, and perhaps even environmentalist parties).

Both KAP and PUP could be classified as both secessionist and aggrieved minorities. They were effectively breakaway micro parties from the existing conservative side of politics, mobilised by well-known personalities who are in their own way charismatic individuals who have gained some respect and a following from a group or groups of voters. In the past there have been many other well-known celebrity personalities who have founded and led minor or micro parties, for example, Vince Gair and the Democratic Labor Party, Gordon Barton and the Australia Party, Don Chipp and the Australian Democrats, Bob Brown and the Australian Greens, as well as Pauline Hanson and One Nation.

Katter's Australia Party

In the case of Bob Katter and the KAP, his grievances were over the policy directions of the National Party that accommodated economic policies favouring market forces at the expense of the financial viability of farmers and small business people. The party was belatedly formed by Katter who, as an existing member of the House of Representatives and a well-known political maverick, had been content to sit on the sidelines of the party system. He had entered the Queensland parliament in 1974 as a Country Party/National Party member rising to become a state minister under the Bjelke-Petersen regime. From 1993 to 2001 he was a troublesome member of the federal parliamentary National Party. In 2001 he resigned from the National Party to sit as an independent because he perceived the Nationals had deserted farmers and small business people in regional Australia. In September 2011 he formed Katter's Australia Party, registering it at both state and federal levels. In 2012 he compiled a book (Katter 2012) which, in addition to providing his personal version of Australian history, attempted to spell out what his new party stood for. Nowra (2013: 28) comments that 'there is raw appeal in his [Katter's] refusal, unlike Julia Gillard or Tony Abbott, to resort to weasel words or hide his own true beliefs.' In other words, Katter is a plain-speaking person and an upfront politician.

Going into the federal election, KAP could boast three members in the Queensland state parliament. In the 2012 state election, Katter's son Rob won the electorate of Mount Isa with 41.61 per cent of the primary vote. Shane Knuth, a former National Party state MP won Dalrymple for KAP with 53.73 per cent of the primary vote. Knuth is the brother of the former One Nation MP, Jeff Knuth. Ray Hopper, also an ex-Nationals member, won Condamine with 58.3 per cent of the primary vote as a Liberal National Party (LNP) MP but resigned from that party in late 2012 to join Katter's new party. All three of those electorates are classified as rural electorates.

Katter was re-elected at the 2013 election but suffered a significant swing against him. Katter was the only candidate from his party to be elected. Ultimately, the advantages of incumbency as a highly-recognisable sitting member of parliament, and with three sitting members of state parliament adding to his profile, did not actually provide much of an advantage to Katter and his party. His decision to preference the Labor Party in the Senate may have also cost his party support in the primary vote.

In fact in the lead-up to the campaign, and indeed throughout the campaign, Katter and his party became heavily embroiled in a relatively marginal issue for his old-style conservative constituency that would only damage their populist support, namely the same-sex marriage debate. Katter had stated at a public pro-marriage rally in August 2011 that 'same-sex marriage should not be taken seriously and deserves to be ridiculed' (Sadler 2011). But matters came to a head when KAP endorsed country singer James Blundell as the party's lead Senate candidate in Queensland. In his first public speech as candidate, Blundell announced that he would vote in favour of gay marriage and, for good measure, also advocated the abolition of penalty rates. This enraged some of the party's backers in the Electrical Trades Union. Blundell's statement on same-sex marriage 'flabbergasted the socially conservative party faithful' and 'the exodus of party members accelerated after Blundell's comments' (Houghton 2013).

A number of members of KAP either resigned or were expelled from the party over their views or comments regarding same-sex marriage. Among those expelled were the party's candidate in Wannon, Tess Corbett, and Queensland Senate candidate hopeful Bernard Gaynor. Gaynor was the National General Secretary of the party, a married father of five children and a former officer in the Australian Army. Gaynor enjoyed a high profile and was forthright in his views against same-sex marriage. The dismissal of Gaynor as a candidate with its resultant adverse publicity was another reason for the party's poor showing at the election as it showed the party to be divided and unsure of its position on same-sex marriage.

Katter, in spite of his years in parliament, was very negligent in laying down the rules and procedures for preselecting candidates for the party. Nowra (2013: 31) observes that:

> Like Pauline Hanson's One Nation party before it, the KAP attracts ratbags, the undistinguished and the plain daffy. Evidently, the KAP's selection process lacks rigour. Katter doesn't seem to be strongly in charge of his own party, but more than that, he doesn't seem to care particularly that he's not.

Katter's new party stands for the same range of protectionist economic issues that Pauline Hanson and One Nation championed, but without any racist overtones. McDonnell (2001: 6) describes Katter as 'an old fashioned protectionist' who is not racist 'and cannot be described as one.' McDonnell goes on to say that 'he is therefore a potential stain free rallying point for ageing conservatives of the right who are turned off Pauline Hanson … [and] who are turned off political parties in general'.

The Palmer United Party

The Palmer United Party is led by Clive Palmer, a flamboyant and well-known political identity in Queensland with a commanding presence. He is a high profile businessman and operates a number of business interests which include mining and tourism. He had been a major financial backer of the conservative parties in Queensland, but fell out with the LNP and especially with the Newman State Government, and so set up his own political party. The party's major concern is the mining industry in Australia and the reduction of red tape for that industry. It supports the abolition of the carbon tax as well as the mining tax. The party also supports free tertiary education and swift on-shore processing of asylum seekers, after allowing them to fly to Australia. Genuine asylum seekers would be allowed to stay in Australia and take up employment and have access to welfare (PUP 2013).

The PUP opted for a tactical advantage on the same-sex marriage issue by declaring in its policies that social issues such as same-sex marriage would be a matter for a conscience vote from the party's parliamentary members. In a press release dated 30 July 2013, Clive Palmer advised that the PUP believes issues such as same-sex marriage, the abortion debate and euthanasia should all come down to the candidates' individual position on the issue. Palmer concluded by saying that:

> the Palmer United Party is committed to offering a voice to all Australians, which is why we promote the individual rights of everyone. There will be no party pressure on any of our candidates and we will respect their thoughts, views and ideas on all social issues including same-sex marriage (Palmer/PUP 2013).

Palmer himself contested and won the federal electorate of Fairfax on the Queensland Sunshine Coast by a slim margin of just 53 votes. His re-election in three years' time is by no means assured. In addition his fledgling party managed to get two Senators elected for the period 2014–20, with one each from Tasmania and Queensland. Before the recount took place in Western Australia, a third PUP candidate, Zhenya 'Dio' Wang, had initially been elected from that state. The April 2014 re-election for the half-Senate seats in Western Australia, ordered by the Court of Disputed Returns, saw him elected to the Senate.

The PUP suffered a small embarrassment in Western Australia that led to the dis-endorsement of its candidate in the seat of Fremantle for 'not toeing the party line'. The candidate, Teresa van Lieshout, was a feisty, opinionated, 'born-again' Christian who claimed that the global financial crisis was a typical 'anti-

Christ' strategy and Hurricane Sandy was God's punishment for globalisation. She was replaced as the PUP candidate by Vashil Vimal Sharma who polled only 3.96 per cent of the primary vote in that seat.

There were claims that the PUP ran an e-campaign over the internet and through social media, and out-spent the other minor parties in the campaign. However, Clive Palmer claimed his party had only spent 'between $8 and $12 million … on everything. That would have been established in the party doing everything'. Palmer went on to claim that 'the Liberals would have spent about $54 million, and Labor probably, you know, not much more than us' ('Palmer Drama' 2013).

The major policies announced by the two parties

Clive Palmer and the PUP policies included the abolition of the carbon and mining taxes and no increase in other taxes. The party also announced the quick processing of asylum seekers and abolition of tertiary fees and Higher Education Contributions Scheme (HECS) payments.

Bob Katter and the KAP included among their policies a national interest test for the privatisation of any public assets and the provision of an arbitrated price for agricultural produce where farmers request it.

A list of PUP and KAP policies can be found in the appendix to this chapter.

What seats did they contest?

Table 1: 2013 election, House of Representatives—number of seats contested

State	Palmer United Party	Katter's Australia Party	Total Seats in HoR
National	150	61	150
NSW	48	14	48
Vic	37	10	37
Qld	30	26	30
WA	15	7	15
SA	11	3	11
Tas	5	1	5
ACT	2	0	2
NT	2	0	2

Source: Australian Electoral Commission.

The PUP contested all 150 electorates in the House of Representatives and fielded Senate candidates in every state and territory. Significantly, while Palmer was wealthy enough to generously fund his party's core campaign, it is truly remarkable that he was able to find people who were able and willing to stand as candidates. By contrast, KAP only contested 40 per cent of the House of Representatives electorates (61 seats) and sometimes struggled to find candidates. The party's choice of seats to contest seems to be without rhyme or reason. For example, they did not contest a number of rural seats such as Farrer in New South Wales, but did stand for the urban electorate of Lilley in Queensland. Surprisingly, while the party contested the Senate in the Australian Capital Territory (not a favourable location), it did not contest the Senate in the Northern Territory where it would have likely done better. This could be because of a lack of finance or a failure to find willing candidates who would stand and make the necessary financial and time commitments. Katter, however, claimed that in the campaign his party 'campaigned all over Australia' but 'we spent no money virtually at all' (Horn 2013). Katter also claimed that 'it's no secret, we had massive disorganisation internally and in relation to the party's finances'. He went on to say in the same report that Clive Palmer's party, which polled strongly, 'was visible all of the time, but we weren't' (*Sydney Morning Herald* 2013).

Throughout much of the campaign the two new micro parties were largely considered as entertainment value. Yet, public opinion polling tracked a late swing to Palmer's party in the last two weeks of the campaign while Katter's stalled.

The performance of the two parties in the election

Tables 2 and 3 show the performance of the two parties both nationally and state-by-state for the House of Representatives and the Senate.

Table 2: 2013 election, House of Representatives—total votes and percentage of formal vote

State	Palmer United Party	Katter's Australia Party
National	709,041 (5.49%)	134,226 (1.04%)
NSW	174,551 (4.20%)	16,534 (0.40%)
Vic	119,623 (3.63%)	15,409 (0.47%)
Qld	278,131 (11.02%)	94,540 (3.75%)
WA	67,332 (5.32%)	4,997 (0.39%)
SA	37,981 (3.78%)	2,268 (0.23%)
Tas	20,026 (6.06%)	478 (0.14%)
ACT	6,788 (2.81%)	0
NT	4,609 (4.63%)	0

Source: Australian Electoral Commission.

The national level of support for Katter was affected by the fact that he stood candidates in only 40 per cent of seats. Significantly, however, except for Queensland (Katter's personal electoral base), the level of support for KAP was below that of its rival micro party in the worst-performing jurisdiction for Palmer (2.81 per cent in the Australian Capital Territory). In only one state did KAP manage to get over 0.5 per cent of the jurisdictional vote. In fact nationally, the PUP won five times the number of votes achieved by KAP, and PUP finished with a national vote of 5.49 per cent—only 3.16 per cent behind the Greens. KAP on the other hand scored a national vote below Family First and well below the combined vote for the Independents (standing 68 candidates).

As can be seen from Table 2, Katter did not stand candidates in either of the two territories and contested only one electorate in Tasmania. By way of contrast, when the Australian Democrats contested their first election in 1977, that minor party scored 9.4 per cent of the vote in the House of Representatives.

Table 3: PUP versus KAP—best results in House of Representatives seats

Palmer United Party			Katter Australia Party		
Electorate	State	Per cent	Electorate	State	Per cent
Fairfax	Qld	26.49	Kennedy	Qld	29.36
Hinkler	Qld	17.65	Herbert	Qld	8.08
Fisher	Qld	17.42	Dawson	Qld	6.74
McPherson	Qld	15.92	Wide Bay	Qld	5.88
Wide Bay	Qld	15.88	Maranoa	Qld	5.59
Fadden	Qld	14.67	Capricornia	Qld	5.54
Wright	Qld	14.48	Wright	Qld	5.37
Maranoa	Qld	13.91	Hinkler	Qld	4.58
Moncrieff	Qld	13.68	Leichhardt	Qld	4.29
Bowman	Qld	12.71	Flynn	Qld	4.13

Source: Australian Electoral Commission.

Significantly, all of the electorates in Table 3—which lists PUP's and KAP's best results—are in Queensland. Katter personally out-polled Palmer—but only just, with 29.36 per cent in Kennedy compared to Palmer's 26.49 per cent in Fairfax. With the exception of Kennedy, Palmer's best electorates received a higher percentage of votes than any of the best Katter electorates. The tenth best Palmer electorate of Bowman captured 12.71 per cent of the vote, compared to the second best Katter electorate of Herbert where KAP only received 8.08 per cent of the vote. In Fairfax and Kennedy, both Katter and Palmer were competing effectively for the same constituency, which affected their respective results.

Table 4: PUP versus KAP—worst results in House of Representatives seats

Palmer United Party			Katter Australia Party		
Electorate	State	Per cent	Electorate	State	Per cent
Melbourne	Vic	0.92	Reid	NSW	0.35
Wentworth	NSW	1.08	Swan	WA	0.51
Melb Ports	Vic	1.38	Throsby	NSW	0.56
Sydney	NSW	1.43	Hindmarsh	SA	0.63
Reid	NSW	1.51	Banks	NSW	0.65
Higgins	Vic	1.59	Hasluck	WA	0.66
Kooyong	Vic	1.60	Indi	Vic	0.69
Chisholm	Vic	1.63	Griffith	Qld	0.69
Grayndler	NSW	1.71	Franklin	Tas	0.71
Bennelong	NSW	1.80	Makin/Barton	SA/NSW	0.71

Source: Australian Electoral Commission.

All of Katter's worst electorates scored significantly more poorly than Palmer's worst seat, Melbourne (an urban seat), where PUP achieved a mere 0.92 per cent of the vote. Significantly, one of the electorates where KAP performed worst was Griffith, which is an electorate in Katter's home state of Queensland. In New South Wales, KAP was out-polled by One Nation in four seats: Hume, Lyne, Barton and Werriwa.

Table 5: 2013 election, Senate

State	Palmer United Party	Katter's Australia Party
National	653,089 (4.91%)	119,550 (0.90%)
NSW	148,281 (3.39%)	19,101 (0.44%)
Vic	123,889 (3.66%)	15,525 (0.46%)
Qld	258,994 (9.89%)	76,918 (2.94%)
WA	59,708 (4.94%)	3539 (0.29%)
SA	27,484 (2.65%)	1,666 (0.16%)
Tas	22,184 (6.58%)	1375 (0.41%)
ACT	5213 (2.11%)	1416 (0.57%)
NT	7386 (7.14%)	0

Source: Australian Electoral Commission.

Neither KAP nor PUP polled exceedingly well in the upper house vote. Palmer scored 4.91 per cent to Katter's 0.9 per cent. By way of contrast, in 1977 the Australian Democrats scored 11.1 per cent of the vote in the Senate election. As micro parties rather than established minor parties, both PUP and KAP have a state in which they are clearly strongest. In this case, that state is Queensland for both parties. On a percentage basis in Queensland, both parties scored well above the national percentage of votes that they received. In fact, PUP polled well in Fisher and Hinkler, and with a little more support the party could have won those two seats. The 2013 federal election saw a general increase in micro parties, making KAP and PUP two of many aggrieved micro parties in a Melbourne Cup field. In this environment, PUP performed poorest in South Australia, where it was up against high profile minor party candidates such as Family First's Bob Day, and Nick Xenophon. A second point to make is that the vote for KAP in the Senate was a lot smaller than that for the PUP—in New South Wales and Victoria KAP's vote was miniscule.

Comparing the votes for the House of Representatives with those for the Senate for each party, it can be seen that nationally both parties received a higher House vote. This is surprising for minor parties, as they tend to poll higher in the Senate (because voters believe the minor party candidate has a better chance of being elected for the Senate). This is true of the Democratic Labour Party (DLP) and the Australian Democrats. However in this election both leaders stood successfully for the Queensland House of Representatives seats. Both would have enjoyed a personal following to some degree, in that people voted for the name of the candidate and not the party as such. However the PUP also had a high profile Senate candidate in Queensland—Glen Lazarus, who is a well-known former rugby league player.

While KAP polled higher for the Senate in New South Wales, Victoria, Tasmania and the Australian Capital Territory, it polled higher for the House of Representatives in Queensland, Western Australia and South Australia. Palmer United polled higher for the Senate in Victoria, Tasmania and the Northern Territory but lower for the House of Representatives in those states, achieving instead a better result in the other states, including Western Australia where it eventually had a Senator elected.

The PUP's higher Senate vote in Tasmania could be a result of their high profile candidate, Jacqui Lambie, who won a Senate seat there. She is a former soldier and a single mother who appealed to the Administrative Appeals Tribunal on an issue of military compensation. This may have won her personal support from voters of a similar demographic who may have identified with her.

Where did PUP/KAP support come from?

This section of the chapter explores the sources for the votes that flowed to these two parties. Did the votes flow from one party, a few parties or several parties? A useful starting point is the electorate of the leader, Palmer, in Fairfax.

Table 6: Number of votes and swing in electorate of Fairfax, by party

Party	Vote	Swing
One Nation	709	+0.84
Independent	1,016	+1.20
Palmer United	22,409	+26.49
LNP	34,959	-8.13
Family First	1,416	-3.57
ALP	15,429	-9.07
Greens	7,046	-9.67
Katter Aust Party	1,623	+1.92

Source: Australian Electoral Commission.

In Fairfax it appears that the swing to Palmer came roughly equally from the established parties, Labor, Liberal and the Greens, and not from one individual source. However, Labor lost government so the swing against the ALP towards minor parties could be seen as a 'protest vote' against the Labor Government. Also of note in this seat is the very small swing to KAP of less than 2 per cent.

As a comparison the swing in Katter's electorate is indicated in Table 7.

Table 7: Number of votes and swing in electorate of Kennedy, by party

Party	Vote	Swing
Palmer United	6,419	+7.63
Independent	571	+0.68
Greens	2,727	-1.25
Katter Aust Party	24,691	-17.35
Rise Up Australia	508	+0.60
Family First	1,064	-0.73
LNP	34,344	+14.24
ALP	13,777	-3.83

Source: Australian Electoral Commission.

As Katter was a sitting member, his 2013 performance is compared to the result he achieved in the 2010 election. He received fewer votes in the 2013 election, suffering a swing against him of 17.63 per cent. Most of that swing went to his LNP rival candidate (14.24 per cent). It would appear the rest of the swing against Katter, along with the swing against the ALP, went in favour of the PUP candidate. A telling point is the significant number of votes won by Palmer's candidate in Kennedy (7.63 per cent) compared to the far fewer votes won by the Katter candidate in Fairfax (1.92 per cent).

In the electorate of Moreton, the sitting Labor member received a small swing in his favour. Most of the swing to KAP (1,070 votes or a 1.30 per cent swing) and to the PUP (4,147 votes or a 5.03 per cent swing) came from other small parties such as Family First and the DLP which did not field a candidate. The swing against the LNP in that seat was -1.16 per cent. The Greens suffered a swing of -5.90 per cent.

Overall, the swing to KAP and PUP did not come from one party (as it did in the case of One Nation) but from a number of parties. In Leichhardt, most of the 8.55 per cent swing to the PUP came from various minor parties, with Labor, Liberals and the Greens suffering swings against them of just over 2 per cent and the Katter candidate receiving a swing in the KAP's favour of 4.29 per cent.

What caused these votes to swing to the two parties? Was it purely a 'protest' against one of the major parties or was the policy of one of the two parties particularly attractive, or was there some other reason? In 2013, Palmer and Katter picked up some of the swing against the ALP and the Greens, but this may not be repeated in the next election and the swing could in fact go back to the major parties. However, some of the votes for KAP and the PUP appear to have come from other minor parties where the minor party did not stand candidates in the 2013 election. Quite likely, these voters searched around for another attractive minor party and settled on either KAP or PUP.

The power of the second preferences

Minor and micro parties derive some of their power from being able to allocate their second preferences to another chosen party, often determining which side wins the seat. However this power is weakened significantly if the second preferences 'leak' to other parties. There was a significant leakage of PUP second preferences. For example, in the Western Australian seat of Hasluck, 38 per cent of that party's preferences went to the Greens, 27 per cent to Labor and 30 per cent to the Liberals. KAP preferences were also dispersed widely with 30 per cent going to the PUP, 20 per cent to the Liberals as well as 17 per cent going to the Australian Sex Party. By comparison, when the Greens candidate was excluded, 70 per cent of the preferences flowed to Labor and 30 per cent to the Liberals—a much tighter flow of preferences.

In Franklin, 45 per cent of PUP preferences flowed to the ALP, 42 per cent to the Liberals and 13 per cent to the Greens. Of the KAP preferences, 29 per cent flowed to the PUP, 17 per cent to the ALP, 22 per cent to the Liberals and 14 per cent to the Greens, with 18 per cent going to Family First. Of the Greens preferences, 85 per cent flowed to the ALP and 15 per cent to the Liberals. In the seat of Hinkler, the Greens candidate was excluded first with 49 per cent of preferences going to the ALP, 54 per cent of KAP preferences then went to Palmer United, 28 per cent to the ALP and 18 per cent to the Liberals. PUP preferences were then split with 55 per cent going to the Liberals and 45 per cent to Labor. In the seat of Corangamite, 52 per cent of PUP preferences flowed to Labor and 48 per cent to the Liberals. Greens preferences were divided with 86 per cent going to Labor and 14 per cent to the Liberals. Eighty per cent of Nationals preferences flowed to the Liberals and 20 per cent went to the ALP.

There was a trend across all electorates of KAP and PUP preferences significantly leaking to other parties while Green preferences flowed strongly to the ALP. One reason for this is that the Greens emphasised the importance of its allocation of second preferences, whereas KAP and PUP largely ignored the issue of preference votes in their campaigns.

Conclusion

In conclusion, the two new micro parties were led by two high profile leaders. However, the Palmer United Party preformed far better than Katter's Australia Party. This is surprising in some ways because Katter had a higher national profile. His policies appealed to his constituency, for example policies to curb the power of the two multinational supermarkets in Australia and low interest loans for farmers. However, Katter was handicapped by a lack of candidates and his poor handling of the same-sex marriage issue. Palmer, on the other hand, stood candidates in every electorate and steered well clear of the same-sex marriage issue, with other policies expressed in very general terms, such as the abolition of tertiary education fees. The swings to both KAP and the PUP did not come from one party alone but from several. These swings even included voters for minor parties whose party stood in the 2010 election but not in the 2013 election—these voters were simply looking for another protest party to express their dissatisfaction with the major parties.

The performance of the two parties varied across Australia. Significantly, both these micro parties only managed to have one candidate elected in the lower house—in both cases their leader in a favourable Queensland seat. In some electorates the level of support for the PUP was very small, in other electorates it was over 20 per cent. In a number of electorates the level of support for KAP was less than 1 per cent, whereas in only one electorate did the PUP poll less than 1 per cent. The low percentages of votes, together with the undisciplined leakage of preferences, meant that the potentiality of these parties to influence the eventual electoral outcome was greatly weakened.

Both Katter and Palmer made an impact in the 2013 election, and made some significant gains; they captured attention and captured some of the disaffected vote from the major parties and from other minor/micro parties. However, their campaign management provided much evidence of their inexperience and capriciousness. While Palmer's hastily assembled party did provide voters with a range of policy options and as a consequence did slightly better than the Katter party, whose policies were more imprecise, both were channels for disaffection across regional Australia. Yet both micro parties are tied to the mercurial personalities of their respective leaders. Whether they can follow-up their election campaigns and go on from here to build more credible political movements remains to be seen.

Appendix

The major policies announced by the two parties

Clive Palmer and the Palmer United Party announced their policy intentions as follows:

- Abolish the Carbon Tax;
- No increase in taxes and abolition of the mining tax;
- Asylum seekers dealt with quickly on arrival and if found to have a legitimate right to asylum then allowed to enter Australia, and have access to welfare like all other Australians;
- Abolish tertiary fees and Higher Education Contributions Scheme (HECS) payments;
- A nationalised school curriculum and a maximum of 30 students to a classroom;
- Introduction of legislation to require former politicians or senior government officials to have left public office for 10 years before they could work as lobbyists;
- A target for 10 per cent of all vehicles to be running on ethanol-based fuel by the end of 2016, rising to 25 per cent by 2020;
- A full review of Australia's voting system;
- A reduction of 50 per cent in income tax on a second job;

- An increase in aged pensions, building more nursing homes and making sure people have adequate help so they can continue to live comfortably in their own homes;
- Payment of funding directly to hospitals, circumventing state governments; and,
- Abolition of the fringe benefits tax on business lunches.

The major policies announced by Bob Katter and the KAP were:

- Mandate a national interest test to the privatisation of any public assets;
- Provide an arbitrated price for agricultural produce where farmers request it;
- Restore irrigation water to agriculture in the Murray Darling Basin;
- Mandate ethanol use in Australia, providing structural support to grain and sugar industries;
- Support and extend the Mandatory Renewable Energy Target;
- An overhaul of the current model used to educate Australia's children, with a focus on providing a solid foundation of reading, writing and mathematics, identify great teaching and reward it;
- Stimulate investment in infrastructure, including roads, rail and ports;
- Mandate the allocation of premium shelf space in supermarkets for Australian produce;
- Reduce interest rates and bring down the Australian Dollar; and,
- Support the right of farmers and other citizens to manage their resources and live without 'uninvited interference'.

References

Horn, Allyson. 2013. 'Big Swing Against Bob Katter in his Seat of Kennedy'. *ABC News,* 8 September, viewed 20 October 2013: <www.abc.net.au/news/2013-09-07/big-swing-againts-bob-katter-in-his-seat-of-kennedy>.

Houghton, Des. 2013. 'Bob Katter's tolerance of star Senate candidate James Blundell's view on gay unions sparks member exodus'. *Courier-Mail*, Brisbane, 10 August.

Katter, Robert. 2012. *An Incredible Race of People: A Passionate History of Australia*. Sydney: Murdoch Books Australia.

Key, Victor, J. 1964. *Politics, Parties and Pressure Groups*. 5th edn. New York: Thomas Y Crowell.

McDonnell, John. 2001. 'Beware the Kattermites'. *Adelaide Review* 215, August: 6–7.

Nowra, Louis. 2013. 'Barramundi Dreaming: The heart and mind of Bob Katter'. *The Monthly,* April: 28–33.

'Palmer Drama'. 2013. *Four Corners*, television programme transcript, ABC TV, Sydney, 25 November, viewed 3 February 2014: <www.abc.net.au/4corners/stories/2013/11/25/3896229.htm>.

Palmer United Party. 2013. 'Palmer United Party announces conscience vote on same sex marriage'. Press release, 30 July.

Sadler, Mat. 2011. 'Gay marriage should be ridiculed, says independent Bob Katter'. *News.com.au*, 16 August, viewed 18 November 2013: <www.news.com.au/national/gay-marriage-should-be-ridiculed-says-independent-bob-katter/story-e6frfkvr-1226116097321>.

Sydney Morning Herald. 2013. 'Bob Katter expects "terrible belting" for his party'. 7 September, viewed 30 October 2014: <www.smh.com.au/federal-politics/federal-election-2013/bob-katter-expects-terrible-belting-for-his-party-20130907-2tcc0.html>.

Part 5. Salient Issues

18. An Impecunious Election: The significance of fiscal and economic issues

John Wanna

This election will be about who the Australian people best trust to lead them through the difficult new economic challenges that now lie ahead.—PM Kevin Rudd, August 2013.

This election is not just about economic management but economic management is the core issue because everything else—national security, border security, the delivery of better schools and hospitals, and the successful implementation of the National Disability Insurance Scheme—needs a strong economy to be sustainable.—Opposition Leader Tony Abbott, September 2013.[1]

Fiscal and economic policy loomed large as a policy contest in the 2013 election, but as an issue or set of issues it failed to capture the public mood or spark much overwhelming interest.[2] Economic issues were more latent than front and centre, when some commentators felt that 'the economy should have been the cornerstone of the whole campaign' (see Harmon 2013). Indeed, the AES survey conducted immediately after the election found, unsurprisingly, that the management of the economy was rated by 94.5 per cent of respondents as very important and 81.4 per cent similarly thought taxation issues were important, but these attitudes did not shape the campaign strategies markedly (Bean et al. 2014: 79, 82).[3] Worries of an impending economic recession were pronounced; escalating job losses occurring in the manufacturing and service sectors and in the public sector, investment trending downward, the mining boom coming off the boil, and fragilities in the retail sector, all added to the sense of nervousness and uncertainty. In addition, the Government's fiscal/budget difficulties and especially the depressed state of revenue returns kept the attention on the Government's performance with respect to economic management. Other

---

[1] Rudd and Abbott quotes taken, respectively, from Abbott and Rudd 2013 and Abbott 2013.
[2] Previous Australian election studies have rarely included separate chapters on the economy, business or fiscal policies; the exceptions in recent years are the collections produced for the 2007 and 2010 elections (see references in the Preface). Overseas electoral studies also rarely include chapters on the salience of economic issues in campaigns.
[3] Moreover, some 27.5 per cent of respondents stated that the management of the economy was the most important issue during the campaign (the highest proportion) and a further 13.9 per cent claimed it was the second most important issue (again the highest combined salience) (see Bean et al. 2014: 86).

'failings' brought on by the Government itself, such as its flawed and inflated estimates of economic growth forecasts, its overly optimistic projections of revenue receipts, and total lack of credibility in its sanguine budget projections of an imminent surplus, only magnified the impression the Government did not really know what it was doing.

Plausible explanations of why the economy was not more prominent as an electoral issue may include the fact that the Australian economy was comparatively not in a bad condition—inflation (+/-2 per cent) and unemployment (around 5.7 per cent) were relatively low, economic growth was positive (2.5 per cent), and the mining boom (commodity markets) had insulated the economy by maintaining export levels and sustained growth in the states of Western Australia and Queensland. Real incomes were rising by 3 pecent per annum. Yet, household cost of living pressures were mounting both in real terms (household utility bills) and as an electoral issue (living affordability); and there were regular media accounts of the increased incidence of poverty and welfare/food handouts. The structural budgetary problem was not something Labor was likely to canvass widely in the campaign, and the Coalition had to be very selective in its attacks because going too hard on this issue would raise fears of the necessary cuts the conservatives would have to make to return to surplus. To keep the issue alive but contained the Coalition proclaimed that Australia faced a real 'budget emergency' and mounting debt levels.

The other important factor about fiscal management was that, because economic activity was relatively flat, there was no real prospect of new money for policy announcements in the campaign or for the foreseeable future. Hence, an impecunious election was fought with virtually no vote buying to leaven the tedium of campaign negativity. The election was fought in a Micawber-like trance with both sides eschewing major spending commitments—only the Greens who were unlikely to be called upon to implement any announcements made extravagant commitments.

By the end of the election campaign the Coalition had made total promises amounting to $33.4 billion but offset by cuts of $42 billion, which over the four-year forward estimates saved the budget some $8 billion. The Coalition committed to spending on new roads ($5.4 billion), a paid parental leave scheme ($3.3 billion), direct action on climate change ($2 billion), and restoring the fringe benefits tax (FBT) concession for company cars ($1.8 billion). It also had to offset the abolition of the carbon and mining taxes ($9.7 billion) and a cut in company tax rates ($4.9 billion). The Coalition announced savings (cuts) to the public service, the school kids bonus, foreign aid, low income super contributions, regional infrastructure, and the refugee intake (and reduced spending by 'stopping the boats') as well as a new levy on companies to pay for the parental leave scheme. Labor by contrast promised a paltry $0.5 billion for better before and afterschool care, and its commitments amounted to a budget neutral stance.

The primacy of economic policy and the disappearing surplus

Economic and fiscal policies had been at the very forefront of the Labor Government's agenda since the early onset of the global financial crisis (GFC) in 2008. Given the severe financial shock hit the Government almost immediately after it assumed office in its first term, economic concerns were a perennial priority for Labor. It implemented a series of five stimulus packages over 2008–09, introduced an expansionary budget in May 2009, and then constantly wrestled with the difficulties of 'fiscal consolidation' with every budget from 2010–11 through to 2013–14—arguably presiding over a deterioration in public finances. The Government took some courageous fiscal measures in its first term that helped prevent Australia from suffering the magnitude of economic woes that afflicted the United States and most of Europe, but difficulties in rebalancing the budget gradually began to hurt the Government's reputation and standing with business.

Treasurer Wayne Swan had pledged to deliver a surplus (absolutely guaranteed, 'come hell or high water') by the end of June 2013. His bravado was pure bluff and exaggeration. When it became impossible to pretend that a surplus would eventuate by that date, Swan quietly announced just before the Christmas break that the surplus commitment would be jettisoned, initially postponing the surplus another year to 2014 before admitting it would not be achieved until 2016–17. Many commentators were either fatalistically resigned to the likelihood of yet another deficit, or were relatively positive about the news because they feared any further contractionary measures would tip Australia into a recession. By 2013 the deficit was around $40 billion for the year, and, counting the 2013–14 budget, Swan had delivered six consecutive deficit final budget outcomes, amounting to over $250 billion in total. On 1 August 2013, after the return of Rudd to the leadership, Chris Bowen, Labor's new treasurer, had to introduce a mini budget and a new budget update (increasing the deficit projections to $58.8 billion over three years), with various 'annoying' tax increases mooted ($5 billion extra in tobacco excise, increases in the FBT, a tax on bank deposits, higher visa charges, and a higher efficiency dividend).

Treasury had to accept some of the blame for the parlous decline in the Government's reputation. The department made significant forecasting errors over the changing magnitude of the deficit (repeatedly overestimating taxation receipts while underestimating the difficulties in re-balancing the books, or achieving 'fiscal consolidation'). Treasury also invited criticism over its wayward miscalculation of the amount of revenues the Mining Resource Rent Tax would generate, with the actual tax delivering only a couple of hundred million dollars by early 2013 and not the $3 billion expected in the budget and nothing close to the $22.5 billion over four years as originally expected. The Treasury Secretary, Martin Parkinson, blamed his department for not having sufficient data on the assumptions the mining companies were making in calculating their liabilities.

Antagonising constituencies

Arguably, the Labor Government made some major economic policy mistakes in its relations with business and households. It repeatedly announced proposals that concentrated the economic pain on powerful constituencies while spreading the benefits thinly. The Mining Super Profit Tax (then the Mining Resource Rent Tax) was guilty of this, as was the Carbon Tax initiative with a bureaucratically-determined high price for emissions passed directly on to household consumers. Other additional levies for floods, health care and disability care were targeted to middle and higher PAYE income earners out of budgetary necessity. The treasurer also seriously proposed increasing the tax on wealthy superannuants, but other senior ministers such as Simon Crean came out publicly and said the Government 'shouldn't be taxing people's [own] surpluses in order to fund our surpluses' (Kelly 2013). Universities were slugged with an overall efficiency dividend raising some $900 million per annum to help offset the initial increased schools funding recommended by Gonski. Later under Rudd's second term as prime minister he announced his intention to remove the tax concessions on leased company cars, not understanding that many of these cars were used in the welfare and caring sectors and not anticipating that the proposals would cause severe disruptions in the car industry (producers and retailers) in its impact on new car orders.

Moreover, the Government continued to increase spending and to make significant long-term financial commitments, leading to an estimated escalation in the public debt burden to $220 billion by 2015–16. This was especially a problem with the Gillard Government (2010–13) which usually chose to spend forecasted funds it *expected* to receive long before it actually received them (and even then often did not receive the projected amount). This was true of both the carbon and mining taxes whose forecasted revenues were allocated before any tax was collected, and of the purported re-bounce in revenues over 2012–13. Long-term impositions on future budgets announced by Gillard as part of her intended legacy included: the increased school funding over seven years under the Gonski recommendations, the National Disability Insurance

Scheme committing increased resources over eight years, as well as schemes to subsidise the wages of low paid workers especially in the carer and early childhood sectors.

The combined effect of these taxing-spending moves often alienated critics and did not appease intended beneficiaries. The mining industry waged an intense advertising war in 2010 with the Rudd Government before gaining concessions from Gillard that made the mining tax virtually ineffectual. Rural communities and small businesses strongly opposed the carbon tax, even though some would not be greatly affected and some would have gained from adaptation measures (afforestation).

Arguments over Labor's economic management

The net effect of the disappearing surplus and Labor's sequential broken promises to fix the budget meant that Labor's economic management record became an electoral liability for the Government, and an opportunity for the Coalition to really target its critique of the Government. Despite effectively combatting the GFC, the Government could not credibly campaign on its performance as an economic manager that had exercised sound fiscal management on public finances (see also AES data on Labor being markedly behind the Coalition as preferred managers of the economy by 22.8 per cent to 43.7 per cent—Bean *et al*. 2014: 86).

The Coalition had been a persistent critic of Labor's economic management since the end of 2008 when Malcolm Turnbull became opposition leader and had argued that the surplus measures were more generous than they needed to be and too costly to the budget. Under Abbott's leadership this criticism moved on to the general profligacy of Labor and inability to rebalance the budget. The shadow treasurer Joe Hockey in particular began to mount a neo-liberal case against 'big spending' and 'big government', promising to 'end the age of entitlement' (Hockey 2012).

Labor's problem in promoting its economic credentials was principally sheeted home to the treasurer Wayne Swan who was a poor communicator and salesman. His stewardship of the economy and particularly the budget came in for criticism from many quarters, and, given he had attached so strenuously his personal reputation to the goal of delivering a surplus, his credibility as an economic manager suffered accordingly. Unlike former treasurers Paul Keating or Peter Costello, but similar to Ralph Willis before him, Treasurer Swan was not a forceful advocate of the Government's economic credentials. He tended to over-promise and then under-deliver rather than the other way around. In speeches, interviews and press conferences he was often flat in his delivery, became tied up in technicalities, or shied away from boasting about his government's achievements. He once famously told an audience of serious journalist and financial writers assembled in the National Press Club after his 2011–12 budget that there was nothing to say about the budget other than that it had been difficult for him to put together and contained no good news. It may have been an honest remark but was not something his predecessors would have been likely to have admitted.

Rudd threw a further 'populist' spanner in the works when he implied that he favoured greater curbs on foreign ownership in Australia. In response to a constituent's question at the third leaders' debate (the people's forum at the Rooty Hill RSL Club) Rudd said he was concerned about the increasing levels of foreign ownership of Australian assets, and proposed to reduce the threshold at which proposed foreign acquisitions of land were vetted by the Foreign Investment Review Board (Abbott and Rudd 2013).

The Coalition's proposals

The Coalition did not promise explicitly to deliver a budgetary surplus; instead Abbott promised about a week out from election day that 'by the end of a Coalition Government's first term, the budget will be back on track to a believable surplus'. It was a calculated 'fudge' but enabled the Coalition to appear virtuous. He also said it might take until 2016–17 before a surplus could be achieved, promising that 'within a decade [by 2023] the budget surplus will be one per cent of GDP' (Berg 2013). These statements significantly watered down Joe Hockey's earlier commitment of January 2013 that he would return a surplus within one year of forming government. Hockey also changed his own tune during the campaign; and after his debate on economic policy with Treasurer Chris Bowen, where he said he would follow in the years ahead the same fiscal plans that Labor had announced, there was talk that the Coalition had belatedly opted for a 'unity ticket' on budgetary issues. Suddenly the structural deficit was not a point of policy difference, largely due to the realisation that there were significant difficulties with imposing major cuts on a fragile economy.

Beyond the issue of the deficit, the Coalition's plans for the economy were dot-point slogans. The widely-circulated *Our Plan* document listed five economic objectives: two million new jobs over ten years; a 'five pillar economy' building on agriculture, mining and manufacturing industries; lower taxes; lower debt levels; and stronger national borders (Liberal Party of Australia 2013).

Squabbles over policy costings

With all the advantages of incumbency and the public service on tap for expert advice, Labor claimed it had accurately costed all its policy changes—which were few and far between. It was less clear that the opposition had similarly managed to produce accurate costings. Previous oppositions had often come unstuck when their announced policy costings were shown by the Government to be flawed or new taxes were likely to hit harder than expected (for example, especially in the federal elections of 1987, 1993 and 1998). Hence oppositions had adopted the practice of delaying any detailed policy announcements until it was too late in the campaign for the Government or Treasury/Finance to produce contradictory costings. In this stand-off the Labor Government constantly challenged the opposition to 'come clean' on its policy commitments and release its own costings so they could be checked and verified or challenged. The Coalition steadfastly refused to comply with Labor's insistence until the end of the campaign, and when it eventually released its policies they were often capped and so the upper limits were declared fixed.

One policy that attracted much debate on the 'fairness' of the costs imposed on the community was the Coalition's paid parental leave scheme (PPL). Unlike Labor's 18-week scheme offered at the minimum wage, the Coalition promised a salary-based or workplace entitlement scheme that set the PPL according to the mother's wage up to a maximum of $75,000 for six months. The Coalition costed this scheme at $5.5 billion when fully operational, and proposed to pay for the policy through an additional temporary levy on big business but with savings offset from Labor's scheme. The ideological argument over this policy revolved around different interpretations of equity. Some Nationals argued that all women (including stay-at-home mums) should get the same benefit set at the level of the minimum wage. Other interests (including some unions and businesses) argued that mothers should have parental leave paid as a workplace entitlement (as many in the professions, the corporate sector and in public employment already enjoyed) with the rate dependent on the income of the employee (there was no provision for non-working mothers). The Greens supported the PPL but thought the Liberals' scheme too generous, and so proposed an income cap of $50,000 over six months. Although the Coalition received much criticism for breaking the 'egalitarian statist spirit' based on minimal means-tested benefits, it persevered with its proposal in defiance of such criticisms. Some unionists and feminists viewing parental leave as an employment entitlement were less critical, as were those who favoured a contributory scheme that would make payments at variable rates. There was also a worry that many existing workplace schemes (in firms, universities, government departments) would transfer their entitlements over to the Coalition's proposed federal scheme which would likely add significantly to its overall costs.

Salience of economic and fiscal issues in the electorate

Many commentators proclaimed in the campaign that 'economic management is by far the most important and influential issue for voters' (Keane 2013). And many thoughtful commentators attempted to urge serious debate on important topics for Australia's future or lamented the lack of meaningful engagement on issues. One former politician, Barry Jones, called it a terrible campaign, devoid of content, and 'the worst [he] could recall' (Jones 2013). This was by no means a novel criticism of recent political campaigns, as campaigns usually came down to strategies oriented towards winning, and were not necessarily about educating the public; indeed, any education of the electorate may have been an unintended consequence.

Yet issue polling demonstrated the economy remained a most pressing issue, and a top priority for many voters. In August, Newspoll found that health, the economy and education were 'very important issues' for voters (scoring respectively 75 per cent, 74 per cent and 73 per cent in importance), followed by 'cost of living' concerns on 65 per cent. The economy was considered best handled by the Coalition (by 49 per cent) compared to Labor (on 33 per cent)—and support for the Coalition's economic management credentials continued to firm slightly over 2013. The Coalition was also regarded as likely to best handle cost of living pressures by 43 per cent to 35 per cent. An *Age*–Nielsen poll reported that 58 per cent of Australians considered the Coalition to be better economic managers compared to 38 per cent who thought Labor was the better manager. According to Colebatch (2013), this finding reflected a consistent pattern evidenced since the 1990–91 recession. However, Galaxy found that after the PPL was taken into account, some 43 per cent had confidence in the Coalition's stewardship of the economy, compared to 35 per cent who opted for Labor. Polls of marginal seats also put the economy and taxation as the main issues that 'would help most', with 40 per cent responding accordingly compared to 18 per cent who nominated welfare, and 8 per cent who opted for health (see Roy Morgan Research 2013).

In addition, a survey of 806 young voters in May 2013 listed jobs for young people entering the workforce (51 per cent) and the high cost of rent or housing generally (47 per cent) as the two most important issues that would affect their vote (Lucas 2013).

An ANUpoll survey released in August 2013 placed the economy/jobs as the most important problem facing Australia today (with 30.3 per cent of respondents indicating it as the top priority—twice the figure for immigration on 15.1 per cent and better government on 12.9 per cent, and well ahead of education (4.2 per cent) and health (3.6 per cent). Moreover, a further 21.2 per cent rated it as the second most important issue, meaning that 'just over half of the survey respondents mentioned the economy and jobs as a priority', a much higher percentage than had mentioned this issue in similar surveys in 2010 or 2011 (ANUpoll 2013). The AES survey also tended to confirm these trends (Bean et al. 2014: 86).

Given then the apparent salience of economic, employment and hip-pocket issues in the electorate, why were these issues latent in the campaign and not more prominent in the promotional strategies of the leaders and parties? Why didn't the economy resonate more noticeably? One factor may be that the media had an 'obsessive emphasis on personalities, stunts and trivia' and shied away from serious debate on issues, whether simple or complex (Jones 2013). Also the 'policy vacuum' may have tended to discourage debate about policy sectoral issues, although the PPL issue and the various elements of the comparable schemes were widely debated in an informed manner. It is also true that some fiscal and budgetary issues may have been hard to comprehend, overly complex and highly technical in nature, and when contradictory assertions or different versions of 'facts' were proffered electors tended to turn off. If complex financial issues appeared unclear and were not relevant to their personal circumstances then voters were likely to become sceptical, find the information tedious and to some extent become bored with issues. Alternatively, the perceptions of electors themselves may have been relevant. Voters may simply have believed that Labor had struggled with its fiscal policies and that the Coalition would do a better job at economic management—and so did not feel the need to get excited about economic issues. Or, perhaps sufficient numbers of voters had made up their minds about their voting intentions months ahead of the polls, and the campaign itself counted for little in terms of political communication or reshaping voting intentions.

References

Abbott, Tony. 2013. 'Address to the National Press Club'. Canberra, 2 September, viewed 15 April 2014: <www.liberal.org.au/latest-news/2013/09/02/tony-abbott-address-national-press-club-election-2013>.

Abbott, Tony and Rudd, Kevin. 2013. 'People's Forum'. Rooty Hill RSL Club, 28 August, viewed 14 October 2013: <www.kevinrudd.org.au/latest3_280813>.

ANUpoll. 2013. *Attitudes to Electoral Reform*. Ian McAllister, ANU College of Arts and Social Sciences, August, viewed 11 April 2014: <politicsir.cass.anu.edu.au/sites/default/files/ANUpoll-report-August-2014-attitudes-electoral-reform.pdf>.

Bean, Clive, McAllister, Ian, Pietsch, Juliet and Gibson, Rachel. 2014. *Australian Election Study, 2013*. Canberra: Australian Data Archive, The Australian National University.

Berg, Chris. 2013. '"On track" for a surplus? Not good enough'. *The Drum*, 3 September, viewed 11 April 2014: <www.abc.net.au/news/2013-09-03/berg-on-track-for-a-surplus/4931502>.

Colebatch, Tim. 2013. 'Taking the prize, losing the plot'. *Sydney Morning Herald*, 4 September, viewed 9 October 2013: <www.smh.com.au/federal-politics/federal-election-2013/taking-the-prize-losing-the-plot-20130903-2t37m.html>.

Harmon, Colm. 2013. 'Election 2013 Essays: It's the economy, stupid'. *The Conversation*, 4 September, viewed 11 April 2014: <theconversation.com/election-2013-essays-its-the-economy-stupid-17470>.

Hockey, Joe. 2012. 'The End of the Age of Entitlement'. Address to the Institute of Economic Affairs, London, 17 April, viewed 11 April 2014: <www.joehockey.com/media-files/speeches/ContentPieces/100/download.pdf>.

Jones, Barry. 2013. 'Virtue and vexation: the policy vacuum in the 2013 election'. *The Conversation*, 16 September, viewed 11 April 2014: <theconversation.com/virtue-and-vexation-the-policy-vacuum-in-the-2013-election-18144>.

Keane, Bernard. 2013. 'Sound and fury signifying not much as both sides embrace unity tickets'. *Crikey*, 28 August, viewed 11 April 2014: <www.crikey.com.au/2013/08/30/sound-and-fury-signifying-not-much-as-both-sides-embrace-unity-tickets/?wpmp_switcher=mobile>.

Kelly, Joe. 2013. 'Simon Crean to fight plan for superannuation tax changes as internal rift deepens'. *The Australian*, 1 April, viewed 11 April 2014: <www.theaustralian.com.au/national-affairs/policy/simon-crean-to-fight-plan-for-superannuation-tax-changes-as-internal-rift-deepens/story-fn59nsif-1226610030006#>.

Liberal Party of Australia. 2013. *Real Solutions for all Australians*. Canberra: Liberal Party of Australia. Available online from the website of the Liberal Party of Australia, viewed 18 March 2014: <lpa.webcontent.s3.amazonaws.com/realsolutions/LPA%20Policy%20Booklet%20210x210_pages.pdf>.

Lucas, Clay. 2013. 'You are not listening, say young voters', *Sydney Morning Herald*, 7 August 2013, viewed 15 October 2014: <www.smh.com.au/federal-politics/federal-election-2013/you-are-not-listening-say-young-voters-20130806-2rdi7 html>

Roy Morgan Research. 2013. 'The Economy, Tax and Welfare rank as top personal issues to electors in Corangamite and Corio'. 26 August, viewed 9 October 2013: <politicsir.cass.anu.edu.au/sites/default/files/ANUpoll-report-August-2014-attitudes-electoral-reform.pdf>.

19. Ethnic Voting and Asylum Issues

James Jupp

In many democratic societies there is a strong tendency for voters from ethnic or religious minorities to support the party of the 'left', however this may be locally defined. This was initially noticed in the United States, where it is an important concern of political scientists and partisans. Similar trends are noticeable in Britain, Canada, Australia and New Zealand. In the seats where immigrant communities have concentrated, ethnic minority support for the ALP is consistently strong (Jupp 1981 and 1984). This support was largely sustained in 2013, despite general swings towards the Liberals. This chapter argues that predictions of a 'wipeout' for Labor in such electorates were unsound, both in Sydney and Melbourne. It does not argue for the overall impact of 'ethnic and immigration issues' as these were heavily focused on asylum seekers rather than immigration as a whole. Campaigning on such issues was aimed at the Anglo-Australian majority. There was very little academic or journalistic debate on immigration issues, as both major parties were in full agreement on 'stopping the boats'.

The two tables in this chapter are both based on the Commonwealth Census of 2006, adjusted to concentrate on those electorates previously described as 'ethnic'. These are defined as having populations in which more than 25 per cent use a language other than English at home. They are confined to Sydney and Melbourne, but constitute almost 20 per cent of the total being contested for the House of Representatives. Significantly they also include nearly all the electorates normally regarded as safe for the ALP; without them Labor would be in permanent opposition. This cannot prove that an 'ethnic vote' exists or is predominantly Labor, but it does suggest that without this reserve (and the Green preferences) there is little hope of change from conservative government nationally and in at least four of the states.

Table 1: Commonwealth elections of 2010 and 2013 in 'ethnic' electorates (defined as those with 25 per cent or more using a language other than English (LOTE) at home)

Electorate	Result 2013	Labor preferences (%)	Swing to Liberals 2010–13 (%)
New South Wales (Boundaries of 22/12/2009)			
Banks	Labor loss	48.07	+3.47
Barton	Labor loss	49.55	+7.45
Bennelong	Liberals retain	41.97	+4.91
Blaxland	Labor retains	62.20	+0.03
Chifley	Labor retains	61.11	+1.36
Fowler	Labor retains	68.12	-8.97
Grayndler	Labor retains	50.48	-0.03
Greenway	Labor retains	53.73	-2.65
Kingsford Smith	Labor retains	53.19	+2.10
McMahon	Labor retains	55.85	+2.21
Parramatta	Labor retains	50.78	+4.10
Reid	Labor loss	49.36	+3.50
Watson	Labor retains	57.5	+1.57
Werriwa	Labor retains	52.65	+4.26
Victoria (Boundaries of 24/12/2010)			
Batman	Labor retains	61.97	-4.17 to Greens
Bruce	Labor retains	51.34	+6.40
Calwell	Labor retains	63.88	+6.18
Chisholm	Labor retains	51.70	+4.39
Gellibrand	Labor retains	66.79	+7.48
Gorton	Labor retains	66.52	+7.10
Holt	Labor retains	60.56	+4.10
Hotham	Labor retains	57.64	+6.47
Isaacs	Labor retains	53.66	+6.70
Lalor	Labor retains	62.11	+10.01
Maribyrnong	Labor retains	61.53	+6.00
Melbourne	Greens retain	45.11	-1.10 to Greens
Menzies	Liberals retain	35.97	+5.75
Scullin	Labor retains	64.63	+5.91
Wills	Labor retains	70.56	+2.98
Northern Territory (Boundaries of September 2008)			
Lingiari	Labor retains	51.07	+2.66

Note: (Most LOTEs in Lingiari are Aboriginal languages)

Source: Australian Electoral Commission (September 2013).

However, nothing lasts forever. At each election those voting are not identical with those who voted last time, nor are the electoral boundaries unchanged. Much prediction, based on uniform national swings, ignores this. Moreover, with a system of transferred preferences (as in Australia) opinion polling can be misleading. Post-election analysis after this election admitted that predictions of a Labor 'wipeout' were wrong, especially the myth of the collapsing Labor heartland of western Sydney. Labor certainly lost and richly deserved to do so (Patrick 2013). But its reliance on the ethnic minorities remained, consistent with the situation in other stable democratic systems. While the Labor primary vote was unsustainably low, Australian elections are won on seats held, not on simple majorities. Of 17 seats lost by Labor only three had large ethnic minorities (Banks, Barton and Reid).

Migration

Immigration is often one of the important, but not dominant, election issues. In 2013 refugees occupied a more central place than immigration numbers or sources. Migration had risen to record levels, without prompting the reaction that Australia was 'full up' as in the past. Labor and the unions were concerned with the numbers being brought into Australia on 457 temporary employment visas. While these were important for the expanding mining operations, many were for less obvious needs such as catering and hospitality. The Liberals responded to employer needs by shifting the intake once more towards skills and employment and away from family reunion and especially refugees and asylum seekers under the UN Convention. The Coalition slogan of 'stop the boats', and its labelling of non-visa arrivals by sea as 'illegal', was thought to be a major issue in the western Sydney suburbs where there was a mix of Australian born and recent arrivals and a strong concentration of Muslims in Blaxland, Parramatta and Watson. There was no comparable situation in Melbourne or anywhere else.

Journalists, broadcasters, party officials, candidates and pollsters had all convinced themselves that there was an explosive situation in western Sydney which would be seriously damaging to Labor. What this overlooked was that the large 'ethnic' electorate might not share the same concerns as the English-speaking majorities and that Labor-held seats often had a very strong residue of habitual Labor voters which would be hard to overturn. The prediction of a Labor 'wipeout' held for Banks, Barton and Reid, but not for another 10 strongholds in Sydney's west, and not for any comparable seats in Melbourne. Swings there certainly were, but 'wipeouts' did not materialise. Given the state of academic research on voting behaviour, there is still very little evidence of the response of immigrants to immigration issues. There might well be a sense that the Liberals are less sympathetic to migrants than the ALP. But the Liberals ran more 'ethnic' candidates and Labor refugee policy had moved very close to the Liberals under Rudd and Gillard.

The 'migrant vote'

Australian national elections are based on compulsory voting with universal suffrage for all citizens in equalised single member electorates for the lower house, in which control of a government majority resides. As more than one-quarter of Australians were born outside the country, this should give considerable power to a 'migrant vote'. However, there is a considerable gap between the proportion of immigrants and the proportion of elected representatives (Jupp 2004). When compared with other English-speaking democracies, such as the UK, US, Canada or New Zealand, the representation of ethnic minorities in Australia is still marginal, especially at the national lower house level. Moreover, frequently quoted figures exaggerate the strength of 'ethnics' by including all migrants. Of these, over 1.5 million are English speakers from the UK, New Zealand and other similar societies, who are not usually regarded as 'ethnics', especially by themselves. A recent increase in temporary 457 visas, student, working holiday and refugee bridging visas (all without voting rights) tends to distort the 'ethnic' composition of electorates. One useful statistic is available in census data for those 'speaking a language other than English (LOTE) at home', which includes second and subsequent generations who are citizens by birth.

Table 2: Major language groups in 'ethnic electorates' of Sydney and Melbourne[1]

Sydney (Boundaries of 22/12/2009)	
Banks	Chinese 30,118; Arabic 8,127; Greek 7,294
Barton	Greek 16,424; Chinese 14,848; Arabic 11,205; Indian Languages 6,756; Macedonian 5,513
Bennelong	Chinese 26,741; Korean 6,803
Blaxland	Arabic 36,697; Chinese 12,709; Vietnamese 17,059
Chifley	Indian Languages 14,153; Tagalog 9,041; Arabic 6,498
Fowler	Vietnamese 29,846; Chinese 13,460; Arabic 9,936; Khmer 5,775; Serbian 4,963

---

1   Notes to Table 2: Chinese is divided in the census between Mandarin (mainly from China and Taiwan), and Cantonese (mainly from Southeast Asia, Hong Kong and the long resident Chinese Australians). Indian languages normally include Hindi, Bengali, Punjabi, Urdu. Tagalog includes Filipino. Only languages totalling more than 5,000 speakers are included. NB: these figures are of inhabitants, including children over the age of five, and not of voters. 'Ethnic electorates' are defined as having more than 25 per cent speaking a language other than English at home. These are not necessarily qualified voters and they are not necessarily of overseas birth or nationality. No official figures are available for citizenship by ethnicity.

Sydney (Boundaries of 22/12/2009)	
Grayndler	Chinese 9,118; Greek 6,375; Italian 5,762
Greenway	Indian Languages 14,362; Vietnamese 5,919
Kingsford Smith	Chinese 13,691; Greek 7,015
McMahon	Arabic 11,646; Assyrian 11,326; Chinese 5,775; Italian 5,120; Vietnamese 8,601
Parramatta	Chinese 20,041; Indian Languages 17,500; Vietnamese 7,714; Arabic 14,111
Reid	Chinese 25,585; Indian Languages 9,572; Korean 8,911; Italian 7,839; Greek 9,864
Watson	Arabic 30,768; Chinese 19,470; Indian Languages 13,907; Vietnamese 6,120
Werriwa	Indian Languages 12,608; Arabic 9,526
Melbourne (Boundaries of 24/12/2010)	
Batman	Italian 11,361; Greek 10 126; Chinese 6445; Indian Languages 5095
Bruce:	Chinese 13,733; Vietnamese 7,886; Indian Languages 6,489; Greek 6,037; Turkish 5,025
Calwell	Turkish 13,681; Arabic 13,023; Assyrian 7,320; Italian 6,505
Chisholm	Chinese 23,554; Greek 6,668
Gellibrand	Vietnamese 9,992; Chinese 6,608
Gorton	Vietnamese 17,049; Tagalog 6,312; Indian Languages 7,361; Chinese 7,123; Macedonian 6,455; Greek 5,725; Maltese 5,511; Italian 5,069
Holt	Chinese 5,051; Sinhalese 5,039
Hotham	Greek 9,857; Chinese 9,468; Vietnamese 6,872; Indian Languages 5,211
Isaacs	Vietnamese 6,041; Chinese 5,346
Lalor	Indian Languages 9,786; Chinese 5,678
Maribyrnong	Vietnamese 12,067; Italian 9,283; Chinese 4,591
Melbourne	Chinese 17,858; Vietnamese 5,438
Menzies	Chinese 16,963; Greek 7,940; Italian 5,886
Scullin	Italian 9,623; Macedonian 9,043; Greek 6,905; Arabic 6,611
Wills	Italian 14,292; Arabic 8,420; Greek 8,050; Indian Languages 6,387

Source: Parliament of Australia Research Paper: *Electoral division rankings: 2006 census (2009 electoral boundaries)*. Figures based on Australian Bureau of Statistics, *2011 Census Quick Stats* and still liable to revision.

This official statistic is elsewhere as defining 'ethnic electorates' when it exceeds 25 per cent of the population. Electorates meeting that criterion are confined to Sydney and Melbourne and numbered 29 (19.3 per cent) in 2013, although there are slightly smaller pockets in Adelaide, Brisbane and Perth. The census of 2011 showed a total of 23 per cent of the population using a language other than English at home, with over 25 per cent for Victoria and New South Wales. These figures have been reorganised into electoral boundaries for the 2013 election by the Parliamentary Library in *Research Paper no. 18, 2009–10*. There is also a wealth of census data arranged for electorates by the Australian Bureau of Statistics and voting by polling stations by the Australian Electoral Commission. While this information is of world standard and very useful to journalists and parties, it is not used by academics as much as it should be. There are no useful official figures for citizens by ethnicity, only by birthplace and religion.

Election results since the readoption of mass immigration in the 1950s show clearly that no effective parties have formed around an ethnic or religious base and related issues, with the exception of the Democratic Labor Party (DLP), which was predominantly Catholic in membership and support. Parties other than the two major contestants—the Australian Labor Party (ALP) and the Liberal Party—have had very limited electoral support for a century. In recent years the One Nation party of Pauline Hanson was strongly but briefly supported in Queensland. All lesser parties reached a vote ceiling of less than 20 per cent and then declined into oblivion. The entirely new Palmer United Party achieved over 600,000 votes (5.53 per cent) at its first outing, which nobody had predicted except Clive Palmer himself. Among the plethora of minor candidates in 2013 only one represented ethnic or religious minorities (Aborigines rather than immigrants).

The strongest minority party, the Greens, are well represented in upper houses elected by proportional representation, but also have a national ceiling of less than 15 per cent. In 2010 and 2013 they held the seat of Melbourne, where 29.2 per cent of the population spoke a language other than English at home. This seat has a very high number of university graduates and a young and transient population. It would be dubious to assume that the Melbourne Greens relied heavily on immigrant voters, although they had a strong following in Richmond and Flemington, parts of which are less gentrified than Fitzroy or Carlton and have substantial ethnic minority populations. The Greens also recorded good returns in those parts of Batman and Wills close to the Melbourne border and long occupied by Italian and Greek settlers. Despite their strong stand on asylum seekers, the Greens usually do no better among immigrant communities than elsewhere.

There is no lasting and consolidated constituency which has produced rivals to the two main parties, either on an ethnic, national or state basis. The prospect for any party based primarily on immigrants is bleak. None have ever succeeded since Federation. The DLP recruited considerable support for a while from refugees from communism who arrived in Australia between 1947 and 1953. The majority of these were Catholics and they were mainly in Victoria. These Eastern Europeans are now an ageing constituency. The ethnic composition of the Green vote is quite unknown, as nobody seems to have asked. Ethnic representation rests with the ALP and the Liberals. Most analysis suggests that Labor has won 'ethnic votes' in working class seats in Sydney and Melbourne, but with Anglo-Australian candidates. Several British migrants have been elected, especially in South and Western Australia, and included the Prime Minister Julia Gillard from 2010 to 2013. Until 2013 the Liberals held very few seats with large immigrant concentrations, but were starting to nominate more migrant and 'ethnic' candidates than Labor in winnable seats. This was already apparent in the 2010 general election (Jupp 2012). Aboriginal voters are concentrated north of the Tropic of Capricorn. Their voters tend towards Labor in remote areas served by mobile polling booths, especially in the Northern Territory seat of Lingiari, which remained with Labor. Aboriginal prominent members have often been politically volatile. There had been a big swing to the Country Liberal Party (CLP) among Aboriginal voters in the 2012 Northern Territory election.

The 'ethnic vote', then, appears to be limited to the major cities in its impact, but favourable to the ALP where concentrated. This judgment must rest on election results, rather than opinion polling, although some surveys support it. There are many complexities in measuring the 'ethnic' vote. These include varying levels of naturalisation, which are highest among former refugees; shifting movements from the inner to the outer suburbs; very many distinct ethnicities and religions even from single birthplaces; the maintenance of cultural differences among Australian-born descendants; differing levels of assimilation and language loss; and political rivalries based on overseas traditions. Creating a viable sample at a reasonable cost has evaded pollsters (McAllister 2011). Attempts have been made in recent Australian Election Study polls to create enhanced samples which reach minorities. The same technique has been used by Andrew Markus in his *Mapping Social Cohesion* reports (Markus 2013). There are a growing number of young immigrants residing here on student or 457 visas who have not yet become citizens, although they are counted in the census. This is particularly relevant to Indian and Chinese residents, who are now more numerous than Europeans in some metropolitan districts.

The basic problems in measuring the 'ethnic' constituency are that it is internally very varied and may behave differently from state to state. It has also been changing its character over the past 20 years, due to changes in the selection criteria for immigrants. These have shifted the emphasis from European manual workers to Asian skilled workers. Naturalisation levels are very high, but a minimum of four years in Australia is required for citizenship. While the degree of allegiance of southern Europeans (Greek, Italian, Maltese, Orthodox Slavs) to Labor is reasonably well established, the same cannot be said for Chinese, Indians, Singaporeans, Koreans, Indochinese or Sri Lankans. The assumption that Muslims gravitate towards Labor has scarcely been tested and covers a wide variety of different nationalities. Blaxland, with a Muslim population of 22.7 per cent, recorded an almost negligible swing to the Liberals in 2013, remaining safe for the ALP despite some pre-election predictions of a possible Labor loss. Calwell in Melbourne (15.9 per cent Muslim) also remained safe. Recently the Lebanese Muslim Association of Sydney has shifted its support towards the Liberals (Jakubowicz 2013).

'Ethnicity' is not confined to the immigrant generation. The children of immigrants do not necessarily remain in the places of first immigrant settlement, nor do they self-evidently vote the same way as their parents or grandparents. English-speaking immigrants do not only come from Britain and New Zealand, even if these constitute one-quarter of the 'overseas born'. 'Ethnic communities' are cut by religious divisions, notably amongst the Arabs, the South Slavs, the Vietnamese, the Koreans, the Indians and the Chinese. Sampling such a varied population may be less informative than 'street wise' local knowledge, which depends on effective local party and ethnic organisations. One must, therefore, assume that local knowledge and unpublished party research was leaking to the media with tales of a Labor wipeout in previously safe electorates. This was reinforced by previous election defeats in New South Wales and the Northern Territory. It created the myth of the dying Labor heartland. This was still puzzling commentators on the ABC election night program and being repeated in the Murdoch press, even after the polls closed (Cater 2013). Of those here defined as 'ethnic electorates', Labor lost three in Sydney (Barton, Reid and Banks) and none at all in Melbourne (see Table 1 above). Labor total losses were 17 electorates, most with small immigrant populations except for Hindmarsh. Half of these were in New South Wales, for understandable reasons (Patrick 2013).

Asylum seekers as a major issue

'Ethnic electorates' are confined to Sydney and Melbourne and the electoral struggle over immigrant and 'ethnic' issues also takes place largely in Sydney and Melbourne. It was muted during this campaign by the high degree of agreement between the two major parties and their common obsession with asylum seekers.[2] In the recent past, One Nation could mobilise considerable support, ably assisted by the tabloid press and talkback radio. But much of that ground had been occupied by the Liberals under John Howard and, increasingly on refugee issues, by Labor under Julia Gillard. The ultimate desertion of the UN Convention on Refugees was sealed in May, with Labor hastily legislating to remove mainland Australia from the 'migration zone'. This followed on from its extension of the 'no advantage principle', which punished asylum seekers arriving by boat with the same delays in processing and detention they would

---

2   For the Coalition's policy, see Liberal Party of Australia/National Party of Australia (2013); Labor's media releases and transcripts on asylum seekers are collected together under the broader topic of immigration at: <pandora.nla.gov.au/pan/22093/20130906-0237/www.alp.org.au/campaign_media_immigration.html>.

have suffered if they had utilised legal channels to obtain a refugee visa. These delays can run into years. By removing the whole of Australia from the 'migration zone' those arriving by boat were further penalised by being denied processing and legal appeals on the mainland. They were to be sent directly to Manus Island (Papua New Guinea) and Nauru. The Liberals endorsed these changes with glee. They had failed to get similar provisions through parliament because of previous Labor and Green opposition. Only the Greens stood firm. Labor voters 'landed on both sides of the debate' with Coalition voters 'comfortably aligned with party policy' (ABC 2013). Australia became the only signatory to the Convention to remove the whole of its territory from the processing system. This avoided the ultimate solution of leaving the Convention altogether, which required a waiting period of a year and would have been embarrassing to Australia as a newly elected chair of the UN Security Council.

While much heat has been generated around the asylum seeker issue, immigration does not normally figure as a dominant issue in national or state opinion polling (McAllister 2003). Thus there are few reliable ways of knowing how 'ethnic' voters feel and behave, except through journalistic impressions or focus groups. These were claiming that asylum seekers were a hot issue in the 'western suburbs' of Sydney, which are among the most 'ethnic' seats in Australia. But their definition of 'western suburbs' often included areas like Penrith (Lindsay) and Campbelltown (Macarthur), which do not have large immigrant populations, and Greenway and Bennelong, which are basically middle class. Nor was there enough difference between the two major parties for a clear-cut choice. The major influences in this region are said to be the (Murdoch) *Daily Telegraph*, Alan Jones and Ray Hadley (both of radio 2GB), all of them fanatically anti-Labor and hostile to asylum seekers. None of these have established much of a following in Melbourne. After the election Bob Carr added his voice to the view that the asylum seeker issue was vital in Labor's 'collapse', without giving any supporting evidence.

Party policies towards asylum seekers had hardened since 1991 with the introduction by ALP minister Gerry Hand of mandatory and irrevocable detention. This was in reaction to a sudden surge in asylum seekers from Cambodia fleeing the terror campaigns of the Khmer Rouge. The genocidal nature of this regime was not fully revealed at the time. While this new policy might have been planned as temporary it has remained in force ever since, with increasing severity (Simms and Wanna 2012: 268–9). Numbers rose as severe crises struck Afghanistan, Iraq and Sri Lanka. The focal point for landings and detention became Christmas Island, which was relatively easy to reach from Indonesia and Sri Lanka. Indonesia's liberal policy towards Muslim immigrants made it the main point of departure. With increasing controversy about the viability and expense of detention centres on the Australian mainland, Australia sought to arrange for several client states to house asylum seekers on their territories with Australian financial and organisational support. East Timor refused to do so, on the reasonable grounds that it was very poor and had many of its own refugees arising from its separation from Indonesia. The Gillard Government developed a plan with Malaysia that would have allowed qualified refugees to be transferred from Malaysia to Australia in exchange for a smaller number who had arrived by boat and would be sent to Malaysia. But the only agreements that came to fruition were for the use of Nauru and Manus Island. Indonesia remained opposed to similar schemes, but gave some undertakings to discourage departures towards Australia.

All these schemes were arguably in breach of the UN Convention on Refugees, of which Australia and New Zealand were the sole signatories in the South Pacific region. Nauru, which is completely dependent on Australia financially, was persuaded to adhere, but Indonesia and Malaysia were not. As one of the smallest and most isolated sovereign states in the world, Nauru seemed an ideal place to remove asylum seekers to. But the logistics of sending refugees, guards, settlement and medical personnel thousands of miles across the ocean proved very expensive and the unhappiness of those dispatched proved very disturbing to the peace of the tiny island. The broad agreement between the main parties that the boats should be stopped and the passengers removed from Australia did not prevent the Greens and many NGOs, academics and lawyers from regular denunciation of bipartisan policies. The main thrust of the Liberal accusation was that the Rudd Government had encouraged the boats by liberalising some of the provisions made by its Coalition predecessor. This may well have been true, but ignored the fact that these changes were more in keeping with the aims of the UN Convention than the alternatives formerly and subsequently implemented. As the election drew nearer both parties escalated their approach. Kevin Rudd claimed that nobody arriving by boat would ever be allowed to secure permanent residence in Australia, which was absurd. Tony Abbott concentrated on the use of Nauru, which was already straining at the seams. However, unlike John Howard, Abbott was not hostile to multiculturalism.

In contrast to Britain and most of Europe there are no Australian parties with electoral support campaigning specifically against immigration, asylum and Muslims. With the passing of One Nation, there was only Pauline Hanson continuing her lonely battle to acquire public funds by contesting elections. The main difference between the major contestants was their competition over who had done better in 'stopping the boats'. On that basis the Liberals were always well ahead, although Kevin Rudd's 'PNG solution' seems to have started working to a limited extent during its short life. This would have settled 'genuine' asylum seekers on Manus Island or elsewhere in Papua New Guinea at Australian expense, but with no right to resettle in Australia. In the rarely used argument about who had upheld the UN Convention, only the Greens had much to claim, especially after the total excision of Australia from the 'migration zone'. Labor simply moved from the liberal approach of Senator Chris Evans in 2010 to the hard-nosed approach of Chris Bowen in the final months of the campaign.

There were, however, a number of organisations criticising Islam, opposing further immigration and calling for the end of multiculturalism. These included the Q Society of Australia, the Salt Shakers, Rise Up Australia and the Stable Population Party. Registered parties specifically opposing Islam, current immigration levels or multiculturalism scored very marginal Representative votes nationwide: One Nation (20,621), Rise Up Australia (44,845), Australia First (6,550), and Stable Population (3,582). Other parties broadly on the right attracted almost one million votes, the largest number being for the Palmer United Party and Katter's Australia Party. Both of these won a lower house seat each in Queensland with very little defined policy. The PUP also won places in the Senate, promising to make things difficult for the government of the day. Neither Palmer nor Katter had detailed policies on immigration or refugees. Palmer suggested flying asylum seekers to Australia for clearance, ending the offshore detention policy endorsed by the Coalition and Labor. This would certainly be cheaper than current policies backed by government and opposition.

The myth of the 'failing' Sydney heartland

The electoral picture in 2010 had been comparatively simple: concentrations of 'ethnic' Australians, including Muslims, Catholics, Asians or Europeans, were to be found predominantly in Labor-represented electorates; British origin majority Australians were to be found most strongly represented in rural, provincial and upper suburban Liberal electorates (Jupp 2012). This basic division was sustained to a significant extent by social, class and occupational factors. The pattern was also clear in the Victorian state elections of 2010. Of 37 seats with more than 25 per cent speaking a language other than English at home, 28 were held by Labor and nine by the Liberals. Of these, four were gains from the ALP. This meant that two-thirds of all Victorian Labor seats were from 'ethnic' electorates, compared with only one-fifth of the Liberals. The same happened nationally in 2013, after the most turbulent period in recent Australian politics and an often divisive and embittered national quarrel about immigration and population. There was much publicised panic about Labor losing Sydney's western suburbs, but little concern about comparable threats in Melbourne, where no comparable seats were lost. This panic proved exaggerated, as only Barton, Reid and Banks were lost in 'ethnic' Sydney, together with marginal

Lindsay, which does not have a high immigrant population. However, it is possible that 'ethnic voters' in Sydney were more dissatisfied than in Melbourne. In particular, the large Chinese communities seemed disaffected, failing even to elect the distinguished Chinese Labor candidate in Bennelong, Jason Yat-Sen Li. Barton, Reid and Banks all had particularly large Chinese-speaking populations. Each also had water frontages with new middle class housing projects. Tony Abbott's early boast that he would have 'several' Nguyens in his parliamentary party was not sustained. None of the three Vietnamese Liberals with that name were elected, even in Fowler, the most Vietnamese electorate in Australia. One, Andrew Nguyen, complained of being treated as a 'second-class citizen' by Liberal organisers in Fowler (Aston 2013).

The concerted Liberal attempt to promote successful 'ethnic' candidates was generally a failure, except in Barton. With more Greek speakers (16,424) than even the better-known Greek strongholds of Melbourne, this mixed bayside suburb was taken from years of Labor control by a Greek-Australian Liberal, despite more than half the population (51.2 per cent) speaking a language other than English at home. Apart from Fowler, usually the safest Labor seat in the country, the Liberals also failed to capture marginal Greenway with a candidate of Filipino descent, although it was the most marginal Labor seat to be held (Green 2013). Blacktown, in which the electorate of Greenway is located, has the largest Filipino population in Australia. However most do not live in Greenway, where they are heavily outnumbered by Indians. Moreover young Jayme Diaz had already failed in 2010. He was pushed into the seat again by his politically powerful and right-wing father, against the advice of Tony Abbott.

For some months before election day there were inspired articles about Labor losing working class western Sydney or the 'ethnic vote' (concentrated in that region) or even the 'Aboriginal vote', which is only significant in half a dozen northern electorates [Solomon, Lingiari (NT); Kennedy, Leichhardt (Qld); Kalgoorlie (WA); and Parkes (NSW)], with Indigenous populations making up over 10 per cent of the total. Aborigines are only close to an absolute majority in Lingiari, the one seat of these six held by Labor in 2010 and 2013. Inferences were wrongly drawn from New South Wales state elections in the first case and Northern Territory elections in the second.

Changed faces but similar policies towards immigration and asylum

Journalists and activists often exaggerate the excitement and changes of an election campaign. Election 2013 was not as exciting or as different as many had expected during the inordinately long campaign. Opinion polling and canvassing wisdom stressed that voters were interested in economic issues, job security and education, health and welfare. They generally saw the ALP as disunited and unreliable and the Liberals as a bit dubious. There was an unusual plethora of disaffected minor parties, most veering towards the right. The left was almost invisible, with the Socialist Alliance recording a minuscule national vote of 4,689. Nobody else could reasonably be described as 'left' in the old sense, unless the Murdoch caricature of the Greens is accepted. The Labor 'heartlands' of Sydney and Melbourne lost a few usually marginal suburban seats for Labor, but not very many. Eight losses were in New South Wales, half of them outside Sydney. Among them were the outer suburbs and retirement centres between Sydney and Newcastle affected by scandals surrounding Labor politicians. Many outer suburbs were also 'ethnic', especially in growing Melbourne. Queensland and Western Australia remained stolidly conservative, except for the intrusions of Bob Katter and Clive Palmer. Little changed in South Australia, with Labor losing only Hindmarsh, with a significant, but not dominant, population of 18.8 per cent speaking a language other than English at home. While there were substantial swings against Labor in many Melbourne electorates, their previous majorities were too large for them to be endangered and Green preferences often saved them.

The elephant in the room was temporarily asleep. Abbott had said 'stop the boats' often enough to get the message over. But his specific policies were provisional and unlikely to appeal to the Indonesian Government. Without negotiation they could not work. Labor politicians from the Sydney heartland were almost panic-stricken. But their fears that asylum seekers were so unpopular that Labor would be slaughtered were not generally justified. Perhaps they spoke only to fellow ALP members. There was essentially no difference on asylum seekers between the parties, except that Labor wanted to lock people up on Manus Island while the Liberals favoured Nauru. Each party claimed to have done a better job in discouraging asylum seekers. Kevin Rudd went further by stating that nobody who came by boat would 'ever' be allowed into Australia. The Liberals did not go as far, knowing that 'never' is a long time in politics. Government money was lavishly spent on full-page horror advertising in the ethnic press (as well as the mainstream publications), which was otherwise less widely used than in the past, except by the Electoral Commission. Seven languages (Tamil, Sinhala, Vietnamese, Arabic, Urdu, Persian and Pushto) were used to explain in very small type that nobody who sought refuge by boat could get Australian permanent residence. What impact this might have on the target groups is not clear. Both major parties fully agreed with the message. Its main impact was likely to be on the majority population. This was no doubt intended, but could not really influence voters when the two main parties were so close. Similar posters in Sinhala and Tamil were displayed in Colombo (Sri Lanka), where their purpose was more obvious. A pictorial booklet aimed at Afghans appeared after the election.

Some of the speculation about immigrant sympathy with bipartisan policy was based on moving successful asylum seekers into the already small humanitarian program. This was seen by some as unfair to those waiting for their families to arrive by official channels and consequently deprived of their places in the never ending 'queue'. Another reaction may have come from Middle Eastern Christians (Maronites, Copts, Assyrians, Chaldeans) who did not welcome Arabic Muslim arrivals. But the consensus between the major parties and the complexity of affected ethnic and religious communities was such that reliable judgment of ethnic reactions proved impossible. It seems likely that differences within specific communities were more important than between communities. The divisions within the large and growing Chinese population were certainly important in Sydney, but much less so in Melbourne. There are very prosperous populations from Hong Kong, Malaysia, Singapore, Taiwan and even China itself, in electorates such as Bennelong, Menzies, Banks, Parramatta and Chisholm, all home to more than 20,000 Chinese speakers each (see Table 2). Chinese interest in the new Significant Investor visa could bring in influential and wealthy potential community leaders. If the Liberals can persuade them to see themselves as prosperous and accepted members of the middle classes, Labor could be in serious trouble in 2016. In 2013, 42 per cent of Labor lower house seats were from the two 'ethnic heartlands', most with large Chinese communities.

Immediate consequences of the election

The immediate consequences of the Liberal/National victory were a restructuring of Commonwealth departments and agencies concerned with immigrants and refugees (Refugee Council of Australia 2013); a strengthening of Operation Sovereign Borders by the creation of a military responsibility for turning back boats when safe and outside Indonesian waters; the transfer of settlement and multicultural affairs from Immigration to Social Services; the absorption of AusAID into the Department of Foreign Affairs and Trade; the movement of Customs and border control, from Attorney General's to Immigration; the transfer of the Adult Migrant English Program to the Department of Industry's vocational training; and the abolition of the small Social Inclusion Board. Of these, the implementation of Operation Sovereign Borders has caused the greatest controversy internationally. In the first week it was already being used to suppress information about boat arrivals and losses at sea, much to the indignation of journalists. The transfer of welfare services and funded organisations to Social

Services might cause the greatest opposition from the normally quiescent service providers, withdrawn from the ambit of the Department of Immigration. Their new minister would initially be the previously controversial Kevin Andrews, supported by the equally controversial Senator Concetta Fierravanti-Wells. There is likely to be less emphasis on multiculturalism and more on national security and integration. Presumably the growth of temporary labour migration will continue, despite trade union complaints. It is not clear that the humanitarian program will be cut back to earlier levels, as threatened by Abbott. Asylum seekers will get only temporary protection visas with no right to permanence or family reunion. Large temporary populations will remain a disfranchised sector of the population. Within a month 25,000 were still in detention awaiting processing.

Within party politics a major impact of Labor's electoral defeat was to get acceptance of Rudd's system for election of the ALP party leader by party branch members and federal caucus. Increased enrolment of party members may improve ethnic candidate selection to a more representative level. But there is likely to be strong opposition to this from interested candidates. Labor has used ethnic branches for the promotion of 'mainstream' hopefuls with influence in the factions, unions and state party offices. A policy innovation, on which partisans from the major parties might well agree, is to reduce the opportunity of minor organisations to benefit from the preferential systems, especially for the Senate. There were far too many minor candidates for a stable system. None were specifically 'ethnic', despite some threats to found a Muslim party and the tiny vote for the Aboriginal First Nation Political Party (AFNPP, 1,783 votes).

In the resulting ministry of Tony Abbott, almost half the members were of Catholic religion. This was a major change from the Liberal ministers of past years, who were predominantly Protestants of English or Scottish origin. Aside from Abbott's birth in London to visiting parents, ministers and parliamentary secretaries of European origin included Eric Abetz (German-born), Mathias Cormann (Belgian-born), Arthur Sinodinos (of Greek origin) and Joe Hockey (of Armenian origin). This too marked a shift in origins from the past, although the dominance of private school and university backgrounds continued. In other parties, Ed Husic (ALP) retained Chifley (5.3 per cent Muslim population) as the national parliament's only Muslim. Zhenya Wang (Palmer United Party) became only the second China-born Senator, after the April 2014 re-election in Western Australia.

This inordinately long and tedious campaign did nothing to resolve the problem of accepting asylum seekers within the terms of the UN Convention. Indeed it returned a government that wanted an even more rigorous approach and began to implement this even before the counting was over, donating two naval vessels to Sri Lanka in November. Labor continued to depend on 'ethnic' metropolitan electorates but this did not produce much overt sympathy for asylum seekers. Both parties had foolishly promised that non-visa arrivals by boat would 'never' be allowed to settle in Australia, which was contrary to the ancient principle that governments cannot determine the policy of their successors. Following the Coalition's first budget, its approval began to sink in opinion polls for Commonwealth and state governments. The issues assuming prominence were jobs and welfare services rather than asylum.

References

Aston, Heath. 2013. 'Liberal candidate Andrew Nguyen says party treated ethnic candidates like "second-class citizens"'. *Canberra Times*, 11 September.

Cater, Nick. 2013. 'How the west was won'. *Weekend Australian*, 17 September.

Green, Antony. 2013. '2013 Federal Election Pendulum'. Australian Broadcasting Corporation, 30 January, viewed 19 December 2013: <blogs.abc.net.au/antonygreen/2013/01/2013-federal-election-pendulum.html>.

Jakubowicz, Andrew. 2013. 'How Labor won the "ethnic vote" in Western Sydney'. *The Drum,* 18 September, viewed 16 January 2014: < www.abc.net.au/news/2013-09-13/jakubowicz-politics-of-ethnicity/4954660>.

Jupp, James. 1981. 'The Ethnic Vote: Does it exist? A Case Study of Melbourne'. *Journal of Intercultural Studies* 2(3): 5–23.

Jupp, James. 1984. 'The politics of "ethnic" areas of Melbourne, Sydney and Adelaide'. In John Halligan and Chris Paris (eds), *Australian Urban Politics*, Melbourne: Longman Cheshire.

Jupp, James. 2004. *How Well Does Australian Democracy Serve Immigrant Australians?* Canberra: Democratic Audit of Australia.

Jupp, James. 2012. 'Immigration Issues in the 2010 Federal Election'. In Marian Simms and John Wanna (eds), *Julia 2010*: *The caretaker election*. Canberra: ANU E-Press.

Liberal Party of Australia/National Party of Australia. 2013. *The Coalition's Sovereign Borders Policy,* viewed 15 December 2013: <pandora.nla.gov.au/pan/22107/20130906-0245/lpaweb-static.s3.amazonaws.com/Policies/OperationSovereignBorders_Policy.pdf>.

Markus, Andrew 2013. *Mapping Social Cohesion National Report*. Melbourne: Monash University.

McAllister, Ian. 1991. 'The Formation and Development of Party Loyalties: Patterns among Australian Immigrants'. *ANZ Journal of Sociology* 27: 195–217.

McAllister, Ian. 2003. 'Border Protection, the 2001 Australian Election and the Coalition Victory'. *Australian Journal of Politics and History* 38(3): 445–63.

McAllister, Ian. 2011. *The Australian Voter*. Sydney: UNSW Press.

Nethery, Amy, Rafferty-Brown, Brynna and Taylor, Savitri. 2013. 'Exporting Detention: Australian-funded Detention in Indonesia'. *Journal of Refugee Studies* 26(1) March.

Parliamentary Library. 2010. *Electoral division rankings: 2006 Census (2009 electoral boundaries)*. Research Paper no. 18, 28 May.

Patrick, Aaron. 2013. *Downfall: How the Labor Party ripped itself apart*. Sydney: Harper Collins/ABC Books.

Refugee Council of Australia. 2013. *Changes to Immigration Portfolio: Update*. Sydney: RCA, 11 October.

Simms, Marian and Wanna, John (eds). 2012. *Julia 2010: The caretaker election*. Canberra: ANU E-Press.

Vote Compass. 2013. 'Kevin Rudd's Asylum Seeker Policy Divides the Labor Faithful'. *ABC News*, 21 August, viewed 15 January 2014: <www.abc.net.au/news/2013-08-21/asylseekers-vote-compass-boats-immigration/4899914>.

20. The Environment in the 2013 Election: Controversies over climate change, the carbon tax and conservation

Nick Economou

The environment has been a major part of the national political debate in Australia since the Franklin Dam dispute in Tasmania became an issue in the 1983 federal election. Labor won that election and subsequently sought to legislate to make good on its campaign promise to stop the Franklin Dam project from proceeding. This decision became the first of a series of conservation-oriented interventions that helped construct the notion that the Australian Labor Party—the party traditionally of blue-collar workers and their trade unions—was also the party most willing to respond to the environmental agenda (Papadakis 1993; Economou 2000). For all the ecological rhetoric employed by both government and environmentalists to rationalise the decision, the real reason for Labor's interest in conservation was electoral. Senior strategists within the Labor secretariat and the caucus were convinced that conservation outcomes could influence the voting choices of electors in marginal seats, especially in the suburbs of Melbourne and Sydney, and that gains in these areas would offset adverse reactions to such decisions amongst the party's traditional blue-collar constituency—after all, Labor failed to win any lower house seats in Tasmania in the 1983 federal election (Warhurst 1983). This electoral outlook drove national Labor environmental policy most of the time during the Hawke Government years.

In the 2013 federal election, Labor was again the party of national government and the environment was again at the forefront of the election campaign, albeit in a form somewhat different from the conservation issues that were around during the Hawke years. This time the matter of climate change was at the fore—an issue that had been dogging the national political debate since the onset of a major national drought, the latter stages of which coincided with the 2007 federal election. In that election the long serving Liberal–National Coalition Government under the prime ministership of John Howard was defeated by the Labor Party and its relatively new leader, Kevin Rudd, who promised to immediately sign Australia up to international agreements on action over climate change (Johnson 2010: 11; Rootes 2008). As part of his approach Rudd sought to reinforce the importance of climate change to his government's policy agenda by declaring the matter to be one of the 'great moral challenges of our time' (van Onselen 2010)—a rhetorical flourish that would haunt him, his party and his successor as prime minister, Julia Gillard, for years to come.

Kevin Rudd was replaced as Labor leader and prime minister by Julia Gillard (Scott 2010), and the first Gillard Government went to an election in 2010. While a number of matters on the environmental agenda to do with water policy did not change markedly under the new prime ministership, climate change policy was altered quite dramatically (Graetz and Manning 2012: 291–4). As will be argued below, the Gillard Government shifted from Rudd's approach of advocating pricing carbon primarily via a market-based emissions trading scheme (but with a fixed price initial period). The Gillard Government moved to a system based on the government directly putting a price on carbon for an extended period—an approach popularly known as the 'carbon tax'—with the eventual introduction of an emissions trading scheme put off for several years. In so doing, Labor policy makers reasoned that they had instituted a market-based method for incorporating the price of carbon production into the economy in order to make alternative methods of low-emissions energy generation more viable. This had been Labor's intention ever since it had been elected to government at the 2007 election under Kevin Rudd's leadership. In the changed political circumstances in which climate change policy was formulated after the 2010 election, however, environment policy began to figure as a major source of voter disillusion with the Government and its prime minister. The Labor Party's downward slide in the polls began almost as soon as Gillard committed her government to 'putting a price on carbon', yet polling on voter attitudes to issues found a persistent majority of respondents who were concerned about climate change and expected government to do something about it (CSIRO 2011; Pietsch and McAllister 2010).

This may have accounted for the approach of the Coalition in opposition. Leader Tony Abbott had previously been associated with that broad group of doubters about the claims of climate science, known colloquially as 'climate change deniers'. The Liberal approach was to align itself with public opinion displaying concern about climate change, but to come up with an alternative 'direct action' approach based on more practical programs such as re-forestation, carbon sequestration and perhaps specific regulation (Graetz and McAllister 2010: 292). This policy had its critics (see Taylor 2011), but the Opposition's main intention was to capitalise on the decline in popular support for the Government and its so-called 'carbon tax'. Promising to repeal the carbon tax became part of the Opposition's election campaign mantra, and the opinion polls suggested that this message resonated with voters (see Thompson 2011).

There was much more to the national environment debate than climate change, of course, and Prime Minister Gillard sought to cleave the issues by giving climate change its own ministry and its own minister in the form of former ACTU secretary and fellow Socialist Left factional ally Greg Combet (who remained in the portfolio until the return of Kevin Rudd to the prime ministership ahead of the 2013 election, at which point Combet resigned and was replaced by Mark Butler). The environment minister, meanwhile, was Tony Burke, a member of the powerful Centre Unity faction from New South Wales and strong supporter of Gillard in her seemingly endless battle to fend off the leadership aspirations of Rudd. In the re-organisation of administration after the 2010 election, Combet's ministry was called 'Climate Change and Energy Efficiency' and Burke's became 'Sustainability, Environment, Water, Population and Communities', which revealed the extensive array of matters other than climate change that came under the general rubric of 'the environment'. As far as the electorate was concerned, however, the Gillard Government's contribution to environmental politics was primarily about the carbon tax, and, in the aftermath of Labor's substantial defeat and the nature of the result in the Senate, its approach to this aspect of the debate looms large as a major contributor to the outcome.

Labor and the environment debate 2010 to 2013

The climate change debate had been a major part of national politics from 2007. Amidst general approval, one of Rudd's first actions as prime minister was to sign Australia up to the international agreements on reducing greenhouse gas emissions that his predecessor Howard had steadfastly refused to agree to. In domestic policy, the Rudd approach to climate change policy was based on trying to establish an emissions trading scheme. This idea had some support from industry (especially from the financial services sector for whom this scheme would provide work and resources) but was opposed by sections of the environmental movement who argued that such trading schemes would not address the problem of carbon pollution directly. These concerns resonated with the Australian Greens whose support would be required if the Rudd policy was to pass the Senate. Indeed, the Greens refused to support the enabling legislation, thereby presenting Rudd with an opportunity to go to a double dissolution election on the issue.

In the process the then Liberal leader, Malcolm Turnbull, was dumped by his colleagues when he indicated a willingness to have the Liberal Party vote with Labor in the Senate to get the emissions trading scheme past the Greens (Kelly 2010). With the Liberals having replaced Turnbull with hard-line conservative (and not particularly popular) Tony Abbott by the narrowest of margins, the moment for Labor to seek a double dissolution and win an election on the climate change issue presented itself. For whatever reason, Rudd demurred. This proved to be a disaster for him. His failure to act decisively had the effect of rendering his rhetorical flourishes about climate change as hollow and hypocritical and soon Labor began to slide in the opinion polls. This, in turn, contributed to a destabilising campaign going on within some sections of the Labor caucus to remove him as prime minister. When this eventually happened in 2010, his replacement—Julia Gillard—nominated the need to resolve the problems the Government was having with this policy as one of her three key objectives. As the 2010 election campaign began, Labor remained committed to its emissions trading scheme, the Greens advocated putting a price on carbon production, while the Coalition advocated a 'practical climate change' policy.

The 2010 general election was held and resulted in Labor losing its lower house majority. On the crossbenches now sat an odd collection of political players, including Adam Bandt who had won the previously safe Labor seat of Melbourne on behalf of the Greens, Andrew Wilkie, a Tasmanian independent, and two other independents, Rob Oakeshott (Lyne) and Tony Windsor (New England). Both Oakeshott and Windsor had indicated that they supported the idea that the best way to deal with climate change would be to have a market-based mechanism that would factor the cost of pollution directly into the production process and that resources should be made available to allow for investment in alternative forms of energy generation. There was an additional political interest for the rural independents in the alternative energy debate, as installations like wind farms and the economic opportunities associated with them invariably occurred in regional Australia. The Gillard Government would formulate a complex policy response to climate change, but the commentary tended to focus on the idea of putting a price on carbon production and the term 'carbon tax' was used to describe this initiative (Thompson 2011). This was potentially dangerous for the Government, as Gillard had already used the term during the 2010 election campaign when she was videoed in Brisbane declaring that a carbon tax would never be part of any policy panacea for climate change under a government led by her (see LiberalPartyTV 2011).

After the election, where the proponents of a climate change policy that included a direct price on carbon now held the balance of power in both parliamentary chambers, the minority Government altered its policy. As part of a broad suite of programs under the general rubric of seeking to achieve 'sustainability', a carbon 'charge' was to be included as an interim impost to be paid by carbon-producing industrial activity ahead of an emissions trading scheme scheduled for some years hence. (By contrast, Rudd's scheme had only a very brief initial fixed-price period before the market would determine the price of carbon via his cap and trade emissions trading scheme). The policy also included assistance for the development of alternative energy and a commitment to achieve a

5 per cent reduction in emissions. The complexity of the Labor approach failed to prevent significant criticism from a range of sources. Some critics noted that the set carbon price was well above international market prices, and alleged that Australian industry would become internationally uncompetitive as a result. Environmental critics meanwhile argued that the emissions cuts weren't extensive enough, and were very concerned at the compensation payments that the Government intended to make to some industries like the coal-fired electricity sector. This was all in addition to the criticism emanating from those ideologues who were as stridently opposed to the idea that humans created climate change as those who were stridently convinced of humanity's complicity in climate change—which, in turn, led to a public debate of ideologically opposed people yelling abuse at each other (and one of the personal targets of a lot of this abuse was Gillard herself). Meanwhile, the prime minister appeared to have broken an election promise. The Liberal–National opposition was delighted to see the opinion polls indicate a big drop in voter support for Labor and Gillard upon the first declarations that a carbon tax might be coming.

The Gillard Government tried to make a virtue of the difficult political position it found itself in on this matter. This took a number of forms, none of which seemed to succeed in halting the downward trend in the opinion polls. Gillard tried to project the decision to 'price carbon' as a triumph of her negotiating skills and as a positive sign of what a minority government could achieve in terms of policy (*Agreement between the Australian Greens and the Australian Labor Party* 2010). Presumably the televised signing of an agreement of co-operation between Labor and the Greens was supposed to reinforce this notion of a co-operative 'new paradigm'. While Gillard and Combet had initially conceded that this measure was effectively a 'tax' they later backtracked and then assiduously avoided the term 'carbon tax' after public demonstrations labelling Gillard as 'Ju-liar'. Gillard's own rhetoric started to utilise the phrase 'it's the right thing to do' to counter those critics who questioned whether it was politically smart to impose a new tax on a community not favourably disposed to the idea of an increasing tax burden. Just to make sure all the bases were covered, however, the Government also mandated an extensive 'household compensation' package in which welfare payments were to be made to offset the cost to households of the new carbon charge even though the Government was also claiming that the impost would be so minor most people would not notice it (Rawson 2011). The Opposition seized on this as muddle-headed logic and stuck with a simple message that clearly resonated with voters that the charge was a 'big new tax' that, if elected to government, the Liberal and National parties would repeal.

These matters dominated the national debate during the tenure of the Gillard Government and tended to obscure other items on the environmental policy agenda. The matters of climate change and water management were related by virtue of the drought that had given such impetus to the climate change debate. The issues of water conservation became very important across the country, but the region where the Commonwealth sought to reconcile competing demands between producers and conservationists was in the Murray-Darling Basin. At issue was the allocation of irrigation water, with conservationists arguing that more water was required for environmental needs while producers were anxious to retain access to as much water as possible for irrigation purposes. The Commonwealth looked to the Murray-Darling Basin Authority (MDBA) to deal with the ecological and economic issues relating to (over) allocations, with the underlying assumption being that, for the sake of the health of the river system, producers would have to relinquish some of their entitlements in the name of conservation.

This was a long administrative process that produced an interim report and recommendations not long after Gillard's new ministries were in place following the 2010 election. The task of explaining the report fell to the head of the MDBA, Mike Taylor, who undertook a tour of communities in the region. What happened next revealed much about conservation politics in Australia. Taylor was met with open hostility wherever he went in the region, with everyone from local politicians to local farmers declaring that the MDBA (and, by extension, the federal Government) was trying to close down agricultural activity leading to the decimation of basin communities. At consultative 'town hall' meetings, aggrieved farmer activists and their supporters set fire to copies of the MDBA report (*PM* 2011). Conservationists were no less dismayed and quickly criticised the Commonwealth for not allocating more water to conservation flows.

The vehemence of the reaction precipitated major political developments. Environment Minister Burke and the Government seemed to back away from the commitment to addressing ecological needs contained in the MDBA report. Taylor responded to the hostile reception by resigning. The Government foreshadowed a parliamentary inquiry into the methods used by the MDBA to try and attach economic values to environmental inputs. The absurdity of the whole exercise was exacerbated by the weather; in early 2011 the basin received unseasonal rains and state politicians suddenly found themselves dealing not with drought but with floods. By late 2012 a number of dams and catchments in the system were full to overflowing. All this seemed to do was confirm the suspicion of locals that city-based technocrats and scientists did not know what they were talking about.

Burke had two other fights going on at about this time. One was with the newly elected Coalition Government of Victoria which was keen to repay support given to the Nationals campaign in the 2010 state election by allowing the resumption of cattle grazing in the state's alpine national park. The Victorian Government argued that cattle grazing would assist in fire prevention—a claim vehemently disputed by conservation groups and the Victorian National Parks Association which led an appeal to the federal Government to intervene (Karvelas 2011). The federal Government duly declared that it would seek further investigation into the fire prevention claims made by the state Government but, in the interim, would maintain the ban on alpine grazing. As is usually the case in such disputes, proponents of grazing declared their outrage at the insensitivity of Canberra-based bureaucrats to the needs of the small and remote communities out in Victoria's far east.

The other fight that was unfolding involved the Gillard Government's decision to expedite the formation of a major marine national park. As the press reported at the time, the new marine park involved the establishment of significant conservation zones that, amongst other things, excluded commercial and some recreational fishing activity. Minister Burke was anxious to herald this decision as an example of significant achievement on the part of the Government, notwithstanding criticism from environmentalists that the park and fishing exclusion zones were too small. In regional centres—especially in New South Wales, Western Australia and Queensland—however, there was anger at the prospect of commercial and recreational fishers being denied access to fishing grounds. The costs associated with the park were assessed at the regional level to be economic in nature, in that they would threaten the fishing industry which would then undermine local employment (Locke 2012).

Once again there was a very strong regional-versus-metropolitan dynamic at play in the politics of this major piece of conservation policy. In the metropolitan centres there was little interest in this policy or the potential economic consequences of the rather esoteric notion of huge tracts of the seabed being included in a national park. In the regions, however, there was growing anger at the way the Government appeared to be seriously constraining recreational choices for people. From the affected states, organisational activity was discernible as a plethora of political parties with charters declaring support for broader access to national parks, greater opportunities for hunters and fishers, and/or opposition to the carbon tax, were being formed to be registered with the Australian Electoral Commission (AEC). The Gillard Government had made an extensive array of enemies in its management of the environmental debate, and these enemies were clearly of a mind to mobilise against it at the next national election. In this campaign the Senate loomed as a major potential battlefield.

The environment and the 2013 election

While there were many issues at work in the 2013 election campaign, the pricing of carbon was particularly contentious and the Coalition sought to put the matter at the centre of the campaign by declaring that it would contest the election as a plebiscite on the 'carbon tax'. Interestingly, Labor had complicated the situation somewhat with its last-minute leadership change, which saw the return of Kevin Rudd. One of the first things the resurrected leader did was to declare that the carbon tax would be terminated well ahead of schedule and that, if returned to government, he would seek to reinstate his preferred emissions trading scheme a year earlier than the Gillard Government had envisaged (Scarr 2013). The impression that Labor was walking away from the 'carbon tax' was reinforced by the resignations of those ministers in the Labor Government who had been the public face of the policy, including Combet and Gillard. Tony Burke also offered to resign but Rudd refused to accept it, although the former environment minister was to lose that portfolio and become Minister for Immigration instead. Despite continuing to espouse the virtues of 'pricing carbon', the reconstituted Rudd Labor Government appeared to have abandoned its signature policy before a single vote had been cast.

Opinion poll data measuring voting intentions by both primary vote and two-party vote between the 2010 and 2013 elections reveal an overall downward trend that commenced from the moment that Prime Minister Gillard announced her government's intention to institute a carbon price as the centrepiece of its climate change policy. The level of two-party support for the Labor Government measured by Newspoll (see Figure 1) shows the extent to which support for Labor fell over the period. However, it is also the case that the same poll found rising levels of support at various points in the timeline in which the Government expedited the carbon tax, and in the period after the carbon tax was actually applied. On the other hand, it is also the case that, while Labor was able to establish a two-party-preferred lead over the Coalition in the short period immediately after Gillard's declared shift in policy, the passage of the Clean Energy Bill in mid-2011 (in the immediate aftermath of the Greens becoming the holders of the balance of power in the upper house) saw support for Labor fall to its lowest point and thereafter it failed to overtake the Coalition.

The Coalition swept to power with a 30-seat majority in the House of Representatives, having secured 17 formerly Labor seats and regaining the two regional seats formerly held by Oakeshott and Windsor. Labor's national two-party vote at the election was 46.5 per cent—a particularly weak performance and commensurate with the trends being monitored by the national opinion polls. Of the 17 Labor seats won by the Coalition, 10 were regional or non-metropolitan districts, suggesting that the metropolitan-versus-regional dynamic at work in the national environmental debate may have been replicated in the transfer of seats. However, it was equally the case that all of these seats bar one (the Tasmanian seat of Lyons) were marginal anyway and had a long history of swinging from one major party to the other in elections producing a change of government (AEC 2013a).

20. The Environment in the 2013 Election

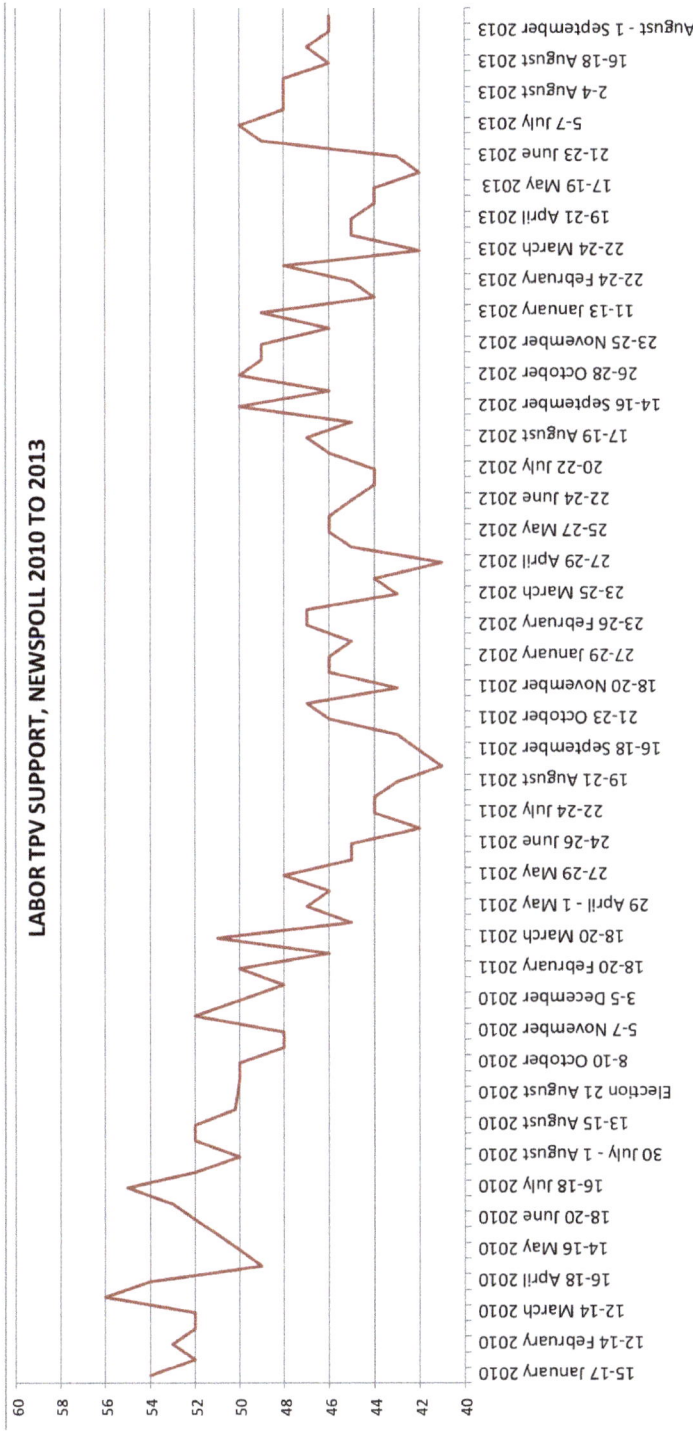

Figure 1: Total primary vote for the ALP, 2010 to 2013

Source: Newspoll.

The result of the half-Senate election, however, was much more complex and provided a little more insight into the strong reaction of the electorate to the nature of the political debate of the previous three years. In the lower house contest, the electoral system allowed the anti-Labor swing to be channelled to the Coalition in most cases (but not all, as the defeat of sitting Liberal Sophie Mirabella in the rural Victorian division of Indi indicated). The Senate contest, with its transferable vote-based proportional system, provided non-major parties with more of an opportunity to make an impact on representational outcomes. This clearly had occurred to a number of political actors who saw the Senate election as an opportunity to exert leverage on the political debate, presumably in opposition to the Labor-Green-Oakeshott-Windsor approach to such contentious policies as climate change (although interestingly Andrew Wilkie survived in the House of Representatives seat of Denison). By the time the deadline for registering parties for the 2013 election had passed, the AEC reported that a record number of parties would be contesting the half-Senate election. In 2010, the total number of registered parties, excluding the various forms of Liberal, National and Labor parties, was 26. In 2013, this number had increased to 50 (AEC 2013b).

Table 1: Anti-Labor/Green minor parties, 2013 half-Senate election

Right-populist, social conservativeImplicit anti-environmental	Explicitly anti-environmental	Others, GTV preferences directed away from Labor-Greens
Democratic Labor Party (DLP) Family First (FF) Country Alliance (CA) Katter Australia Party (KAP) Palmer United Party (PUP) One Nation (ON) Christian Democratic Party (CDP) Citizens Electoral Council (CEC)	Australian Fishing and Lifestyle Party (AFLP) Australian Motoring Enthusiasts Party (AMEP) Shooters and Fishers Party (SFP) Stop the Greens (STG) Stable Population Party (SPP) Australian Sports Party (SPORT)	Australian Independents (AI) Australian Sex Party (SEX) Rise Up Australia Party (RUAP) Liberal Democratic Party (LDP) Smokers Rights Party (SRP) Senators On Line (SOL) Australian Voice Party (AVP) Pirate Party (PP) Australian Republicans (AR) Uniting Australian Party (UAP) WikiLeaks Party (WP) Australia First (AF) Australian Protectionist Party (AP) Carers' Alliance Party (CAP)

Source: Australian Electoral Commission data: <results.aec.gov.au/17496/Website/Default.htm>.

Table 1 lists all those parties (other than the major parties) registered for the 2013 half-Senate election which lodged group ticket votes (GTV) with preferences directed to each other (that is, they were part of a cross-preference arrangement these days referred to in the press as 'preference harvesting') before being directed to the Liberal and/or National parties. These parties could be thought of as being anti-Labor/Green. The table categorises these parties under three sub-headings: first, general right-populist or socially conservative parties that had either contested previous Senate elections or, in the case of the Palmer United Party (PUP), had been receiving significant media attention during the campaign. Opposition to the 'carbon tax' was a policy position commonly taken by these parties. The second heading lists those parties whose nomenclature made specific reference to their opposition to aspects of Labor's environmental policies including the various sporting, shooters and fishers parties, the Australian Motor Enthusiasts Party (AMEP), the No Carbon Tax Party and the Stable Population Party. The third heading lists all the other parties whose GTVs directed preferences to each other and thereafter to anti-Labor/Green candidates. This list includes some minor parties that might generally have been identified with the left of politics, including the libertarian Sex Party and the WikiLeaks Party. Table 1, thus, lists a total of 28 out of the 50 minor parties aligned against Labor. In terms of GTV allocations Labor's only allies in the Senate contest were the Greens and a handful of parties (six in total) like the Animal Rights and Justice Party and doctrinaire parties such as the Socialist Equity Party.

Table 2: Anti-Labor/Green minor party performance by state, 2013 half-Senate election

	NSW	Vic	Qld	WA	SA#	Tas
Number of anti-left minor parties	25	24	25	19	20	19
Explicit anti-environment party vote %	20.4	8.9	17.8	18.5	10.1	12.1
Total explicit and implicit anti-environment vote	27.7	14.3	21.4	22.3	15.4	17.9
Right minor party elected	LDP	AMEP	PUP	SPORT*	FF	PUP

#Result here excludes Nick Xenophon Group.
*Result here at original declaration. At a re-count, this seat was won by the PUP. The result was later voided by the High Court after which a by-election was held.

Source: Australian Electoral Commission data: <results.aec.gov.au/17496/Website/Default.htm>.

The significance of the nature of the party system for the Senate contest only becomes apparent when the total vote for the plethora of minor parties is aggregated. Table 2 presents Senate results for each state by recording the number of parties directing their GTV preferences away from Labor and the Greens. It then shows the total vote won by those minor parties that were explicitly branded as anti-environmental and those right-populist and socially conservative parties whose opposition to the carbon tax was well known. The table indicates the total right-of-centre minor party vote which demonstrates quite clearly the impact the surge in party registrations had on voter behaviour. While it is true that on their own none of these minor parties achieved a significant primary vote, with only the Liberal Democratic Party (LDP) in New South Wales and the PUP candidate in Queensland winning a primary vote greater than 4 per cent (the threshold for public funding and for regaining the candidate deposit), their accumulated vote was very large. The combined effect of the large number of parties was a total primary vote that was big enough in all states except Victoria to exceed the 14.4 per cent required to secure a seat (in Victoria the total vote of 14.3 per cent was only just under quota). Given the nature of the Senate voting system, this meant that instead of assisting the Coalition in winning an extra seat, the total right-of-centre minor party vote was strong enough to get one of their number returned, and Table 2 lists those minor parties that won the sixth seat in each of the state contests.

Table 3: Left versus right-of-centre contests, half Senate election 2013

	NSW	Vic	Qld	WA	SA#	Tas
Left-of-centre vote %	40.2	44.9	36.9	38.3	31.9	45.0
Quota	2.79	3.1	2.5	2.6	2.2	3.1
Seats	2.0	3.0	2.0	2.0	2.0	3.0
Right-of-centre vote %	58.0	54.4	62.7	61.5	42.8	55.4
Quota	4.0	3.7	4.3	4.2	2.9	3.8
Seats	4.0	3.0	4.0	4.0	3.0	3.0

#SA result excludes Nick Xenophon Group.

Source: Australian Electoral Commission data: <results.aec.gov.au/17496/Website/Default.htm>.

Table 2 disaggregates the total primary vote won by explicitly and implicitly anti-environmental and anti-carbon tax minor parties from the rest of the minor parties whose motives for contesting the election were not immediately clear but which still directed their preferences away from Labor and the Greens. The table shows that anti-environmental and anti-carbon tax parties achieved an accumulated primary vote in excess of the quota in New South Wales, Queensland and Western Australia. In Tasmania the vote won was 0.84 of a quota and in South Australia 0.70 of a quota. The weakest anti-environment performance was in Victoria, yet one of the anti-environmental parties, the AMEP, secured a seat nonetheless. In addition to the AMEP, the LDP secured a seat in New South Wales while the PUP and Family First won seats in the other states.

These results were the clearest expression of voter reaction to Labor's approach to the environmental policy debate. The sense of a rightward shift in the electorate as a whole is reinforced when the Coalition vote is factored into the result. The commonly held view amongst Senate election analysts is that the equal allocation of seats between the collective left-of-centre and right-of-centre is the norm and that any variation from this is significant (see Economou 2006; Bowler and Denemark 1993; Mackerras 1993). Table 3 outlines the Senate contest as a left-of-centre (that is, Labor, Greens and those directing their GTV preferences to these two parties) versus right-of-centre contest by way of aggregated primary vote, quota won and seats won. The table is quite clear in what it reveals: in four states the right-of-centre won four out of a possible six seats. In two states—South Australia and Western Australia—Labor could win only one seat. The significance of this for post-election politics in Australia was delayed by the constitutional provision that new Senators wait until 1 July the following year to take their seats.

Conclusion

Election outcomes are rarely the result of voters responding to a single issue or even a small number of issues gathered under a single rubric such as 'the environment'. On the other hand, the environment (if the climate change debate is included) loomed large in national politics between the 2010 and 2013 elections, and the way in which the Gillard Government dealt with it was something voters reflected upon when they went to the polls in 2013. The election result suggests that voters rejected the Gillard Government's approach to the issue even though opinion polling indicated that a majority of Australians still saw climate change as an important issue that the Australian Government needed to address. Indeed, a Lowy Institute poll outlined the problem for the Government and its crossbench parliamentary supporters when it found that, while support for doing something about climate change was still strong, 58 per cent of respondents rejected the Gillard Government's carbon pricing scheme, and 57 per cent said they agreed with the Coalition's policy of abolishing the program (Lowy Institute 2013). In short, the Government had saddled itself with an unpopular policy.

The problems did not end there. In addition to being an unpopular program, the way in which the Gillard Government had reached its decision also contributed to its declining support. Here, Gillard's promise not to introduce a carbon tax during the campaign and what looked like a breaking of an election promise hurt the standing of both the Government and the Prime Minister. The election result indicated that no amount of rhetoric about doing the right thing and no attempt at sophistry by calling the scheme a 'price on carbon' rather than a 'carbon tax' was able to ameliorate the electorate's hostile response to the Gillard Government's decision to run with the carbon price/tax option. As if all of this was not deleterious enough, by at least appearing to have adopted an approach previously associated with the Greens, the Gillard Government gave the very strong impression that it had handed leadership of the climate change debate to the minority interests in the House of Representatives and the Senate. Given this, a voter could choose from an array of reasons why she or he would be opposed to the Gillard Government's approach to climate change policy but still think that climate change was happening and that government should do something about it.

The other items on the national environmental policy agenda played out in ways that students of environmental policy politics would be very familiar with (Stewart 2010: 536–7; Downs 1972). The Government would find itself trying to mediate between polarised sectional interest groups, and any decision was bound to alienate at least one side of the ecology-development divide. In the case of the Murray-Darling Basin, both conservationists and producers were dissatisfied with outcomes, although the producers tended to be more hyperbolic in venting their outrage. The marine park decision was also criticised by both sides. For a Labor Government, such matters do not usually have a major electoral impact. These conservation or resource management controversies generally occur in remote communities in electoral districts that tend to be safe for the Coalition parties and involve a small number of constituents, the majority of whom would not vote for the ALP anyway.

The difference this time, however, was that the Gillard Government had found a way through its approach to climate change to universalise the politics of environmentalism to the extent that swinging voters in marginal urban electorates had become involved. This also allowed the otherwise marginalised players in other land use and resource use disputes to have their campaigns resonate in the national debate. The next thing that happened was that these dynamics impacted on the national election, especially in the Senate where the anti-Gillard forces beyond the mainstream centre-right had a lot of success at the expense of the collective left-of-centre which had been in the unfamiliar position of having a majority in the upper house. The Labor caucus knew its approach to climate change was a political disaster—that was one of the reasons why Gillard was removed as leader ahead of the 2013 election. By then it was all too late.

References

Australian Electoral Commission (AEC). 2013a. 'Seats Which Changed Hands'. *Election 2013: Virtual Tally Room*, 4 November, viewed 20 December 2013: <results.aec.gov.au/17496/Website/HouseSeatsWhichChangedHands-17496-NAT.htm>.

AEC. 2013b. 'Record number of candidates to contest the 2013 federal election'. Media release, Canberra, 16 August: <www.aec.gov.au/media/media-releases/2013/e08-16a.htm>.

Australian Greens and the Australian Labor Party. 2010. 'Agreement'. 1 September, viewed 16 January 2014: <resources.news.com.au/files/2010/09/01/1225912/745814-greens-alp-deal.pdf>.

Bowler, Shaun and Denemark, David. 1993. 'Split ticket voting in Australia: dealignment and inconsistent voting reconsidered'. *Australian Journal of Political Science* 28(1): 19–37.

CSIRO. 2011. 'Australian views of climate change'. Social and Economic Sciences Program Paper, 10 March.

Downs, Anthony. 1972. 'Up and down with ecology: the issues attention cycle'. *The Public Interest* 28: 38–50.

Economou, Nick. 2000. 'Labor and the environment: greening the workers' party'. In John Warhurst and Andrew Parkin (eds), *The Machine: Labor Confronts the Future*, Sydney: Allen & Unwin.

Economou, Nick. 2006. 'A right-of-centre triumph: the 2004 Australian half-Senate election'. *Australian Journal of Political Science* 41(4): 501–16.

Graetz, Geordan and Manning, Haydon. 2012. 'Environmental issues and the 2010 campaign'. In Marian Simms and John Wanna (eds), *Julia 2010: the caretaker election*, Canberra: ANU E-Press.

Johnson, Carol. 2010. 'The ideological contest'. *Australian Cultural History Special Edition* 28(1): 7–14.

Karvelas, Patricia. 2011. 'Commonwealth overrides Victoria on issue of grazing in alpine park'. *Sydney Morning Herald*, 18 March, viewed 16 January 2014: <www.theaustralian.com.au/news/nation/commonwealth-overrides-victoria-on-issue-of-grazing-in-alpine-park/story-e6frg6nf-1226024063731>.

Kelly, Joe. 2010. 'Kevin Rudd delays emissions trading scheme until Kyoto expires in 2012'. *The Australian*, 28 April, viewed 16 January

2014: <www.theaustralian.com.au/national-affairs/policy/kevin-rudd-delays-emissions-trading-scheme-until-kyoto-expires-in-2012/story-e6frg6xf-1225858894753>.

Leviston, Zoe, Leitch, Ann, Greenhill, Murni, Leonard, Rosemary and Walker, Ian. 2011. *Australians' views of climate change.* CSIRO Report, Canberra: <www.csiro.au/Outcomes/Climate/Adapting/Annual-Survey-of-Australian-Attitudes-to-Climate-Change.aspx>.

LiberalPartyTV. 2011. *Gillard says 'NO' to Carbon Tax—August 2010.* Online video, 24 February, viewed 16 January 2014: <www.youtube.com/watch?v=KMVc0IbtyAQ>.

Locke, Sarina. 2012. 'Fishermen stage marine parks protest'. *ABC*, 27 June, viewed 16 January 2014: <www.abc.net.au/site-archive/rural/news/content/201206/s3534015.htm>.

Lowy Institute. 2013. 'The Lowy Institute Poll 2013'. Lowy Institute, 24 June, viewed 20 December 2013: <www.lowyinstitute.org/publications/lowy-institute-poll-2013>.

Mackerras, Malcolm. 1993. *The Mackerras 1993 Election Guide.* Canberra: AGPS.

Papadakis, Elim. 1993. *Politics and the Environment: The Australian Edition.* Sydney: Allen & Unwin.

Pietsch, Juliet and McAllister, Ian. 2010. '"A Diabolical Challenge": Public Opinion and Climate Change Policy in Australia'. *Environmental Politics* 19(2): 217–36.

PM. 2011. 'Protest against basin plan'. Radio program transcript, ABC Radio, Sydney, 28 November, viewed 16 January 2014: <www.abc.net.au/pm/content/2011/s3378328.htm>.

Rawson, Jane. 2011. 'The carbon tax package'. *The Conversation*, 11 July, viewed 16 January 2014: <theconversation.com/the-carbon-tax-package-2290>.

Rootes, Christopher. 2008. 'The first climate change election? The Australian election of 24 November 2007'. *Environmental Politics* 17: 473–80.

Scarr, Lanai. 2013. 'Kevin Rudd axes carbon tax in favour of Emissions Trading Scheme'. *News.com.au*, 16 July, viewed 16 January 2014: <www.news.com.au/national/kevin-rudd-axes-carbon-tax-in-favour-of-emissions-trading-scheme/story-fnho52ip-1226680043190>.

Scott, Andrew. 2010. 'From Rudd to Gillard: why the Australian leadership has changed'. *Social Europe Journal*, 25 June, viewed 1 April 2014: <www.social-europe.eu/2010/06/from-rudd-to-gillard-why-the-australian-leadership-changed/>.

Stewart, Jenny. 2010. 'Environmental policy'. In Dennis Woodward, Andrew Parkin and John Summers (eds), *Government, Politics, Power and Policy in Australia*, 9th edn, Sydney: Pearson.

Taylor, Lenore. 2011. 'Experts doubt Coalition plan'. *The Sydney Morning Herald*, 3 March, viewed 16 January 2014: <www.smh.com.au/environment/climate-change/experts-doubt-coalition-carbon-plan-20110302-1bext.html>.

The 7.30 Report. 2011. 'Gillard explains carbon scheme'. Television program transcript, ABC, 24 February, viewed 8 April 2014: <www.abc.net.au/7.30/content/2011/s3148281.htm>. Interview with Julia Gillard, presented by Heather Ewart.

Thompson, Jeremy. 2011. 'Gillard reveals carbon price scheme'. ABC, 11 July, viewed 16 January 2014: <www.abc.net.au/news/2011-07-10/gillard-reveals-carbon-price-scheme/2788842>.

van Onselen, Peter. 2010. 'Politics trumps a moral challenge'. *The Australian*, 29 April, viewed 16 January 2014: <www.theaustralian.com.au/news/features/politics-trumps-a-moral-challenge/story-e6frg6z6-1225859592923>.

Warhurst, John. 1983. 'The impact of conservation and anti-abortion groups in politics'. *Current Affairs Bulletin* 60(2): 19–31.

Wong, Penny. 2008. 'Climate Change: A responsibility agenda'. Speech to the Australian Industry Group Luncheon, 6 February, Melbourne. Transcript available online: <www.france.embassy.gov.au/pari/SpeechCC6Feb.html>.

Wong, Penny. 2009. '2020 targets are only the first step'. *The Sydney Morning Herald*, 23 February, viewed 8 April 2014: <www.smh.com.au/environment/climate-change/2020-targets-are-only-the-first-step-20090222-8eof.html>.

Wong, Penny. 2009. 'ETS better than tax'. *The Australian*, 23 February, viewed 8 April 2014: <www.theaustralian.com.au/opinion/columnists/ets-is-better-than-tax/story-e6frg7ef-1111118932471>.

21. Unstable Bipartisanship or Off the Agenda? Social issues during the 2013 election campaign

Rob Manwaring, Gwen Gray and Lionel Orchard

Introduction

The 2013 federal election was dominated by economic issues, carbon policy and the controversies surrounding asylum seekers, driven by the Abbott Coalition's campaign to damage the economic and political credibility of the Rudd–Gillard governments. As a result, the role and place of social policy issues during the campaign was uncertain and had less prominence. With the exception of the issue of paid parental leave, traditional social policy issues such as education and health did not play a decisive and direct role in the outcome. In part, this was the result of a deliberate strategy by the Coalition to neutralise key social issues, often perceived as the ALP's traditional areas of strength (McAllister and Pietsch 2011: 19–20). Nevertheless, there was some social policy convergence between the two major party groupings but this was for tactical rather than ideological reasons.

This chapter offers a detailed analysis of the role of social policy during the election campaign, by setting out the broader context and then focusing on the key policy issues, including the paid parental leave (PPL) scheme, the Gonski reforms to secondary education, the National Disability Insurance Scheme (NDIS), health policy, indigenous policy and welfare policy.

Generally, the prominence of social policy issues at federal elections waxes and wanes over time. Like other policy domains, social policy is subject to Downs' 'issue attention cycle', where a confluence of fashion, events, and interests can combine to elevate some issues to the policy agenda while other issues receive less prominence (Downs 1972). For instance, industrial relations policy was a key factor at the 2007 election (Wanna 2010) but not in 2010 or 2013, largely because Abbott claimed *WorkChoices* was now 'dead, buried and cremated' (Karvelas 2010). Survey data tends to show that health and economic policies are the dominant issues for most people, although followed closely by education (Bean and McAllister 2012). Data from the 2013 Australian Election Study (AES) shows that health and education were the two key issues for voters, with over 60 per cent of respondents indicating that these were 'extremely important' issues for them (Bean *et al*. 2013; Figure 1 sets out the most important policy issues for respondents). Despite the importance of social services for citizens, Australia's federal system means that many of these services are delivered at the state level. This tempers their overall impact on voting behaviour at federal elections. Accordingly, in the political discourse of the 2013 campaign, social policy provided important 'atmospherics' but was not decisive in a government-changing election.

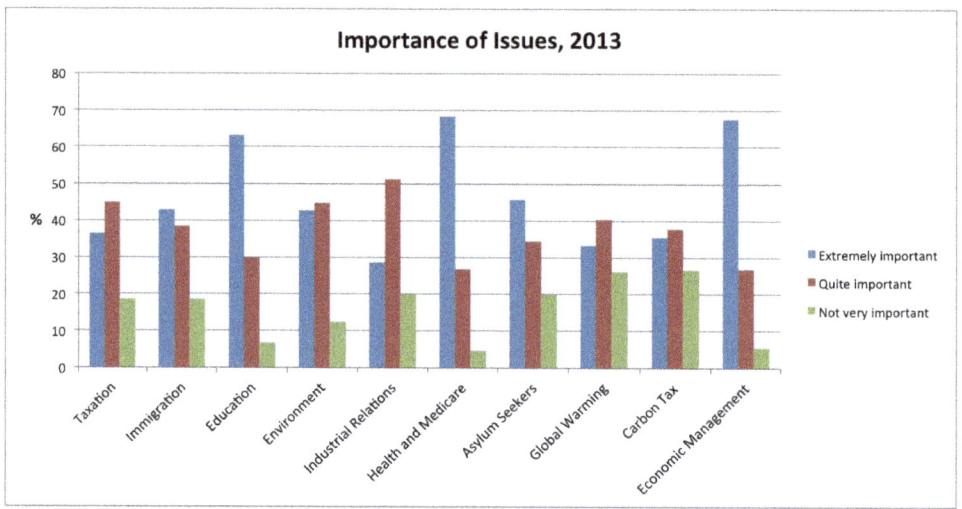

Figure 1: Importance of issues, 2013 Australian Election Study

Source: Bean *et al*. 2014.

Despite limited media coverage, social policy was a vexed issue for the major parties. For the ALP, the two most significant reforms were the NDIS, and the 'Better Schools Plan'—a commitment by Kevin Rudd to fund for six years a new school education formula based on the review by David Gonski. However, the ALP was tactically caught up in selling these policies in the face of the protracted leadership change. Kevin Rudd was hamstrung in promoting these two major reforms given that they had been introduced and implemented by his predecessor Julia Gillard. It is striking that in his acceptance speech, Rudd praised Gillard as a 'radical reformer' citing her main achievements as the *Fair Work Act* and the national education test reforms (introduced during his term as prime minister), but not her (prime ministerial) role in either the NDIS or Gonski reforms (ABC 2013). The issue for Rudd was how to consolidate these popular reforms and, at the same time, offer a new distinctive agenda. In part, his relabelling of what were commonly called the 'Gonski reforms' as the 'Better

Schools Plan' reflected this dilemma. The other dilemma for Rudd was how to ensure that disaffected ALP supporters did not defect to the Greens—who generally claim to have a more progressive social policy agenda.

For the Coalition, social issues also raised a series of dilemmas. AES data shows that the public generally views the ALP as a better custodian of the health and education policy areas (McAllister and Pietsch 2011). Whilst clearly making an impact on the electorate with his strong economic message and his pledge to repeal the carbon tax, Opposition Leader Tony Abbott had to ensure that social policy did not damage his campaign. In this respect, Abbott's response was the so-called 'small target' strategy, pursuing policy convergence with the ALP, with the exception of the PPL scheme, where it sought to outflank Labor from the left. Abbott also advocated the need to refocus efforts in indigenous policy, albeit in an embryonic way. In this, Noel Pearson and his allies played a key advisory role.

Schools education policy: Neutralising Gonski

The political and policy debates about school education in Australia have always been riven by conflict between public and private priorities and interests. This continues to be so. Equity and social inclusion in education policy have proven to be difficult to achieve despite the strong reforming efforts of the Rudd–Gillard governments in this area.[1] In 2007, education was a critical policy area for the newly installed Prime Minister, Kevin Rudd. Earlier, in the 2007 election campaign, he had promised an 'education revolution'. The lack of progress in transforming Australia's secondary education performance was a factor in portraying Rudd in his first term as PM as strong on symbolic policy (for example, the Apology to the Stolen Generations of Indigenous children and ratifying the Kyoto Protocol on carbon emissions) but less able to demonstrate substantive policy advances. Not without controversy and strongly shaped by advice from influential think tanks like the Grattan Institute (for commentary, see Ashenden 2013), the ALP's education achievements included introducing the National Assessment Program—Literacy and Numeracy (NAPLAN) tests and the *My Education* website (along with the subsequent perception that this was a 'backdoor' introduction of school league tables). By the time of Rudd's second tilt as prime minister, the 'Gonski' reforms were at the top of the Government's education policy agenda. In April 2010, Julia Gillard as Minister of Education commissioned businessman David Gonski to chair an expert panel on schools funding. Among its findings, the Gonski review highlighted declining educational outcomes for Australians, and suggested a new, simpler funding

---

1   For recent surveys, see Keating (2010); Watson and Liu (2014).

model with increased funds from both state and federal governments (ABC 2012). Julia Gillard, as prime minister, attempted to make the Gonski reforms a centrepiece of her case for re-election. Initially, the Gonski reforms were met with resistance from the federal Opposition. Moreover, since most of the large states were also held by the Liberals, Gillard was struggling to persuade the state Liberals to sign up to the new funding agreements.

When Rudd assumed the prime ministership in June 2013, he sought to both consolidate this agenda and remake it as the 'Better Schools Improvement Plan'. At the outset of the campaign, only New South Wales under Barry O'Farrell had broken Liberal ranks to sign up to the new model, promising the state much-needed additional funding. Deals with the Labor jurisdictions were brokered on the cusp of the election with the Tasmanian, Australian Capital Territory and South Australian governments.

The significant moment came on 2 August when the Abbott Coalition announced support for Rudd's 'Better Schools Plan' after all, but would only commit to funding for four rather than six years. Abbott described this as a 'unity ticket' with the Government. Labor sensed this was purely for narrow electoral reasons (AAP 2013a). Yet, the Coalition's reversal changed the dynamics of the debate. For Labor the pressure to sign up the major states increased, and eventually Victoria also agreed, albeit on somewhat different terms. The refusal of both Queensland and Western Australia to sign up meant this was only a limited achievement for the ALP.

The Coalition, by partially accepting the 'Better Schools Plan', also marginalised the ACTU's 'I give a Gonski' campaign, which the union movement hoped would have the same impact as its successful 2007 anti-*WorkChoices* campaign. Hence, the ALP lost its policy 'edge' on this issue. Nevertheless, the overall level of commitment by the Coalition to the Gonski agenda was open to question and indeed, post-election, its failed attempt to reverse its position suggested that tactical considerations outweighed any ideological ones in the context of the campaign.

Interestingly, the Coalition's policy U-turn on the Gonski reforms during the campaign masked some of the details and differences between the main parties. Significantly, the ALP committed to continuing the School Kids Bonus whilst the Coalition pledged to abolish it. The Coalition, with a preference for introducing greater forms of localism, also pledged to establish a $70-million fund to encourage state schools to become independent, along with a commitment to review the curriculum—in effect seeking to relaunch the so-called 'history wars' that characterised the Howard era (Blake 2013). It was also clear that, despite the rhetoric, the ALP was only partially meeting the full suite of Gonski recommendations (Caro 2013); some see the period as one in which education policies continued to be shaped by neoliberal priorities, albeit mixed with some social democratic and equity effort (Watson and Liu 2014).

Bipartisanship over disability policy

Disability policy did not feature as prominently as education policy during the election campaign. To a large extent, the issue had been de-politicised when both the major parties pledged to support the introduction of the ALP's NDIS, which was the outcome of well-organised and well-articulated advocacy over a long period of time (Steketee 2013). Enjoying widespread support across the Australian public, it was a key policy area where Abbott had departed from his usually stronger oppositional stances. This meant that, by the time of the election campaign, the scheme had bipartisan support and both parties were committed to rolling out pilot schemes throughout the nation. The model of NDIS broadly fitted with the recommendations arising from the Productivity Commission's reforms to improve support for people with disabilities. The Coalition's endorsement of the NDIS reflected its commitment and was less of a tactical ploy than its response to the Gonski recommendations.

Yet, throughout the campaign there were some issues arising with the disability scheme. There had been some disquiet in the wider disability community services sector when NDIS was renamed *DisabilityCare Australia* in March 2013, and the Coalition committed itself to reverting back to the original NDIS (AAP 2013b). There was also a wider debate about how the disability scheme (along with other increased spending proposals such as Gonski) would be funded. Demographer Bernard Salt suggested that unless tax revenues increased the quality of public services might suffer (Mitchell 2013), and the CEO of the Business Council of Australia accused the parties of 'jumping the gun' on financing the scheme (Carswell 2013).

The most damaging aspect of the *DisabilityCare* reforms for the ALP was in respect to negotiations and dealings with state governments over the roll-out of pilot schemes. To the dismay of Barry O'Farrell in New South Wales, the ALP announced, without consultation, 11 sites for the disability scheme rollout. The New South Wales disabilities minister accused Labor of seeking 'political gain' in their announcement, suggesting that the pilots were in key marginal seats and the timing was designed to maximise another of Labor's flagship policy areas (AAP 2013c). The accusation of politicisation was also made when Labor announced the seven pilots in Queensland, with the state minister claiming to have learned of the sites only via Labor's press release. Significantly, the last state to sign up to the *DisabilityCare* package was Western Australia. Interestingly, the Western Australian Government runs a well-regarded scheme called 'My Way' and the subsequent deal brokered with the federal Government meant that the schemes would run alongside each other, providing fruitful comparison. Overall, Labor's lack of negotiating finesse with the state governments meant that its flagship policy was somewhat tarred, and the broad bipartisan support meant that it had limited scope to draw policy advantage over the Coalition. Disability, like schools education, was successfully neutralised by the Coalition.

Outflanked on the left over paid parental leave?

If there was broad policy consensus on disability and education, the issue of paid parental leave (PPL) was far more divisive. Historically, Australia has been one of the few remaining advanced industrial nations without such a scheme, although during the Howard era the universal cash 'baby bonus' was the main policy response (Ray, Gornick and Schmitt 2009). Following an inquiry by the Productivity Commission, the Gillard Government had introduced a PPL scheme paid at the minimum wage for 18 weeks whether or not the parent was in the workforce (Productivity Commission 2009). Labor had also promised to increase wages for child care workers, and to scrap the baby bonus and replace it with a $2,000 supplement to Family Tax Benefit A.

To some surprise, at Abbott's insistence the Coalition retained the 'signature policy' it took to the 2010 election offering a far more generous scheme than the ALP, promising women their full salary for 26 weeks capped at $75,000. Women earning over $150,000 would still receive the capped benefit but women not in the workforce would not. Abbott's scheme was to be funded by a 1.5 per cent levy on the top 3,000 companies in Australia, although the same companies would be compensated by a reduction in the company tax rate from 30 to 28.5 per cent. In total the scheme was estimated to cost $5.5 billion per year (Coorey 2013a). The Western Australian premier, Colin Barnett, was perhaps emblematic of those on the Coalition side who supported the PPL but considered it 'overly generous' (Coorey 2013b). The Coalition scheme was also seen to be at odds with the simultaneous concerns about the overall budget 'crisis' (Coorey and Daley 2013). This was further complicated for the Coalition as it became clear that the levy on business would only foot some of the PPL bill, and there was inevitably some vocal concern from the wider business community about the Coalition's scheme (Mitchell 2013).[2]

---

2   The Greens announced a similar scheme to the Coalition's proposal but capped theirs at $100,000.

Not surprisingly, this policy, more than any other social policy issue, dominated the public debate, and Figure 2 gives some impression of how the issue dominated media coverage, when compared to other key social policy issues.

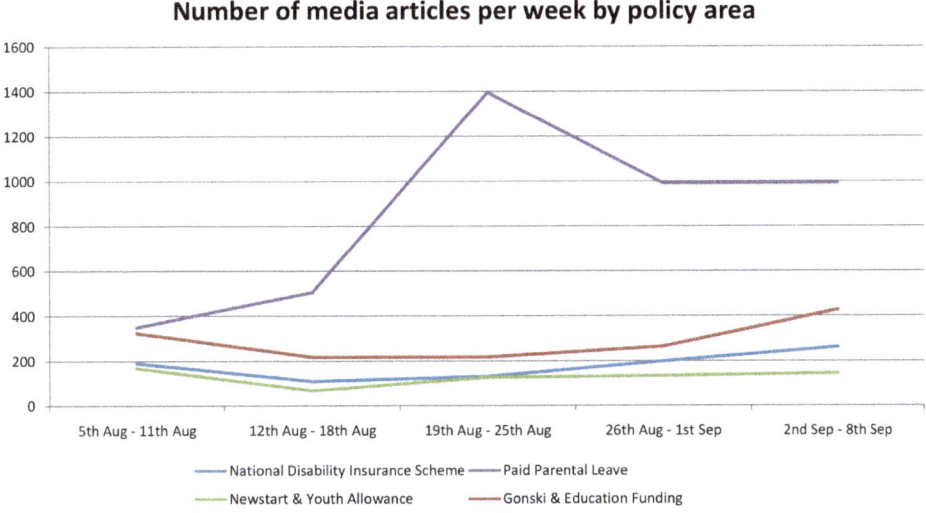

Figure 2: Social policy media articles (5 August to 8 September 2013)

Source: Factiva. Data extracted 11 November 2013.

The arguments between the major parties over their rival PPL schemes raised wider ideological and policy issues. The parties made competing claims about the types of equity being offered in the different schemes, and how low-paid families would fare, especially as the cash baby bonus was abolished. The PPL also raised critical issues about gender, employment and work-life issues, and elicited feminist (and other) responses, notably when public intellectual Eva Cox supported Abbott's scheme as a workplace entitlement (Karvelas 2013a). In many respects, the Coalition seemed to outflank Labor from both the left *and* the right on this issue. With the support of some feminists, the Coalition's more generous scheme for working women resembled similar Scandinavian social democratic models. Yet, there was also a strong argument that this scheme was an important aspect of both Tony Abbott's conservative thinking and his campaign strategy. Using the government to protect the family unit economically at this time of need was an expression of state activism and a deliberate attempt to deal with Abbott's so-called 'women problem'. Abbott mostly faced criticism from both classical liberals and conservatives within his party who prefer a small state and fiscal constraint (Coorey and Heath 2013).

Some commentators argued that the debate over the PPL displayed some old fashioned 'class warfare' between the parties. During the campaign, Rudd described it as a 'dog of a policy' in that it would penalise self-funded retirees and their superannuation savings. Labor, caught mainly on the back foot, raised the spectre that a Coalition Government would be forced to raise the GST to fully fund the scheme—an initial scare tactic which failed to take hold (Coorey and Daley 2013). Accordingly, in a social policy area that should have benefitted the Labor Government, and indeed where the ALP had arguably led the Coalition, they were out-manoeuvred by Abbott's PPL scheme.

Indigenous social policy

Indigenous policy is an area of continuing controversy and change, and indeed turbulence. In recent times, the Howard Government's Northern Territory Intervention, Rudd's apology to the Stolen Generations, and the Rudd–Gillard *Closing the Gap* strategies have been the dominant national initiatives in this area. The 'intervention' and 'closing the gap' policy approaches have had a reasonably close association, with the former commencing in 2005 and the second developed over 2006–07 and adopted by the Council of Australian Governments (COAG) in December 2007. There have been some elements of bipartisan consensus in recent national policy approaches, particularly in the Rudd–Gillard acceptance of key elements of the intervention about welfare quarantining whilst pursuing higher levels of housing and related investment through 'closing the gap' policies, an approach shaped through Indigenous Affairs Minister Jenny Macklin's leadership (Karvelas 2013b).

Contemporary indigenous policy is an area of vigorous exchange between advocates. Noel Pearson and Marcia Langton have a strong presence in the debates. Pearson advocates the idea of a 'radical centre' which reconciles liberal, conservative and progressive principles. Pearson's approach brings together Amartya Sen's capability and 'development as freedom' ideas, conservative critiques of passive welfare, and liberal views about the importance of education and mainstream economic participation of indigenous people. This remains perhaps the most dominant framework shaping the public debate about indigenous issues. Nevertheless, other views also have a strong presence in indigenous debates (Altman and Kerins 2012). Some argue that the whole area is powerfully shaped by neoliberal precepts and priorities (Altman 2014). There is also an ongoing division of opinion about the assumptions and impacts of the 'intervention' and the 'closing the gap' strategies. The strong 'advocacy' voice of Murdoch's *Australian* newspaper in commentary and analysis of indigenous policy, including reinforcing and publishing Pearson's views and supporting the 'intervention', should also be noted.

Indigenous issues had some presence in the 2013 election campaign. In the lead-up to the campaign, some commentators highlighted the ongoing difficulties and failures in dealing with indigenous disadvantage and development, particularly in remote Australia. According to one commentator, land reform, welfare, education and the impact of alcohol abuse in remote indigenous communities were 'the four chief areas of crisis and systemic policy failure bedevilling the indigenous societies of the inland and the north', suggesting that these issues needed further attention in the election campaign (Rothwell 2013a).

Tony Abbott's speech in federal parliament in February 2013 on indigenous recognition was significant in giving some indication about future indigenous policy. In a major shift from recent Coalition stances on reconciliation with indigenous people, particularly under John Howard, Abbott's speech noted the past injustices done to indigenous peoples and the importance of Paul Keating's Redfern speech, and defended the need for constitutional recognition of Aboriginal people. In March, Abbott announced that he would become the 'Prime Minister for Indigenous Affairs' and his February speech was seen by some as providing the 'moral framework' for his leadership in this area (Manne 2013).

Some fundamentals in indigenous policy were debated as the election campaign unfolded. Some commentators associated with Howard's previous policies highlighted the ongoing failures of passive welfare and the excessive bureaucracy associated with the 'intervention'. For instance, Peter Shergold (2013) argued that 'diversity, choice and flexibility' in policy design have been ignored. Indigenous advocates such as Noel Pearson (2013a and 2013b) agreed with these assessments, highlighting the need for indigenous leadership and ownership as a condition of policy success.

By mid-August, the policy positions of the major parties were clearer. In launching the Coalition's policy, Abbott highlighted the continuing crisis in remote indigenous communities and the need for policy reform to be taking 'reconciliation to a new level and embedding the idea of personal responsibility' (Shanahan and Karvelas 2013). He committed to establishing a new indigenous advisory board under the leadership of former ALP president Warren Mundine, which would rationalise bureaucracy and priority-setting in the indigenous area. Abbott spoke of Noel Pearson's leadership and influence on his thinking. He committed to expanding the Pearson/Cape York 'empowered community' approach in indigenous policy (AAP 2013c; Karvelas and Kelly 2013). Some journalists suggested Abbott's approach lacked clarity about where ultimate responsibility for indigenous policy would lie (Rothwell 2013b). For his part, Pearson supported Abbott's plans for constitutional recognition of indigenous peoples, arguing that 'only a highly conservative leader can deliver change' in this area given the difficult history of change through referenda in Australia (Karvelas 2013c).

On the Labor side, Rudd made the case for greater bipartisanship in indigenous policy, highlighting the need for a more apolitical approach. The Minister for Indigenous Affairs, Jenny Macklin, put the case for new 'closing the gap' targets for indigenous incarceration, participation in higher education and coverage of disabled indigenous people by *DisabilityCare Australia* (AAP 2013b; Karvelas 2013d). In contrast to the Coalition, the ALP's policies were not all that inspiring and could be viewed as incremental additions to existing unproven policies. Key indigenous leaders, some with previously strong Labor connections, were now in the Coalition circle and the Abbott policies on reconciliation and recognition had a greater freshness and energy, even if there were doubts about a Coalition government's longer-term commitment to them (Strakosch 2013). Immediately post-election, some commentators argued that while the difficulties remained great, Abbott's quest for a new indigenous compact giving emphasis to Pearson's views represented the best hope (Rothwell 2013c). In the event, the Coalition's and Abbott's capacity to develop an indigenous agenda integrating liberal, communitarian and conservative perspectives during the election campaign trumped Labor's more traditional social democratic policy model.

Accommodation in health policy

The Coalition's attempts to neutralise contentious social policy issues were particularly evident in the area of health policy. Both sides had gradually come to an accommodation over Medicare, bulk-billing, improving the performance of public hospitals, and urging the privatisation of health care via private health insurance. Both major parties supported the existing public/private mix with a strong private insurance scheme and private providers operating alongside Medicare and the public hospital system. This mix pays insufficient attention to equity impacts and social needs and tends to favour the private sector (Lewis 2010; Baum and Dwyer 2014). Hence, for the first time since the 1940s, health was a low-key issue during the 2013 election campaign and, for some, it was the 'missing election debate' (Russell 2013). No significant new policies were announced and, instead of presenting competing health programs, both major parties supported the status quo. This was a very marked change from the vehement disagreements that produced radical policy changes over previous decades. In 2013, Labor was content to run on its record while the Coalition quickly retreated from any proposition that might become controversial. Only the Greens proposed major reforms, drawing attention to some of the structural problems of the system. Greens ideas, however, never reached centre stage, so the major parties were able to slip through the campaign, avoiding issues that might offend major interest groups and sidestepping the concerns of community members and health experts.

One acknowledged health expert described health policy during the 2013 campaign as 'anodyne, soporific and vapid' (Duckett 2013). Abbott, for his part, said very little about health in his campaign launch speech (Abbott 2013), while Rudd made only a few scattered references. Labor's promise to restore the Commonwealth's share of hospital funding to 50 per cent was a major new commitment (Rudd 2013), although neither side was prepared to address the issue of health spending increasing at a rate faster than GDP growth (AIHW 2013a: 6–7). Other promises were either too broad to be meaningful or were trivial in terms of policy contours.

The health debate between Minister Tanya Plibersek and Shadow Minister Peter Dutton revealed little about party intentions. Both agreed on the importance of Medicare and a strong private health sector. The Coalition announced it would retain Labor's National Health Reform Agreement with the states and territories, through which the Commonwealth's share of hospital funding would ostensibly be increased.

Although critical of 'unnecessary bureaucracy', the Coalition avoided comment on the future of Labor's new national agencies. Both parties promised to fund new cancer care programs and both expressed support for medical research and for the improvement of Aboriginal health. In mental health, both promised small additional pots of funding, seen as a missed opportunity by the sector (Hickey 2013). Mr Abbott committed to maintaining the overall level of hospital and medical funding and to retaining Labor's $4 billion dental package for children and low income adults, due to begin in 2014. The Greens called for universal primary dental care under Medicare but the proposal attracted little attention.

Labor promised to continue its reform agenda if re-elected. The main Rudd–Gillard structural initiative had been the introduction of Medicare Locals: primary health care organisations charged with planning and coordinating improved primary health care for designated populations, with supporting providers to improve services and fill gaps. The Coalition's initial plan to abolish them gave way during the campaign to a commitment to review them and, finally, to a promise that none would be closed. The closest that party competition came to emerging was when Abbott promised to restore universal eligibility to public subsidy for private insurance which Labor had means-tested.

On the whole, then, bipartisanship in health prevailed, allowing the major parties to ignore the problems that consumers, the Greens and reform groups have identified (such as over-reliance on fee-for-service, user-charging for patients, over-servicing by hospitals, and an under investment in primary health care and preventative care—see AIHW 2013b: 133; Commonwealth of Australia 2009a: 51, 102–4; Gray 2009: 66–76; Gray Jamieson 2012: 317; Elshaug *et al*. 2012).

Conclusion

By astutely adopting a strategy of accommodation over a number of social policy issues, the Coalition was able to neutralise them as issues that could play to Labor's strengths. The Coalition thereby ensured that the main focus of the election campaign remained on fiscal and economic policies and their critique of the Government's (mis)management. Despite some attempts to reframe its social policy agenda, Labor was unable to campaign effectively on what have traditionally been seen as its 'natural' areas of policy strength. Labor attempted to resuscitate policy differences tangentially by claiming that the Coalition's budgetary cuts would disproportionately fall in the education, health and social policy areas. The Coalition effectively countered this argument once Abbott gave an undertaking to quarantine these areas from the cuts, retaining Commonwealth spending at existing levels. And Labor may have undermined its own case because it was already making cuts to public services as a result of its own budgetary difficulties.

References

Abbott, Tony, 2013. 'Tony Abbott's campaign launch speech: full transcript'. 25 August, viewed 5 November 2013: <www.smh.com.au/federal-politics/federal-election-2013/tony-abbotts-campaign-launch-speech-full-transcript-20130825-2sjhc.html>.

AIHW. 2013a. *Health Expenditure Australia 2011–12*. Health and Welfare Expenditure Series, Number 50, viewed 5 November 2013: <www.aihw.gov.au/publication-detail/?id=60129544658>.

AIHW. 2013b. *Australian Hospital Statistics 2011–12*. Health Services Series Number 50, viewed 5 November 2013: <www.aihw.gov.au/WorkArea/DownloadAsset.aspx?id=60129543146>.

Altman, Jon. 2014. 'Indigenous policy: Canberra consensus on a neoliberal project of improvement'. In Chris Miller and Lionel Orchard (eds), *Australian Public Policy: Progressive Ideas in the Neoliberal Ascendency*, Bristol: Policy Press.

Altman, Jon and Kerins, Sean (eds). 2012. *People on Country: Vital Landscapes, Indigenous Futures*. Sydney: Federation Press.

Ashenden, Dean. 2013. 'The Grattan line'. *Inside Story*, 2 July, viewed 16 July 2014: <inside.org.au/the-grattan-line/>.

Australian Associated Press (AAP). 2013a. 'Abbott scared of schools backlash: Shorten'. 2 August.

AAP. 2013b. 'FED: Make indigenous policy bipartisan: Rudd'. 10 August.

AAP. 2013c. 'FED: Abbott speaks about his indigenous journey'. 10 August.

AAP. 2013d. 'FED: Open to dump DisabilityCare name'. 20 August.

AAP. 2013e. 'O'Farrell upset over Labor's NDIS plan'. 28 August.

Australian Broadcasting Corporation (ABC). 2012. 'What's in the Gonski report?'. *ABC*, 27 August, viewed 5 November 2013: <www.abc.net.au/news/2012-08-27/whats-in-the-gonski-report/4219508>.

ABC. 2013. 'Kevin Rudd aims to "forge consensus" in politics after victory over Julia Gillard'. *ABC*, 27 June, viewed 5 November 2013: <www.abc.net.au/news/2013-06-27/kevin-rudd-responds-to-leadership-win/4784040>.

Baum, Fran and Dwyer, Judith. 2014. 'The accidental logic of health policy in Australia'. In Chris Miller and Lionel Orchard (eds), *Australian Public Policy: Progressive Ideas in the Neoliberal Ascendency*, Bristol: Policy Press.

Bean, Clive S and McAllister, Ian. 2012. 'Electoral behaviour in the 2010 Australian federal election'. In Marian Simms and John Wanna (eds), *Julia 2010: The Caretaker Election*, Canberra: ANU E-Press.

Bean, Clive, McAllister, Ian, Pietsch, Juliet and Gibson, Rachel. 2014. *Australian Election Study, 2013*. Canberra: The Australian Data Archive, The Australian National University.

Blake, Sarah. 2013, 'Policies on education a major battleground'. *Adelaide Advertiser,* 6 September.

Caro, Jane. 2013. 'Getting past Gonski: school equity beyond the election'. *The Conversation*, 5 September, viewed 13 January 2014: <theconversation.com/getting-past-gonski-school-equity-beyond-the-election-17467>.

Carswell, Andrew. 2013. 'NDISaster as Costs Soar'. *Daily Telegraph,* 5 August.

Commonwealth of Australia. 2009a. *A healthy future for all Australians*. Final Report of the National Health and Hospitals Reform Commission, Canberra, June.

Commonwealth of Australia. 2009b. *Australia: the healthiest country by 2020*. Report of the National Preventive Health Task Force, Canberra, 30 June.

Coorey, Phillip. 2013a. 'Abbott's $5.5bn baby bill'. *Australian Financial Review*, 19 August.

Coorey, Phillip. 2013b. 'Critics fear scheme cost blowouts'. *Australian Financial Review*, 21 August.

Coorey, Phillip and Daley, Gemma. 2013. 'Row over GST, parental leave'. *Australian Financial Review,* 8 August.

Coorey, Phillip and Heath, Joanna. 2013. 'Abbott dismisses criticism of paid parental leave'. *Australian Financial Review*, 6 May, viewed 14 February 2014: <www.afr.com/p/national/drop_abbott_paid_parental_leave_otoRi9yP6nej1pkwnHEfVJ>.

Downs, Anthony. 1972. 'Up and down with ecology: The issue attention cycle'. *Public Interest 28*(1): 38–50.

Duckett, Stephen. 2013. 'Bland is best? Bipartisan health platform left no room for policy'. *The Conversation*, 10 September, viewed 2 January 2014: <theconversation.com/bland-is-best-bipartisan-health-platform-left-no-room-for-policy-17881>.

Elshaug, Adam, Watt, Amber, Mundy, Linda and Willis, Cameron. 2012. 'Over 150 potentially low value health care practices: an Australian study'. *MJA* 197(10): 556–60.

Gray, Gwen, 2009. 'Health Policy'. In Dennis Woodward, Andrew Parkin and John Summers (eds), *Government, Politics, Power and Policy in Australia*, 9th edition, French's Forest, NSW: Pearson.

Gray Jamieson, Gwendolyn. 2012. *Reaching for Health, The Australian women's health movement and public policy*. Canberra: ANU E-Press.

Hickey, Ian. 2013. 'Mental health is largely missing from the election campaign'. *The Conversation*, 2 September, viewed 2 January 2014: <theconversation.com/mental-health-is-largely-missing-from-the-election-campaign-17684>.

Karvelas, Patricia. 2010. 'Tony Abbott signs contract on Work Choices but muddles message on workplace laws'. *The Australian*, 19 July, viewed 21 July 2014: <www.theaustralian.com.au/national-affairs/tony-abbott-signs-contract-on-work-choices-but-muddles-message-on-workplace-laws/story-fn59niix-1225893906267>.

Karvelas, Patricia. 2013a. 'Abbott delivers his baby'. *The Australian,* 21 August.

Karvelas, Patricia. 2013b. 'How Macklin took on the Left to transform indigenous policy'. *Weekend Australian*, 23–24 November, *Inquirer*: 15.

Karvelas, Patricia. 2013d. 'Change needs a conservative: Pearson'. *The Australian*, 26 August: 1.

Karvelas, Patricia. 2013e. 'Labor commits to new targets to help close indigenous gap'. *The Australian*, 9 August: 1.

Karvelas, Patricia and Kelly, Paul. 2013. 'Abbott to fund Pearson gap plan'. *The Australian*, 24 August: 1.

Keating, Jack. 2010. 'Education Policy and Social Inclusion'. In Alison McClelland and Paul Smyth (eds), *Social Policy in Australia: Understanding for Action*, 2nd edn, Melbourne: Oxford University Press.

Lewis, Jenny. 2010. 'Health Policy: Tackling the Gaps?' In Alison McClelland and Paul Smyth (eds), *Social Policy in Australia: Understanding for Action*, 2nd edn, Melbourne: Oxford University Press.

Manne, Robert, 2013. 'Lest we forget'. *The Monthly* 88: 10–4.

McAllister, Ian and Pietsch, Judith. 2011. *Trends in Australian political opinion: results from the Australian Election Study, 1987–2010*. Canberra: Australian National Institute for Public Policy and ANU College of Arts and Social Sciences.

Mitchell, Sue. 2013. 'Tax base can't support level of services'. *Australian Financial Review*, 24 August.

Pearson, Noel. 2013a. 'Recent indigenous policy failures can't be pinned on Aborigines'. *The Australian*, 15 June: 19.

Pearson, Noel. 2013b. 'Yes Minister, we're trapped in bureaucracy'. *The Australian*, 20 July: 19.

Productivity Commission. 2009. *Paid parental Leave: Support for Parents with Newborn Children*. Productivity Commission Inquiry report no. 47, February. Canberra: Australian Government.

Ray, Rebecca, Cornick, Janet and Schmitt, John. 2009. 'Parental Leave Policies in 21 Countries: Assessing Generosity and Gender Equality. Washington: Center for Economic and Policy Research.

Rothwell, Nicolas. 2013a. 'The great unmentionables of remote life'. *Weekend Australian*, 2–3 February, *Inquirer*: 18.

Rothwell, Nicolas. 2013b. 'Indigenous merry-go-round keeps spinning'. *The Australian*, 31 August: 21.

Rothwell, Nicolas. 2013c. 'Abbott's remote chance the best there is'. *Weekend Australian*, 12–13 October, Inquirer: 17.

Rudd, Kevin. 2013. 'Kevin Rudd's election campaign launch speech, full text'. *Guardian Australia*, 1 September, viewed 2 January 2014: <theguardian.com/world/2013/sep/01/kevin-rudd-launch-speech-text>.

Russell, Lesley. 2013. 'Health: the missing election debate'. *Inside Story*, 20 August, viewed 16 July 2014: <inside.org.au/health-the-missing-election-debate/>.

Shanahan, Dennis and Karvelas, Patricia. 2013. 'Abbott: my pledge to close the gap'. *The Australian*, 10 August: 1.

Shergold, Peter. 2013. 'The best of intentions, the worst of outcomes for indigenous people'. *The Australian*, 8 June: 19.

Steketee, Mike. 2013. 'How a decades-old proposal became a movement for change'. *Inside Story,* 22 October, viewed 15 December 2013: <inside.org.au/national-disability-insurance-scheme/>.

Strakosch, Elizabeth. 2013. 'Will Tony Abbott be a "prime minister for Aboriginal affairs"?'. *The Conversation,* 11 September, viewed 15 December 2013: <theconversation.com/will-tony-abbott-be-a-prime-minister-for-aboriginal-affairs-17985>.

Wanna, John. 2010. 'Business and Unions', in Special Issue: Kevin 07—the 2007 Australian Election, *Australian Cultural History*, Vol 28 (1), April: 15–22.

Watson, Louise and Liu, Charlotte. 2014. 'Mixed messages in the new politics of education'. In Chris Miller and Lionel Orchard (eds), *Australian Public Policy: Progressive Ideas in the Neoliberal Ascendency*, Bristol: Policy Press.

22. Gender and the 2013 Election: The Abbott 'mandate'

Kirsty McLaren and Marian Sawer

In the 2013 federal election, Tony Abbott was again wooing women voters with his relatively generous paid parental leave scheme and the constant sight of his wife and daughters on the campaign trail. Like Julia Gillard in 2010, Kevin Rudd was assuring voters that he was not someone to make an issue of gender and he failed to produce a women's policy. Despite these attempts to neutralise gender it continued to be an undercurrent in the election, in part because of the preceding replacement of Australia's first woman prime minister and in part because of campaigning around the gender implications of an Abbott victory.

To evaluate the role of gender in the 2013 election, we draw together evidence on the campaign, campaign policies, the participation of women, the discursive positioning of male leaders and unofficial gender-based campaigning. We also apply a new international model of the dimensions of male dominance in the old democracies and the stages through which such dominance is overcome. We argue that, though feminist campaigning was a feature of the campaign, traditional views on gender remain powerful. Raising issues of gender equality, as Julia Gillard did in the latter part of her prime ministership, is perceived as electorally damaging, particularly among blue-collar voters.

The prelude to the election

Gender received most attention in the run-up to the election in 2012–13 rather than during the campaign itself. Prime Minister Julia Gillard's famous misogyny speech of 2012 was prompted in immediate terms by the Leader of the Opposition drawing attention to sexism in what she perceived as a hypocritical way. He also enraged her by saying the Government should have 'died of shame', a phrase used about the recent death of her father. In broader terms, the speech appeared to be a delayed but passionate response to both sexism and the campaign of sexual vilification she had experienced. When she became Australia's first female prime minister, Gillard had studiously avoided reference to gender, claiming instead that it was a 'great day for redheads'. Her caution about drawing attention to gender issues was illustrated by the long delay in deploying Abbott's pronouncements on women. They had already been tested on focus groups under the Rudd Government and found to produce an 'intense reaction'. Rudd's advisor, Bruce Hawker, had been disappointed that when he sought to have them used in parliamentary debates: 'the response of many female ministers was to stand back' (Hawker 2013: 3). When Gillard eventually delivered her misogyny speech it was largely dismissed in Australian print media as 'playing the gender card' or engaging in a 'gender war', perhaps justifying her previous caution. The YouTube video of the speech went viral, however, and was watched by two million viewers within ten days (Sawer 2013: 114).

Since 2011 at least, when the 'Julia Gillard—worst PM in Australian History' Facebook page was created, Gillard had been the subject of obscene depictions in the social media as well as having cartoons of herself naked and wearing a dildo emailed to federal parliamentarians. This was in addition to the narratives being circulated by talkback radio hosts and by the Opposition depicting Gillard as a 'liar' ('Juliar') and as 'treacherous' for replacing an elected prime minister. The Opposition Leader famously spoke to carbon tax protesters in 2011 in front of banners reading 'Juliar … Bob Brown's Bitch' and 'Ditch the Witch'—an image often used to illustrate the Opposition's sexism and disrespect for the Prime Minister.

There were gendered overtones and double standards involved in both the 'Juliar' and 'treachery' narratives: the 'treachery' of her ousting of Kevin Rudd was judged more harshly because ambition is often regarded as at odds with feminine characteristics (see Hall and Donaghue 2013). The gendered nature of other violent and sexualised language being used to describe Gillard, including references to her genitals and menstruation, was even more explicit (Summers 2013). It was Gillard's misogyny speech, however, which sparked commentary in the media about a 'gender war'.

There was a marked disjuncture between the mainstream media response to the speech and the response of online communities and alternative outlets. Within the dominant narrative, which was also taken up by the Opposition, Gillard was responsible for beginning a gender war that then rebounded on her leadership. Women cabinet ministers who defended her were described by Opposition members as the 'handbag hit squad', suggesting it was illegitimate for senior ministers to openly discuss sexism in politics and confirming received wisdom that women in public life will be penalised for doing so (Johnson 2012). The media-constructed idea that any reference to gender inequality was divisive in the electorate was reflected in adverse opinion polls and, in particular, a loss of male support (*Vote Compass* 2013).

The gender war narrative stood in contrast to the narratives found on feminist blogs such as *Hoyden About Town* (www.hoydenabouttown.com) and in publications targeted at women, such as the *Sydney Morning Herald*'s 'Daily Life' site. There, Gillard's speech was covered as a continuation of debates about sexism in politics. Commentary was overwhelmingly positive and coverage was more extensive. A second peak in 'gender war' stories occurred after a 2013 speech at the launch of 'Women for Gillard', where the then Prime Minister again made reference to gender equality issues, including abortion and women's representation in government.[1] The same contrast in how the speech was framed—as an instrumental, political tactic in newspapers, and as a part of ongoing discussion of sexism and politics in online communities—was evident once more (Table 1).

Table 1: Media framing of and commentary on Gillard's sexism speeches of 9 October 2012, 11 June 2013

	Online communities*		Crossover publications*#		Newspapers#	
	Sexism/ gender frame	Political strategy frame	Sexism/ gender frame	Political strategy frame	Sexism/ gender frame	Political strategy frame
Positive	31	2	8	0	24	29
Neutral	2	0	1	0	5	24
Critical	4	2	2	5	25	120
Total	37	4	11	5	54	173

*fcollective, feminaust, 'Destroy the Joint' (Facebook), The Hoopla, Hoyden about Town, Mamamia.

*#'Daily Life' (*Sydney Morning Herald*), The Drum (ABC).

#*Australian, Courier-Mail, Daily Telegraph, Sydney Morning Herald*.

Sources: As indicated above.

As Gillard stated in her resignation speech after being defeated in the caucus ballot, gender did not explain everything about her prime ministership, but it explained some things. She ended this speech on an optimistic note: that it would be easier for the next woman and the woman after that. However there was nothing in her experience to suggest it would be any easier for a woman prime minister who raised issues of gender equality—on the contrary it might have 'become harder for the next feminist and the feminist after that' (comment by Fabrizio Napoleoni responding to Elam and Esmay 2013). To counter such an effect, *GetUp!* ran a campaign asking Australians to submit their own 'gender card' calling out sexism, and naming issues that affected women unfairly. Thousands responded. EMILY's List also circulated their own gender card to be handed out for sexist offenses—modelled on yellow and red penalty cards in football.

---

1 A former Labor Party staffer had been given a brief to set up 'Women for Gillard', funded by the New South Wales State Office of the ALP. There was no attempt to seek input from bodies such as EMILY's List, which was promoting the power of gender-based online campaigning, nor from the creators of the successful 'Destroy the Joint' Facebook and Twitter campaigns. It lacked credibility and gained no traction.

Beyond the issue of sexism that mired her prime ministership, Gillard's policy legacy remained highly contested. On the one hand, many commented on her failure to communicate the range of policy achievements her government successfully made in difficult circumstances; on the other hand, there was much criticism of specific policies such as moving sole parents onto the inadequate NewStart allowance. The Victorian Women's Trust, while disagreeing with her sole parent and asylum seeker policies, took out full-page newspaper advertisements in July 2013 under the heading 'Credit Where Credit Is Due' to draw attention to the record legislative achievements of the Gillard Government.[2] Her supposedly dysfunctional government had seen 561 pieces of legislation through to royal assent, considerably more than the Rudd Government (Singleton 2014: 45).

A week after his overthrow of Australia's first woman prime minister, Kevin Rudd announced a new cabinet, with an unprecedented number of women (six out of 20). When asked if this was to stem a possible backlash from women voters he pointed to his previous record of appointing women but also said, in what was clearly intended as a critique of Gillard: 'I'm not one to make an issue of gender. I don't see things through the prism of gender, I never have, never will' (Rudd 2013). This commitment to avoid gender issues was carried into the 2013 Labor election campaign, which did not include a women's policy or any gender equality commitments apart from a token gesture in the campaign launch speech: 'We want an inclusive Australia where there is no discrimination on the basis of your race, your gender or your sexuality.'

The retreat from commitments to women in key election policy speeches has been evident at both state and national levels since the 1990s. This trend is also apparent in other democracies, although it is sometimes balanced by a desire to depict gender equality as a core national value to be contrasted with the values of Muslim immigrants (Dahlerup and Leyenaar 2013).

The campaign

Official campaigning was characterised by a contradiction: there was a studied evasion of the topic of gender by the major parties, yet campaigning was strongly gendered. Examining media coverage shows how consistently both leaders were striving to project themselves as masculine leaders. Beyond this

---

2 After the election was over, sold-out tribute events were organised by Anne Summers and the Victorian Women's Trust in venues such as the Sydney Opera House and the Melbourne Town Hall. Again thousands expressed their determination that the achievements of Julia Gillard's prime ministership not be written out of history nor her resilience in the face of three 'leaders of the opposition': Tony Abbott, the Murdoch press and—on her own side of politics—Kevin Rudd.

tacit competition, less powerful political actors attempted to raise gender issues, and especially women's interests, but had limited success. As such, the election saw the 'blokiness' of Australian political discourses reassert itself.

As we have already discussed, the major political actors made little mention of gender during the campaign. Instead, both Tony Abbott and Kevin Rudd presented themselves as men of action and as family men. For Tony Abbott, the emphasis on his wife and daughters—and even Peta Credlin, his chief of staff—was not new. Abbott and Coalition politicians have for years referred to the women in his life as evidence that Abbott has no 'problem with women'. This 'problem' with women was partly a reference to a gender gap in Abbott's approval ratings (see, for instance, Sawer 2012). It was also a reference to Abbott's many comments indicating a belief in traditional gender roles.

Tony Abbott's views on women were kept alive as an issue by feminist and progressive campaigning online. Yet this was also a consequence of Abbott's own comments: most notably he referred to the 'sex appeal' of candidate Fiona Scott as a reason to vote for her. Then, in a video message to the Big Brother house, he referred to the sex appeal of his own daughters: 'If you want to know who to vote for, I'm the guy with the not bad-looking daughters' (Badham 2013). There were a series of other sexist comments, which the Abbott campaign framed as 'daggy dad' moments. Thus, Abbott's family allowed him to emphasise his paternal role, and diminish perceptions of a more aggressive masculinity. This image of a 'fatherly and husbandly protective masculinity' was well rehearsed and strategic: it had allowed Abbott to draw flattering contrasts between himself and both Gillard and Rudd (Johnson 2013: 22).

Rudd, too, used his family members in his campaign, with his daughter Jessica taking an active role. Like Abbott, Rudd sought to project an image of strong and active leadership. Though Abbott used his sporting pursuits to do this, Rudd relied on seeming busy, decisive and efficient. Both leaders thus used masculinity in their attempts to appear relatable and personable.

Campaign policies

As already noted, the Labor Government did not take a women's policy into the election. For its part, the Coalition did release a women's policy, albeit only two days before the election and with its only spending commitment being $1 million additional funding for the White Ribbon Campaign, a men's campaign against gender-based violence. However the first item of the policy did indicate that the Coalition Spokeswoman on Women, Senator Michaelia Cash, had been listening to the concerns of the Women's Alliances. The Alliances are the peak bodies funded since 2010 to represent to government the views of different sectors of women, including rural, immigrant and Indigenous women, as well as to represent the views of advocacy coalitions around issues of equal rights, economic security and violence against women. They received a renewal of their triennial operational funding in 2013. The Alliances, like preceding women's advocacy coalitions, had been pressing for the return of the Office for Women to Prime Minister and Cabinet from its exile in the line department of Family and Housing, Community Services and Indigenous Affairs, 20 kilometres away from the heart of government.

As the Coalition policy stated, location in the Family and Community Services portfolio had implied that the women's portfolio was a welfare concern rather than underpinning a whole-of-government approach to improving government outcomes for women. Within a month the Office had moved back to Prime Minister and Cabinet from where it had been exiled since the Howard Government moved it out in 2004, a move that had not been countermanded by the Rudd or Gillard governments. Its previous exile had come under the Fraser Government and had lasted from 1977 to 1983 when its return had been a high point of the Hawke Government's women's policy. The 2013 Coalition women's policy was the first time since 1983 that a commitment relating to the actual structure of government had been a lead feature of women's policy. The return of the portfolio to Prime Minister and Cabinet was of satisfaction both to advocates and bureaucrats, providing much more timely access to Cabinet proposals for the purpose of advice on gender impacts. It also provided a stronger base for the Interdepartmental Committee on Women, responsible for a whole-of-government approach to improving gender outcomes. The Women's Safety Branch remained in the renamed Department of Social Services along with the National Plan for Reducing Violence against Women and Children and related functions. The potential gain from the return of women's policy to the heart of government was offset by the abolition in December 2013 of the last vestige of women's policy machinery within the framework for intergovernmental decision-making—the COAG Select Council on Women's Issues.

Moreover, the return of women's policy to Prime Minister and Cabinet received a very mixed reception thanks to Tony Abbott's misogynist reputation (Harris Rimmer 2013). The 'Destroy the Joint' movement helped spread the word through Facebook and Twitter that the Prime Minister was now 'Minister for Women' and an electronic petition stating that this was unacceptable promptly gathered 10,000 signatures. EMILY's List used its new social media capability to create a meme: 'The new Minister for the Status of Women in his own words…'. It had 200,000 views and was doubtless shared with many more.

This reputation meant that the Coalition's paid parental leave policy—first unveiled before the 2010 election—was received somewhat cynically in the media as an attempt to repair Abbott's sexist image (e.g. McGuirk 2013). However it was well received by a number of women's advocacy groups including the Women's Electoral Lobby (WEL), which surveyed the parties on key policy areas (WEL 2013). The Coalition policy was more generous than the scheme introduced by the Labor Government in 2011, providing for 26 weeks of leave (rather than 18 weeks); income replacement rather than the minimum wage, up to a cap of $75,000 over the six months; and a superannuation component. It was subject to criticism on a number of grounds, including expense and policy details, but most notably from the Nationals who saw it as discriminating against homemakers.

Both major parties received low ratings from WEL on support for sole parents, despite some minor improvements made by the Labor Government after an outcry over the shift of sole parents onto NewStart. The Coalition did particularly badly on the equal pay issue. Labor had both supported and funded the equal pay increases for community service workers and also committed $6 million over four years in the 2013–14 Budget to the Pay Equity Unit in Fair Work Australia. The Coalition, on the other hand, had supported neither the equal pay increases nor the Pay Equity Unit.

Furthermore, in relation to pay equity, the Coalition made it clear in their childcare policy (released on the same day as their women's policy) that they would be making no new payments from the Labor Government's Early Years Quality Fund, established in June. This fund was to raise the pay of childcare workers for two years, until an equal remuneration decision could be handed down by Fair Work Australia. Early childhood educators were earning only $19.00 an hour. After the election the Government wrote to childcare providers, saying that if they had not already implemented the wage increases the offer of funding was 'hereby revoked'. More broadly, the Coalition commitment to cuts in public sector expenditure inevitably carried with it a disproportionate impact on women, due to female employment patterns in public sector and community service employment.

One area to which the new Minister Assisting the Prime Minister for Women, Senator Michaelia Cash, appeared committed was the National Action Plan on Women, Peace and Security, adopted in 2012 as part of the implementation of Security Council Resolution 1325 on women in conflict and conflict resolution. Although somewhat slow to develop its national action plan (the 36th country to do so), Australia's bid for Security Council membership supplied some momentum. Senator Cash enthusiastically launched the first annual civil society report card on the plan (prepared with funding from the Office for Women and the Australian Civil/Military Centre) and called on women's advocacy organisations to continue holding government to account. Julie Bishop, as the new Foreign

Affairs Minister, also highlighted issues of sexual violence in conflict and the crucial part women play in peacekeeping and peacebuilding, notably in her first speech to the UN General Assembly.

Even the Australian Greens, who had succeeded the Australian Democrats in the role of championing gender equality, were relatively muted in 2013. The section on women in their election policy did point out that Labor had put the political promise of a surplus above the wellbeing of single parents while the Coalition was intending to cut health, education and welfare spending affecting the most vulnerable. One commitment clearly directed against an incoming Coalition Government and any repeat of Howard-era policies was to 'maintain Australian foreign aid programs that support women's reproductive health'. The Greens platform (and that of the Australian Sex Party) also included strong support for women's right to choose abortion. The other micro-parties, especially those on the right of the political spectrum, generally paid little attention to gender. However, it is important to note that the Family First Party, which has socially conservative views on issues such as abortion and believed that Labor's parental leave scheme discriminated against stay-at-home mothers, won a Senate spot in South Australia.

Contenders and representation

In terms of the parliamentary presence of women, the election brought little change. Overall the entry of women into Australian parliaments plateaued around 2005 (see Figure 1). This is similar to the stalling effect noted in other Westminster countries such as Canada (Trimble *et al*. 2013) and has contributed to Australia's slide down the international league table of the representation of women in national parliaments. Australia dropped from 15th place in 1999 to 49th place by 1 May 2014, with 52 countries ranked above it (IPU 2014). Coalition victories contributed to a halt in progress, while only repeated media interventions by EMILY's List prevented the Labor Party from falling further below its own quota. By July 2014 women constituted 21 per cent of Coalition parliamentarians around Australia compared with 43 per cent of Labor parliamentarians.

This standstill in progress deserves further discussion: to what extent have women overcome men's dominance of politics in Australia? A major comparative study published in 2013 provides an especially helpful way of conceptualising such dominance. Drawing together case studies of 'old' democracies, Drude Dahlerup and Monique Leyenaar developed a model that included six dimensions of politics: the numbers of women in politics; politics as a workplace; vertical and also horizontal sex segregation of roles; discourses about women in politics; and public policy which takes account of gender issues (Table 2).

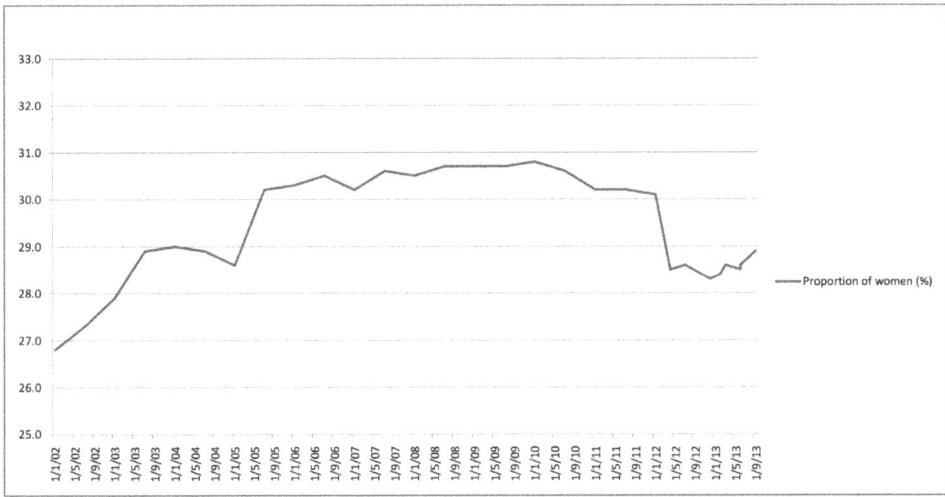

Figure 1: Women as a percentage of MPs across Australia since 2002

Source: Parliamentary Library.

Table 2: Multidimensional model of male dominance/gender balance in politics

Dimensions	Male dominance	Gender balance
1. Representation	Women's numerical underrepresentation	A continuous 40–60 per cent representation for either sex
2. Politics as workplace	Male-coded norms and practices	Gender-neutral codes and family-friendly practices; crèches
3. Vertical sex segregation	Unequal gender distribution in political hierarchies	Leadership positions shared equally (40–60 per cent)
4. Horizontal sex segregation	Limited access of women to full range of portfolios and committees	Portfolios assigned without gender bias but according to expertise and interest
5. Discourse and framing	Gendered perceptions of politicians	Dominating discourse that gender balance is normal and required for democracy
6. Public policy	Policies biased in favour of men. No concern for gender equality	Gender mainstreaming, i.e. action taken to ensure policies reflect needs of both sexes and promote gender equality

Source: Adapted from Dahlerup and Leyenaar (2012: 8, 302).

Within the first dimension of the Dahlerup/Leyenaar model, the parliamentary representation of women, four stages of progress towards gender equality were identified. Australia sits within the third of these four stages—in other words progress has stalled before gender balance has been achieved and while women still make up less than a third of parliamentarians. In terms of parliament as a workplace, progress has also been slow, with the first (small) childcare centre in an Australian parliament only opened in 2009 and with babies and toddlers still being regarded in Standing Orders as 'strangers in the house' (Holland 2003; Rodrigues 2009).

Turning to vertical and horizontal segregation, the 21st century has seen some improvement, with an increased number of women serving as heads of government—for the first time at the federal level as well as in New South Wales, Queensland, Tasmania and for the third time in the Australian Capital Territory. Women have also been moving into non-traditional portfolio areas, such as Julie Bishop as both Foreign Affairs Minister in the Abbott Government and Deputy Leader of the Liberal Party, Tanya Plibersek as Shadow Foreign Affairs Minister as well as Deputy Leader of the Opposition, and Senator Penny Wong as Shadow Minister for Trade and Investment as well as Opposition Leader in the Senate. However other women in the Abbott ministry were allocated more traditional 'nurturing' portfolios such as Assistant Minister for Health (Fiona Nash), Assistant Minister for Education (Sussan Ley) and Minister for Human Services (Marise Payne). Where progress has been limited, as illustrated during the Gillard prime ministership, is in discourse around women in politics and in substantive policies directed towards gender equality.

Looking more closely at gender and partisan effects, as in previous elections the Greens had the largest proportion of women candidates (46 per cent), followed by the Labor Party (33 per cent) and then the Coalition parties (21 per cent) (AEC 2013). While the number of Coalition women in the House of Representatives went up by four, their presence in the Coalition parliamentary parties continued to be much lower than the proportion of women within the parliamentary Labor Party (Tables 3 and 4; Figure 2). The continuing failure of the Coalition parties to field a significant number of women candidates has meant that incoming Coalition governments have an inadequate pool of women to draw on for frontbench positions. This has resulted in significant falls in the representation of women in government following recent Coalition victories, most dramatically in Western Australia and Queensland, but also in New South Wales. Because the pool of eligible candidates for appointment to ministerial positions consists of members of the government party or parties, the highly uneven representation of women across parliamentary parties creates a real problem for maintaining women's presence in the executive (Curtin and Sawer 2011: 50). In the United Kingdom, for example, this uneven representation has contributed to Conservative Prime Minister David Cameron's 'woman problem'—a problem worsened by the effects the Cameron Government's public sector cuts have had on women.

Table 3: Gender breakdown of the House of Representatives after the 2013 election

Party	Male	Female	Female (%)
ALP	35	20	36.4
Liberals/LNP/CLP*	58	17	22.6
Nationals/LNP*	14	1	6.6
Independents	1	1	50.0
Greens	1	0	0.0
Palmer United Party	1	0	0.0
Katter's Australia Party	1	0	0.0
Total	111	39	26.0

*MPs allocated according to their party room.

Source: Parliamentary Library.

Table 4: Gender breakdown of the Senate, 1 July 2014

Party	Male	Female	Female (%)
Greens	3	7	66.7
ALP	11	14	56.0
Nationals/CLP*	4	2	33.3
Liberals	22	5	18.5
Other	7	1	12.5
Total	47	29	38.2

*Senators allocated according to their party room.

Source: Parliamentary Library.

There was a great deal of critical commentary on the absence of women from the new Abbott cabinet, where the only woman is Foreign Minister Julie Bishop (Table 5). Media stories adversely compared Australia to many countries including Afghanistan and were perhaps best summed up in the headline 'Is this what Abbott means by having a "mandate"?' (Kenny 2013). The extensive media criticism was reflected in the polls, although with a gender and partisan inflection. Essential Research found 51 per cent of women (but only 39 per cent of men) were concerned that there was only one woman in cabinet; 90 per cent of Greens voters were concerned, compared with 67 per cent of Labor voters and only 17 per cent of Liberal voters (Bowe 2013). Abbott's remark that he was 'very disappointed there are not a lot more women in cabinet'—an oddly passive way to describe his own decision—helped earn him the Clinton Award for Repeat offenders at the 2013 Ernies Awards for sexist remarks.

Despite his 'disappointment', implying that there was no way to appoint more women, Abbott claimed that there were many women 'knocking on the door' and this led to some public discussion about whether the door was really open on the conservative side of politics. Outgoing Liberal parliamentarians such as Judi Moylan, Senator Sue Boyce and former Senator Judith Troeth (who had advocated quotas for the Party in 2010) cited structural and cultural problems within the Party. Boyce went so far as to describe the cabinet composition as 'shocking' and 'embarrassing' (Crowe 2013). Interestingly, one potential ministerial candidate, Bronwyn Bishop, was instead nominated to be Speaker of the House of Representatives. This continued a pattern whereby new Coalition governments in New South Wales and Queensland also compensated for shortfalls in their cabinets by appointing women as Speakers.

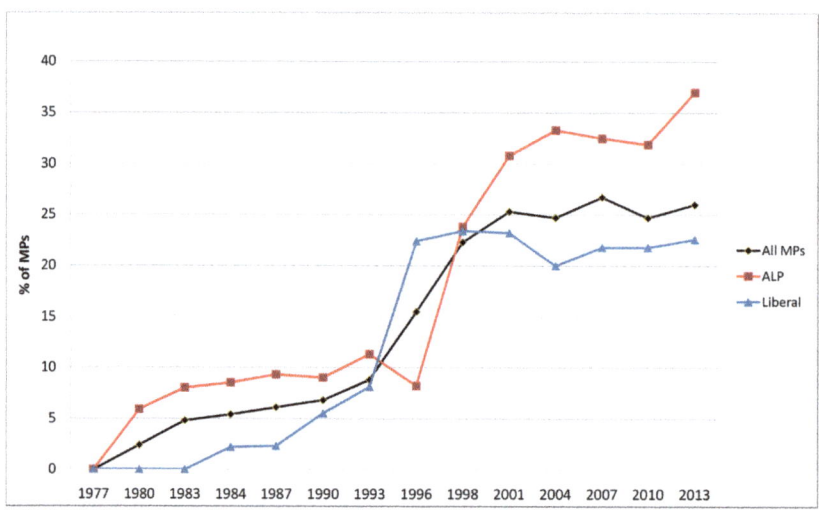

Figure 2: Women as a percentage of parliamentary parties and of all MPs, House of Representatives, 1977–2003

Source: Parliamentary Library.

While it seemed a great leap backward for there to be only one woman in cabinet, the picture was somewhat more gender balanced on the other side of the chamber (Table 5). There was a greater pool of women to draw from in the parliamentary Labor Party and the representation of women in the shadow ministry almost mirrored their representation in caucus. It was notable, however, that most of the women in caucus and in the shadow ministry (eight out of 11) were from the Left faction. These included Tanya Plibersek who, as we have seen, became Deputy Leader and Senator Penny Wong who continued as Labor Leader in the Senate.

Table 5: Gender breakdown of the Abbott ministry and the opposition shadow ministry, September 2013

Ministry category	Male	Female	Female (%)
Cabinet	18	1	5.3
Whole ministry	25	5	16.6
Parliamentary secretaries	11	1	8.3
Shadow Cabinet	14	5	26.3
Shadow ministry	19	11	36.7
Shadow parliamentary secretaries	7	8	53.3

Source: *Parliamentary Handbook, 44th Parliament of Australia.*

Conclusion

Julia Gillard's prime ministership led to increased visibility of sexism in politics, and also brought to light considerable unease about the way in which that sexism was discussed. Although Gillard was removed from the leadership, this unease continued to influence the 2013 election. Notably, the campaign tactics of both major leaders placed significant value on masculinity. To what extent, then, does Australian federal politics remain strongly masculine, as measured against the Dahlerup/Leyenaar typology of masculine dominance?

Despite an increase in women reaching leadership positions such as head of government or presiding officer of parliament, the entry of women into Australian politics has stalled since 2005. Even raising this issue has been construed as divisive and, as we have seen, the major parties have difficulty in articulating an overarching commitment to gender equality, at least for domestic purposes. High profile women's policies are no longer taken to elections. There remains, moreover, an undercurrent of sexism in political discourse. The machismo of both Abbott's and Rudd's campaigning indicates a widespread assumption that leadership requires the attributes of traditional masculinity. The 2013 election saw many political actors protesting that gender—that is, gender inequality—is not a significant issue. Campaign tactics, however, continued to suggest otherwise.

References

Australian Electoral Commission (AEC). 2013. 'House of Representatives Nominations by Gender'. Viewed 1 April 2014: <results.aec.gov.au/17496/Website/HouseNominationsByGender-17496.htm>.

Badham, Van. 2013. 'Tony Abbott's daughters: Are women just ornaments?' *Guardian Australia*, 4 September, viewed 16 January 2014: <www.theguardian.com/commentisfree/2013/sep/04/tony-abbott-daughters-big-brother>.

Bowe, William. 2013. 'Morgan and Essential polls'. *Crikey!* 24 September.

Crowe, David. 2013. 'Liberals "despair" at jobs for the boys'. *The Australian*, 17 September.

Curtin, Jennifer and Sawer, Marian. 2011. 'Oceania'. In Gretchen Bauer and Manon Tremblay (eds), *Women in Executive Power: A Global Overview*, London: Routledge.

Dahlerup, Drude and Leyenaar, Monique (eds). 2013. *Breaking Male Dominance in Old Democracies*. Oxford: Oxford University Press.

Elam, Paul and Esmay, Dean. 2013. 'Julia Gillard, feminist hatemonger: You're fired!!' *A Voice for Men*, 26 June, viewed 16 January 2014: <www.avoiceformen.com/feminism/julia-gillard-feminist-hatemoger-youre-fired/>.

Hall, Lauren J and Donaghue, Ngaire. 2012. '"Nice girls don't carry knives": Constructions of ambition in media coverage of Australia's first female prime minister'. *British Journal of Social Psychology* 52(4): 631–47.

Harris Rimmer, Susan. 2013. 'The distortion of Abbott's "women problem"'. *Public Sector Informant*, October: 4.

Hawker, Bruce. 2013. *The Rudd Rebellion: The campaign to save Labor*. Melbourne: Melbourne University Press.

Holland, Ian. 2003. 'Strangers! Non-Members in the Parliamentary Chamber'. Parliamentary Library Current Issues Brief, 15 April. Canberra: Parliament of Australia.

Inter-Parliamentary Union (IPU). 2013. 'Women in National Parliaments: World Classification'. Viewed 16 January 2014: <www.ipu.org/wmn-e/classif.htm>.

Johnson, Carol. 2012. 'Tony Abbott and women: How both sides have played the gender card'. *The Conversation*, 8 October, viewed 16 January 2014: <theconversation.edu.au/tony-abbott-and-women-how-both-sides-have-played-the-gender-card-10019>.

Johnson, Carol. 2013. 'From Obama to Abbott: Gender identity and the politics of emotion'. *Australian Feminist Studies* 28(75): 14–29.

Kenny, Mark. 2013. 'Is this what Abbott means by having a "mandate"?' *The Sydney Morning Herald*, 17 September.

McGuirk, Rod. 2013. 'Australian opposition leader fights sexist image with generous parental leave policy'. *Associated Press Online*, 21 August.

Rodrigues, Mark. 2009. *'Children in the Parliamentary Chambers, Parliamentary Library Research Paper*. Canberra: Parliament of Australia, 19 November.

Rudd, Kevin. 2013. 'Response to question at media conference'. *SBS News*, 1 July.

Saville, Margot. 2013. 'Brough, Jones, Riewoldt, Albrechtsen: our most sexist crowned'. *Crikey!* 10 October.

Sawer, Marian. 2012. 'Managing gender: The 2010 federal election'. In Marian Simms and John Wanna (eds), *Julia 2010: The caretaker election*. Canberra: ANU E-Press.

Sawer, Marian. 2013. 'Misogyny and misrepresentation: Women in Australian parliaments'. *Political Science* 65(1): 105–17.

Singleton, Gwynneth. 2014. 'The Legislative Record of a "Hung" Parliament'. In Chris Aulich (ed.), *The Gillard Governments*. Melbourne: Melbourne University Press.

Summers, Anne. 2013. *The Misogyny Factor*. Sydney: NewSouth Publishing.

Trimble, Linda, Jane Arscott and Manon Tremblay (eds). 2013. *Stalled: The Representation of Women in Canadian Governments*. Vancouver: UBC Press.

Vote Compass. 2013. 'Rudd vs Gillard, according to gender'. *ABC News*, 15 August, viewed 16 January 2014: <www.abc.net.au/news/2013-08-15/vote-compass-analysis-kevin-rudd-julia-gillard-gender/4890086>.

Women's Electoral Lobby (WEL). 2013. 'Federal Election Scorecard'. Viewed 16 January 2014: <wel.org.au/election-2013>.

Part 6. The Results

23. Explaining the Results

Antony Green

Labor came to office in 2007 with its strongest hold on government in the nation's history—it was, for the first time, in office nationally and in every state and territory. Six years later Labor left national office with its lowest first preference vote in a century. For only the third time since the First World War, a governing party failed to win a third term in office. From a clean sweep of governments in 2007, by mid-2014 Labor's last bastions were minority governments in South Australia and the Australian Capital Territory.[1]

Based on the national two-party-preferred vote, Labor's 2013 result was less disastrous than previous post-war lows in 1966, 1975, 1977 and 1996. Labor also bettered those four elections on the proportion of House seats won. The two-party-preferred swing of 3.6 percentage points was also small for a change of government election, equal to the swing that defeated the Fraser Government in 1983 but smaller than those suffered by Whitlam in 1975, Keating in 1996 and Howard in 2007. Even over two elections from 2007 to 2013, the two-party-preferred swing of 6.2 percentage points was below that suffered by Labor previously over two elections (1961–66 and 1972–75), and smaller than the swing against the Coalition between 1977 and 1983. By the measure of first preference vote share, the 2013 election was a dreadful result for Labor, its lowest vote share since 1904.[2] Labor's vote share slid from 43.4 per cent in 2007 to 38.0 per cent in 2010 and 33.4 per cent in 2013.

Despite success at the 2013 election, the Liberal and National party coalition was not the major vote beneficiary of Labor's decline. The Coalition's vote share rose from 42.1 per cent in 2007 to 45.6 per cent in 2013, attracting only a third of the fall in Labor's vote share over two elections. The most notable feature of the 2013 election was the surge in support for third parties and independents, on top of Green support that remained stable over two elections. In both the House and Senate, support for non-major party candidates rose to levels never previously recorded at an Australian national election.

With a disastrous decline in its first preference vote, the Labor Party only remained competitive at the 2010 and 2013 elections through strong preference flows from an enlarged pool of votes from electors who first voted for third

---

1 Unless otherwise noted, the historical comparisons in this chapter have been calculated from the tables of historic federal election results in Barber (2011).
2 The federal Labor Party polled 27.1 per cent of the vote at the 1931 election, but Labor's overall vote that year was 37.7 per cent if the breakaway New South Wales Lang Labor Party is included in the Labor total.

parties and independents. Concentrating on the two-party-preferred result overlooks the long-term impact of a low first preference vote on the Labor Party and the competitiveness of the Australian party system.

State of the House

The 2013 election was fought on largely unchanged boundaries with only minor redistributions taking place in Victoria and South Australia to bring enrolments back within permitted variation. No electorate changed notional party status based on the new boundaries, and no by-elections were held in the life of the 43rd parliament. Twenty-five House members retired at the 2013 election compared to 20 in 2010 and 21 in 2007. Thirteen Labor and 10 Coalition members retired, as well as the two independents who put the Gillard Government back into office in 2010, Tony Windsor and Rob Oakeshott. Eight of the Coalition's retirees had long careers as backbench members and were older than Labor's oldest retiree, 64-year-old former leader Simon Crean. Of Labor's 13 retirements, nine had been cabinet ministers within the previous 12 months,[3] a bitter harvest of Labor's leadership battles.

Oakeshott's and Windsor's decisions to retire gifted their seats to the Coalition. Effectively Labor went into the election with 72 seats to the Coalition's 75. The Coalition needed a net gain of one seat for majority government; Labor needed a net gain of four seats in an electoral climate where polls in several keys states indicated Labor was certain to lose seats.

After the election there were 37 new parliamentarians in the House of Representatives, including two former members returning[4] and three senators transferring from the other chamber.[5] Seventeen members were defeated: 14 Labor, one Liberal and the two party members who had moved to the crossbenches, Craig Thomson and Peter Slipper.[6] The only Liberal member defeated was frontbencher Sophie Mirabella, who lost her Victorian seat of Indi to independent Cathy McGowan. The Liberal Party lost the Queensland seat of Fairfax to Clive Palmer but regained O'Connor from the Nationals.

---

3   The nine were Greg Combet, Simon Crean, Craig Emerson, Martin Ferguson, Peter Garrett, Julia Gillard, Robert McClelland, Nicola Roxon and Stephen Smith.
4   Former Howard Government minister Mal Brough in Fisher and Liberal Jason Wood winning back his seat of La Trobe.
5   Labor's David Feeney and Matt Thistlethwaite and Nationals Deputy Leader Barnaby Joyce, who won Tony Windsor's former seat of New England. Joyce became only the sixth federal member to represent two states, the first in six decades, and the first to do so representing two states in different chambers, having been a Queensland Senator since 2005.
6   Both Thomson and Slipper fell short of the 4 per cent barrier required to recover deposits and receive election funding. Slipper recorded 1.6 per cent, possibly the lowest vote ever for a sitting member. Both members left parliament facing criminal charges.

Parties and candidates

Political parties have been central to Australian politics since Federation, but it was not until 1984 that parties were registered and party names appeared on ballot papers. Julia Gillard's January announcement of a September election established a generous timetable for new party registration, and in the two months before the register was closed by the issue of writs, 19 new parties had registered. This was an increase of around 50 per cent since January and meant a record number of parties were registered and able to contest the 2013 election, as shown in Table 1.

Table 1: Number of registered parties at Australian elections 1984–2013

Election	Number registered	Contesting House	Contesting Senate
1984	18	11	13
1987	23	12	16
1990	32	22	20
1993	27	16	22
1996	28	18	23
1998	41	25	30
2001	38	22	29
2004	34	26	30
2007	27	19	26
2010	25	22	25
2013	54	34	51

Source: Compiled from party registration data on AEC website and from past election results. Separate state Green parties at elections before 2001 have been counted as a single party.

A total of 1,188 candidates were nominated for the 150 House contests, more than the previous record of 1,109 candidates for 148 seats in 1998. This was an increase from 859 House candidates in 2010, much of this due to new parties. The newly formed Palmer United Party contested all 150 electorates, Katter's Australia Party 63 and the Rise Up Australia Party 77.

The increase in Senate candidates was more dramatic, a total of 529 candidates nominating, well up on the previous record of 367 in 2007. Record numbers of candidates contested every state. The New South Wales Senate ballot paper had 110 candidates and 45 columns on a ballot paper one metre wide, with column widths reduced to two centimetres and font size to six points. In the larger states the AEC made magnifying sheets available to assist voters in reading their ballot papers. Between 1949 and 1987 more than half of House electorates had been contested by four or fewer candidates, whereas in 2013 more than half had eight or more and a general election record of 16 candidates contested Melbourne. Table 2 shows the average number of candidates per vacancy at House and Senate elections since 1974.

Table 2: Average number of candidates per vacancy, Australian elections 1974–2013

Election	House	Senate	Election	House	Senate
1974	3.9	4.1	1993	6.4	6.7
1975	3.8	4.2	1996	6.1	6.4
1977	4.1	4.4	1998	7.5	8.2
1980	4.0	5.4	2001	6.9	7.1
1983	4.2	3.8	2004	7.3	8.3
1984	4.2	4.4	2007	7.0	9.2
1987	4.1	3.4	2010	5.7	8.7
1990	5.3	5.6	2013	7.9	13.2

Source: Calculated from published Australian Electoral Commission statistics.

Full preferential voting for House elections requires that all squares on the ballot paper be correctly numbered. Past research has shown that the rate of informal voting increases with the number of candidates, rates of informal voting also being higher in electorates with high concentrations of voters born overseas and speaking a language other than English at home. Confusion also arises with the '1' only ticket voting option allowed on Senate ballot papers, and with the use of optional preferential voting for state elections in New South Wales and Queensland (Australian Electoral Commission 2011).

Informal voting in the House of Representatives rose from 5.5 per cent in 2010 to 5.9 per cent in 2013, with New South Wales recording the highest rate at 7.6 per cent as well as the largest increase. Research on the 2013 informal vote is not yet available, but its geographic pattern was similar to that recorded in 2010, being highest in high migrant and non-English speaking parts of western Sydney, above 13 per cent in the electorates of Blaxland, Chifley, Fowler and Watson, and passing 20 per cent in individual polling places.

Two-party-preferred results and swings

The Coalition won the 2013 election with 53.5 per cent of the national two-party-preferred vote, an overall swing of 3.6 percentage points with all states and territories swinging to the Coalition. The Coalition recorded two-party-preferred majorities in four states and the Northern Territory, Labor the majority party in the Australian Capital Territory, Victoria and Tasmania.

23. Explaining the Results

The historic scale of the Coalition victory varied. In Victoria, Queensland and South Australia, the Coalition's two-party-preferred vote was down on John Howard's final victory in 2004. The Coalition recorded its highest two-party-preferred vote in Tasmania since 1990, in Western Australia since 1977, and New South Wales since the 1966 landslide. The Labor Party recorded its lowest proportion of seats in New South Wales since 1934.

The Coalition gained 17 seats from Labor as differential state swings delivered five seats more than would have been expected with a uniform national swing. The Nationals gained Lyne and New England from their retiring independent MPs, the Liberal Party lost Fairfax to the Palmer United Party and Indi to an independent, but gained O'Connor from the National Party. Of the 150 electorates, 137 recorded swings to the Coalition. Figure 1 shows the average swing in each state, the variance of the swing as well as swing outlier electorates in each state.

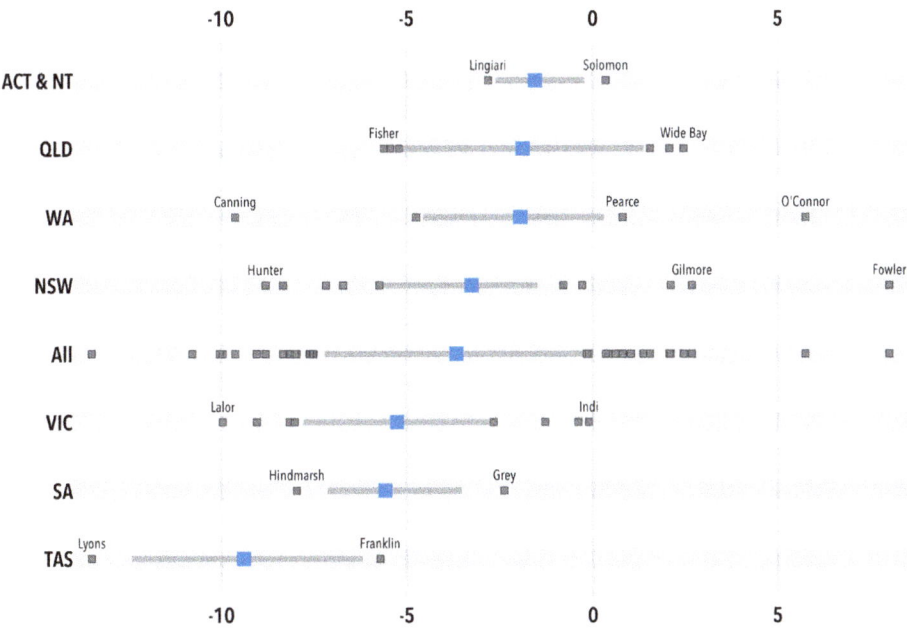

Figure 1: Average swing, swing variance and swing outlier electorates by state

Note: Lines cover 10th to 90th percentiles; blue squares are means.

Source: Data from the Australian Electoral Commission; computed and graphed by Simon Jackman.

The election's three largest swings were in Tasmania, where an unpopular state Labor Government helped deliver Lyons (margin 12.3, swing 13.5), Braddon (margin 7.5, swing 10.0), and Bass (margin 6.7, swing 10.8) to the Liberal Party. Of the 13 seats that swung to Labor, seven were in Queensland, a state where the return of Kevin Rudd and the rise of the Palmer United Party may have combined to ameliorate the swing predicted by polling earlier in the year. Labor lost only one seat in South Australia and three in Victoria despite state-wide swings of more than 5 percentage points.

In 2010 Labor had won a majority of New South Wales seats with a minority of the two-party-preferred vote. The 2013 results corrected the ledger, with the Coalition gaining 10 seats, eight from Labor plus the former independent seats of Lyne and New England. Despite predictions of a dire Labor result in western Sydney, only the bellwether electorate of Lindsay was lost, while Greenway was retained with a swing towards Labor thanks to the problems of the hapless Liberal candidate Jaymes Diaz. Labor lost the inner Sydney seats of Banks and Reid for the first time ever, and Barton for the first time since 1983.

The divergence from any uniform swing is explained by the overall pattern of state swings. As shown in Table 3, the swings against Labor in 2013 were *largest* in the states that had swung *to* Labor in 2010, and *smallest* in the states where there had been large anti-Labor swings in 2010.

Table 3: Two-party-preferred swings by state 2007–13

Category	Swing 2007–10	Swing 2010–13	Swing 2007–13
NSW	-4.9	-3.2	-8.1
Vic	+1.0	-5.1	-4.1
Qld	-5.5	-1.9	-7.4
WA	-3.1	-1.9	-5.0
SA	+0.8	-5.6	-4.8
Tas	+4.4	-9.4	-5.0
ACT	-1.7	-1.8	-3.5
NT	-4.7	-1.0	-5.7
National	-2.6	-3.6	-6.2
Range of swings	9.9	8.4	4.6

Note: '+' indicates a swing to Labor, '-' a swing away from Labor and to the Coalition.

Source: Calculated from published Australian Electoral Commission statistics.

The final row of Table 3 shows the range of state swings at the 2010 and 2013 elections, much larger than recorded at recent elections, 5.5 percentage points in 2007, 3.6 in 2004, 3.2 in 2001 and 3.9 in 1998. The smaller range of swings over two elections in the final column points to Labor's defeat in 2013 being a levelling out of the swing over two elections. The 2010 swing laggards caught up with the mood of the nation in 2013.

Changing party fortunes in New South Wales and Victoria were an important dynamic of both the 2010 and 2013 elections. Victoria was once 'the jewel in the Liberal crown', but the state is increasingly a stronghold for Labor. Labor has recorded a majority of the two-party-preferred vote in Victoria at 11 of the 13 elections since 1980, a better record for Labor than any other state. Victoria was also the only state to deliver a majority of seats for Labor in 2013, whereas in New South Wales Labor recorded its lowest proportion of seats since 1934. Labor's two-party-preferred percentage was higher in New South Wales than Victoria at every election from 1954 to 1977, but since 1980 it has been Victoria with the higher Labor two-party-preferred vote at 11 of the last 13 elections.

Between the 2010 and 2013 federal elections, Labor lost local office in both states. In Victoria the Coalition's victory was narrow and unexpected, and the new Government has since struggled in opinion polls. In New South Wales the Coalition won the 2011 state election with the biggest landslide in the state's history and opinion polls have indicated little resurgence in support for the once dominant New South Wales Labor Party. At both state and federal levels, it appears the Labor Party's historical weakness in Victoria is over, while in New South Wales the Coalition has improved its electoral performance in what was once a Labor-leaning state.

Changing first preference vote share and analysis of preference flows

Table 4: Change in first preference vote and two-party swing by state 2007–13

Category	Labor	Coalition	Greens	Others	2PP Swing
NSW	-9.6	+6.8	-	+2.8	8.1 to Coalition
Vic	-9.9	+1.6	+2.6	+5.7	4.1 to Coalition
Qld	-13.1	+1.2	+0.6	+11.3	7.4 to Coalition
WA	-8.0	+3.8	+0.8	+3.4	5.0 to Coalition
SA	-7.5	+2.7	+1.4	+3.4	4.8 to Coalition
Tas	-8.0	+2.1	-5.2	+11.1	5.0 to Coalition
ACT	-8.2	+1.4	+0.2	+6.6	3.5 to Coalition
NT	-10.2	+3.5	-0.1	+6.8	5.7 to Coalition
National	-10.0	+3.5	+0.8	+5.7	6.2 to Coalition

Source: Calculated from published Australian Electoral Commission statistics.

Table 4 sets out the change in first preference vote over the two terms of the Labor Government. Labor lost more than 7.5 percentage points of vote share in every state and territory, but only in New South Wales did more than half of this re-appear as a lift in Coalition vote share. In most states the two-party-preferred swing against Labor was substantially smaller than its loss of first preference share, the two-party-preferred swing against Labor ameliorated by the flow back of preferences from an increased pool of votes for minor parties and independents.

The rise in support for non-major party candidates is shown clearly in Figure 2. Support for non-major alternatives passed 10 per cent at only four elections between 1949 and 1987,[7] but has been above 10 per cent at every election since 1990, reaching highpoints of 17.1 per cent in 1990, 20.4 per cent at One Nation's first election in 1998, and a record 21.1 per cent in 2013. As Figure 2 shows, minor party and independent voting has been consistently higher in the Senate, reaching 32.2 per cent in 2013.

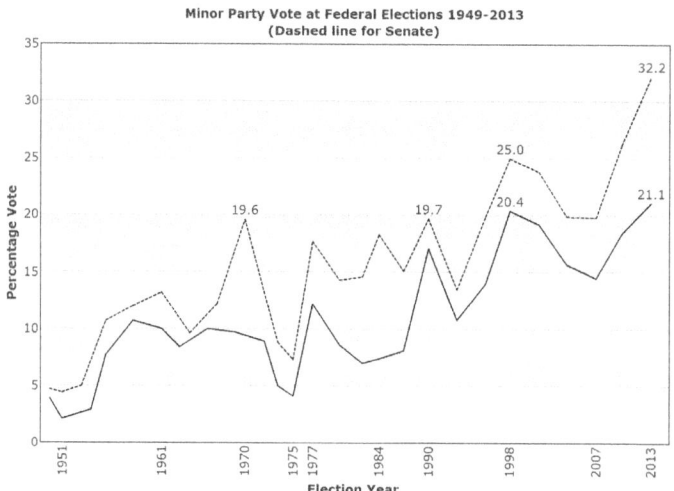

Figure 2: Minor party vote at federal elections, 1949–2013

Source: Author's work, from Australian Electoral Commission data.

The rise in support for non-major party candidates has been at the expense of Labor rather than the Coalition. The first preference vote share of both Labor and the Coalition was above 40 per cent at every election from 1949 to 1987. Since 1990, the only election where the Coalition vote share failed to reach 40 per cent was One Nation's first contest in 1998, while Labor has been below

---

7 Three times in the heyday of the DLP (1958, 1961, 1966) and a then record 12.2 per cent at the Australian Democrats' first election in 1977.

40 per cent at six of the past nine elections. The 1987 election was the first national victory by Labor with a lower first preference vote share than the Coalition, a feat since repeated in 1990 and 2010.

While Labor has been losing vote share to minor parties and independents, it has been attracting an increasing proportion of these votes back as preferences. The availability of accurate two-party-preferred counts since 1983 makes it possible to analyse the overall direction of distributed preferences. Table 5 provides two estimates of this. The second and third columns estimate the overall proportion of distributed preferences that flowed to Labor and the Coalition. The fourth and fifth columns show the percentage of the two-party-preferred vote for Labor and the Coalition that was derived as second and higher preferences rather than first preferences.

Table 5: Split of national preferences House of Representatives elections 1984–2013

Election	% preferences to Labor	% preferences to Coalition	% Labor 2PP from preferences	% Coalition 2PP from preferences
1983	54.3	45.7	7.0	6.8
1984	56.7	43.3	8.2	6.7
1987	61.8	38.2	9.8	6.3
1990	61.2	38.8	21.0	13.3
1993	60.3	39.7	12.7	8.8
1996	54.4	45.6	16.4	11.9
1998	53.4	46.6	21.3	19.4
2001	58.5	41.5	22.9	15.6
2004	61.5	38.5	20.4	11.4
2007	64.1	35.9	17.7	11.0
2010	66.0	34.0	24.2	12.6
2013	62.3	37.7	28.2	14.8

Source: Calculated from published AEC results.

Preferences for Labor in the tables may be inflated in the 1980s by the leakage of Coalition votes in triangular contests, but the number of such contests has fallen since 1990.[8] As Table 5 shows, Labor now consistently attracts more than 60 per cent of preferences from other candidates, the rate heavily influenced by strong preferences to Labor from the Greens since 2001. Using the final two columns, the election where the Coalition most relied on preferences was 1998, when 19.4 per cent of the Coalition's two-party-preferred vote came via

---

8   Triangular or three-cornered contests take place where both Coalition parties nominate candidates against Labor. There were 64 triangular contests in 1984, 72 in 1987 after the breakdown of the federal Coalition, but fewer than 20 at each election since 1996. There were 10 triangular contests at the 2013 election.

preferences. Labor's reliance has been higher than this figure at six of the nine elections since 1990. In 2010 and 2013, preferences as a proportion of Labor's two-party-preferred were around twice that of the Coalition.

The change in preferences is reflected in Labor's increasing ability to win electorates after trailing on first preferences. Table 6 identifies the number of trailing candidate victories for all parties since 1949 without taking into account triangular contests.

Table 6: Electorates where preference distribution changed the result 1949–2013

Election	% changed on preferences	Won by Labor	Won by Coalition	Won by others
1949	7.4	1	8	-
1951	1.7	1	1	-
1954	1.7	-	2	-
1955	0.8	-	1	-
1958	6.6	-	8	-
1961	5.7	1	6	-
1963	6.6	-	8	-
1966	4.1	-	4	1
1969	9.6	-	12	-
1972	11.2	-	14	-
1974	7.9	1	9	-
1975	5.5	-	7	-
1977	3.2	-	4	-
1980	4.8	3	3	-
1983	1.6	-	2	-
1984	8.8	-	13	-
1987	2.7	-	4	-
1990	6.8	7	3	-
1993	8.2	4	6	2
1996	4.7	2	4	1
1998	4.7	4	3	-
2001	4.0	4	2	-
2004	5.3	8	-	-
2007	6.0	9	-	-
2010	9.3	8	4	2
2013	10.0	12	-	3

Source: Re-calculated from election results, based on Rydon (1986), Hughes (1997) and Bean (1997).

The trend to Labor winning from behind is even starker if the figures in Table 6 are adjusted to take account of triangular contests. Between 1955 and 1972 at the highpoint of the breakaway Democratic Labor Party, Labor won only three seats after trailing the combined Coalition first preference vote, whereas the Coalition won 36 victories after trailing Labor. Since 1990 a very different picture has emerged, with Labor winning 71 contests after trailing the combined Coalition first preference vote, compared to just two such trailing victories for the Coalition. Labor won eight seats from second place at the 2010 election, making it one of the few elections where preferential voting would have changed the overall outcome. Labor would also have lost had optional preferential voting been used (Green 2013a).

In 2013 the Coalition won 46 seats with a first preference majority compared to Labor's seven. The Coalition won a further 44 seats after leading on first preferences, Labor won 36 and others two. Labor won 12 seats in come-from-behind victories, almost one in four of its elected members and more seats than it won on first preferences. Labor closed first preference gaps ranging from 1.1 to 9.3 percentage points. Three crossbench members were elected from second place on strong flows of Labor and Green preferences, with Clive Palmer closing a 14.8 percentage point gap to defeat his Liberal–National opponent in Fairfax.

Since 1996, the AEC has published 'preference flow' data, tallies of the two-party-preferred destination of ballot papers for excluded candidates, without the intermediary exclusions in traditional preference distribution tables. Table 7 extracts the preference flow data for significant parties at all elections since 1996. The table shows the very strong flows of preferences to Labor from the Greens, increasingly strong flows of Australian Democrat preferences to Labor in that party's latter years as a significant force, and the more evenly divided preferences of Coalition-leaning minor parties.

Table 7: Preference flows from significant minor parties to major parties 1996–2013

Party	Election	% first preferences	% preferences to Labor	% preferences to Coalition
Australian Democrats	1996	6.8	54.0	46.0
	1998	5.1	56.7	43.3
	2001	5.4	64.1	35.9
	2004	1.2	59.0	41.0
Greens	1996	2.9	67.1	32.9
	1998	2.6	73.3	26.7
	2001	5.0	74.8	25.2
	2004	7.2	80.9	19.1
	2007	7.8	79.7	20.3
	2010	11.8	78.8	21.2
	2013	8.6	83.0	17.0

Party	Election	% first preferences	% preferences to Labor	% preferences to Coalition
One Nation	1998	8.4	46.3	53.7
	2001	4.3	44.1	55.9
	2004	1.2	43.8	56.2
Family First	2004	2.0	33.3	66.7
	2007	2.0	39.7	60.3
	2010	2.3	40.2	59.8
	2013	1.4	41.7	58.3
Palmer United Party	2013	5.5	46.3	53.7

Note: Totals for 1996–2004 exclude a small number of electorates that did not finish as Labor–Coalition contests.

Source: Calculated from AEC preference flow data.

In the 139 electorates where preference flow data is available for the 2013 election, Green flows to Labor ranged from 58.0 per cent to 91.1 per cent. The flow was greater than 70 per cent in 135 electorates, greater than 80 per cent in 85 electorates, and greater than 85 per cent in 36 electorates.

By actively distributing how-to-vote material outside polling places and recommending preferences to Labor, there should be a relationship between a higher Green first preference vote and higher flows of preferences to Labor. The electorate level preferences show that the higher the Green vote, the stronger the flow of preferences to Labor. When the Greens experimented with issuing open how-to-vote material with no recommendation of preferences in 2010, the flow of preferences to Labor was weaker by three percentage points on average where open tickets were issued (Green 2011).

The 2013 election's new entrant, the Palmer United Party (PUP), displayed weaker flows of preferences. Despite its how-to-vote material recommending preferences to the Coalition in every electorate, only 53.7 per cent of PUP voters followed the recommendation. Preferences favoured Labor in 43 electorates and the Coalition 96. Preference flows to the Coalition ranged from 39.3 per cent in Labor-held Calwell, to 64.7 per cent in National-held Gippsland. There was only a weak relationship between the flow of preferences to the Coalition and the PUP first preference vote share.

Why was the flow of PUP preferences so different to the Greens? One possibility is that PUP distributed less how-to-vote material, though the lack of relationship between PUP's vote share and the flow of preferences suggests how-to-vote material may not have been a strong influence. Another possibility is that voters may make up their own minds. At the 2010 Victorian state election, the Victorian

Electoral Commission undertook research on whether ballot papers exactly followed a party's how-to-vote recommendation. In three inner-Melbourne electorates where the Greens finished second ahead of the Liberal candidate, between 21.6 per cent and 27.4 per cent of ballot papers exactly matched the Green how-to-vote recommendation (Victorian Electoral Commission 2011:71). Examination of the distribution of preferences in these electorates reveals that more than 80 per cent of Green preferences reached the Labor candidate ahead of the Liberal, which suggests more than half of Green voters devised their own sequence of preferences to complete their ballot papers to achieve the same purpose.

The pattern of Green preferences, the party's ideology and the geographic and historic pattern of Green support suggest that the Greens draw overwhelmingly from left-aligned voters. Having voted Green, the pattern of preference flows suggest these electors give preferences back to Labor as being aligned with their personal ideology. The geographic distribution of PUP support provides fewer clues on the previous party allegiance of its supporters. The PUP's highest first preference vote share by state was 11.0 per cent in Queensland, the only state where the Coalition's first preference vote share declined at the 2013 election. It appears the PUP drew support from past supporters of both major parties. The lack of strong preference flows to the Coalition, despite PUP's recommendation, suggests many voters may have voted for PUP candidates and then directed preferences back to the party they traditionally supported. PUP may have provided an opportunity for voters to send a message to their traditional party without having to traverse the two-party political divide, especially in the case of traditional Labor voters.

One significant change in preference strategy at the 2013 election was made by the Coalition. At previous elections the Coalition recommended preferences for their 'enemy's enemy', putting the Greens ahead of Labor. In 2013, as part of a strategy to paint Labor as doing deals with the 'extremist' Greens, the Coalition reversed its position and recommended its lowest preferences to Labor ahead of the Greens. In 2010 Liberal preference flows had been 77.9 per cent to the Greens in the three electorates where its preferences counted, but in 2013 only 34.2 per cent flowed to the Greens in the three seats counted. In 2010, Liberal preferences lifted Greens' candidate Adam Bandt from second place to victory over Labor in Melbourne. Had the Liberal Party's 2013 preference strategy applied in 2010, Labor would never have lost Melbourne. In 2013, a first preference shift from Labor to the Greens in Melbourne nullified the change in Liberal preferences and Bandt was re-elected.

The strange contest for the Senate

The use of preferential voting in single member House electorates may have protected Labor from the consequences of its low vote share in 2013, but no such protection was afforded by the Senate's proportional form of preferential voting.

Table 8: Summary of 2013 Senate result

Party	Continuing Senators	New senators	Total	Change
Liberal–National Coalition	16	17	33	-1
Labor Party	13	12	25	-6
Australian Greens	6	4	10	+1
Democratic Labour Party	1	-	1	-
Palmer United Party	-	3	3	+3
Nick Xenophon Group	-	1	1	-
Liberal Democratic Party	-	1	1	+1
Family First	-	1	1	+1
Motoring Enthusiasts Party	-	1	1	+1

Note: These figures incorporate the result of the Western Australian Senate re-run in April 2014, at which the Palmer United Party won a third seat at the expense of the originally elected Australian Sports Party. Note that Senate changes apply from 1 July 2014.

Source: AEC data.

The Labor Party lost six Senate seats, one in each state, and was reduced to single seats in both Western Australia and South Australia. Whereas in the existing Senate Labor's 31 seats plus nine Greens gave them an absolute majority in the 76-seat chamber, the combined Labor and Greens numbers in the new Senate will be 35, short of the 38 votes required to block Abbott Government legislation. With new Senators taking their seats in July 2014, the balance of Senate power will generally be with eight Senators on an expanded crossbench.

The Coalition aim was to maximise its Senate numbers so it could legislate to meet its election commitments. Instead, confusion created by the record number of candidates and parties cost the Coalition one of its existing Senate seats (in Victoria) and prevented it from gaining one and possibly two extra seats. In New South Wales, the largely unknown Liberal Democrats (LDP) benefited from drawing the left-hand column on the ballot paper, creating confusion with the Coalition's group labelled 'Liberal and National' in the 25th column.[9] The LDP

---

9 Comparing New South Wales Coalition support in the House and Senate suggests voters were confused. The Coalition's first preference vote in the House rose 2.7 percentage points but fell 4.8 in the Senate. The gap between Coalition support in the two chambers was a record 13.1 percentage points. The Coalition recording its highest House vote share since 1975 but its lowest in the Senate since 1943.

polled 9.5 per cent, triple its support in other states. Successful LDP candidate David Leyonhjelm won his seat at the expense of Labor, blocking the Greens who had won the equivalent seat in 2010.

The Greens recorded their highest Senate vote in 2013 in Victoria and took Labor's third seat. The surprise Victorian result was the defeat of third-placed Liberal Senator Helen Kroger by Ricky Muir of the Australian Motoring Enthusiasts Party (AMEP). The Coalition led the field with 40.1 per cent of the vote or 2.81 quotas against the 13th-placed Motoring Enthusiasts with 0.5 per cent or 0.04 quotas. Muir was elected through the extraordinary preference deals arranged by the micro party alliance (see below).

In both Queensland and Tasmania Labor lost its third Senate seat to the PUP. The Liberal Party had expected to gain a third Tasmanian seat, but minor party preferences delivered the final seat to the PUP. Green Senator Peter Whish-Wilson was re-elected, but with the lowest Tasmanian Green Senate vote since 1998.

The popularity of independent Senator Nick Xenophon complicated the South Australian Senate race. Xenophon's group nearly doubled its vote, polling 24.9 per cent—the highest vote ever recorded for a Senate independent—and pushing Labor into third place. With 1.74 quotas Xenophon's vote would have elected his second candidate Stirling Griff, except that Labor and the Greens chose to put Family First ahead of Griff on their preference tickets. Labor lost its second Senate seat by attracting only 22.7 per cent of the vote, but helped elect Family First's Bob Day.[10]

The Western Australian Senate produced the most remarkable result. Initially, Greens' Senator Scott Ludlam was defeated, losing his seat to the PUP's Zhenya Wang. As explained below, the closeness of the count at a key point resulted in a re-count at which Ludlam was re-instated in place of Wang. More remarkably, Labor's second Senator Louise Pratt was defeated, losing her seat to the Australian Sports Party's Wayne Dropulich. This was despite Labor polling 26.6 per cent or 1.86 quotas compared to just 0.23 per cent or 0.016 quotas for the Sports Party. The Sports Party finished 21st of the 27 parties on the ballot paper. Twenty different parties contributed votes through preference tickets to the party's victory, with 15 of those parties having recorded a higher share of the vote. At three points during the distribution of preferences Mr Dropulich had the second lowest vote tally of remaining candidates, only to survive by gaining ticket preferences on the exclusion of the only candidate with fewer votes (Green 2013b).

---

10   Labor right faction power broker Don Farrell had originally been chosen to lead the Labor ticket, but stood aside to let Finance Minister Penny Wong lead the ticket. That gesture plus Labor's low vote cost him his seat.

The extraordinarily complex nature of the count and the determining power of ticket preferences were revealed by a 'choke point' in the count that determined the final two seats. At a point where only 10 candidates remained in the count, the two lowest polling candidates were from the Australian Christians and the Shooters and Fishers Party. Both had 1.8 per cent of the vote at this point, and on the first completed count, the Shooters and Fishers led the Australian Christians by 14 votes, resulting in the final two seats being won by Labor and the PUP. This 'choke point' was so close that the AEC ordered a re-count. During the re-count, it was determined that 1,370 ballot papers included in the initial count could not be located. The distribution of preferences on this second count saw the Australian Christians finish 12 votes ahead of the Shooters and Fishers at the critical count, resulting in Dropulich and the Greens winning the final two seats. If the missing ballots were included based on their first count totals, then the Shooters and Fishers would have finished one vote ahead of the Australian Christians, resulting in Labor and PUP winning the final two seats. The AEC referred the count to the Court of Disputed Returns and a fresh election was ordered for the Western Australian Senate, at which the Liberal Party retained its three seats, Labor again failed to win a second seat, and the PUP and the Greens made up the complement.

The giant ballot papers and strange preference deals were a deliberate strategy by minor and 'micro' parties to try and win election to the Senate. One of the participants in this was the Australian Sex Party, whose registered officer and Tasmanian Senate candidate Robbie Swan (2013) described the process as follows:

> Formed in Sydney by the man known as 'the preference whisperer', Glenn Druery, the Minor Party Alliance allowed minor and micro parties the chance to win a Senate seat off the back of a small primary vote, as long as all the parties in the Alliance preferenced themselves above the three major parties.[11] It was a plan that most small parties wanted to be in on but it also required them to place some parties above others, which may not have reflected their own core values.
>
> Would your party's stated policies and philosophies be more advanced by getting you elected, even though that may come at the risk of supporting another small party with an opposing political outlook? That was the question.

---

11 Note that Swan is here including the Greens as a major party.

The Pirate Party and the Secular Party did not join the group. Animal Justice, Australian Independents, HEMP and the Democrats were all committed. Wikileaks were players who made a couple of genuine administrative errors in their final preferences.

The Sex Party were open about having one foot in the Alliance and one foot out. This hokey-pokey, each way bet approach was the one that I supported. The Sex Party refused to preference the religious right anywhere but at the very bottom of our ticket. For this we were penalised within the Alliance and yet still allowed to stay, because we preferenced mostly progressive small parties at the top and were considered to be one of the major minor parties that delivered a substantial primary vote.

With the Minor Party Alliance running across the political spectrum from the left-libertarian Sex Party to the various conservative Christian parties, parties that sat to the political centre of this grouping were the main beneficiaries. The success of the Motoring Enthusiasts in Victoria, the PUP in Tasmania (and initially the Sports Party in Western Australia) and to a lesser extent the Liberal Democrats in New South Wales, stems from this tactic by the minor party participants to manipulate group ticket voting to accumulate votes within the alliance and win seats ahead of the Greens and the major parties. In 1984, with the Nuclear Disarmament Party, and in 1998 with Pauline Hanson's One Nation, the larger parties used preference tickets to deny those new parties entry to the Senate. In 2013, the Minor Party Alliance used the same rules to engineer victory by participants in the alliance. The Minor Party Alliance 'gamed' the system, but they did no more than use the rules as they existed and as they had been used by the major parties in the past.

However, the election of two unknown candidates with extremely low vote shares via labyrinthine preference tickets built on strategy rather than ideology has raised serious questions about the Senate's electoral system as well as the rules governing the registration of political parties. Changing the rules will be a challenge for the Abbott Government given that its ability to legislate on all other matters will depend on a Senate crossbench elected under the existing rules.

References

Australian Electoral Commission (AEC). 2011. *Analysis of Informal Voting, House of Representatives, 2010 federal election*. Research Report Number 12, 29 March.

Barber, Stephen. 2011. *Federal Election Results 1901–2010*. Parliamentary Library Research Paper No. 6, 2011–12, Canberra: Parliament of Australia.

Bean, Clive. 1997. 'Australia's Experience with the Alternative Vote'. *Representation* 34(2): 103–10.

Green, Antony. 2011. 'Does it Matter if the Greens do not Direct Preferences to Labor?' *Antony Green's Election Blog*, 7 November, viewed 14 January 2014: <blogs.abc.net.au/antonygreen/2011/11/does-it-matter-if-the-greens-do-not-direct-preferences-to-labor.html>.

Green, Antony. 2013a. '2010 Federal Election—Would Optional Preferential Voting Have Changed the Result?' *Antony Green's Election Blog*, 10 January, viewed 14 January 2014: <blogs.abc.net.au/antonygreen/2013/01/2010-federal-election-would-optional-preferential-voting-have-changed-the-result.html>.

Green, Antony. 2013b. 'The Remarkable Path to Victory of Wayne Dropulich'. *Antony Green's Election Blog*, 21 December, viewed 14 January 2014: <blogs.abc.net.au/antonygreen/2013/12/the-remarkable-path-to-victory-of-wayne-dropulich.html>.

Hughes, Colin A. 1990. 'Rules of the Game'. In Clive Bean, Ian McAllister and John Warhurst (eds), *The Greening of Australian Politics: the 1990 Federal Election*, Melbourne: Longman Cheshire.

Hughes, Colin A. 1997. 'Individual Electoral Districts'. In Clive Bean, Scott Bennett, Marian Simms and John Warhurst (eds), *The Politics of Retribution: the 1996 Federal Election*, Sydney: Allen & Unwin.

Mackerras, Malcolm. 1990. 'Election Results'. In Clive Bean, Ian McAllister and John Warhurst (eds), *The Greening of Australian Politics: the 1990 Federal Election*, Melbourne: Longman Cheshire.

Rydon, Joan. 1986. *A Federal Legislature: The Australian Commonwealth Parliament 1901–1980*. Melbourne: Oxford University Press.

Swan, Robbie. 2013. 'The Greens Vs the Micro Party Alliance'. *New Matilda*, 17 October, viewed 14 January 2014: <www.newmatilda.com/2013/10/17/greens-vs-micro-party-alliance>.

Victorian Electoral Commission. 2011. *Report to Parliament on the 2010 Victorian State Election*. Melbourne, August.

24. Documenting the Inevitable: Voting behaviour at the 2013 Australian election

Clive Bean and Ian McAllister

In late June 2010, with the federal election looming, Kevin Rudd was replaced by his deputy, Julia Gillard, in a now infamous move against the serving prime minister (Simms and Wanna 2012). The election was held less than two months afterwards. Almost exactly three years later, in an ironic reversal of fortunes, the Australian Labor Party caucus reversed its stance and replaced Gillard with Rudd. As in 2010, the 2013 election also followed just over two months later.

The latter move, in particular, was a culmination of the disunity that had been evident within the Labor Government for most of its term of office. For a time the switch back to Rudd gave some hope that the Government's fortunes might be revived sufficiently to win the election, but the more realistic prospect was that Rudd's reintroduction as leader would reduce the size of the defeat that the Government would inevitably suffer.

The 2013 election was also held amid a backdrop of trenchant policy debates and criticism of the Government over its handling of issues such as the carbon tax, the ongoing arrival of boats carrying asylum seekers, the national school curriculum, the cost of health care, the introduction of the National Disability Insurance Scheme, government expenditure and the balancing of the federal budget, and the Government's general ability to manage the economy in an ongoing context of fiscally challenging times.

This chapter uses data from the 2013 Australian Election Study (AES), conducted by Clive Bean, Ian McAllister, Juliet Pietsch and Rachel Gibson (Bean *et al*. 2014) to investigate political attitudes and voting behaviour in the election. The study was funded by the Australian Research Council and involved a national survey of political attitudes and behaviour using a self-completion questionnaire mailed to respondents on the day before the 7 September election. The sample was a systematic random sample of enrolled voters throughout Australia, drawn by the Australian Electoral Commission. Respondents were given the option of returning the completed questionnaire by reply-paid mail or completing the survey online. Non-respondents were sent several follow-up mailings and the final sample size was 3,955, representing a response rate of 34 per cent. The data were weighted to reflect population parameters for gender, age, state and vote.

Voter engagement with the election

The three years of government prior to the 2013 election was both tense and intense as the political fortunes of a rare minority government at the federal level in Australia waxed and waned. Seldom did the Government appear far from collapse and the status of its leader, Gillard, was under continual threat. It would have been difficult to say whether the political machinations of the parliamentary term would have turned the electorate off politics, to the extent that the 2013 election aroused little attention, or whether interest would have been piqued, as voters rallied to see how the election would resolve the political situation.

Table 1, which shows a set of voter orientations towards the election campaign and compares the current election with the preceding three, suggests the patterns of voter attention to the election were broadly similar in 2013 to other elections of the recent past, albeit towards the lower end of the interest range with, for example, 33 per cent of AES respondents taking a good deal of interest in the election campaign and 68 per cent caring a good deal which party won. Television remained the main medium through which voters followed the campaign, after which came newspapers, radio and the internet. Although the order of attention to these different media types remained the same as previously, the degree of attention to the two leading media dipped in 2013 compared to the two previous elections. On the other hand, the internet, while remaining the fourth and least popular source through which attention was paid to the campaign, continued to grow as a political news medium. Over 40 per cent now report using the internet for election news or information, 10 times the proportion of voters who reported doing so when this question was first asked after the 1998 election (Bean and McAllister 2000: 176). An examination of the figures from 2007, 2010 and 2013, however, shows that the rate of growth in the uptake of the internet for campaign news has slowed.

Table 1: Voter attitudes towards the election campaign 2004–13 (percentages)

	2004	2007	2010	2013
Took 'a good deal' of interest in the election campaign overall	30	40	34	33
Cared 'a good deal' which party won	72	76	68	68
Paid 'a good deal' or 'some' attention to the campaign: • in newspapers • on television • on radio • on the internet	57 69 44 -	61 77 50 16	62 77 48 29	50 70 45 34
Used the internet for election news or information	12	20	36	41
Watched the televised leaders' debate	35	46	47	32
Thought Howard (2004, 2007)/Gillard (2010)/Rudd performed better in the debate	25	13	37	30

Sources: Australian Election Studies 2004 (n=1,769), 2007 (n=1,873), 2010 (n=2,061) and 2013 (n=3,955).

The bottom section of Table 1 shows that just under a third of the electorate reported watching the televised leaders' debate held on 11 August (a significantly lower proportion than for the equivalent event before the previous two elections). Respondents saw the debate as being roughly even, with 30 per cent saying they thought that Rudd performed better than the Opposition Leader, Tony Abbott, 31 per cent saying they thought Abbott performed better and 39 per cent saying the two leaders did about equally.

Table 2 contains several indicators which address the question of the relative stability versus volatility of electoral behaviour in Australia. In many countries, an increase in the number of voters not deciding how to vote until during the election campaign has been apparent (McAllister 2002), although in Australia the proportion has tended to vary with the nature of the election, so that, for example, most people had made up their minds before the campaign in 2007, while in 2010 nearly half the electorate was still to decide when the campaign began. The figure for 2013 of 41 per cent saying they did not definitely decide how to vote until during the election campaign is in the middle of the range. Some 30 per cent said they seriously thought of voting for a party other than that which they did eventually vote for, while 46 per cent said that they have always voted for the same party.

Table 2: Measures of electoral stability and partisanship 2004–13 (percentages)

	2004	2007	2010	2013
Decided definitely how to vote during campaign period	39	29	47	41
Seriously thought of giving first preference to another party in the House of Representatives during election campaign	25	23	29	30
Always voted for same party	50	45	52	46
Identifier with one of the major parties	77	77	78	73
Not a party identifier	16	16	14	17
Very strong party identifier	21	25	19	21

Sources: Australian Election Studies 2004 (n=1,769), 2007 (n=1,873), 2010 (n=2,061) and 2013 (n=3,955).

One of the key indicators of stability in modern democracies is party identification, the tendency of voters to support one or other of the major political parties consistently over a long period of time, a phenomenon that has been particularly strong and persistent in Australia (Aitkin 1982; McAllister 2011), while in many other countries it has declined (Dalton and Wattenberg 2000; Webb, Farrell and Holliday 2003; Dalton 2008). After some signs of decline in the second half of the 1990s (Bean and McAllister 2000: 183), the level of party identification again steadied throughout the first decade of the 21st century, with the proportion of voters identifying with one of the major parties consistently hovering at just under 80 per cent (Bean and McAllister 2012: 343). In 2013, there is the first sign for seven elections that party identification may be declining further in Australia. Only 73 per cent—less than three-quarters—

of AES respondents reported an identification with one of the major political parties in 2013, a drop of 5 per cent from 2010. Minor parties soak up some of the remainder, but the proportion not identifying with any party at all has increased to 17 per cent, still low by world standards, but higher than ever before in Australia. Among those who are party identifiers, the percentage that supports their party strongly persists at around 20 per cent.

Social structure and electoral choice

There is little doubt that patterns of partisan attachment relating to socio-demographic groupings have changed and weakened over time in Australia (McAllister 2011). Yet, there remains some variability from election to election and examination of these relationships can aid understanding of the ebb and flow of the political fortunes of the major parties. Accordingly, Tables 3 and 4 set out the patterns of support for the parties in 2013 by various measures of social structure. Table 3 begins with gender. A clear reversal of the traditional gender gap had been evident in 2010 (Bean and McAllister 2012: 344). In 2013 we appear to have returned to the more common pattern of recent years in which there has been little or no gender gap (Bean and McAllister 2009; McAllister 2011: 115). The only sense of gender being a factor in party support in this election relates to the Greens, which drew more support from women than men.

Table 3: Vote by gender, age, region and religion in 2013 (percentages)

	Labor	Liberal–National	Greens	Other	(N)
Gender					
Male	34	46	7	13	(1,735)
Female	33	45	10	12	(1,862)
Age group					
Under 25	36	35	12	17	(362)
25 to 44	34	42	12	11	(1,167)
45 to 64	35	45	8	12	(1,266)
65 and over	29	56	3	11	(777)
Region					
Rural	30	47	7	16	(987)
Urban	35	45	10	11	(2,570)
Religious denomination					
Catholic	35	52	4	9	(829)
Anglican	28	56	3	13	(655)
Uniting	27	55	5	14	(369)
Other	34	46	6	15	(567)
No religion	39	33	18	12	(1,153)
Church attendance					
At least once a month	27	54	4	14	(580)
At least once a year	30	54	7	9	(704)
Less than once a year	32	48	8	12	(555)
Never	38	38	11	13	(1,731)

Source: Australian Election Study 2013 (n=3,955).

Younger voters disproportionately supported minor parties in 2013. This was true not only for the Greens, but also for the substantial group of 'other' minor party supporters, a category capturing a diverse range of votes but in which the largest group is the Palmer United Party. Older voters opted very strongly for the Coalition Liberal and National parties, as they had done in 2010 (Bean and McAllister 2012). The patterns of urban versus rural support for the minor parties was arguably also a more interesting feature in 2013 than the persistent, if modest, urban-rural divide in support for the major parties. Rural voters supported the other minor parties more strongly but the Greens less strongly than urban voters.

For the second election in a row, more Catholic voters supported the Coalition than Labor, this time by a substantial margin. Although Labor is still favoured by Catholics more than Protestants, it derives more electoral support from those with no religion than from any religious denomination. Much more starkly, this situation is also true for the Greens. The bastion of religious support for the Coalition continues to be Protestant members of the electorate and also those who attend church more frequently, whereas support for both Labor and the Greens rises as church attendance declines. The dominance of the Coalition in this election, however, is reflected in the fact that the Coalition attracted the support of as many voters who never attend church as Labor.

Table 4: Vote by socio-economic indicators in 2013 (percentages)

	Labor	Liberal–National	Greens	Other	(N)
Education					
No post-school qualifications	34	48	6	12	(1,012)
Non-degree qualifications	33	48	6	14	(1,380)
University degree	35	39	16	11	(1,139)
Occupation					
Manual	38	41	7	14	(948)
Non-manual	32	48	10	10	(2,192)
Employment					
Self-employed	23	57	8	12	(564)
Government employee	39	38	12	11	(820)
Trade Union Membership					
Union member	46	31	12	12	(695)
Not a union member	30	50	8	12	(2,670)

Source: Australian Election Study 2013 (n=3,955).

Table 4 contains the equivalent figures for the socio-economic variables of education, occupation, employment and union membership. Education is significant for the strong support for the Greens of those with tertiary degrees and for the relatively low support for the Coalition among the same group. The figures for occupation and vote allow us to calculate the index of class voting (the manual vote for Labor minus the non-manual vote for Labor). Class voting has become much weaker in Australia than in years gone by and it has been quite variable in recent elections. In 2013 it registered at 6 per cent, which is a reduction from the previous election, but not as low as it has gone on occasions in the past two decades (McAllister 2011: 152). Other minor parties appear to have eaten into Labor support among blue-collar voters, with 14 per cent of manual voters opting for such parties as opposed to 10 per cent of non-manual voters. Again, the Greens profile is the reverse, in that they attracted more support from non-manual than manual voters.

Further down, Table 4 shows that clear patterns of differential party support continue to be evident based on employment status or sector. The self-employed are much more likely to vote Liberal–National, while those employed in the public sector are more likely to support Labor and also the Greens. The data in the last section of the table contain some concerning messages for the Labor Party. While a clear divide continues to be apparent in the political leanings of union members compared to non-union members, Labor on this evidence no longer receives the vote of a majority of unionists. The Greens, in particular, have eaten into this support base, so that only 46 per cent of union members gave their first preference vote to the Labor Party in the 2013 federal election.

The party leaders

Analysis of the 2010 election had concluded that, while no party leader was particularly popular, Abbott's lack of rapport with voters and greater unpopularity made a substantial contribution to the Coalition's narrow loss of a closely fought contest. With the Labor Government in such disarray over its leadership and the time Abbott had to establish himself as a credible leadership figure over the three years since, it was possible that in 2013 the tables might be turned. There is some evidence in the section that follows that this may indeed have been the case.

Table 5: Leader and party evaluations in 2013 (means on 0–10 scale)

Leader	Mean	Standard deviation	Party	Mean	Standard deviation
Kevin Rudd	4.1	3.2	Labor	4.8	3.0
Tony Abbott	4.3	3.4	Liberal	5.0	3.4
Warren Truss	4.3	2.2	National	4.5	2.7
Christine Milne	3.8	2.5	Greens	3.8	3.0
Julia Gillard	4.0	3.1			

Source: Australian Election Study 2013 (n=3,955).

As Table 5 demonstrates, none of the leaders was seen in a positive light by the respondents in the 2013 AES. Even compared to 2010 (Bean and McAllister 2012: 347), the leadership ratings were generally low. Abbott himself, however, with a mean rating of 4.3, scored no worse than he had done three years previously. By contrast, the mean scores for both of the key protagonists on the Labor side—the newly restored Rudd and the recently deposed Gillard—had fallen substantially. The result was that Abbott was now narrowly ahead of his principal opponent in terms of his leadership rating. Rudd's evaluation stood at 4.1, on a scale in which zero represents a strong dislike, five represents a neutral position and 10 represents a strong liking for the leader. Both leaders, however, lagged well behind the equivalent ratings of their parties, although again, neither of the major parties could be called popular with the electorate, the highest party score being 5.0 for the Liberal Party. The Greens' reversal of fortunes in this election is reflected in the low scores for both the Party and its leader, Christine Milne.

Table 6 further explores the composition of voter evaluations of Abbott and Rudd. In 2010, Abbott had trailed Gillard on every one of the nine leadership characteristics listed in Table 6 (Bean and McAllister 2012: 348). In 2013, he headed Rudd in five of the nine. Abbott was seen as more competent, more sensible, as providing stronger leadership, as more honest and more trustworthy than Rudd. One qualification is that on several of these qualities, notably honesty and trustworthiness, while ahead of Rudd, Abbott himself did not score highly and indeed there is no one quality for which a very large proportion of respondents did say it described him extremely or quite well. Rudd stands out as having been rated highly for his intelligence and knowledge, while few saw him as trustworthy.

Table 6: Perceived leadership qualities of Kevin Rudd and Tony Abbott in 2013 (percentage saying quality describes leader extremely well or quite well)

Quality	Kevin Rudd	Tony Abbott
Intelligent	84	68
Compassionate	48	46
Competent	51	57
Sensible	49	52
Provides strong leadership	40	60
Honest	38	45
Knowledgeable	80	58
Inspiring	33	31
Trustworthy	29	40

Source: Australian Election Study 2013 (n=3,955).

Issues in the 2013 election

As described in the introduction to the chapter, there was no shortage of (often controversial) policy issues on the agenda in the lead up to the 2013 election, including the carbon tax, refugees and asylum seekers, education, health care and management of the economy. A growing body of research has also been documenting how voters have their own issue agendas, which may or may not coincide with the emphasis placed on these issues by the political parties during the election campaign (Goot and Watson 2007; Bean and McAllister 2012; McAllister, Bean and Pietsch 2012). Thus, health, education, economic management and taxation repeatedly feature as election issues of significance. So it was in 2013.

Table 7 shows that health and Medicare, and management of the economy scored equally as the issues rated by the most voters as being extremely important (68 per cent). These were followed by education (with 63 per cent rating it an extremely important issue), but then there was a considerable gap, with no other issue rated as extremely important by a majority of the AES sample. Refugees and asylum seekers, immigration and the environment rated in the mid-40s, followed by taxation, the carbon tax and global warming, in the mid-30s, and finally industrial relations, with only 29 per cent rating it as an issue of extreme importance.

Table 7: Importance rating of election issues (percentage describing issue as extremely important) and party differential (percentage saying Labor closer on issue minus percentage saying Liberal–National closer) in 2013

Issue	Importance					Party differential
	All voters	Labor voters	Liberal–National voters	Green voters	Other voters	
Taxation	37	32	43	16	35	-9
Immigration	43	36	51	36	35	-16
Education	63	73	56	70	61	+17
The environment	43	53	27	82	44	+13
Industrial relations	29	34	26	20	28	+0
Health and Medicare	68	75	65	65	63	+10
Refugees and asylum seekers	46	41	50	51	40	-22
Global warming	33	46	16	72	34	+12
The carbon tax	36	32	37	45	34	-9
Management of the economy	68	6	81	37	63	-21

Source: Australian Election Study 2013 (n=3,955).

The breakdown of issue importance by party shows that, for the two leading issues, health mattered more to Labor voters and management of the economy to Coalition voters. Labor voters were also particularly concerned about education, while both taxation and the issue of refugees and asylum seekers were more important to Coalition voters. The most distinctive issue profile was for Greens supporters, who predictably rated the environment and global warming as far more important than any other party group (with 82 per cent of Greens voters saying they thought the environment was an extremely important issue and 72 per cent similarly rating global warming) and management of the economy as far less important (only 37 per cent said it was extremely important). The level of concern about global warming among Greens voters has risen considerably since 2010 (Bean and McAllister 2012: 349). Both Greens and Coalition voters gave the issue of refugees and asylum seekers an elevated level of importance, but almost certainly with quite different policy outcomes in mind. Voters for 'other' parties largely mirrored the electorate as a whole, displaying more or less equal concern about health, the economy and education.

At the far right of Table 7, the column headed 'party differential' shows in summary which of the two major parties appears to have had an advantage on each issue in terms of the proportion of voters saying the party's policies came closer to their own views. When there is a plus sign the advantage lay with Labor; a negative sign means the balance was in favour of the Liberal–National parties. For one issue (industrial relations) there was no advantage to either party. Of the remainder, the Coalition had an advantage on five and Labor on four. Of the two highest rating issues, the Coalition had the advantage on economic management while Labor had the advantage on health and Medicare. The Coalition's lead was greater on the economy than Labor's on health, but in addition Labor had the advantage on the next highest rated issue, education. Interestingly, the Coalition also had a large advantage on the hotly debated issue of refugees and asylum seekers.

Conclusion: Weighing all the factors together

While the raw issue data provide pointers to which issues may have mattered in the election, what they cannot do on their own is reveal which issues and other variables actually influenced people's votes, independent of all other considerations. What is required to achieve this is a multivariate analysis to assess the net impact of all the relevant factors and this is the task of the final section of the chapter. This will allow us to conclude, for example, which of the issues really did make a difference to the election outcome. The multivariate procedure isolates the separate influence on the vote of the variables examined earlier in the chapter, including the socio-demographic measures, party identification, the summary leadership ratings and the 10 campaign issues discussed in the section above. The results are shown in Table 8. Only those variables with statistically significant effects appear in the table. Methodological details are outlined in the appendix.

Of all the factors examined, nine feature in the table. Of these, only one is a socio-demographic variable (gender). Five of the 10 issue variables had significant effects on the vote, as did the two-party leader evaluations and party identification. The effect for gender, though statistically significant, is small, indicating that when other factors are controlled, men were around 3 per cent less likely to vote for the Liberal–National Coalition, as opposed to Labor, than women. What is interesting about this result is that it reverses the direction of the effect found in the equivalent study of the last election, in which men were, by the same percentage, *more* likely than women to vote for the Coalition (Bean and McAllister 2012). The 2013 pattern returns us to the more common direction of association between gender and partisan support, while also reinforcing the small size of the gender gap in contemporary Australian politics. In addition, the finding gives further weight to the view that the atypical relationship between gender and the vote found in 2010 related to the presence of Australia's first female prime minister (Tranter 2011; Denemark, Ward and Bean 2012).

Table 8: Significant influences on voting behaviour in 2013 (multiple regression)

	Unstandardised regression coefficient		Standardised regression coefficient
Gender (male)	-0.03		-0.03
Party identification	0.42		0.41
Kevin Rudd	-0.17		-0.12
Tony Abbott	0.23		0.17
Taxation	0.06		0.04
Education	0.07		0.05
Health and Medicare	0.09		0.08
Refugees and asylum seekers	0.07		0.05
Management of the economy	0.09		0.08
R-squared		0.69	

Note: Entries in the table are statistically significant at $p < .05$ or better. Further methodological details can be found in the appendix.

Source: Australian Election Study 2013 (n=3,955).

Party identification routinely has the largest electoral impact by far and this election was no exception. However, consistent with the evidence of decline in the level of partisanship noted earlier in the chapter, there was a noticeable reduction in the size of the party identification effect compared to previous elections (Bean and McAllister 2009 and 2012).

By contrast, leadership effects, while much smaller than the party influence, remained at similar levels to the last election and again reinforced their persistence over time in Australian elections (Senior and van Onselen 2008). For example, the unstandardised regression coefficient for Abbott shows that voters who strongly liked the Opposition Leader were some 23 per cent more likely to vote for the Coalition parties than for Labor compared to those who strongly disliked him. Voters who strongly liked Rudd were around 17 per cent more likely to vote Labor than those who strongly disliked the Prime Minister.

All of the five significant issue variables had similarly modest effects, led by the two that had registered as being of most concern to voters—management of the economy and health and Medicare—but also featuring two that, although topical, had in the initial assessment of issues above seemed less obviously important to voters—refugees and asylum seekers and taxation—as well as education. Four of these five issues, economic concerns, tax, health and more latterly education, repeatedly stamp themselves as important in the electoral decision-making of the Australian electorate (Bean and McAllister 2009 and 2012).

While the size of the issue effects, in particular, and also the leader effects is small, these factors nonetheless potentially have a significant role to play in explaining the election outcome, depending on the extent to which the electorate favoured one side over the other. We have seen, for instance, from Table 7 that the balance of opinion on the issues of refugees and asylum seekers, management of the economy and taxation all favoured the Coalition, while the balance favoured Labor on the issues of education and health. We also saw that voter evaluations of both leaders were relatively low. It is possible to calculate the effect of each variable on the net balance of the party vote at the election by combining the size of the effect on individual voters (the regression coefficient) with the size and direction of the balance of voter opinion (derived from the mean of the variable). Details of the method of these calculations are given in the appendix.

As it turns out, the negative appraisals of the two major party leaders more or less cancelled each other out. The calculations show that Abbott effectively cost the Coalition just over 1.5 per cent of the vote, while Rudd cost the Labor Party a similar percentage and thus the two effects largely neutralised each other. With respect to issues, the largest impact on the party balance came from management of the economy which, when the combination of its effect and the balance of opinion is taken into account, conferred a net advantage of 1 per cent of the vote to the Coalition. The net effects of refugees and asylum seekers and taxation together added almost another 1 per cent to the Coalition's vote, but this was counteracted by the combined effects of health and education, which delivered just over 1 per cent to Labor. Overall, these issue effects left the Liberal–National parties a little under 1 per cent of the vote better off than they would have been if none of these factors had been in play. These calculations thus give some insight into the policy issues that drove voter behaviour in an election at which defeat for the Government was virtually inevitable.

Appendix

The equation in Table 8 was estimated by ordinary least squares regression analysis with pairwise deletion of missing data. The dependent variable, first preference vote for the House of Representatives in the 2013 federal election, was scored zero for Labor, 0.5 for minor parties and one for Liberal–National. Party identification was likewise scored zero for Labor, 0.5 for minor parties or no party identification and one for Liberal–National. Apart from age, scored in years, all other independent variables were either 0–1 dummy variables or scaled to run from a low score of zero to a high score of one.

The issue variables were computed by combining the importance ratings with the party closer to the respondent, so that at one end those who rated the issue as extremely important and felt closer to the Labor Party on the issue were scored zero and at the other end of the scale those who rated the issue as extremely important and felt closer to the Coalition on the issue were scored one.

For both the issue and leader variables, the calculations showing the impact of these factors on the party balance were made by multiplying the unstandardised regression coefficient by the amount by which the mean of the variable deviated from the neutral point of 0.5. For management of the economy the deviation was +0.11, for refugees and asylum seekers it was +0.09, for taxation it was +0.05, for health and Medicare it was -0.05 and for education it was -0.09. In the case of the leadership variables, the deviation for Rudd was -0.09 and for Abbott it was -0.07.

References

Aitkin, Don. 1982. *Stability and Change in Australian Politics*. 2nd edn. Canberra: Australian National University Press.

Bean, Clive and McAllister, Ian. 2000. 'Voting Behaviour'. In Marian Simms and John Warhurst (eds), *Howard's Agenda: The 1998 Australian Election*, St Lucia: University of Queensland Press.

Bean, Clive and McAllister, Ian. 2009. 'The Australian Election Survey: The Tale of the Rabbit-less Hat. Voting Behaviour in 2007'. *Australian Cultural History* 27: 205–18.

Bean, Clive and McAllister, Ian. 2012. 'Electoral Behaviour in the 2010 Australian Federal Election'. In Marian Simms and John Wanna (eds), *Julia 2010: The caretaker election*, Canberra: ANU E-Press.

Bean, Clive, McAllister, Ian, Pietsch, Juliet and Gibson, Rachel. 2014. *Australian Election Study, 2013: Codebook*. Canberra: Australian Data Archive, The Australian National University.

Dalton, Russell J. 2008. *Citizen Politics: Public Opinion and Political Parties in Advanced Industrial Democracies*. 5th edn. Washington, DC: CQ Press.

Dalton, Russell J. and Wattenberg, Martin P (eds). 2000. *Parties without Partisans: Political Change in Advanced Industrial Democracies*. Oxford: Oxford University Press.

Denemark, David, Ward, Ian and Bean, Clive. 2012. 'Gender and Leader Effects in the 2010 Australian Election'. *Australian Journal of Political Science* 47: 563–78.

Goot, Murray and Watson, Ian. 2007. 'Explaining Howard's Success: Social Structure, Issue Agendas and Party Support, 1993–2004'. *Australian Journal of Political Science* 42: 253–76.

McAllister, Ian. 2002. 'Calculating or Capricious? The New Politics of Late Deciding Voters'. In D M Farrell and R Schmitt-Beck (eds), *Do Political Campaigns Matter? Campaign Effects in Elections and Referendums*, London and New York: Routledge.

McAllister, Ian. 2011. *The Australian Voter: Fifty Years of Change*. Sydney: UNSW Press.

McAllister, Ian, Bean, Clive and Pietsch, Juliet. 2012. 'Leadership Change, Policy Issues and Voter Defection in the 2010 Australian Election'. *Australian Journal of Political Science* 47: 189–209.

Senior, Philip and van Onselen, Peter. 2008. 'Re-examining Leader Effects: Have Leader Effects Grown in Australian Federal Elections 1990–2004?' *Australian Journal of Political Science* 43: 225–42.

Simms, Marian and Wanna, John (eds). *2012. Julia 2010: the caretaker election*. Canberra: ANU E-Press.

Tranter, Bruce. 2011. 'Gendered Voting at the 2010 Australian Election'. *Australian Journal of Political Science* 46: 707–17.

Webb, Paul, Farrell, David and Holliday, Ian (eds). 2003. *Political Parties at the Millennium: Adaptation and Decline in Democratic Societies*. Oxford: Oxford University Press.

Conclusion: Reflections on Abbott's Gambit—Mantras, manipulation and mandates

Carol Johnson and John Wanna

The chapters in this volume chart the 2013 federal election in some depth: acknowledging the economic and social context in which it occurred; exploring its immediate history and the political context of a hung parliament; highlighting the role of an outright adversarial opposition intent solely on displacing the Labor Government; focusing on the leadership contest between the main protagonists, each marred in some way in the eyes of the electorate; examining the media coverage and often partisan commentary; reporting the frantic attempts to stage manage the main campaign; even following the meanderings and peccadillos of the campaign as they transpired in the eventuality, and explaining the results and swings recorded along with survey data reporting what factors drive voter attitudes. Across 24 chapters the contributors have provided a detailed descriptive account of the election, mainly for a general readership but using analytical themes and concepts when and as appropriate. The coverage of the campaign here is generally much wider and richer than in similar compilations undertaken in comparative overseas democracies, as is the range of contributors included in this volume. Whereas much of the international literature on elections and campaigning involves specialist scholars analysing campaign techniques and outcomes using academic models and theories (see the British Election Series from the University of Essex and the Nuffield series), our collection combines not just electoral specialists but also policy experts, political practitioners and party officials, political and media commentators and observers of Australian politics. Some of these contributors are explicitly partisan providing flavour, colour and insight. The compilation aims primarily to be accessible to general readers as well as specialists.

So how might we conclude this volume, drawing together the analyses from the many and varied chapters? The election brought to an end a tumultuous period of Labor Government and ushered in their conservative adversaries who appeared very under-equipped for government. As many chapters have argued, the election saw an unpopular Labor Government lose the election itself and become trapped in the pathology of defeat (see Chapters 1, 3, 10, 11, 12 and 24). Here was another example of the truism of 'governments losing elections rather than oppositions winning them'. Opinion polls and other forms of electoral prediction had for months consistently reported the electorate's desire for a change of government, but also high levels of disaffection especially with the three political leaders: Abbott, Gillard and Rudd. While much of the national campaign strategies focused on the leaders and their images, as many polls showed and the AES confirmed, there was a strong dislike factor weighing against both Abbott and Rudd (see Chapters 3 and 24). As we discuss below, the narrow target strategy adopted by the Coalition, which highlighted merely a few 'wedge issues' in its campaigning, provided the new Abbott Government with a constrained mandate—a clear electoral mandate to abolish two controversial taxes (the carbon and mining taxes), to address boat people arrivals, to reduce the size of the public service and to introduce a generous paid parental leave scheme—but little else. Hence, the election was not so much a contest of policy ideas (and indeed some of the stranger announcements appeared as little more than 'thought bubbles') as it was a contest over which side of politics could provide the most competent majoritarian government, but with crossbenchers deliberately awarded the balance of power in the Senate and none of the main party blocs being able to dictate legislative outcomes alone.

To explain the electoral contest of 2013 that brought the experiment of the hung parliament to a close, we have chosen to conclude the analysis of this volume by focusing on three themes:

- the contest over campaign messages (the repeated *mantras*);
- the various ways in which the main political players attempted to seek partisan advantage (attempts at *manipulation*); and,
- the eventual nature of the *mandate* that came out of the election given the political context and counter-claims made.

We discuss each of these in turn.

Contending but uninspiring mantras

Unlike the 2010 federal election, which was contested over rival leadership credentials (see Simms and Wanna 2012), the 2013 election was largely fought over the battle of the slogans, simplistic catchphrases regularly repeated by leaders, frontbenchers, backbenchers and major party candidates. The resort to sloganeering was in one sense a rational (but cynical) political response to three phenomena: the growing proclivity for asserting headline statements often lacking in specificity and devoid of detail; a shrewd response to the risk-averseness of hyper-adversarial politics (concentrating on simply attacking one's opponents and allowing no chinks in one's own armour); and, as a preferred campaign tactic in a situation where many voters had made their mind up about their voting intentions some months out from the poll (reminding voters not persuading them). Mantras dominated the campaign and arguably were seen by all sides as a 'least worst' tactic to adopt.

From the outset of the campaign proper, all major parties promoted the concept of 'change' and renewal—a new beginning, a 'new way', or a 'new plan'. The consistency of these aspirational mantras suggests that all the parties were reading that the electorate was exasperated with the previous period in politics and especially the in-fighting of the Labor ministry. But when these messages failed to resonate, they were quickly jettisoned (especially by the ALP) in favour of direct negative attacks on opponents and negative advertising generally. Some of the minor parties also promoted change and renewal, feeding on a general sense of disaffection.

The lack of policy detail was an intentional ploy adopted by both sides at times, but particularly by the Coalition (see, Australian Labor Party 2013a; Department of Finance and Deregulation and The Treasury 2013). When slogans substitute for detailed policy, the electorate is asked to agree with the sentiment, not analyse whether the policy 'stacks up' plausibly or seems reasonable and acceptable (see Johnson's chapter). Moreover, when few or no details were provided there was less chance of exciting pockets of opposition and voices of dissent which might perhaps question what was in it for them personally. Keeping policy to mere slogans was meant to convince voters of the general benefits rather than allow opponents to nit-pick at the specifics. The proposal to abolish the carbon tax was one clear example of this investment in a particular mantra without providing policy detail that might upset potential supporters. Equally, it is hard to cost or quantify slogans. Labor, in particular complained that, while it had provided detailed Department of Finance costings for key policies, the Coalition had not provided equivalent information (see Australian Labor Party 2013b). Nonetheless, the Coalition did release some information and claimed that its policies had been rigorously costed (Hockey and Robb 2013).

Among their more prominent policy commitments there were some areas of major disagreement (such as over the carbon tax, the resource rental tax, the dimensions of the fiscal problem, and the better parental leave scheme) but also some surprising areas of agreement—which did not necessarily neutralise issues in the minds of voters. Both parties out-bid each other on the need to get tougher on asylum seekers and conduct off-shore processing of boat people, on the importance of better infrastructure, stronger defence, better schools and increased educational funding, a more productive economy, and skills and training for the labour market, and the need to fund a national disability carer scheme based on client choice.

Both sides had announced cuts to public services and to the number of public servants employed by the Commonwealth. For Labor these reductions (of 12,000 to 14,000) announced well before the election campaign period were presented as prudent government policy imposed through the 'efficiency dividend'; but when their conservative opponents announced they were going to make further cuts, they were denounced as irresponsible and heartless. The Coalition implied it would cut as many as 15,000 to 16,500 public servants and reduce the number of agencies, and it was often assumed that this figure was in addition to the Labor cuts—making reductions of up to 25,000 officials possible, as the public sector unions often claimed. However, later the Coalition clarified it was seeking 16,500 redundancies or separations in total. The fear of job losses and counter-threats over proposed public sector cuts consumed much of the election 'heat', although the fact that both sides were engaged in the same exercise largely neutralised it as a negative for either side.

Mantras were also directed explicitly at adversaries and protagonists. While Rudd painted his opponent as an untrustworthy adversary who had a secret austerity agenda, Abbott continued to specialise in the repetition of pithy three word slogans, such as 'stop the boats', 'turn back boats', 'axe the tax', 'big new tax', and occasionally 'just say no'. His strategy was to frame the wedge issues he had chosen to campaign upon and relentlessly drill them into the electorate's consciousness. Rudd responded with a counter-slogan accusing Abbott of seeking 'cuts, cuts, cuts'.

With the election underway, Joe Hockey, Tony Abbott and Andrew Robb all began to emphasise that Australia was facing a 'budget emergency' caused by the looming fiscal problems that the Labor Government had failed to rectify. The persistence of a sizeable deficit and growing levels of debt were sufficient to underscore this message in the minds of voters, despite Labor's attempts to argue that they were relatively small in international terms. Both Abbott and Hockey then promised to balance the budget well before the date by which Labor had committed to do so. To provide some reassurance that any government he would lead would not impose outright austerity on ideological grounds, Tony Abbott promised that there would be 'no unnecessary tax increases' and infamously said to the SBS TV audience on the eve of the election that there would be 'no cuts to education, no cuts to health, no change to pensions, no change to the GST and no cuts to the ABC or SBS' (see also Hockey and Robb 2013). So, although these commitments were meant to reassure vacillating voters they had nothing to fear, these statements would come to haunt the Government, and later in 2014 expose it to claims it had broken its election commitments—just as Gillard had earlier done. Here was one of the dilemmas at the heart of Abbott's gambit, going hard and negative in opposition helped him to win government but also shaped voters' perceptions of how he was meant to behave in government.

Despite honing their mantras, there were so many comments made during the campaign that ultimately few of them resonated; there were no 'cut-through' messages or consistent themes, such as John Howard managed in 2001 with his 'we will decide who comes to this country and the circumstances in which they come ...', or the momentum Kevin Rudd generated in 2007 with his *Kevin07* brand (see Snow 2013). In that sense the 2013 election campaign became a lackadaisical affair where both sides, for different reasons, went through the motions without expecting a fundamental turnaround, though Labor at least hoped to contain losses.

Attempts at manipulation

As in previous elections, the party campaign strategies for the federal election of 2013 were highly stage managed. Centrally planned strategies and schedules around the leader dominated the main campaign trajectories while bottom-up campaigns from local electorates enhanced candidate recognition and reinforced certain messages. Protagonists relentlessly stayed on script almost to the point of tediousness (or, as in the case of Jaymes Diaz, who could not recall the six-point border protection policy, were airbrushed from view); 'Noddy shots' all had the local candidate looking serious and nodding sagely with every utterance of the leaders when in camera; fake images were everywhere with candidates desperately trying to 'fit in' with the local communities they visited; flimsy gimmicks and disingenuous photo opportunities for the nightly news underscored the blandness of the contest and further dumbed down the contest.

Image manipulation again proved powerful. In his post-election analysis included in this volume, Brian Loughnane, Federal Director of the Liberal Party of Australia, argues that the Coalition won the 2013 election because of a combination of factors, and cites: Labor's broken commitment not to introduce a carbon tax; its inability to deal with border security; issues of economic management; and, the soap opera saga of Labor disunity while in government, which culminated in Julia Gillard being supplanted by the leader she had previously replaced, namely Kevin Rudd. Loughnane readily acknowledges the important role played for the conservatives by support groups for local candidates, including improved use of social media technology and micro-targeting of key voters. Furthermore, Loughnane wishes to emphasise that the Liberals also ran a positive agenda, concluding that 'while Labor's internal crisis provided opportunity for the Coalition, it was not inevitable that we would win the election. The community wanted something to vote *for* not just *against*'.

Needless to say, there are aspects of Loughnane's analysis which politicians from opposing parties and some academic commentators would find contentious. For example, the role played by Labor disunity is widely acknowledged, including by George Wright, National Secretary of the Australian Labor Party, in this volume. However, Loughnane's depiction of the image of 'chaos, instability and dysfunction' associated with the Labor Government in the public mind, fails to adequately acknowledge the key role of the Opposition in successfully promulgating and manipulating that image for its own ends, given that the Gillard Government alone actually passed over 500 pieces of legislation. Furthermore, no government bills were defeated in the House of Representatives (although some that might have been were not put forward or were allowed to lapse) and the Gillard minority Government was far more successful at passing legislation than was the case with many past governments facing a hostile Senate. Though as George Wright admits, while he might claim that the Rudd and Gillard governments 'kept Australia out of a world recession', and pursued worthwhile policies in regard to education, information technology and disability, the Labor Government did not manage to sell its reform credentials well. The analysis here suggests that Labor failed to adequately sell its legacy of reform not only because of poor communication strategies and major issues with implementation, but because of Labor's internal machinations—for example, Rudd was loathe to acknowledge Gillard's achievements. By contrast, the Coalition was more successful at selling its framing of the successive Labor governments as dysfunctional and chaotic.

Despite predictable disagreements between the three partisan analyses from the party officials, all three provide essential insights into modern campaigning, emphasising the presidentialisation of campaigns and the growing professionalisation of politics that is analysed in more depth in the chapters by Young and Reece amongst others, and the increasing use of social media that is analysed by Chen. Meanwhile the leadership issues alluded to by both Loughnane and Wright are analysed in more depth by Walter and Strangio, who argue the increasing personalisation of politics, and the mediatisation of politics that it partly reflects, has resulted in increased voter volatility. Bean and McAllister's analysis reinforces Walter's and Strangio's arguments regarding the influence of attitudes towards political leaders on party identification. Manning and Phiddian also note the focus on leadership in their analysis of political cartoons. Meanwhile, as Errington points out, the traditional media also played a key role in both propagating and reinforcing particular framings of issues and particular depictions of the Labor Government, the Coalition and their respective leaders.

However, a key message of this book is that election outcomes are normally decided by a complex combination of factors and the 2013 Australian election was no exception. Institutional factors and the ways in which the various actors attempt to manipulate the system for partisan advantage tend to come into play and shape the eventual outcomes. The preferential nature of the Australian voting system is wide open to this sort of manipulation and preference swapping has become a dark art and a science. As Antony Green points out in his chapter, the role of preferences was essential in keeping Labor at all competitive given a 'disastrous decline' in its first preference votes. The Greens survived in the upper house largely on preferences. But other minor players also got in on the act. Green notes that 'in both the House and Senate, support for non-major party candidates rose to levels never previously recorded at an Australian national election' and candidates were elected with infinitesimally small primary votes and with many other voters not being aware their votes were being channelled to these candidates. Once again institutional factors, including the 'light touch' regulation of campaign financing and the relative ease with which minor parties can be formed, played a role as is pointed out in our introduction to this volume.

Reactions to continuous opinion polling can also be an influential institutional factor. Generally regular polling tends to focus on calculating the likely two-party-preferred outcome, and this can affect not only the behaviour of the principal contestants but also shape the expectations of the electorate as to the likely outcome. (As Jackman points out in his chapter, other predictions of voting outcomes, such as the betting markets, often draw on polling information too). Who voters think will win can have a marked impact on the directions of their own voting intentions. Yet, as Goot points out, even though the polls were accurate in predicting overall trends, they were often less successful at predicting outcomes in selected regions and specific seats (for example, western Sydney and some battlefield seats across the nation). It is here that the complex regional factors analysed by Robinson, Jaensch, Wear and Miragliotta, along with other factors such as the ethnic voting analysed by Jupp, come into play. As does the success of the major parties in sand-bagging individual seats that are vulnerable, using traditional methods such as door-knocking as well as new methods such as social media and sophisticated databases that allow micro-targeting, including the individualised massaging highlighted in Young's chapter. Meanwhile the role of minor parties, including exceptionally well-funded new ones such as the Palmer United Party (see the chapter by King), and the unexpected successful local campaigns run by independents such as Cathy McGowan (see chapter by Curtin and Costar) , are further wildcards that can influence the outcomes in particular seats and in the Senate. In the case of the 2013 election, the Greens also had a notable success in retaining Adam Bandt's seat of Melbourne. Some Greens felt that other winnable seats were sacrificed in order to shore-up Bandt's seat for symbolic reasons.

The marketability of specific policy issues was carefully assessed by campaigners, as Reece eloquently describes in his chapter. The importance to the parties of economic management issues is emphasised in both Loughnane's and Wanna's chapters, while Johnson identifies the significant roles in party discourse played by the fear of government debt and concerns over personal financial security. Economou emphasises the importance of the carbon tax as an iconic economic issue. Bean and McAllister's analysis confirms the role of issues made more salient by the parties themselves: promises to solve the issues of economic management, stem the flow of asylum seekers and reduce taxation influenced support for the Coalition, while the Labor Party's record and commitments to education and health continued to influence support for its candidates in the campaign. Interestingly though, Gray, Manwaring and Orchard outline the Coalition's success in partially neutralising issues that might have worked to their disadvantage, such as health and education, thereby cauterising Labor's scare tactics about cuts under an Abbott Government. Meanwhile, as McLaren and Sawer note, both major parties attempted to mobilise the masculinity of the two leaders in their stage-managed campaigning, and in the process some important gender issues involving women were marginalised.

An afflicted mandate

There was some commentary in the aftermath of the 2013 election of the result not being quite as devastating a defeat for Labor, and conversely not quite a convincing win for the conservatives. Malcolm Mackerras (2013) opined that the final result was a 'respectable loss'—implying that Labor's defeat was not as dire as some had expected or that one opinion poll of marginal electorates had implied some six months out from the poll (see JWS Research 2013, covering 54 marginal seats with margins under 6 per cent). However, such a view has limited plausibility and only holds up if the 2013 election is looked at totally in isolation, whereas we would argue the 2010 and 2013 elections should be judged together in terms of a two-stage trajectory that removed Labor from government. The combined swing to the Coalition from 2007 to 2013 was 3.78 per cent in the primary vote and 6.19 per cent in two-party-preferred terms.

Moreover, Labor's primary vote was the lowest recorded in 110 years (since 1903). In the 28 federal elections since 1943, Labor's vote had only fallen below 40 per cent on six previous occasions (in 2010, 2004, 2001, 1996, 1990 and 1977), which suggests a serious structural malaise in recent decades. In 2013 it fell to 33.38 per cent—a further swing of 4.61 per cent from Labor's result in 2010, and a combined swing of exactly 10 per cent since the *Kevin07* election of 2007. Its two-party-preferred vote was 46.51 per cent, a swing against the party of 3.61 per cent. Labor's two-party-preferred vote was almost identical to that of its loss in 1996 (a mere 0.14 per cent difference at 46.38 per cent in 1996) and one would have to go back to the spectacular losses in 1975 and 1977 to find lower two-party-preferred votes. In the 24 elections since 1949, Labor's two-party-preferred vote was higher than in 2013 on 18 occasions, and only on six was it lower (in 1955, 1958, 1966, 1975, 1977 and 1996). Labor's sanguineness at the election result, reflected in George Wright's chapter, was probably due to the fact that it expected to be mauled more severely and was relieved that its frontbench talent managed to survive the defeat (except David Bradbury in Lindsay, and Mike Kelly in Eden-Monaro). Labor was far less sanguine about its Senate vote where it lost six Senate positions and was reduced to 12 returning Senators—and with only one position re-elected from two mainland states (SA and WA), reducing their total representation to 25 from July 2014—less than one-third of the chamber.

The Coalition's primary support was far from their highest winning margin. In terms of primary votes, Abbott's gambit win was close to the party's average result, but *lower* than 11 previous election victories since the previous hung parliament of 1941–43 (namely, in 2004, 1996, 1980, 1977, 1975, 1966, 1963, 1958, 1955, 1954 and 1949). Significantly, it was also a result *below* that of two Coalition losses (the elections of 1987 and 1974). Moreover, in two-party terms the Coalition did not manage to attract a consistent nationwide swing towards it, and did not achieve a majority in three out of the eight jurisdictions (Victoria, Tasmania and the ACT). The Coalition also lost one Senate seat in Victoria to the Motoring Enthusiasts Party.

Hence, the 2013 election was a further defeat for Labor and part of a longer trend in sliding support, but not a spectacular win for the Coalition. That 21.07 per cent of the electorate either voted for parties/candidates other than the major parties, or voted informally, suggests a high degree of voter disaffection. If the fact that some 1.5 million Australian adults are entitled to be on the electoral roll but have not registered because they are not interested in politics is taken into account, then there is a substantial measure of societal disaffection with the politics on offer. This feature is not so much evidence of a 'democratic deficit' as of a deep-seated disaffection with the current state of democracy and political parties and politicians. Opinion polls of younger voters especially have indicated a high degree of questioning over the value of democracy or its effectiveness as a preferred system of government.

The Greens similarly could not be content with their level of electoral endorsement; they suffered a 3.11 per cent swing against them in the lower house and a swing of -4.46 in the Senate. Although their representation increased by one additional Senator, their upper house representation was almost totally dependent on preference flows in each state from the Labor Party and some smaller minor parties. In 2013 the Greens seemed to have inherited the status of 'least worst' among the minor parties, a position once held by the Australian Democrats.

Of course in Australia the notion of a 'dual mandate' is highly pertinent; the government is formed and claims a given mandate through its control over the House of Representatives, but the upper house Senate also enjoys an elected mandate—they are usually expected to scrutinise executive government and allow for different voices and preferences in the legislature. While Abbott managed a comfortable majority (of 30 seats) in the lower house, his side of politics fell short of gaining a majority in the Senate. Eight Labor Senators retired or were defeated from among the outgoing members compared to four from the Coalition benches; Labor managed to elect two new Senators as replacements to the Liberals' three, while the Greens gained an extra Senate position (in Victoria). In addition, three Palmer United Senators were elected for the first time, plus a Family First candidate, a Liberal Democrat and a Motoring Enthusiast. The final composition of the Senate after July 2014 was: Coalition 33 seats (down one seat); Labor 25 seats (down six seats); the Greens with 10 Senators (up one seat); Palmer United with three new Senators; plus one Senator each from Family First, Liberal Democrats, Democratic Labor, the Australian Motoring Enthusiast Party and Nick Xenophon. The Coalition would require the votes of at least six additional Senators to pass their legislation if Labor and the Greens oppose their measures.

The other aspect of the mandate that has attracted attention is the way in which Tony Abbott campaigned and led the Opposition parties to victory. His 'relentless negativism' and pillorying of Julia Gillard for reversing her commitment not to introduce a carbon tax, was widely seen as strident and uncompromising. The Coalition also made some of its own commitments in the lead up to the 2013 election and, given what it had railed so vehemently against since 2010, voters could reasonably expect it to be bound to honour these commitments to the letter (especially the commitments to stop the boats, abolish the carbon and mining taxes, introduce no new taxes and not change the GST, not cut pension benefits or education and health budgets, and preserve the funding for the public broadcasters). In many ways Abbott painted himself into a tight corner with his 'preserve the status quo' commitments, leaving his government little room to manoeuvre without being forced to break his commitments.

To the next instalment …

So, if elections are normally decided by a complex combination of factors, an extraordinary combination came together to determine the outcome of the 2013 election, both in terms of the formation of a new Coalition Government, the plight of the out-going Labor Party, the survival of the Greens and inauguration of the Palmer Party, as well as in terms of the unexpected outcomes in the Senate and some individual seats. In an era of perpetual election cycles and constant campaigning, the parties have already begun to assess how they should be positioning themselves for the next election, whenever that takes place, and under whatever circumstances. It is often observed that parties, like military generals, fight the next campaign according to their own post mortem of their performance in the last one; building on what aspects they did well and rectifying those aspects that went badly. It constitutes a form of 'rear vision' campaigning or backward mapping. Going forward, therefore, we might expect the Coalition to include greater policy detail and be more forthcoming in their appeal to voters; Labor to stress unity, stability and consistency; the Greens to become less amorphous and prone to ambulance chasing; and Palmer and some of the other fringe jester parties to better hone their appeals to the disaffected while continuing to entertain.

But these are more volatile times. The previous conservative government lasted four successive terms, looked competent for most of that time and frequently out-manoeuvred its Labor opponents. The Abbott Government began office somewhat shakily (as did Howard in 1996 and Rudd in 2008) and as yet does not appear to have fully mastered the art of government. The Coalition's party discipline and unity in opposition helped to deliver it victory, but the imperatives of government are more pressing, especially in a time of reduced revenues, and likely to re-open old divisions and internal debates. In 2013 Labor appeared to be partially successful in its strategy of saving the furniture and the cherished careers of its frontbench team, but does that provide a sufficient base on which to rebuild the party's fortunes without some major internal changes, a reassessment of what the party stands for and the cultivation of a more attractive appeal to voters? Labor's disastrously low primary vote may remain an enduring concern for it into the future, particularly given the Greens long-term goal of challenging the 'century-long' stranglehold that the major parties have on the Australian political system. Yet the Greens are not the only party fighting for the 'protest vote' and peeling voters from the major parties. The initial spectacular showing of the well-resourced Palmer group captured protest votes from the major parties and from other minor parties alike.

In their respective chapters in this volume, both national campaign directors of the major parties argue that their respective sides of politics have the better vision for the future. For Wright, issues such as tackling climate change, disability, education and broadband will not go away and Labor, he argues, is well-positioned as the party committed to pursuing them. In Loughnane's view the Liberals' policy positions in regard to issues such as economic management and border security are 'much more closely aligned to the concerns of the community than Labor's'. But whether the new Coalition Government can continue to stay tightly focused and deliver electorally desirable outcomes, or whether Labor can rebuild as a competitive force in opposition in very difficult and uncertain economic and social times, remains to be seen. That will be one of the tasks for the next book in this series to assess.

References

Australian Labor Party. 2013a. 'What we're for: A stronger and fairer Australia'. Viewed 16 May 2014: <pandora.nla.gov.au/pan/22093/20130810-0000/www.alp.org.au/what_we_re_for.html>.

Australian Labor Party. 2013b. 'Groundhog Day: Hockey and Robb Costings Circus'. Media release, 5 September, viewed 16 May 2014: <www.alp.org.au/cm25_050913>.

Department of Finance and Deregulation and The Treasury. 2013. 'Election Commitment Costing, Federal Election 2013'. Canberra, viewed 16 May 2014: <electioncostings.gov.au/>.

Hockey, Joe and Robb, Andrew. 2013. 'Final update on Federal Coalition Election Policy Commitments', viewed 16 May 2014: <pandora.nla.gov.au/pan/22107/20130906-0245/www.liberal.org.au/latest-news/2013/09/05/final-update-federal-coalition-election-policy-commitments.html>

JWS Research. 2013. 'ALP set to lose Federal election with loss of 10+ seats in NSW'. *JWS Research*, January, viewed 15 May 2014: <jwsresearch.com/news_files/alp-set-to-lose-federal-election-with-loss-of-10-seats-in-nsw.pdf>.

Mackerras, Malcolm. 2013. 'My reaction to the election—a landslide?' *Switzer News*, 20 September, viewed 15 May 2014: <www.switzer.com.au/the-experts/malcolm-mackerras---political-expert/my-reaction-to-the-election---a-landslide/>.

Simms, Marian and Wanna, John (eds). 2012. *Julia 2010: The caretaker government*. Canberra: ANU E-Press.

Snow, Deborah. 2013. 'How Kevin Rudd's 2013 election campaign imploded'. *The Sydney Morning Herald,* 9 September.

www.ingramcontent.com/pod-product-compliance
Lightning Source LLC
Chambersburg PA
CBHW061947240426
43669CB00055B/2988